Handbook on Parent Education

EDUCATIONAL PSYCHOLOGY

Allen J. Edwards, Series Editor
Department of Psychology
Southwest Missouri State University
Springfield, Missouri

In preparation:

James H. McMillan (ed.). The Social Psychology of School Learning

Published

M. C. Wittrock (ed.). The Brain and Psychology
Marvin J. Fine (ed.). Handbook on Parent Education
Dale G. Range, James R. Layton, and Darrell L. Roubinek (eds.). Aspects of Early Childhood Education: Theory to Research to Practice
Jean Stockard, Patricia A. Schmuck, Ken Kempner, Peg Williams, Sakre K. Edson, and Mary Ann Smith. Sex Equity in Education
James R. Layton. The Psychology of Learning to Read
Thomas E. Jordan. Development in the Preschool Years: Birth to Age Five
Gary D. Phye and Daniel J. Reschly (eds.). School Psychology: Perspectives and Issues
Norman Steinaker and M. Robert Bell. The Experiential Taxonomy: A New Approach to Teaching and Learning
J. P. Das, John R. Kirby, and Ronald F. Jarman. Simultaneous and Successive Cognitive Processes
Herbert J. Klausmeier and Patricia S. Allen. Cognitive Development of Children and Youth: A Longitudinal Study
Victor M. Agruso, Jr. Learning in the Later Years: Principles of Educational Gerontology
Thomas R. Kratochwill (ed.). Single Subject Research: Strategies for Evaluating Change
Kay Pomerance Torshen. The Mastery Approach to Competency-Based Education
Harvey Lesser. Television and the Preschool Child: A Psychological Theory of Instruction and Curriculum Development

The list of titles in this series continues on the last page of this volume.

Handbook on Parent Education

Edited by

MARVIN J. FINE

Department of Educational Psychology and Research
School of Education
University of Kansas
Lawrence, Kansas

1980

ACADEMIC PRESS

A Subsidiary of Harcourt Brace Jovanovich, Publishers

New York   London   Toronto   Sydney   San Francisco

217245

ACADEMIC PRESS, INC.
111 Fifth Avenue, New York, New York 10003

United Kingdom Edition published by
ACADEMIC PRESS, INC. (LONDON) LTD.
24/28 Oval Road, London NW1 7DX

Library of Congress Cataloging in Publication Data
Main entry under title:

Handbook on parent education.

(Educational psychology series)
Includes bibliographies and index.
1. Parenting--Study and teaching--United States.
I. Fine, Marvin J.
HQ755.7.H36   649'.1'07   79−8871
ISBN 0−12−256480−4

649.107
Har

Contents

PART I INTRODUCTION

Chapter 1

The Parent Education Movement: An Introduction 3
MARVIN J. FINE

PART III   APPLICATION TO VARIED GROUPS

Chapter 11

Parent Education: One Strategy for the Prevention of Child Abuse 245

SUELLEN FRIED AND PENNI HOLT

Chapter 12

Parenting Education for Youth 271

KAREN W. BARTZ

PART IV   IMPLEMENTATION AND EVALUATION

Chapter 13

Parent Education Programs: Ready, Set, Go! 293

JERRY L. WYCKOFF

Chapter 14

Evaluating Parent Education Programs   317

MARVIN S. KAPLAN

List of Contributors

Numbers in parentheses indicate the pages on which the authors' contributions begin.

KAREN W. BARTZ (271), Camp Fire, Inc., Kansas City, Missouri 64112

OSCAR C. CHRISTENSEN (53), Department of Counseling and Guidance, College of Education, University of Arizona, Tucson, Arizona 85721

MARVIN J. FINE (3), Department of Educational Psychology and Research, School of Education, University of Kansas, Lawrence, Kansas 66045

SUELLEN FRIED (245), Kansas Committee for Prevention of Child Abuse, Topeka, Kansas 66603

THOMAS GORDON (101), Effectiveness Training Incorporated, Solana Beach, California 92075

PENNI HOLT (245), Department of Educational Psychology and Research, School of Education, University of Kansas, Lawrence, Kansas 66045

MARVIN S. KAPLAN (317), Department of Counseling and Personnel Services Education, Kent State University, Kent, Ohio 44242

MERLE B. KARNES (201), Institute for Child Behavior and Development, Colonel Wolfe School, University of Illinois, Champaign, Illinois 61820

DENNIS H. KARPOWITZ (27), Department of Psychology, University of Kansas, Lawrence, Kansas 66045

C. E. KENNEDY (181), Department of Family and Child Development, Kansas State University, Manhattan, Kansas 66506

JOSEPH LAPIDES (227), Merrill Palmer Institute, Detroit, Michigan 48202

RICHARD C. LEE (201), Institute for Child Behavior and Development, Colonel Wolfe School, University of Illinois, Champaign, Illinois 61820

PAMELA C. MARR (181), Department of Family and Child Development, Kansas State University, Manhattan, Kansas 66506

ARTHUR R. ORGEL (75), Department of Psychiatry, University of Rochester School of Medicine and Dentistry, Rochester, New York 14642

RICHARD L. SIMPSON (153), Department of Special Education, University of Kansas Medical Center, Kansas City, Kansas 66103

STEPHEN T. SIRRIDGE (123), Department of Education and Psychology, Avila College, Kansas City, Missouri 64145

CARROLL R. THOMAS (53), Adlerian Psychological Institute, Tucson, Arizona 85716

JERRY L. WYCKOFF (293), Education Clinic, University of Kansas, Shawnee Mission, Kansas 66208

Preface

This year, 6 million Americans will take a step that will significantly change their own lives and profoundly affect the next generation: They will have children. How they raise these youngsters will have a greater impact on American society than the way they vote, the technologies they produce, the wars they wage, or the art they create. [K. L. Woodward and P. Malamud. The parent gap. *Newsweek*, 1975, *86* (12), 48.]

These observations dramatize the importance of both parenting and the programs aimed at helping parents. Too often we read tragic accounts in the newspapers of parents who abuse or neglect their children. The professional literature has frequently pointed out that these parents are often simply repeating the negative parenting patterns that they experienced as children. For disturbed parents, an intensive therapy experience may be needed; but for many other parents, systematic exposure to ideas and skills about parenting, along with opportunities to ventilate and share feelings and experiences, holds the promise of facilitating healthy parenting.

The parent education movement is still in its childhood. Therefore, the many new ideas and programs being presented to the public today are often controversial. What programs are available? What do they accomplish? When should parent education begin? With what groups is parent education useful, and are different programs needed for different groups? The intention of this book is to offer some answers to such questions and, in effect, to present a contemporary picture of the state of the parent education movement.

Part I of the book presents a historical and contemporary perspective on the parent education movement and the American family. Part II elaborates on different models of parent education, highlighting a number of popular approaches. Part III details the application of parenting programs for specific groups, including parents of handicapped children, foster parents, parents of preschoolers, abusive parents, as well as parenting programs for youth. Part IV, the last section, offers some practical "do's" and "don'ts" on planning and implementing a parent education program and includes an important chapter on program evaluation.

The contributors to this book have all been involved for many years with various aspects of parent education. Thus they bring a high level of professional competence to their respective chapters, along with a commitment to enhancing the quality of family life and parent–child relationships in the future.

Acknowledgments

My personal interests in parenting and parent education prompted the idea for this book. I did not believe that this book was ahead of its time, given the growing interest in parent education today. However, a number of publishers were not so easily convinced. I am appreciative of the good judgment shown by Academic Press and its editors in supporting this project.

Several of my graduate students made significant editorial–proofing contributions and I would like to single out Jacalyn Wright and Penni Holt for their involvement.

Finally, the contributors responded to their tasks in a responsible, professional manner and considerably eased my task as editor. The outgrowth of the efforts by all involved is, I believe, a worthwhile contribution to the expanding literature on parent education.

PART I

INTRODUCTION

Chapter 1

The Parent Education Movement:
An Introduction

MARVIN J. FINE

The American family has been undergoing major changes recently that have had direct effects on parent–child relationships and on the growing up experiences of children.

While this statement could have been expressed in almost any country in any period of history, it is perhaps more valid today because of the phenomenal technological progress that our society has made over the last few decades. Many of us will be raising our children under substantially different societal conditions than we experienced as children. We are more "nomadic" than ever, with the figures increasing on the number of home moves per family. In growing up, the children of today will experience a great deal of mobility; they will live in different communities and come into contact, either directly or vicariously, with many life-styles. The burgeoning divorce rate and related increase in single-parent families testifies to this turbulence on the American family scene. The statement, "That's the way I was raised," becomes a tenuous anchor for contemporary parenting. A common retort from today's child is, "This isn't then; this is now!"

Bronfenbrenner (1973) described some of the major changes affecting the American family. From 1948 to 1971, the incidence of working mothers rose from 18 to 43%. This means that more than one out of every three mothers with children under six is working today. The number of single-parent families has more than doubled in the last

3

HANDBOOK ON
PARENT EDUCATION

decade and the number of other adults in the home who could care for the child has substantially decreased.

These data represent a trend that is continuing, if not accelerating; this leads to the image of children spending minimal amounts of time with their parents, children being raised by baby-sitters or day-care workers, and children spending time with different families (e.g., with mother and stepfather and with father and stepmother). This is certainly a different picture from that of 50 years ago, when two-parent families and nonworking wives were more common and parents had considerably more contact with their children.

Understandably, many parents and parents-to-be are questioning the goals and techniques of parenting. What values are enduring and should be passed on to our children? How can we get our children to accept certain beliefs and ways of behaving? On a more basic level, children ask questions such as, "How do I get my child to obey?" or "What do I say when he tells me the other kids do it?" For some people it may seem hard to believe that such questions are really raised. For them the what, why, and how of parenting are clear-cut—or so it seems. But for many others, the questions are relevant.

On the heels of the changing American family scene has come the parent education movement. The growing popularity of parent education programs is evidenced by just one organized program, Parent Effectiveness Training, which claims to have trained over 8000 instructors and 250,000 parents (Brown, 1976). Organized parent education, simply defined as "instruction on how to parent," is not new on the American scene. The influx of new immigrants early in the century created a host of adjustment problems for families and children. Jane Addams, the founder of Hull House in Chicago and a pioneer social worker, was acutely sensitive to the needs of the immigrants in their new land. Many of her programs focused on one or another aspect of family life (Addams, 1942). Rudolph Dreikurs, a disciple of Alfred Adler, promoted neighborhood parent discussion groups many years ago (Dreikurs & Soltz, 1964). Indeed, Dreikurs' viewpoint and writings on parenting and family life are still immensely popular.

No discussion of parent education would be complete without mentioning Benjamin Spock and his original book on infant and child care (Spock, 1957). For millions of mothers, his book was and still is a "bible" on the "how to's" of parenting infants and young children. The Gesell Institute has published several books on child development (Gesell & Ilg, 1946; Ilg & Ames, 1955). Like Dr. Spock's book, these were also widely read and assisted parents in understanding what essentially was normal, to-be-expected behavior. One could go on and on here identifying individuals and books that were concerned with the growth of children and the parenting process. Selma Fraiberg's excellent book, *The Magic Years* (1959), is a good example of how some important and complex ideas have been presented to the layperson.

The clinical professions of psychiatry, psychology, and social work have also addressed themselves to the question of parenting. Therapy groups for parents sharing common problems have been in existence for some time. For example, mental health clinics have offered groups for parents of children in treatment. There have been groups for parents of retarded children and children with many other disorders. The orientation of these groups is therapeutic in that either the parents are considered to be causal agents of the child's problem, or it is believed that they are being seriously affected by the child's problem. For example, this would be the case in relation to the parents of dying children; often in such cases, the parents get together under professional direction to sort out their feelings and to learn how to cope with the child's impending death.

It has been mainly over the last two decades, however, that systematic approaches to parent education have emerged as distinct from parent or family therapy and from the popularized presentations on child development. The preparation of this book was prompted by the recognition that there has recently been a rapid growth of systematic and conceptually based approaches to parent education, which in turn raises the need for a current, comprehensive statement on the topic. Some of the historical antecedents to formalized parent education curricula have already been reviewed. The remainder of this chapter will give an overview of several prototype programs, distinguish education from therapy, consider some ethical issues, and describe parent education with special interest groups. In addition, problems of research and evaluation and a projection for the future will be presented. The subsequent chapters will examine these topics in greater detail, including some specifics on how to initiate a parent education program.

What Is Parent Education?

The term "parent education" was earlier defined as "instruction on how to parent." This definition properly applies to organized programs rather than to informal get-togethers. Parent education, as we will be using the term, refers to a systematic and conceptually based program, intended to impart information, awareness, or skills to the participants on aspects of parenting. These programs usually take the form of a weekly meeting of a few hours over several weeks.

The format usually includes the presentation of specific ideas, some group discussion, sharing or processing of ideas and experiences, and some skill-building activities. A given parent education program may stress one aspect over others. For example, behavior modification programs usually focus more on the mechanics of selecting problem behaviors and programming reinforcement, whereas Parent Effectiveness Training as developed by Gordon (1970) gives ample opportunities for discussion and for communication skill-building activities. Other programs might stress the sharing of developmental information, raising questions and answers on the order of "What do you do with a child who . . . ?" One program might use a great many audiovisual activities, such as films, slide programs, and audiotapes, whereas another might emphasize discussion and sharing of personal experiences.

Some programs are offered without charge through churches, schools, or community agencies. Often there is a charge ranging from a small registration fee up to $75 for a series of several sessions. In some cases, where the program is franchised, the instructor keeps some of the fee with the rest sent to the franchising source. This is the case with Parent Effectiveness Training (P.E.T.).

"Homework" is an important aspect of many programs. It is recognized that a once-a-week experience will be of limited value if the ideas and skills discussed are not tested in real situations. The nature of homework will of course vary from program to program. In some instances it will be required, whereas in others the participants are invited and encouraged to try out the ideas and to report on their experiences the following week. The extent of record keeping will also vary. Some programs may require detailed weekly reports or logs, whereas for others it will be considered sufficient just for the parents to have attempted some application that they are willing to discuss.

Popular Parent Education Programs

The following is an overview of several popular themes and programs in parent education. A detailed description of some of these programs will be presented in later chapters. This section is a preview of what is to come and an orienting experience for the reader. In addition to the programs discussed here, there are of course many other programs being initiated and developed. The programs described in this section were selected because they have either existed for a period of time, have a related body of literature, or have achieved some significant degree of popularity.

Haim Ginott: Caring, Communicating, and Being Real

The late Haim Ginott wrote two books that were best-sellers and became the "bibles" for many parent discussion and education programs. *Between Parent and Child* (Ginott, 1965) and *Between Parent and Teenager* (Ginott, 1969) reflected Ginott's emphasis on how the needs of parents could coexist with the needs of their children. The book *Liberated Parents/Liberated Children* (Faber & Mazlish, 1974) was written by two parents who actively participated in a lengthy parent workshop offered by Ginott.

Ginott's two books raised the problems and techniques of parenting in ways that presented "permissions" to parents to have and even express feelings, such as anger and sadness.

> We used to think a good parent was a patient parent—calm, logical. He never yelled.
> Now we feel no need to bottle up our anger. We express it fully, but instead of hurling insults, we hurl our feelings, our values, our expectations [Faber & Mazlish, p. 227].

It was important to Ginott for the parents to be self-aware, to know what and why they were feeling. He wanted parents to see their children accurately and not to project roles and characterizations onto them. Children's self-esteem would be built from success experiences and what they learned about themselves from important people such as parents. Ginott stressed parents listening to children and reducing the amount of telling, ordering, and admonishing. Giving children choices and encouraging them to think was recommended as valuable experience. For Ginott, who was a trained therapist, how people felt (and that included children) and what they perceived at a point in time was valid for them. Telling them something different or insisting that they should feel differently would only mobilize the child's energy to defend his or her viewpoint.

Ginott wanted parents to feel good about themselves in their parenting role and not to feel guilty when they made decisions. He understood that children often prefer to manipulate parents through guilt into a course of action. Ginott's approach might be summed up by saying that he believed healthy childrearing practices would emerge from a self-aware parent who was able to accept the child, including the child's feelings and actions, and who was able to offer the child the experience of a parent as a "real" person.

Behavior Modification:
A Child Management Emphasis

Behavior modification techniques have become very popular in clinical and educational settings over the last 15–20 years. The basic principles, stated simply, involve operationally defining a behavior, observing its occurrence, then modifying or introducing reinforcement procedures and continuing to observe them, so as to determine if the behavior has been affected by the reinforcement. These procedures can be elaborated or added to in terms of actually recording and charting frequencies or durations of behavior, getting inter-rater reliability, systematically stopping and reintroducing the reinforcement so as to give proof that the behavior is indeed being controlled by the reinforcement, and phasing out or phasing in reinforcements. Probably one of the most commonly used behavioral principles is that of extinction. The parent who ignores a child's temper tantrum is hoping that without getting attention for such behavior, the child will no longer exhibit the behavior; without reinforcement, the behavior has no reason to occur.

Over the last several years these basic principles of behavior modification have been presented in parent education format. A number of books are available for parents, many of them in workbook or programmed learning format (Becker, 1968; Hall, 1978; Madsen & Madsen, 1972; Miller, 1975; Patterson, 1976; Smith & Smith, 1976). The Responsive Parent Training Program (Hall, 1978) is one of the most elaborate in terms of organization of instructional units and audiovisual materials.

What all behavioral programs have in common is the belief in positive reinforcement as the *sine qua non* of behavior management. The goals include helping parents to understand behavior in reinforcement terms with the decided emphasis, as indicated, on the use of positive reinforcement. These programs all express an awareness that parents, especially those having problems with their children, are often involved in a negative response pattern with their children. "Good behavior" gets taken for granted and is not reinforced, whereas "bad behavior" gets a lot of negative parent attention. This pattern of reinforcement actually leads to maintenance of the undesirable behaviors. Thus, in order to modify the child's behavior, the first step is for the parents to change their behavior. This point is often overlooked by critics of behavior modification who believe that the parent remains unchanged while the focus is completely on changing the child's behavior.

Behavior modification does seem to receive more criticism than any other approach to parent education. Some of the criticisms have to do with the rights of children; the seeming ignoring of developmental processes or issues; the lack of generalizability of the behavior change in the child to other settings or behaviors; and the procedural demands on parents to observe, record, and pay off children. The proponents of behavior modification counter with disclaimers of unethical behavior and claims of success. They hold that it is the straightforward, albeit simplistic, thinking of the procedures and the parent success in managing behavior that reinforces the growth of this approach to parent education.

Parent Effectiveness Training: Facilitating Communication

The most widely taught parent education program seems to be that of Tom Gordon's Parent Effectiveness Training, or P.E.T. (Gordon, 1970). It is also a successful commercial enterprise with a sequence of instructor training programs leading to licensing and an organized instructional and payment format. It has also been widely promoted in lay and professional journals and its most vocal proponents seem to be the parents who have completed the course and find themselves relating in different and more satisfying ways with their children.

The theoretical roots of P.E.T. derive from Carl Rogers' client-centered therapy, with its emphasis on the therapist being accepting and nonjudgmental of the client. Gordon uses a similar orientation to communication as the basis of his program. He believes that parents historically have erected roadblocks to communicating with their children through the use of 12 nonproductive verbal responses. These include such responses as commanding, threatening, lecturing, blaming, and moralizing.

When the parent is aware that it is the child's, rather than the parent's problem, the parent can be most helpful through "active listening." Operationally, this is a nonjudgment response that communicates that the parent is listening, caring, and understanding. An example would be a parent who responds to a child's complaints about another child by saying, "I can see you really are upset by what Billy did." Such statements assist the child in becoming aware of his or her feelings and thoughts and in permitting the child to work out a solution to the problem. When the parents believe that they are involved and need to actively intervene, then Gordon describes the use of "I messages." These messages are expressed as statements of personal concern that are connected to some tangible reference. For example, "I am concerned because if you throw the ball in the den you could break the window." Gordon also advocates and describes a no-lose method of conflict resolution. The techniques of "active listening" and "I-messages" are used by the parent in initiating a discussion with the child over the issue. It is important in this process that all parties have an opportunity for input, are heard by the other person, and understand the other person's viewpoint and the realities of the situation. The solution that ideally emerges is one that is agreeable to all parties and that all parties feel good about, so that it does not turn into a situation where one person is the winner and the other the loser.

The appeal of Gordon's program seems to lie in its humanistic values, its clear presentation of some potentially effective communication strategies, and its promotion of a mutually gratifying style of human interaction. The organizational aspects of the program, its packaged units with well-tested group activities and exercises, and the instructor training program are also key factors adding to both the popularity and the claims for the effectiveness of P.E.T.

Transactional Analysis—Promoting "OK'ness"

The late Eric Berne originated Transactional Analysis, referred to as TA, as a theory of personality and a frame of reference for psychotherapy. The subsequent popularization of TA occurred through such books as *Games People Play* (Berne, 1964), *I'm OK—You're OK* (Harris, 1969), and *Born to Win* (James & Jongeward, 1971). Each of these books was a best-seller, testifying to the public's receptivity to the ideas and techniques of TA.

While there are "schools" within Transactional Analysis, some of the basic tenets are as follows:

1. All persons are born "OK" but may learn to feel "not OK."
2. Each person has three parts to his or her personality: the Parent, Adult, and Child ego states.
3. The developmental processes that people go through can lead to healthy or unhealthy personality organization.
4. People can become self-aware and actively participate in facilitating their own personality development.
5. Children make decisions about themselves early in life (before age 6) that influence their perceptions, beliefs, and behaviors.
6. The giving and receiving of positive strokes (touching, caring, listening, complimenting, loving, etc.) is crucial for healthy personality development.

As stated, there are different schools within TA, and these are reflected in the content and structure of parent education programs. Transactional analysis is group oriented to begin with. That is, even as a mode of therapy it is oriented toward therapy groups rather than individual treatment. In many communities there are TA study groups where people come together to study and experience what TA can offer them. This orientation to group involvement and self-growth readily lends itself to parent education programs.

One theme of TA, reflected in *Raising Kids OK* (Babcock & Keepers, 1976), is strongly developmental. The emphasis in the book is on the process of child development and how parenting can support a healthy developmental sequence leading to a healthy adult. An important TA developmental concept, similar to psychoanalytic theory, is that a child needs to progress successfully through the developmental tasks at each stage of life or (*a*) the child will not progress satisfactorily through subsequent tasks; or (*b*) the child may seemingly progress in terms of psychological development but may experience conflicts in later life associated with the unresolved developmental problem or issue. The exercises that Babcock and Keepers suggest assist parents in better understanding what it is like to be a child at a certain age and also help them to understand what internal "pushes and pulls" parents experience as they relate to their children.

Another TA theme, related to developmental issues, focuses more on the parents and their needs (James, 1974). The emphasis here is on the parents understanding their own personality structures, maintaining self-awareness as they interact with their children, and relating healthily with their children. Both views are sympathetic to the experiences of childhood, the strengths and vulnerabilities of the child facing the world, and the importance of the parenting process.

Parent programs built around TA tend to be fun and experientially oriented. A great deal of modeling usually occurs through the leaders giving strokes, being open and spontaneous, and relating helpfully to group members. There is no standard format for TA parent education programs. The individual leaders organize the curriculum, often an intensive two-day workshop or a series of weekly meetings over several weeks. The existence of an organization devoted to furthering TA (International Transactional Analysis Association) gives some assurance that group leaders have themselves experienced appropriate TA training.

Rudolph Dreikurs: Democracy and Adequacy

One of the pioneers and major figures in the parent education movement has been Rudolph Dreikurs. While he has published a great deal on parent–child and teacher–child relationships, his main book on parenting remains *Children: The Challenge* (Dreikurs & Soltz, 1964). This book, along with the instructor's manual (Soltz, 1967), has been the mainstay of countless parent education and study groups.

Rudolph Dreikurs based much of his thinking on the works of Alfred Adler, a contemporary of Freud. Adler broke with Freud because, among other reasons, he felt the "social nature" of people was not considered important enough in Freud's approach to personality development and psychotherapy. Dreikurs is very concerned with the social nature of the child and the child's quest for adequacy. He views misbehavior as the function of a child whose goals are misdirected. The goal of parenting is to help a child become an adequate human being who uses constructive means to obtain his or her own sense of significance and status.

The family is where the child establishes his or her sense of self, makes early decisions about himself or herself, and begins to develop a social nature. Dreikurs, who came from an authoritarian cultural background, stressed democracy in the home. The concept of a "family council" was one means Dreikurs promoted for helping to establish a caring, trusting atmosphere in the home where mutual respect could be expressed.

In relation to formal parent education programs, there is Soltz's study manual (1967), which details the leader's role, techniques of coping with problem group members, how to organize the group, and an actual study outline. Dreikurs expressed a great deal of faith in people helping each other, and he believed that with some basic training and the use of his book and the study manual, most parents could lead a parent study group. He wanted the group sessions to focus on the principles of parenting as presented in the handout materials and in his book. Presumably parents would attempt to apply these principles, such as the use of logical and natural consequences, avoiding power struggles, recognizing and responding to the needs of children, and offering children encouragement. It was expected that parents would be eager to share their experiences with each other, ask questions, and receive support and encouragement in the group. The group leader's function was not viewed as that of a lecturer but rather that of a good discussion leader, question asker, and when necessary, refocuser. Indeed, in Dreikurs' groups it is appropriate for group members to assume leadership at different times in terms of sharing information, expertise, or experiences.

As with other points of view on parent education, Dreikurs' approach recognized that while the ultimate goal has to do with the child's growth as a person, the key steps to achieving that goal require that the parents make some changes. Dreikurs was aware that giving up old ideas and trying new ones would be difficult for many parents, but he saw the group experiences as supporting parents in acquiring and applying new ideas.

Systematic Training for Effective Parenting (STEP)

The STEP program is a comprehensive, organized, and sequenced parent education program, developed by Dinkmeyer and McKay (1976). It is gaining in popularity because of good promotion by its publisher, its clear structured guidance for instructors, and most importantly, its very worthwhile content.

The senior author, Donald Dinkmeyer, has collaborated with Rudolph Dreikurs (Dinkmeyer & Dreikurs, 1963) in the past, and the influence of Dreikurs' ideas is readily apparent in the program. For example, some of the topics covered include the goals of behavior, encouragement, applying logical and natural consequences, and implementing the family meeting. In addition, the authors have incorporated some of Gordon's ideas on active listening and sending I-messages. The program is humanistically oriented and focuses on building a positive relationship between parents and their children.

The instructor's guide is quite detailed and the authors claim that any person from the helping professions or layperson who reads the material carefully can lead the group. The organization and structure of the program certainly offers an instructor a great deal of concrete direction. There are posters, charts, cassettes, and a parent's handbook. The materials are colorful, well done, and appealing to parents.

Parent Involvement Program (PIP):
Coping with Reality

From his early work with delinquent girls, William Glasser developed his model of Reality Therapy (Glasser, 1965). The initial applications of Reality Therapy in treatment situations eventually extended into a model for discipline in the public schools (Glasser, 1969) and more recently into a model of parent education, the Parent Involvement Program (PIP).

In the paper entitled "Teaching Parents about Reality Therapy" (McGuiness, 1977), the author states, "The goal of Reality Therapy is to help people become responsible and self-disciplined so they can face their problems and find pleasure in their life [p. 2]." The Parent Involvement Program is a structured 18-hour seminar program that introduces parents to Reality Therapy, family involvement practices, and effective communication techniques.

Glasser highly values close, involved family relationships that include as mainstays, courtesy, laughter, and communication. He espouses a problem-solving and personal responsibility orientation for day-to-day living that the parents exemplify in their own lives so that their attempts to transmit that orientation to their children is not contrived or mechanical.

Listening emphatically, the heart of Gordon's Parent Effectiveness Training, is also highly valued by Glasser. The development of warm, communicative family relationships paves the way to deal, as necessary, with problem areas. Glasser advocates a training process of several steps that moves the parent and child from problem identification to a planned problem resolution. The steps tend to be quite behavioral in nature, with a consistent and repetitive focus on "What's happening? Is it helpful? and What are you going to do?" The skills that are necessary for the parent to interact nonpunitively with the child are taught as part of the PIP curriculum.

There is also a leadership training program available to prepare certified PIP instructors. This seems to represent some quality control on the dissemination of the PIP program.

Parent Education versus Parent Therapy

One question that is frequently asked is, How does therapy for parents differ from parent education? There are important distinctions as well as commonalities between the two. If we were to examine a random group of therapists and a random group of parent educators, we would find some readily apparent differences. The therapist group would probably be mainly psychiatrists, psychologists, and social workers; the parent educator group would be more heterogeneous and include teachers, ministers, nurses, counselors, and persons without any formal titles but who have been trained specifically as parent educators. In many states certification and licensure requirements have to be fulfilled before anyone can sell services to the public as a therapist, but this is not the case with parent education. Parent education to date seems to be offered by persons and institutions that view themselves as appropriate to do so, without any external monitoring by professional organizations or public laws.

While therapy and parent education take many forms and reflect varied theoretical frames of reference, the therapist usually seeks to establish a relationship with his or her clients different from that of a parent educator. The therapist communicates by word and attitude an invitation to the client to share "secret" information, and also sends the message that the client can count on the therapist to be trustworthy, caring, and available. The parent educator is interested in sharing information and skills on parenting and is usually willing to problem solve some specific parenting problems as presented by participants. But the extent of involvement in a parent's personal problems will be more limited. The parent educator is likely to have an agenda to pursue and will not be willing to dwell extensively on any one person's situation. The competence of the parent educator to deal helpfully with serious personal or family problems may also be limited.

While therapy might continue indefinitely or until the therapist or client chooses to terminate the relationship, parent education programs are typically time limited, running 6–10 weeks, with one or two meetings per week. The time structure does limit the support that the parent educator has to offer parents.

The therapist often uses the other group members as a part of the therapeutic process. They participate in confronting, advising, and supporting one another. This might also occur in a parent education group, but probably with some clear limits on how involved each person can become with the other. The parent educator may act out a more protecting and structuring role in relation to how the group members may react to a member presenting a problem.

The goals of therapy vary with the frame of reference. In dynamic therapies, the goals may include personality reintegration or reeducation. In more behavioral therapies the goals focus on the person acquiring new behaviors or extinguishing old behaviors. Parent education does not attempt to promote personality reintegration, but through the information and skills imparted does aim at achieving some behavior changes. Parent education often deals with values clarification and the resolution of values conflicts. For example, a parent who is resistant to offering a child certain freedoms may be acting from an outdated belief system. Some group discussion and experiential activities might help parents to become aware of the source of their beliefs and to reach an understanding that certain beliefs need to be updated.

An additional differentiation between therapy and parent education has to do with the seriousness and pervasiveness of the problem that a parent or child is experiencing and how that problem impacts on the family. In the case of child-abusing parents, the parent is usually quite troubled, has long-standing psychological problems, and often was abused as a child. To simply offer such parents better communication skills, or teach them how to set limits, would ignore and deny their own serious problems. A parent therapy experience for such persons would focus both on the nature of their own disturbances and on some specific parenting skills, especially at those times when the abusive behavior gets triggered.

Ethical Considerations

Parents commonly attend parent education programs out of a sense of need for new information or perhaps help with a particular problem at home. They have an emotional investment in their children and in viewing themselves as "good" parents. This creates a vulnerability on their part and contributes toward an aggrandizement of the leader, someone who presumably is "expert" on parenting.

As any group leader knows, while some group members are highly susceptible to being influenced by the group leader, others come seemingly to engage the leader in a power struggle. In any event, the leader is in a position of potency as far as affecting the thinking, feelings, and behavior of the group members. This raises a number of ethical issues that need to be considered in relation to parent education programs.

Leader Qualifications

As stated earlier, a sampling of leader qualifications would reveal a wide range of professional preparation. There is no national organization nor are there any legal statutes governing who may call themselves a parent educator. There are some instructor training programs, for example Parent Effectiveness Training, and Glasser's Parent Involvement Program, that train and certify instructors. But for the most part a person decides that he or she is appropriate to lead a parent group and then moves to initiate a program, either through some organization or privately. Different program orientations may require different kinds of skills and knowledge. Some persons use a discussion leader format, without claiming special expertise. Other leader models explicitly or implicitly project that the leader is an expert, can be counted on to give accurate information, and can skillfully lead a group.

The lack of recognized standards for parent education leaders opens the door for unqualified persons to lead groups. Such people assuming leadership roles could misrepresent their qualifications. The consequence is that incorrect or highly biased information may be presented as if it were "truth," group members may be instructed or encouraged to engage in parenting practices that are inappropriate or even harmful, and parents may not be adequately emotionally supported.

Claims and Promises

Professional groups such as physicians, psychologists, and lawyers have recently been concerned with the question of advertising in their respective fields. What claims and promises are acceptable and what claims are "ballyhoo"? Parent education programs face the same dilemma. What can realistically be promised? Most parent education programs hope to achieve at least some of the following goals: (a) offer parents greater self-awareness; (b) help parents to use effective discipline methods; (c) increase parent–child communication; (d) encourage families to have more fun together; and (e) give parents useful information on child development.

All of these may sound worthwhile, but on what basis can any of these objectives be guaranteed? Promotion of parent education programs often takes place via newspaper ads or articles, brochures, posters, or announcements at other meetings such as PTA gatherings. It seems appropriate to give prospective members some reasonable idea of what they might expect by way of group format (lecture, small-group experiences, workbook activity, etc.) and what the goals of the program will be. But to guarantee anyone that they will achieve a happier home or improved family relationship by attending the group is unprofessional and could become problematic when people do not in fact achieve those goals.

Permission and Protection

The leader does possess some potency simply because of the designated leadership role. Parents who come looking for answers to home difficulties may grab very quickly at the ideas and techniques being presented, eager to try anything to alleviate a problem. Also, even if parents question the appropriateness of a particular technique in their family, they may be persuaded by the instructor's surety or the group's endorsement of the procedure.

In essence, what happens in groups is that members are given a "permission" to do something because of the potency of the leader or group process. The permission to engage in certain behaviors, for example, building in certain tangible consequences when a child misbehaves in certain ways, may run counter to the parent's ideas and values, or may conflict with some internalized prohibition the parent has against that kind of behavior. Parents are entitled to "protection" within the parent group. This protection should include (a) not being required to change their behavior if they do not feel comfortable doing so; (b) being made aware of why certain techniques are suggested; (c) knowing they can depend on the instructor to advise them against attempting some technique that may be inappropriate; (d) knowing that the instructor, who is an adequately trained and ethical person, will not encourage people to make changes that could be harmful to relationships and people; and (e) knowing that the instructor, in encouraging changes, will make people aware of and prepare them for some of the consequences of that change.

Acceptance versus Rejection of Values

One criticism of some of the existing parent education programs is that they are basically white and middle-class oriented in terms of values. Many of the techniques depend on verbal skills and are based on a democratic value structure, emphasizing that everyone in the family should participate in the family process; the leaders of these programs also tend to be against corporal punishment and supportive of the human rights of each family member. Not all parents would subscribe to these values, and this raises questions of whether some values are better than others, whether we can have a pluralistic value system regarding raising children, and what are the rights of parents to act out their value systems within their families.

The awareness that a group of parents will hold differing values on childrearing and family life has prompted many parent education programs to include a section on values clarification. Parents may not be sensitive to their own beliefs and where those beliefs originated; yet those beliefs may be the heart of childrearing practices in their home. Awareness of values does not mean that everyone will agree on a common set of values. How do value differences get resolved or treated within a parent education group? Is a family to be told that their values are wrong?

Most persons, regardless of cultural background, would be against open examples of child abuse in the form of physical, psychological, or sexual exploitation of children. Within legal limitations, there is an active arena of value judgments to be considered. What are the ethical implications of a parent educator promoting "middle-class values" on families that are culturally different? One suggestion is that the instructor communicate the value base of the program to the participants so that they are able to understand and evaluate the procedures accordingly. This kind of explicitness by an instructor could also include recognition that people do have different value positions, as do different parent education programs. Such acknowledgments and even legitimizing of different value positions might reduce the conflict and anxiety some parents feel and help them to more comfortably decide on what values and techniques are appropriate for them.

Parent Education with Special Parents

Raising children is challenging with normal children, but for parents of "special" children, the parenting process can be additionally problematic. Thus, it is understandable why professionals have often addressed themselves through parent education programs specifically to the needs of such parents. Indeed, there is even a journal devoted to those parents, *The Exceptional Parent*.

A handicapped child can put a great deal of stress on a family. Parental expectations may be unrealistic and the parent may have many feelings about their responsibility for the child's condition that can affect the parent–child relationship (Farber, 1968; Richardson, 1971; Warnick, 1969). Parents of exceptional children may also be in need of information and sometimes may not even know how to ask the relevant questions. For parents of retarded children, there may be questions about the child's intellectual growth: Will he ever be normal? What is an IQ? Will he be employable? What can we do to help him or her now? Parents of children with marked behavior problems will want assistance in acquiring management skills and in dealing with their own feelings about the child's acting-out. Parents of learning disordered or brain-damaged children may also need developmental information and an understanding of their child's unusual learning pattern.

There is an extensive literature on the challenge of parenting exceptional children (Barsch, 1968; Kroth, 1975; Love, 1970; Ross, 1964). Fine (1978) has written of the difficulties that parents sometimes face with gifted children, itemizing suggestions. Stock (1977) reviewed the literature on parent education programs with parents of neurologically impaired children, underscoring the problems these children can create within a family structure. Simmons-Martin (1975) reported on a parent education program for parents of deaf children, using a simulated apartment life setting. Rossett (1974) also reported on a communications-based parent education program for parents of learning impaired adolescents. Carkhuff and Bierman (1970) trained parents of emotionally disturbed children in interpersonal skills and found that these parents gained in communication skills over a treatment and control group. They argued that systematic skills training was a preferred mode of treatment of these parents over involving them directly in therapy. For some time there has been great interest in training parents of retarded children in behavior management techniques to help them better manage their children at home (Heifetz, 1975), usually with good results.

The references cited previously on parenting exceptional children are only samples of the extensive literature in this area. Parent education programs with special populations are likely to increase with the greater attention to preschool development. Also, federal laws such as PL 94-142 that mandate the full education of all handicapped children are likely to promote more auxilliary services, such as parent education programs.

Parent Education in the Schools

Concurrent with the rising of parents' interest in parent education programs, there is growing interest in teaching parenting skills to school-age children. More and more it is being recognized that many persons enter parenthood woefully ignorant of vital information on the needs of infants and young children and lacking the most rudimentary knowledge of how to develop a healthy parent–child relationship.

In addition, with the number of teenage marriages and unwed mothers increasing, education for parenting seems as necessary in the schools as the basic academic subjects. Consequently, more junior highs, high schools, and youth organizations are offering structured educational experiences on child development and parenting. The potential outcomes of such programs could conceivably be to lower substantially the role of child abuse among frustrated parents, and to increase greatly the number of children being raised under more optimal conditions.

In the past, home economics courses have been the traditional base of such instruction, often given in dry, textbook form. The growing awareness of the importance of parenting education for younger persons, however, has prompted the development of some exciting and experientially oriented programs. Significant impetus to the movement was offered in 1972 through a joint program of the U.S. Office of Education and the Office of Child Development. Under federal funding, the Education Development Center of Newton, Massachusetts developed a comprehensive course for grades 7 through 12, entitled

Exploring Childhood (Education Development Center, 1978). It is in the form of a 1-year elective course and utilizes actual observation of children as well as case studies, workbooks, audiotapes, and films.

The use of these curricular materials was extended in 1973 to such youth and community agencies as the National Federation of Settlements and Neighborhood Centers, Boys' Clubs of America, Save the Children Federation/Appalachian Program, the Salvation Army, Girl Scouts of America, Boy Scouts of America, and the National 4-H Club Foundation of America. The extensive ways in which these organizations implemented the program and developed additional materials is written up in a U.S. Government pamphlet (Ogg, 1975).

A logical target of parenting courses in the schools is teenage parents. Many of these are unwed mothers, but even when there are two parents, the confusion and anxiety over the parenting role is evident. Often the young mother is a product of an unhappy parenting experience and lacks an adequate model to imitate. Disturbing feelings about herself in the parenting role, coupled with a history of her own emotional needs not being met, increase the probability that a child-abusing situation will occur. The programs for these young parents ought to consider some personal therapeutic experiences as well as directed study on aspects of child development and parenting.

The parent education movement in the public schools has not met with the same volatile reaction that sex education programs have encountered. Many parents are ambivalent and even reactive to the role of the school in sex education, fearing that children will obtain "wrong" information, will be encouraged into promiscuity, or that home values will be violated. Arguments and data to the contrary seem to do little to ease the anxiety of these parents. Community acceptance of parenting courses in the schools is indicative of the awareness of "moms and dads" that parenting is important, that they might not have entered parenthood as prepared as they would have wished, and that classes in parenting may assist their children toward a fulfilling experience when they become parents.

Does Parent Education Make a Difference?

The testimonials by parents are legion as to how they enjoyed and were helped by parent education programs. If we were to look only at the testimonials, we would have to conclude that parent education programs are highly successful. But is there any research evidence for such a conclusion?

One difficulty with obtaining research data is that most parent education leaders are practitioners, not researchers. Consequently consumer satisfaction, which indeed is often achieved, is the main criterion by which effectiveness gets judged. In addition, much of the literature, even in professional journals, is of a descriptive nature, advocating some form of parent education or speaking to certain problems.

Well-controlled studies are difficult to obtain for a number of reasons. The dynamic interplay among the leader(s) and group members makes every group a unique experience. Instructor personality and competency affects outcomes as could duration of the program, prior attitudes of the participants, and socioeconomic and cultural factors. Accordingly, caution needs to be exercised in generalizing from the results of a single study.

A review of literature on the efficacy of parent education programs primarily highlighted behavioral models. Johnson and Katz (1973), O'Dell (1974), and Berkowitz and Graziano (1972), reported on studies wherein parents were trained in behavioral techniques. The evidence generally showed that parents were able to effect positive, although often limited, changes in their children. Most of the reported studies involved parents acting on their children via implementing reinforcement strategies rather than by communicating with and involving children actively in the behavior change process.

There are some data available on the effects of some more humanistically oriented parent programs. Hanley (1974) reported that Parent Effectiveness Training did increase the parents' acceptance of their children and their children's behavior, that the parents were able to communicate more clearly, and were able to allow their children greater autonomy. Wunderlin (1973) utilized a communications training program with adolescents and their parents and found that generally, communication patterns in the family improved. A number of studies reported negative findings, however. For example, Stock (1977) failed to find the expected positive changes in parent attitudes and behavior as a result of a humanistic–relational program. Mahoney (1974) reported only limited success with an Adlerian approach, which sought to help parents better recognize why their children were misbehaving and how to effectively intervene. Mahoney found that the parents' attitudes toward discipline did not change, nor was there a decrease in parent overprotectiveness.

An advantage of the behaviorally oriented research is that it focuses on actual behavior, so that conclusions can be drawn as to what happens with parents and with their children. The more humanistic, relational, and communication-based training programs tend to look at changes in parent attitudes, beliefs, and values, with less focus on what they actually do differently with their children or if their children benefit.

From a family systems viewpoint, the changing of one member's behavior changes the system. If mother no longer yells and threatens, but instead sets clear limits and avoids endless arguments, how would these changes affect parent–child, husband–wife, and child–child interactions? There is a need for research that looks at changes in families from a systems perspective. Systems have an "elasticity," and while the system may shift, there is often a tendency for former patterns to get reestablished. This raises questions as to the permanence of changes that might be noted while the parent is in the program or immediately afterward.

While there is a growing body of research findings on the effects of different parent education programs, more systematic study is necessary to answer questions about these programs. Such research will require clearer statements by practitioners as to their goals and their procedures for achieving those goals. Questions regarding instructor competence and instructional formats also need to be researched.

The findings to date are mainly that parents like parent education programs, each type of parent education program has its devotees, and many parents report that they are being helped. More empirical evidence is needed to support or refute these impressions, to discriminate among the input variables in parent education programs in relation to outcomes, and to study more holistically the effects of parent participation on family structure. Such research will inevitably lead the practitioner to develop and implement more effective parent education programs.

The Future

The parent education movement is here to stay; it is needed, and it is likely to expand and change in the years ahead. Thus far, there have been numerous models and programs of parent education developed and implemented, but more data are required in order to establish what in fact is being accomplished. Clearly one of the major needs for the future is to develop more adequate testing of the applicability and efficacy of the different models with different populations.

The most obvious target population is parents. Even "intact" traditional families are under increasing stress. Nontraditional families, such as single-parent or foster familes, often experience additional stress and may require somewhat different information and parenting strategies.

Parent education for teenagers is on the upswing as a result of programs offered in the public schools and other youth agencies. These programs are seen by the community as being valuable because they seek to educate children in parenting skills before they become parents. Once teenagers become parents (married or unmarried) the importance of their acquiring healthy parenting skills is even more evident. The future is likely to witness the development and extension of parenting programs that are sensitive to the values of different cultural and ethnic groups. More efforts to meet the needs of parents of handicapped children are also occurring.

Little has happened, however, by way of preparing and evaluating instructors. There are currently no national standards; the persons leading parent groups range from expert to adequate to bunglers and charlatans. What criteria are reasonable and necessary if one is to instruct others in parenting—that you have parented effectively?—that you have parented poorly but know your mistakes?—that having parented is helpful but not mandatory if you have other kinds of awareness, knowledge and skills? Are formal academic credentials necessary? Do different parent education models require different leadership training programs in terms of personality or value variables? Also, as stated, parent education for parents of atypical children is likely to increase. What are the needs of these parents and who will serve them?

The public schools seem to be expanding their coverage of educational and human needs. Today, schools frequently offer educational and skill development programs from preschool through adult education. More and specialized personnel are being located in the schools— counselors, social workers, psychologists, child development experts and special education personnel, to name the more visible professional groups. Many of these persons in addition to teachers are excellent candidates for parent education leadership training. Programs offered through the schools may be more palatable to the public than programs offered through clinical settings.

Yet, mental health clinics are striving to offer more comprehensive services, and preventive and educational programs are assuming higher priorities. Churches with their historical concern for family life are another center for parent education programs. The number of private organizations offering instruction in parenting is also increasing.

Parent education is a challenging, exciting, and vital movement. It truly supports the American ideal of creating the most fortuitous circumstances for children to achieve their potential. The outcomes in terms of more effective parenting resulting in more psychologically healthy children seems well worth the efforts being made by the professional and lay communities.

References

Addams, J. *Twenty years at Hull House.* New York: MacMillan, 1942.

Babcock, D., & Keepers, T. *Raising kids OK.* New York: Grove Press, 1976.

Barsch, R. *The parents of the handicapped child: The study of child rearing practices.* Springfield, Ill.: Charles C. Thomas, 1968.

Becker, W. C. *Parents are teachers.* Champaign, Ill.: Research Press, 1968.

Berkowitz, D. P., & Graziano, A. M. Training parents as behavior therapists: A review. *Behaviour Research and Therapy,* 1972, *10,* 297–317.

Berne, E. *Games people play.* New York: Grove Press, 1964.

Bronfenbrenner, U. How will we raise our children in the year 2000? *Saturday Review of Education,* 1973, *1,* 32.

Brown, C. C. It changed my life. *Psychology Today,* 1976, *10,* 47–57; 109–112.

Carkhuff, R. R., & Bierman, R. Training as a preferred mode of treatment of parents of emotionally disturbed children. *Journal of Counseling Psychology,* 1970, *17,* 157–161.

Dinkmeyer, D., & Dreikurs, R. *Encouraging children to learn: The encouragement process.* Englewood Cliffs, N.J.: Prentice-Hall, 1963.

Dinkmeyer, D., & McKay, G. *Systematic training for effective parenting.* Circle Pines, Minn.: American Guidance Services, 1976.

Dreikurs, R., & Soltz, V. *Children: The challenge.* Des Moines, Iowa: Meredith Press, 1964.

Education Development Center. *Exploring children: Program overview and catalog of materials.* Newton, Mass.: Education Development Center, 1978.

The Exceptional Parent. Boston: Psych-Ed Corporation.

Faber, A., & Mazlish, E. *Liberated parents/liberated children.* New York: Grossett & Dunlap, 1974.

Farber, B. *Mental retardation: Its social context and social consequences.* Boston: Houghton Mifflin, 1968.

Fine, M. J. Facilitating parent–child relationships. *Gifted Child Quarterly,* 1978, *21,* 487–500.

Fraiberg, S. *The magic years.* New York: Charles Scribner's Sons, 1959.

Gesell, A., & Ilg, F. L. *The child from five to ten.* New York: Harper & Row, 1946.

Ginott, H. *Between parent and child.* New York: MacMillan, 1965.

Ginott, H. *Between parent and teenager.* New York: MacMillan, 1969.

Glasser, W. *Reality therapy, a new approach to psychiatry.* New York: Harper & Row, 1965.

Glasser, W. *Schools without failure.* New York: Harper & Row, 1969.

Gordon, T. *Parent effectiveness training.* New York: Peter H. Wyden, 1970.

Hall, M. C. *The responsive parenting program.* Lawrence, Kans.: H. & H. Enterprises, 1978.

Hanley, D. F. Changes in parent attitudes related to parent effectiveness training and a family enrichment program. *Dissertation Abstracts,* 1974, *34,* 7044-A.

Harris, T. *I'm OK—you're OK—A practical guide to Transactional Analysis.* New York: Harper & Row, 1969.

Heifetz, L. J. Toward freedom and dignity: Alternative formats for training parents of retarded children in behavior modification. *Dissertation Abstracts,* 1975, *35,* 4175–4176.

Ilg, F. L., & Ames, L. B. *Child behavior.* New York: Harper & Row, 1955.

James, M. *What do you do with them now that you've got them?* Menlo Park, Calif.: Addison-Wesley, 1974.

James, M., & Jongeward, D. *Born to win.* Reading, Mass.: Addison-Wesley, 1971.

Johnson, C. A., & Katz, R. C. Using parents as change agents for their children: A review. *Journal of Child Psychology & Psychiatry,* 1973, *14,* 181–200.

Kroth, R. L. *Communicating with parents of exceptional children: Improving parent–teacher relationships.* Denver, Colo.: Love Publishing, 1975.

Love, H. D. *Parental attitudes toward exceptional children.* Springfield, Ill.: Charles C. Thomas, 1970.

Madsen, C. K., & Madsen, C. H. *Parents/children/discipline: A positive approach.* Boston: Allyn and Bacon, 1972.

Mahoney, K. F. The effect of Adlerian groups on the authoritarian childrearing practices of parents. *Dissertation Abstracts,* 1975, *35,* 4161-A.

McGuiness, T. P. *Teaching parents about reality therapy.* Los Angeles: Educator Training Center, 1977. (Mimeograph)

Miller, W. *Systematic parent training.* Champaign, Ill.: Research Press, 1975.

O'Dell, S. Training parents in behavior modification: A review. *Psychological Bulletin,* 1974, *81,* 418–433.

Ogg, E. *Preparing tomorrow's parents.* New York: Public Affairs Committee, 1975.

Patterson, G. *Living with children* (Rev. ed.). Champaign, Ill.: Research Press, 1976.

Richardson, S. A. The effect of physical disability on the socialization of a child. In D. A. Goslin (Ed.), *Handbook of socialization theory and research.* Chicago: Rand McNally, 1971.

Ross, A. O. *The exceptional child in the family.* New York: Grune & Stratton, 1964.

Rossett, A. Special strategies for a special problem: Improving communication between hearing impaired adolescents and their parents. *Volta Review,* 1974, *76,* 231–238.

Simmons-Martin, A. Facilitating parent–child interactions through the education of parents. *Journal of Research and Development in Education,* 1975, *8,* 96–102.

Smith, J. M., & Smith, D. E. *Child management: A program for parents and teachers.* Champaign, Ill.: Research Press, 1976.

Soltz, V. *Study group leader's manual for children: The challenge.* Chicago: Alfred Adler Institute, 1967.

Spock, B. *Baby and child care.* New York: Pocket Books, 1957.

Stock, H. V. *The effects of a humanistic–relational parent education group on neurologically impaired children and their parents.* Unpublished doctoral dissertation, University of Kansas, 1977.

Warnick, L. The effects upon a family of a child with a handicap. *New Outlook for the Blind,* 1969, *63,* 299–304.

Wunderlin, R. F. The effects of communication training on verbal communications and relationship ratings of parents and adolescents. *Dissertation Abstracts,* 1974, *34,* 6400-A.

Chapter 2

A Conceptualization of the American Family

DENNIS H. KARPOWITZ

What forces have shaped the American family? How has family life affected society? Is the American nuclear family in trouble? How are the changing roles of men and women affecting family life? Will alternatives to the family such as communal living and group marriages replace more traditional forms of the family? Are the pressures of a modern technological society too much for the continued existence of the nuclear family? These questions and many more like them have raised important issues regarding the state of the nuclear family in American society today. This chapter selectively evaluates some of these issues in an effort to conceptualize, at least partially, the American family of the 1970s.

A clear picture of the American family is clouded by many emotionally impassioned pleas that have no basis in either the biological, social, or behavioral sciences. Examples of such unsupported statements include, "the nuclear family is dead," "marriage has become obsolete," and "the spiraling divorce rate demonstrates the failure of the family as an institution in modern society." They are in fact speculation. As a result, much misinformation abounds. Many myths have become "truths." There is a need to return to the solid footing of research from which to generate hypotheses concerning the family (Rossi, Kagan, & Hareven, 1978). There are as yet few definitive answers to the questions posed earlier, but there are some hypotheses that have been confirmed

27

HANDBOOK ON
PARENT EDUCATION

in a number of studies; others have been found wanting or have been disconfirmed. One purpose of this chapter is to clarify directions in the study of the family that seem to have some empirical footing or that would have pragmatic benefits. Many of the references in this chapter provide further sources of information and reflect the author's bias toward methodologically sound studies and findings that have been at least minimally replicated. Theories have been labeled as such.

A major thesis of this chapter is that the American nuclear family is alive and strong (Graubard, 1978). The family has been and is besieged by forces that change and alter the functioning of the family unit. But the family has also been a determining factor in the shaping of many of these same forces. For example, the family changed to meet the demands of the Industrial Revolution and migration to the cities. But the family also initiated change that helped to precipitate these very events (Hareven, 1978). The family is not a static entity but a changing, coping, developing, adapting, acting, involving social organism. No other social institution has adapted to such a wide variety of social changes over such an extended time period.

The presence of these many strengths does not eliminate the many problems now impinging on the family. The staggering divorce rate (Glick, 1975), the constant mobility, the perfectionistic expectations within spouse and parent–child relationships, and pluralistic values in relation to family matters are just a few of the challenges that modern families have to face (Joint Commission on Mental Health of Children, 1970). Means for helping families deal with the common and the uncommon problems that beset them need further exploration. Parent education is one of those means.

The chapter begins with some working definitions: the family, the nuclear family, the extended family, the one-parent family, and the reconstituted family. The history of the family in Western culture is briefly reviewed. The impact of modern American society on the family is selectively examined. The effects of the mass media, poverty, and wealth, two parents working outside the home, government interventions, and value and role pluralism are given particular attention. Factors directly affecting the stability of the family such as child abuse, mobility, divorce, one-parent families, and reconstituted families are surveyed. Systems theory is presented as one vehicle for examining and understanding family interaction. An outline of the change that families undergo over time follows next. Finally, some conclusions are drawn about the future viability of the family in American society.

The literature concerning American families is replete with definitions of what constitutes a *family* (Melville, 1977; Williamson, 1972). A working definition that incorporates some of the breadth found in American society is that a family is a multigenerational unit in which people live "under the same roof." Family members have either a biological relationship or a legal relationship or an irrational attachment to one another. They may have two or all three of the preceding attachments.

The *nuclear family* usually consists of a mother and/or a father and "their children." When one speaks of grandparents, cousins, aunts, or uncles as being part of the family, this defines the extended family. Such additional family members may live in or outside the nuclear family's home. The family of origin is the family in which the person being referred to was a child. This, then, is the family in which one was raised.

One-parent families constitute an ever-increasing proportion of all families (Glick, 1975). A one-parent family is one in which a single parent (father or mother) is the head of the household and in which there is at least one child. When a single person with one or more children marries, that family becomes a reconstituted family. The other spouse may or may not have children.

A Brief History of the Family in Western Cultures

Colonial America

Several histories of childhood and the family are now available (e.g., Aries, 1962; Gordon, 1978). From the discovery of America until well into the nineteenth century, most American families sustained themselves by farming. This agrarian economic foundation affected the total organization and functioning of the family. In contrast to modern society in the last half of the twentieth century, in the agrarian society of the colonial period, most of the available time was spent producing the food necessary to sustain life. The whole family, even relatively young children of 5 or 6 years of age, had to perform duties necessary to the family's economic survival.

What little time was available for recreational activity was quite well organized in typical farm communities. Many social skills were learned through such activities as doing the old barn dance, the Virginia Reel.

Value systems during the colonial period reflected a narrower range and were acknowledged more firmly by the total community. Thus, a neighbor might have disciplined a child with full assurance that the parents would concur. Family and community rules of behavior were so universal and accepted as to be almost unspoken.

The roles of men, women, and children were much more narrowly defined. Contrary to some recent literature describing traditional women's roles (e.g., Van Dusen & Sheldon, 1977), the role of the woman in the pre-Industrial Revolution family was neither unequal nor subservient. Her contribution to the family in economic terms was crucial to maintaining economic stability. She was also viewed as the caretaker of education and culture. As reflected in attitudes and behavior, the woman was highly esteemed.

Many of the farms of this early period of American history were family farms. As children grew to adulthood, they were given a portion of the farm for their own. As a result, many of the neighbors were in fact relatives. The extended family was always close at hand. Childrearing responsibilities were shared by grandparents, aunts, uncles, and other relatives. Because the nuclear family was considerably larger than it is today, older children also helped care for their younger siblings.

The Industrial Revolution

At the close of the eighteenth century and the beginning of the nineteenth century, the Industrial Revolution began to have a major impact on all aspects of life. Its impact would change family life-styles for at least two centuries. Two major forces of the Industrial Revolution became immediately apparent: migration toward the city, and the influx of women and children into the industrial work force (Goode, 1971; Marx in Skolnick & Skolnick, 1977). Families were also active agents in the changes associated with the Industrial Revolution. According to Hareven (1978), families participated as "agents of change, socializing and preparing their members for new ways of life, facilitating their adaptation to industrial work and to living in complex urban communities [p. 58]."

Several immediate effects on family functioning resulted from the influx into metropolitan areas. Space and space usage changed drastically. Apartments were smaller in the cities and had little or no space around them for recreation and other activities. Contact with other families increased exponentially. The peer group became a much more potent influence in the lives of adults and especially children. The availability of food and other necessities became totally dependent on employment; this was in contrast to the availability of gardens on the farm.

Financial exigencies forced women and children into the factory. Father and often mother, as well as older siblings, were absent from the home for long hours each day. Tasks within the home setting became convenience matters rather than necessities. For example, doing the dishes and cleaning the house were not seen in the same functional light as milking the cows and making bread. It is at this point that the value of the role of women in the home changed drastically.

If the wife and mother stayed at home, her responsibilities for caring for the children and managing the household were not given the same prestige as had previously been the case in a more agrarian society. The home management role declined in social status faster than the role of child caretaker. Even into the twentieth century the latter was seen as an important, if not prestigious, activity. But more and more, homemaker became housewife, and the referent image became a harried, unkempt, bedraggled woman on her knees scrubbing the floors.

Men's roles became more distinct from that of the housewife. If anything, the man's power became greater because of the greater dependence of the family on his income (Anderson, 1978). However, his influence within the home began to diminish if only by his greater absence (Biller, 1974). In families where the wife remained at home, there was an increasing role differentiation with father as provider and mother as child caretaker. Even in families where the wife and mother was employed, she was still expected to care for the home and children.

Although the city family lived near more people, their family lifestyle became more and more isolated. The established rural patterns of community "get-togethers" did not transfer to the city life-style. Extended family social contacts decreased drastically, especially among white Americans.

One way of tracing this trend toward greater isolation of the nuclear family is to examine size of household. According to Kobrin (1978) 35% of households in 1870 had seven or more members. This percentage dropped to 20.4, 5.8, and 4.1 in 1900, 1950, and 1973, respectively. During the same time, the percentage of households with only one member rose from 3.7 to 18.5. These data allow Kobrin to conclude,

> The great increase in persons living separately from families, and the concentration of these people at the youngest and oldest stages of the adult life cycle, indicate two major changes: that a process of age-segregation is going on, and that there is a decreasing tolerance for family forms which include nonnuclear members [p. 79].

In addition to the influence of the Industrial Revolution, more recently World Wars I and II, and the women's movement of the 1960s and 1970s have all resulted in greater and greater numbers of women entering the work force. In 1940, 15% of married women living with their husbands were employed. By 1960 this figure had doubled to 31%, and in 1970 it rose to 41% (Leslie, 1973).

Summary

In summarizing the trends that have deeply affected the family structure and function from American agrarian society through the first half of the twentieth century, the following seem to be particularly relevant.

1. The nuclear family had become more and more isolated.
2. The role of women in the home had decreased in prestige.
3. The social value placed on childrearing functions had decreased.
4. The peer influence on children had increased.
5. Dependence on the economic role of the father had increased.
6. Greater numbers of married women living with their husbands had entered the work force.
7. Family space both in the home (apartment) and outside the home had decreased.

The Impact of Modern American Society on the Family

Television

Since the turn of this century, methods of communication have revolutionized the public transmission of information. There are more radios and more televisions in America than there are dwellings. Families play their television sets an average of 6–7 hours each day (U.S. Office of Management and Budget, 1973, p. 221). Some of the effects of television have been studied empirically with some support found for the following hypotheses:

1. Television viewing of violent material may increase aggression in children (*Television and Social Behavior,* 1972).
2. Television may prevent communication and the effective learning or practice of social skills (Robinson, 1972).

3. Television may prevent or delay conflict resolution or conflict instigation (Rosenblatt & Cunningham, 1976).
4. Television may also give people unrealistic expectations in regard to typical family functioning.

The most common sequence in family situation comedies begins with a "happy" family that faces some obstacle and by the end of the 25–50-minute presentation, it miraculously overcomes the problem and everyone lives "happily every after." Even soap operas follow a more subtle version of this same sequence. Expectations can easily be built up that are unattainable in a typical marriage or family.

Poverty

Although the United States is the richest country in the world by some standards, and its standard of living is unparalleled, there are still many in this country who suffer malnutrition and are poor by any standard. Gordon (1977) reported that 26.9% of the families living in the U.S. in 1976 had an annual income of less than $7000, and 17.9% had income less than $5000. For families headed by a female, these figures are even more staggering: 38% of white female-headed families and 65% of nonwhite female-headed families had an annual income of less than $3000 in 1964 (Joint Commission on Mental Health of Children, 1970). The contrast of wealth and poverty side by side creates tremendous anger and resentment among the poor.

Unfortunately much of middle-class America is shielded from the reality of poverty through the segregation of the poor. The blight of poverty is especially evident among nonwhites (Frost & Hawkes, 1970). The family life-styles and childrearing patterns correlated with poverty are grossly different from those of the middle class (Chilman, 1966). Childrearing patterns and family life-styles more prevalent among the poor include: (a) inconsistent, harsh physical punishment; (b) fatalistic attitudes and magical thinking; (c) an orientation to the present; (d) rigid, authoritarian family structures with strict definitions of male and female roles; (e) constricted experiences with society and an alienated, distrustful approach to society; (f) limited verbal communication with little attention to abstract concepts; (g) human behavior seen as unpredictable; (h) low self-esteem, passivity, and acceptance of impoverished conditions; (i) distrust for the opposite sex (Joint Commission on Mental Health of Children, 1970, p. 191). Thus, there are tremendous differences in the psychological and social functioning of middle-class families and poverty stricken families in America.

Maternal Employment

As suggested earlier, homemaking and mothering roles have been devalued, at least in the media and in the actions of government programs in the third quarter of this century. There has been a tremendous upsurge of government spending for child day-care programs in the decade of the 1970s. However, when parents were asked their preference in a 1975 national child-care consumer study reported by Woolsey (1978), they suggested greater flexibility of work hours, more part-time, but long-term employment opportunities, and a preference for caring for children within the context of the family, including the extended family.

For many families the only way to maintain the economic life-style that they have enjoyed from the family of origin is for both husband and wife to work. In the early stages of marriage this is seen as a temporary situation. Also many women today want to use their skills and capacities in the world of work rather than in the home. But as financial indebtedness becomes a fact, the decision for both to be employed becomes a necessity. The birth of children increases the need for greater financial stability, which again acts as a force to return the wife to full- or part-time employment. Younger children especially may suffer from the inconsistency produced by the usual necessity of many caretakers. Here the suffering may not come in the form of gross emotional instability (Hoffman & Nye, 1974), but rather in the failure to fulfill their potential in areas of personality, social, and cognitive functioning (Biller, 1974). It may be asking the impossible of parents to work hard all day and then come home in the evening and be expected to meet all of the needs of growing children. It is little wonder that such working parents are so frustrated with the dissonance between expectation (their own and society's) and actual functioning.

The work of Lois Hoffman and her associates (e.g., Hoffman & Nye, 1974) makes clear the relationship between a mother's attitude about employment, whether she works outside the home or not, and the effect of the situation on children. Where attitudes and behavior are harmonious, benefit to the child is maximized. Where attitudes and behavior are in conflict, the child is affected negatively. In other words, mothers who genuinely desire to work outside the home and do work outside the home, and mothers who desire to focus their energies within the home and are able to expend their energies in the home benefit the child more than the two discrepant conditions. Unfortunately, social and economic pressures often force maternal employment even though mother may prefer to be at home.

Government Programs

While government intervention is supposed to reflect concern for the family, the actual programs have often functioned in a way that offers "encouragement to divorce, separation and desertion" (Blaydon & Stack, 1978). Welfare assistance has grown from $17 billion in 1944 to $177 billion in 1975, while at the same time there has been no decline in the proportion of poverty, unemployment, and other major indices that might reflect that the tremendous financial outlay is in any way encouraging solutions to the problems.

It appears that many government social programs function in such a way as to make the "cure worse than the disease." The following steps illustrate the vicious cycle that often prevents a social reform program from being effective.

1. A problem or need is identified that adversely affects a large number of people but a small proportion of the total population. For example, the mid-1960s saw a rapid increase in the number of illegitimate births among teenagers. This observation was linked with poor sex education in the homes of these young parents.

2. A social reform program is developed to correct the problem. To continue the illustration suggested previously, sex education programs were developed.

3. The program is often implemented within the structure of an existing system. Since the existing system already has the population "captive" and the administration unit is already available, using the existing system makes economic sense. Thus, a sex education program was implemented in the public school systems across the nation. It might be noted that implementation often precedes proper evaluation of either the appropriateness of the program or its effectiveness. For example, at what ages should certain sex education information be introduced? Will such a program decrease illegitimacy?

4. Although the program was developed to meet the needs of a small proportion of individuals who have the need or problem, the majority as well as the minority take advantage of the program. So parents who normally would have taken the responsibility for teaching their children sexual processes and values turn this function over to the schools.

5. The cost of the program becomes inflated because of use. Price goes up. Quality goes down. No group education system can be as effective as the individualized instruction that can take place in the home. At home, level of development can be considered individually rather than on a group basis, and values can be taught as well as mechanics and information.

6. The public responds negatively to the program as they witness the effects of the increased cost and as the program does not offer any real solution to the problem. The credibility of government decreases. To conclude the illustration, reports of outrage in communities all over the country in response to sex education programs have been typical. The rate of illegitimacy has not only not decreased, it has increased. Other negative side effects have included the increase of sexual interest prior to appropriate emotional development and the separation of sexual information and values considerations. There is an increasing gap between schools and the communities they serve. Family functioning has given up another of its responsibilities, one for which it is aptly suited.

This example is only one of many that might be cited. Our present welfare assistance system reflects the same cycle. The point here is not to devalue government intervention per se, but to recognize that such assistance must be implemented in a way that actually affects the problem for which it was designed and in a way that does not produce more problems than it solves (Rossi *et al.*, 1978). For example, if parents of "high-risk" children were given information regarding sexual functioning and taught to teach their children this information, many of the negative side effects of the cycle described might have been avoided.

Values and Roles

Political pluralism has had a positive effect on the American system of government. However, the increase in alternatives regarding values and family roles seems to have created more confusion than help. One reason for this is that often life-style alternatives to the family are experimented with by large numbers of individuals and families long before the short- and long-term consequences of such alternatives have been effectively evaluated. Stinnett and Birdsong (1977) have recently examined dispassionately the evidence regarding such alternatives to more traditional family life-styles as cohabitation, swinging, extramarital relations, communes, and group marriage. Although these alternatives will undoubtedly continue to be pursued by a small proportion of the population, the authors found them wanting along such variables as commitment, trust, security, deep personal relationships, friendship, maturity, harmony, longevity, and responsibleness. If these variables are valued, then the family provides greater opportunity for their development than the proposed alternatives.

As a specific example, research regarding the effects of communal living on children almost uniformly finds neglect, deprivation, mal-nourishment, unhappiness, and lack of education to be commonplace (Berger, 1972; Rothchild & Wolf, 1976).

With the advent of the feminist movement of the 1960s and 1970s came the cry of equality regardless of sex. Demands for equal rights in education and employment have been very justified. However, some demands have been ridiculous, while others have failed to examine the total consequences of the proposed action. One error has been the suggested equivalence of "equal" with "same." This equation's weak-ness is demonstrated in government building contracts that have spec-ified that restrooms must be the "same" for both sexes. Thus, the men's room has a sanitary napkin dispenser and the women's restroom has urinals.

The suggestion that infant care can be done equally well by mother, father, or another caretaker scrupulously avoids research findings re-garding mother–infant biosocial attachments and their effects on emo-tional and relationship attachments (Kagan, 1978). Rossi (1978) con-cludes,

> It is more likely that the emotional ties to the children are more important to mothers than to fathers. . . . If a society wishes to create shared parental roles, it must either accept the high probability that the mother–infant relationship will continue to have greater emotional depth than the father–infant relationship, or institutionalize the means for providing men with compensatory exposure and training in infant and child care in order to close the gap produced by the psychological experience of pregnancy, birth, and nursing. Without such compensatory training of males, females will show added dimensions of intensity to their bonds with children [p. 18].

Lamb (1976), in his excellent review of the role of the father in child development, concludes that the effects of maternal and paternal child-rearing are different and that both are needed for maximum child growth and development. He summarizes, "All the evidence we have suggests that childrearing is most enjoyable, most enriching, and most successful when it is performed jointly by two parents, in the context of a secure marital relationship [p. 33]."

Unfortunately much of the stress on women's rights has focused on adult male and female rights and needs, and little on the rights and needs of children or the family as a whole. Failure to examine these consequences may have undesirable effects on the family and all of its members, effects that are unforeseen and unwanted by all family mem-bers. One cannot look at family members in isolation.

Too frequently acceptance of a new trend precedes rather than follows the evaluation of the effects of the new behavior. Clearer definitions of alternative values and roles and a better understanding of the consequences of each will greatly enhance the effectiveness of family decisions in these areas.

Several factors have directly affected the stability of family relationships. They include child abuse, mobility, separation and divorce (one-parent families), and reconstituted families.

Child Abuse

Helfer and Kempe (1976) have recently summarized the now vast literature in the area of child abuse. Two decades of voluminous study in this area seems to indicate that the problem is larger and the effects more severe than first suspected. Child abuse may include physical abuse, physical neglect, emotional abuse and neglect, and sexual abuse. According to studies reported by the Office of Child Development (U.S. Department of Health, Education and Welfare, 1976) incidence rates range as high as 4 million per year in the U.S. A study done in Florida found that the incidence rate increased from 8.8 cases per 1000 children to 13.4 per 1000 with improved reporting procedures. Sixty percent of the reports were subsequently confirmed as child abuse (Nagi, 1975). There is no doubt that abuse adversely affects the child's growth and development and may make family life a living "hell" for all concerned (Segal & Yahraes, 1978). Programs to alter this tragic reality have been developed, and there is evidence that more families are taking advantage of the available help (Kempe & Kempe, 1978), but such programs must increase in number and scope.

Mobility

Family relationships are also drastically affected by the mobility of our society. Statistics on house mortgages indicate that the average home owner remains in a house for less than 5 years, and home owners are probably less transitory than apartment dwellers. When a move requires the development of new friendships, adjustment to new school situations, and the development of other support systems, stress is focused on every family member. When such moves come with limited time to develop "roots" in-between, the stress may have long-term negative effects on both adult and child family members (Joint Commission on Mental Health of Children, 1970).

Migrant workers and business executives alike are subjected to these sudden and frequent moves. Their adverse effects on families touch all segments of society. Mobility has contributed greatly to the isolation of the nuclear family. The ability of the family to use available resources in its extended family relationships and in the community is hindered through such constant relocation. Where home relocations are necessary, methods for inoculating family members or at least preparing them with skills that might be helpful to dealing with this particular stress would be very welcome.

Divorce, One-Parent Families, and Reconstituted Families

The increasing rate of separation and divorce is staggering (Glick, 1975). The probability of a marriage ending in divorce is 1 in 3 today. Among some groups and in some locations the percentage exceeds 50%. Divorce has increased seven-fold since the turn of the century (Segal & Yahraes, 1978). For many children and spouses the adverse effects of divorce are most difficult during the first year following the divorce. But for 25% of the children, the negative effects may persist much longer (Wallerstein & Kelly, 1976). The one-parent experience is often overwhelming for both the parent and the child. Women in particular are often not prepared for economic survival when the divorce occurs. The challenge of parenting is deeply felt when two parents can support each other in the process. When one parent must bear the full brunt of the economic and childrearing responsibilities, the stress increases exponentially.

Remarriage rates have kept pace with the divorce rate (Melville, 1977). This factor indicates that marriage has maintained its popularity; but when children are involved in the subsequent marriage, the reconstituted family often suffers severe developmental stress. Several of the stages of family development (see discussion later in this chapter) must be dealt with simultaneously instead of successively (Duberman, 1975). As yet, few clear-cut and substantial guidelines are available, but the need is clear.

Premarital and preparental education programs are needed on a much larger scale than is presently available. Specific programs to deal with foreseeable stress, such as the stress resulting from relocation, separation, or divorce, have been helpful where tried, but these programs have not reached the vast majority of individuals who undergo these experiences.

Summary

Summarizing the impact of modern American society on the family, the following conclusions seem reasonable:

1. Television may increase aggression, prevent communication, prevent or delay conflict instigation or resolution, and help to create unrealistic expectations about typical family life.

2. Poverty is still a part of our society. Poverty adversely affects family functioning and hinders effective child growth and development. Poverty creates anger and resentment. Many middle-class Americans are shielded from the reality of poverty.

3. Economic and social conditions have increased drastically the number of married women with young children who have entered the work force. The needs of children have been overlooked in this area. Whether the mother really wants to work and enjoys her employment is an important factor in the effects of such employment on the child.

4. Government intervention programs in education, welfare, industry, and health may have had good intentions toward the family, but in many cases the operationalization of these programs has adversely affected children and families.

5. Changing roles and values in American society have created ambiguity and uncertainty for many parents. Social "fads" have often been embraced by both the public and some social scientists before sufficient information became available with which to evaluate the consequences of such fads. When the data are impartially evaluated, it becomes clear that there is as yet no viable alternative to the nuclear family. The biological and constitutional forces involved in family relationships must be considered along with psychological, social, political, and economic factors.

6. Child abuse affects many American families.

7. Mobility can have adverse effects on family life and child growth and development, especially when relocation is frequent.

8. Divorce is increasingly affecting larger numbers of children. For more than a quarter of these children the negative effects may be long-lasting.

9. One-parent and reconstituted families face all of the stresses of two-parent, first-marriage families plus the stresses of their own unique experiences. There is increasing need for research and programs to better understand and help the one-parent and reconstituted family. Prevention of unnecessary divorce and inappropriate marriages through education and premarital and preparental counseling is needed.

Each of these factors has been reviewed separately, but in fact many of these factors interact together. In reality it is the total constellation of factors that affect and are affected by the family.

Systems Theory and Family Interaction

Virginia Satir (1972) has suggested an interesting game that illustrates how the family functions as a system. Members of the family tie ropes around their waists connecting each family member with the others. The ropes are usually 15–20 feet in length. Once the family is tied together, one family member is asked to fulfill a request, such as getting a drink of water. It becomes immediately apparent that the movement of one individual affects the whole family. This is a basic concept of systems theory.

Levels of Family Functioning

The family system functions at several levels simultaneously. The core level of the system is the intrapsychic or personal subsystem. Next is the interpersonal subsystem. The outermost level is the family unit subsystem. Outside the family there are also exterior systems that affect the family and its subsystems. Such exterior systems include schools, churches, social organizations, work places, and friends, to list just a few. Each system and subsystem has its own rules, goals, and strategies. It is at the interface of two or more systems or subsystems "where the action is." How each subsystem develops its own strategies for dealing with other subsystems determines the smoothness or roughness with which the total system functions (Kantor & Lehr, 1975). No event takes place without its effects being felt in two or more subsystems.

Like individual personality theorists, family systems theorists have developed concepts to clarify the functioning of the various subsystems beyond the intrapsychic level. At the interpersonal level Kantor and Lehr (1975) have suggested four roles or player parts that family members adopt when interacting with each other. These player parts include the mover, the opposer, the follower, and the bystander. These player parts bear remarkable resemblance to Satir's (1972) four patterns of communication: the blamer, the placator, the computer, and the distractor. At the family unit subsystem level Kantor and Lehr describe three family types: the open system, the closed system, and the random system. Each system has the capacity to function effectively or flaws may develop that get in the way of family functioning. Families develop goals or targets along the dimensions of affect, power, and meaning. They develop methods for reaching these goals along dimensions of space, time, and energy.

Depending upon the family type, different target ideals and access criterion variables are employed. The closed system values durability, fidelity, and sincerity in the affect dimension; authority, discipline, and preparation in the power dimension; and certainty, unity, and clarity in the meaning dimension. The closed family seeks to achieve these ideals by employing the access dimensions of fixed space, regular time, and steady energy.

In contrast, the open family system values responsiveness, authenticity, and latitude as target effect ideals; resolution, allowance, and cooperation as target power ideals; and relevance, affinity, and tolerance as target meaning ideals. Open family systems seek to achieve these ideals by using the access dimensions of movable space, variable time, and flexible energy. Likewise the random family system has its own target ideals and access criterion variables.

Thus, it is not enough to think of a family simply in terms of a group of individuals who live under the same roof. Powerful ties connect family members together. The action of any individual or subgroup affects the whole. The family has much in common with a living organism; each part can help or hinder itself, each other part, and the organism as a whole. Like a living organism, the whole is greater than the sum of its parts (Ritterman, 1977).

When considering a program designed to have an impact on the family, systems theory suggests that it is necessary to examine the effects of that program on the various subsystems in the family, including the spouses, parent–child interaction, sibling interaction, individual development, and systems outside the family that in turn impact upon the family. For example, if one spouse enters psychotherapy and achieves some personal growth through that experience, such change in that spouse may positively affect the spouse subsystem (improve relations) or may negatively affect that system (lead to divorce). Simultaneous and chaining effects may also be seen in the other subsystems of the family.

Change and Resistance

From the material reviewed earlier in this chapter it may seem as if the family is a static entity being acted on by forces outside of itself. It is the case that forces outside the family influence it. It is also true that the family is often very resistant to change. From the colonial era to the present, the nuclear family has remained the most important force in relationship to development and childrearing. The nature of family interaction has changed, the size of the family has decreased, timing of important family events have changed (age at marriage, spacing of children, etc.), the family has relocated in urban industrial centers; but through all of these changes, the nuclear family has remained powerful (Hareven, 1978).

All of the factors affecting this stability within change are not clearly understood. One concept that has been used to better understand this phenomenon is equilibrium. The family establishes interactions among its members and with extrafamilial systems that create a balance. The family strives to maintain this state of equilibrium and resists any force that would disturb the balance (Winter & Ferreira, 1969).

The power structure within the family also resists change. Members of the family form coalitions with each other that work to prevent change. At any point in time the family has developed its own history, which includes rules for what will be done, by whom, and how it will be done. These rules are often implicit and unspoken (Bowen, 1976). Anyone who attempts to either understand or change the family must be aware of these internal forces as well as the external forces described earlier.

Stages of Family Development

Just as families differ in regard to size, socioeconomic level, location, ethnicity, etc., so does each family undergo change depending upon the particular phase of development it is in. Families are continually developing. Dividing the course of that development into stages serves to highlight some major differences that can be identified at each stage (Haley, 1973). Solomon (1973) suggests that there are specific tasks associated with each stage. Failure to accomplish the task or tasks of any one stage produces problems in the course of family development and also hinders the accomplishment of tasks associated with subsequent stages. The theoretical conceptualization of the stages of family development is still in development. Thus, most of the supporting data are clinical rather than empirical.

Marriage

The first stage of family development is marriage. There are two tasks associated with this stage. First, it is necessary to relinquish the family of origin as the major source of emotional gratification. Each spouse must, so to speak, "cut the apron strings" with their parents. Parents may continue to play an important role, but the relationship with them cannot be the major relationship in the lives of the couple. This task may be partially or wholly accomplished before the marriage in situations where the spouses have been living away from their family of origin for some time. The second task of the marriage stage is the development of the spouse relationship as the single most important source of emotional strength for the couple. Couples vary according to the number and strength of other relationships, such as friends and career, but the spouse relationship should take priority (Solomon, 1973).

Problems at this stage occur when, for example, the wife "goes home to mama" before the couple really learns to resolve differences. Or perhaps the husband seeks his parents' economic advice, but fails to consult his wife. Some couples delay resolution of the tasks of this stage through economic dependence on one of their families of origin.

Birth of the First Child

The second stage of family development comes with the birth of the first child. Two tasks in this stage also represent challenges to continued family development. The first task is to effectively maintain the spouse relationship. With the birth of a child, time commitments change radically. The infant requires considerable time and energy. Energy levels are partially dependent upon the patterns of interaction developed that are necessary to the care of the newborn. Although husband and wife typically find they have less time together, according to the demands of this task, they must work out ways of maintaining their own relationship. The second task of this stage is to develop effective relationships with the infant. The needs of the infant cannot be ignored without deleterious consequences. These needs include providing not only physical necessities, but also opportunities to develop strong emotional attachments, feelings of security, and trust (Erikson, 1963).

Examples of failure to develop at this stage include one parent diverting all of his or her emotional energies to the child while withdrawing from or neglecting the spouse. The parents may compete with each other for the attention of the child. If one parent overinvests in the child, the other may withdraw into a career or social institutions, and so on. When a child comes to a couple only weeks or months after marriage, the task of the second stage may be thrust upon the couple well before the tasks of the first stage can be dealt with effectively. Couples may falsely assume that a child will help them solve some of the tasks and problems associated with their relationship. This is seldom the case. The birth of a child into a "rocky" marriage often simply exacerbates the problems (Lederer & Jackson, 1968).

Role Change

The third stage of family development is the most ambiguous and poorly defined. It covers the period of time in which the children grow to maturity. The task is simply expressed but more difficult to achieve: changing parental roles to meet the changing needs of maturing children. For example, parents can greatly enhance the ease with which children develop independence by slowly and steadily reducing their control of the child and giving him or her opportunities to make decisions. Methods of effective discipline vary greatly as a function of the age of the child. Whereas placing the child on a chair facing the corner may be effective as a discipline measure in early and middle childhood, it may encourage resentment and rebellion in adolescence.

Some parents may find they have a natural affinity to infants and toddlers but are "turned off" by the mannerisms of the latency-age child. Other parents are offended when peers increase in importance in the life of the child. The parent feels rejected and may be resentful. Still other problems arise when parents try to be "buddies" with their teenagers and give up the role of parent completely. Teenagers are often "turned completely off" by such role changes and actually prefer parents to remain parents (Ginott, 1969).

Last Child Leaves Home

The fourth stage of family development occurs when the last child leaves home. The first of the two tasks associated with this stage is the relinquishing of the child. In some families the role of "the baby of the family" may be overemphasized, making the dependence–independence conflict exaggerated. The adolescent may feel he or she is deserting the nest, while the parents feel the child is too immature to face the rigors of adult life on his or her own. Parents who have invested many years in the parenting role see the home and the future as barren and lonely without children at home.

Thus, the second task of this stage is the reinvestment of greater time and energy in the spouse relationship. Failure to accomplish this task may at least partially explain the divorces that often occur at this point after 25 or more years of marriage (Glick, 1975). Spouses who have not maintained some important aspects of their relationship while the children were in the home find this task particularly difficult. Other spouses look forward with anticipation to doing many things they were unable to do while the children were at home or while the financial burdens of helping a child through college were borne.

Loss

The last stage of family development occurs as loss becomes an increasing consideration in the lives of the couple. There are many types of loss, including loss of physical capacities (gradual or sudden), loss of friends and loved ones, loss of future opportunities, recognition that some goals may not be achieved, loss of respect in a youth-oriented culture. The task of this stage is to cope effectively with loss. There are few guidelines available in this area (Haley, 1973). Only recently have the social sciences become more aggressive in understanding the psychosocial functioning and the needs of the elderly (Goldberg & Deutsch, 1977). Erikson (1963) was one of the first to recognize that individuals at this stage can develop a sense of integrity or a sense of despair. Lederer and Jackson (1968) suggest that often the most effective type of marital relationships (the "heavenly twins" or the "collaborative geniuses") do not develop until the couple has reached full maturity. Problems at this stage are often real, such as physical disability, chronic pain, the repetition of mourning. However, many problems could be more effectively dealt with such as chronic depression, isolation, and loneliness.

In the context of parent education the stages of family development become an important, even crucial consideration. The needs of the parents with their first infant are vastly different from those of a large family with children of several ages or a family in which teenagers are about to depart from the home. Focusing the parent education program to meet the present needs of a particular family according to their stage of development and preparing them for subsequent stages is now lacking in many programs (Gordon, 1970; Patterson, 1971).

There are limitations in our present understanding of family development. As is clear from the preceding outline, only a few dimensions have been explored and these mostly at the theoretical level. More research and testing of hypotheses is needed. It seems clear that often the stages overlap and that sometimes the order is even reversed, for example, by reconstituted families and the early death of a family member. Nonetheless these stages can help clarify some of the particular and relevant needs of families at various stages of development (Haley, 1973; Solomon, 1973).

Conclusions

There is no such thing as "the" American family. Much evidence is available to show that many different factors interact to affect family functioning. Specific causal links have not been well established. What is clear is that both intrinsic and extrinsic factors affect family functioning in complex and idiosyncratic ways. Uniformity among American families is a myth perpetuated by our need to simplify and our drive toward the ideal. From one perspective this diversity is a great strength. It appears, for example, that there may be many "good" ways to rear children. The diversity, however, makes both understanding families and helping them change a more complex situation. There may be principles of effective family functioning that bridge some of this diversity. In childrearing, for example, there is some evidence that clarity of communication, salience, and warm acceptance facilitate effective growth and development (Lamb, 1976; Segal & Yahraes, 1978).

The effects on the family of such events as the Industrial Revolution and migration to large cities have too often been described in simple, linear, and causal terms. There is a growing body of historical research that clearly demonstrates that the interaction of these events with family functioning is much more complex than earlier, oversimplified explanations had indicated. This does not lessen the importance of these events; it is only that their relationship to the many factors affecting family functioning is changed.

Historically the family has probably been overidealized. The three-generation extended family of rural, nineteenth-century America was actually much less common than we sometimes imagine. For one thing, life expectancy figures show that most people didn't live that long. Migrations to America and then West also affected the extended kin concept. Such extended family resources were no doubt much less available than sometimes suggested. The nuclear family played a basic role in the nineteenth century, as it does now (Hareven, 1978).

It is important to view the family as a process, not as a static entity. It is constantly being affected by external stresses and support systems. The family in turn is an active agent in the creation of these stresses and support systems. The family is in the process of developing, becoming. It is also holding on and resisting change. Just as the family affects and is affected by these external factors, forces within the family and its members shape the family and are shaped by the family.

Seen in this light, one cannot but be impressed by the strength and survival capacity of the nuclear family in America. However, such a statement is not an invitation to sit back and simply "let the chips fall where they may." There is much that can be done to prevent some stresses, to cope and deal with some other stresses, and to resolve and eliminate still others. More and better research is absolutely necessary. Many questions remain unanswered or incompletely answered. There is an equally great need to communicate what we do know to couples and families. The productive possibilities in parent education seem almost limitless.

References

Anderson, M. Family, household, and the Industrial Revolution. In M. Gordon (Ed.), *The American family in social-historical perspective*. New York: St. Martin's Press, 1978.

Aries, P. *Centuries of childhood*, London: Jonathan Cape, 1962.

Berger, B., Hackett, B., & Millar, R. M. The communal family. *The Family Coordinator*, 1972, *21*(4), 419–428.

Biller, H. B. Paternal deprivation, cognitive functioning, and the feminized classroom. In A. Davids (Ed.), *Child personality and psychopathology: Current topics*. New York: Wiley-Interscience, 1974.

Blaydon, C. C., & Stack, C. B. Income support policies and the family. In A. S. Rossi, J. K. Kagan, & T. K. Hareven (Eds.), *The family*. New York: W. W. Norton & Co., 1978.

Bowen, M. Family therapy and family group therapy. In D. H. L. Olson (Ed.), *Treating relationships*, Lake Mills, Iowa: Graphic Publishing, 1976.

Chilman, C. *Growing up poor*. Washington, D.C.: U.S. Department of Health, Education and Welfare, Government Printing Office, 1966.

Duberman, L. *The reconstituted family*. Chicago: Nelson-Hall, 1975.

Erikson, E. H. *Childhood and society*. New York: W. W. Norton & Co., 1963.

Frost, J. L., & Hawkes, G. R. (Eds.). *The disadvantaged child: Issues and innovations*. New York: Houghton Mifflin, 1970.

Ginott, H. G. *Between parent and teenager*. New York: Avon Books, 1969.

Glick, P. C. A demographer looks at American families. *Journal of Marriage and the Family*, 1975, *37*(1), 15–27.

Goldberg, S. R., & Deutsch, F. *Life-span individual and family development*. Monterey, Calif.: Brooks/Cole Publishing, 1977.

Goode, W. J. World revolution and family patterns. *Journal of Marriage and the Family*, November 1971, pp. 624–635.

Gordon, M. (Ed.). *The American family in social-historical perspective*. New York: St. Martin's Press, 1978.

Gordon, M. J. Business and the economy: The U.S. economy in 1977. In T. B. Dolmatch (Ed.), *Information please almanac, atlas, and yearbook 1978*. New York: Information Please Publishing, 1977.

Gordon, T. *Parent effectiveness training*. New York: Peter Wyden, 1970.

Graubard, S. R. Preface to the issue, "The family." In A. S. Rossi, J. K. Kagan, & T. K. Hareven (Eds.), *The family*. New York: W. W. Norton & Co., 1978.

Haley, J. The family life cycle. *Uncommon therapy*. New York: Ballantine Books, 1973.

Hareven, T. K. Family time and historical time. In A. S. Rossi, J. K. Kagan, & T. K. Hareven (Eds.), *The family*. New York: W. W. Norton & Co., 1978.

Helfer, R. E., & Kempe, C. H. (Eds.). *Child abuse and neglect: The family and the community.* Cambridge, Mass.: Ballinger, 1976.

Hoffman, L. W., & Nye, F. I. *Working mothers.* San Francisco: Jossey-Bass, 1974.

Joint Commission on Mental Health of Children. *Crisis in child mental health: Challenge for the 1970s.* New York: Harper & Row, 1970.

Kagan, J. The child in the family. In A. S. Rossi, J. K. Kagan, & T. K. Hareven (Eds.), *The family.* New York: W. W. Norton & Co., 1978.

Kantor, D., & Lehr, W. *Inside the family.* San Francisco: Jossey-Bass, 1975.

Kempe, R. S., & Kempe, H. C. *Child abuse.* Cambridge, Mass.: Harvard University Press, 1978.

Kobrin, F. E. The fall in household size and the rise of the primary individual in the United States. In M. Gordon (Ed.), *The American family in social-historical perspective.* New York: St. Martin's Press, 1978.

Lamb, M. E. (Ed.). *The role of the father in child development.* New York: John Wiley & Sons, 1976.

Lederer, W. J., & Jackson, D. D. *The mirages of marriage.* New York: W. W. Norton & Co., 1968.

Leslie, G. R. *The family in social context* (2nd ed.). New York: Oxford University Press, 1973.

Marx, K. On family life under the factory system. In A. S. Skolnick & J. H. Skolnick (Eds.), *Family in transition.* Boston: Little, Brown and Co., 1977.

Melville, K. *Marriage and family today.* New York: Random House, 1977.

Nagi, S. Z. Child abuse and neglect programs: A national overview. *Children today.* Washington, D.C.: Office of Child Development/Office of Human Development, May–June 1975, pp. 13–17.

Patterson, G. R. *Families: Applications of social learning to family life.* Champaign, Ill.: Research Press, 1971.

Ritterman, M. K. Paradigmatic classification of family therapy theories. *Family Process,* 1977, *16*(1), 29–48.

Robinson, J. P. Television's impact on everyday life: Some cross-national evidence. In E. A. Rubinstein, G. A. Comstock, & J. P. Murray (Eds.), *Television in day-to-day life: Patterns of use* (Vol. 4 of *Television and Social Behavior*). Washington, D.C.: U.S. Government Printing Office, 1972.

Rosenblatt, P. C., & Cunningham, M. R. Television watching and family tensions. *Journal of Marriage and the Family,* 1976, *38*(1), 105–114.

Rossi, A. S. A biosocial perspective on parenting. In A. S. Rossi, J. K. Kagan, & T. K. Hareven (Eds.), *The family.* New York: W. W. Norton & Co., 1978.

Rossi, A. S., Kagan, J. K., & Hareven, T. K. (Eds.). *The family.* New York: W. W. Norton & Co., 1978.

Rothchild, J., & Wolf, S. B. *The children of the counterculture.* New York: Doubleday, 1976.

Satir, V. *Peoplemaking.* Palo Alto, Calif.: Science and Behavior Books, 1972.

Segal, J., & Yahraes, H. *A child's journey.* New York: McGraw-Hill, 1978.

Skolnick, A. S., & Skolnick, J. H. *Family in transition.* Boston: Little, Brown and Co., 1977.

Solomon, M. A developmental conceptual premise for family therapy. *Family Process,* 1973, *12*, 179–188.

Stinnett, N., & Birdsong, C. W. *The family and alternative life styles.* Chicago: Nelson-Hall, 1977.

Television and Social Behavior (5 vols.). Washington, D.C.: U.S. Government Printing Office, 1972.

U.S. Department of Health, Education and Welfare. *Child abuse and neglect: The problem and its management.* Washington, D.C.: HEW Office of Human Development/Office of Child Development, 1976.

U.S. Office of Management and Budget. *Social indicators, 1973.* Washington, D.C.: U.S. Government Printing Office, 1973.

Van Dusen, R. A., & Sheldon, E. B. The changing status of American women: A life cycle perspective. In A. S. Skolnick & J. H. Skolnick (Eds.), *Family in transition* (2nd ed.). Boston: Little, Brown and Co., 1977.

Wallerstein, J. S., & Keely, J. B. The effects of parental divorce: Experiences of the child in later latency. *American Journal of Orthopsychiatry,* 1976, 46(2), 257–269.

Williamson, R. E. *Marriage and family relations* (2nd ed.). New York: John Wiley & Sons, 1972.

Winter, W. D., & Ferreira, A. J. *Research in family interaction: Readings and commentary.* Palo Alto, Calif.: Science and Behavior Books, 1969.

Woolsey, S. H. Pied piper politics and the child-care debate. In A. S. Rossi, J. K. Kagan, & T. K. Hareven (Eds.), *The family.* New York: W. W. Norton & Co., 1978.

PART II

PARENT EDUCATION—
THEORETICAL FRAMEWORKS

217245

Chapter 3

Dreikurs and the Search for Equality

OSCAR C. CHRISTENSEN
CARROLL R. THOMAS

Background: The Adlerian Influence

Sigmund Freud (1856–1939) and Alfred Adler (1870–1937) were contemporaries in Vienna just after the turn of the century. Both Freud and Adler were practicing physicians prior to each developing an interest in psychology. Although they lived during the same period of time and in the same place, their positions could hardly have been more dissimilar. During their lifetimes Freud's psychoanalysis was rapidly accepted and Adler's individual psychology was overshadowed. However, Freud's theories have since been modified, largely by his followers, and numerous new schools of psychology have been developed whose tenets are increasingly compatible with Adler's original views.

In 1902, Freud invited Adler to join a small discussion group, which became the illustrious Vienna Psychoanalytic Society. Adler accepted the invitation and became an active member but never considered himself Freud's pupil or disciple. Adler actually joined Freud in the Vienna discussion group as a co-equal, contrary to most Psychology 1-A textbooks, which indicate that Adler was a student of Freud. As time passed, Adler's position diverged more and more from that of Freud, and he resigned from Freud's circle in 1911 to formulate and found his own school.

In 1919, Adler established a child guidance center in Vienna and also

53

HANDBOOK ON
PARENT EDUCATION

became a lecturer at the Pedagogical Institute. He was probably the first psychiatrist to apply mental hygiene principles in the schools. In the child guidance centers he established, Adler developed his innovative counseling approach for restricted audiences and dealt with parents and teachers as well as children. His was perhaps the first official use of "family therapy" and "community psychiatry" on record (Ansbacher, 1973, p. 53). Adler believed that the goal of psychology, psychiatry, and guidance was to educate the whole community toward more effective social living. He said, "During all my life it was my endeavor to bring people together [Rom, 1976, p. 5]." And he emphatically stated: "The study of human nature cannot be pursued with the sole purpose of developing occasional experts; only the understanding of human nature by every human being can be its proper goal [Adler, 1927a, p. 15]." Thus, Adler was not only concerned with helping children, but also with conveying knowledge and skills to others. Adler would discuss with the child, in a hypothetical problem-solving fashion, the child's situation and his or her mistaken goals (Adler, 1930). Most important, Adler explored with the child useful, alternative behaviors. Adler discovered unexpected benefits of counseling the child before a group:

> I found that treating the child as part of his group was very effective. It made the child realize that "no man liveth unto himself alone," and that the mistakes of every individual affect many lives and are of public concern. The boys and girls could be brought to see themselves as social beings, not as isolated units [Adler, 1927b, p. 491].

Adler's dream was to generate a true community of committed parents, teachers, and other adults who would work together to foster courage and social responsibility in children and youth. Before long the enthusiasm of the teachers infected the parents, especially through parent associations, and as a result, a number of child guidance centers were opened to the general community for parents and other interested parties (Terner & Pew, 1978).

By 1927, there were 22 child guidance centers in Vienna plus 20 in the rest of Europe (Adler, 1978). In 1931, the Individual Psychological Experimental School was founded. This school was a secondary school for boys aged 10–14 where Adler's psychological and educational principles could be comprehensively applied (Terner & Pew, 1978). Unfortunately, the school and the centers in Vienna, which by that time numbered over 30, were closed by the Austrian fascists in 1934. The German centers had already been closed or taken over by the Nazis a year earlier when Hitler came to power (Adler, 1978).

The Impact of Rudolf Dreikurs

During the last 11 years of Adler's life he spent most of his time in the United States, eventually making his home here. Due to the course of events in Europe before World War II, Adler decided to promote his ideas in America. However, the person who largely made Adler a household word in many families in the United States was Rudolf Dreikurs of Chicago. Dreikurs' inpact on childrearing practices and his contribution to individual psychology was recently acknowledged by Paul Rom, a prominent Adlerian (Rom, 1976).

> Among the most important developments in Adlerian Psychology has been the establishment of family counseling centers and family education study groups, dedicated to helping families develop a democratic life style guided by the principles of social equality and social interest. Much of the inspiration for this movement came from the writings and personal enthusiasm of Rudolf Dreikurs [p. 11].

Dreikurs was one of Adler's early students and colleagues who participated in the child guidance centers in Vienna. He was very well known throughout Europe before the fascists gained power. In 1939, he fled to the United States by way of Brazil and eventually established a practice in Chicago. In the years between his arrival in the United States in 1939 and his death in 1972, Dr. Dreikurs made a profound impact upon parent education, marriage and family counseling, the field of education, and the practice of psychotherapy, not only in the United States, but throughout the world. While his extensions and expansions of Adlerian theory and practice were profound, he resolutely opposed those of his students who would rename the Adlerian movement as Dreikurian or in any way detract from the originator, Alfred Adler. For the rest of his life "following his move to America his goal was to see Adler's psychology restored as a viable, actively practical, and dynamic school of thought [Terner & Pew, 1978, p. 374]."

Dreikurs' major contributions were not only to refine the open-centered family counseling concepts first demonstrated by Adler in Vienna prior to World War I, but also to demonstrate the multiple therapist concept long before it was presented in the general psychological literature, as well as various aspects of group counseling for which he received relatively little credit. He also developed a system of democratic conflict resolution to be used in the family, in the school, in industry, or in any other situation where people live and interact with each other (Dreikurs, 1970, 1972a, 1972b).

Dreikurs first established a parent counseling center at the Abraham Lincoln Center in Chicago in 1939. The history of the early years in

Chicago is indeed an intriguing one and demonstrates the tremendous resistance that Dreikurs had to overcome, including active opposition by the psychoanalytic community (Terner & Pew, 1978). Dreikurs considered his early breakthrough in teacher education to be the result of a summer session appointment to the faculty of the College of Education at the University of Oregon in 1957. Dr. Dreikurs went to Oregon at the invitation of Dr. Raymond Lowe, and it was there that many of his active followers had their first exposure to the Adlerian model. Dr. Lowe established a Parent Teacher Education Center at the University of Oregon in the winter of 1958, which has remained in operation ever since (Lowe, 1974). *Adlerian Family Counseling: A Manual for Counseling Centers* was published in 1959 and has served as the basic format for establishing centers elsewhere (Dreikurs, Corsini, Lowe, & Sonstegard, 1959).

Dreikurs' View of the Child and Parent–Child Relationships

Dreikurs work gave a great deal of emphasis to the importance of the socialization process that takes place in the family.

> One can understand a person's style of life when one recognizes his relationship with the other members of the family in his particular family constellation. The family constellation does not force a child to behave in a certain manner; it merely indicates how he arrived at his conviction. He's not the victim of the other, since he very early participates in shaping his relationships with them. The most important person in the development of his personality is the sibling who is most different from him [Dreikurs, Grunwald, & Pepper, 1964, p. 45].

> The family atmosphere—the attitudes, values, and relationships within the immediate family . . . provides the initial, critical medium through which the child's personality takes shape. From his experience of it, the child creates a picture of himself, of others, and of the world at large. It shapes his values and provides the testing ground for actions that will give him a sense of belonging and significance [Terner & Pew, 1978, p. 5].

By and large, all children are influenced by the family atmosphere, which is established by father and mother. Through their parents, children are exposed to cultural and social influences. Racial, religious, economic, educational, and other social factors are perceived by children through experiences with their parents. The similarity of siblings expresses their common experience at home, the values to which they were exposed, and the patterns of behavior in which they were trained. It is within this social unit that the child learns to adapt (Dreikurs, 1955).

The child who endlessly strives for better security, better orientation, better adaptation, must and will formulate for himself ideals, concepts, however vague, or an ideal goal of absolute security, or perfect orientation, of total and complete adaptation. Such a goal becomes a necessity for him as a guiding light for which to direct all his strivings for better adaptations. As this goal becomes fixed, then the goal will direct all the strivings and will determine, therefore, how he sees reality, what he feels about reality, and how he should act to come closer to his ideal goal. This ideal goal also contains his idealized self-image, the way he should be, the way he should act, the way he should feel in order to reach his ideal goal or come closer to it [Adler, 1977, pp. 21–22].

Adlerian concepts have supported the family unit as the primary group wherin the child first formulates ideals and goals and where vital behavior patterns are first learned. In particular, Dreikurs emphasized the educational nature of counseling and developed methods to help families learn to foster an environment leading to the selection of constructive life goals and interactional skills.

The assumption that underlies Adlerian parent education is that assisting parents is an educational endeavor rather than a medical procedure. The model alluded to here is essentially an educational one, which makes the assumption that the lack of knowledge, information, or experience, rather than illness, is the basis of maladaptive behavior. Whereas counselors, and indeed schools, are poorly equipped to cure illness, they are well designed to provide information, experiences, or education. It is assumed that people, if provided with new or pertinent information, are capable of applying the new information to their situation in order to make the corrections necessary to bring about change (Christensen, 1969).

While recognizing the risk of overgeneralization, it is relatively accurate to state that, by and large, parents today are confused about how to rear their young. This phenomenon is novel inasmuch as this is the first generation of parents for whom the traditional childrearing methods have proven less than effective. To understand the breakdown in childrearing methods, it is helpful to trace the changes that have taken place in our society that have rendered the traditional approaches ineffective.

It is safe to say that most of our childrearing approaches were brought to this country from middle Europe and represent almost exclusively autocratic methods. These childrearing traditions were developed originally in a feudalistic system that produced an atmosphere of superior–inferior interpersonal relationships. An essential component of any autocratic social system is that some people are always better than other people. Within such a system children would be taught "to know their place" and to learn to show deference to "their betters," inasmuch as they would be expected to play a similar role in adult life. The superior–inferior relationship between adults and children was politically endorsed and also sanctified by religion.

With the emergence of the democratic social system and the striving for social equality, evident in the human rights movement, the concept of equality has permeated our entire social structure to the extent that the last minority group to demand equal status has been children. In brief, children today see themselves as being social equals to adults, and for this reason autocratic training methods are doomed to failure. The age-honored disciplinary techniques of reward and punishment are no longer effective, primarily because children view reward and punishment from the position of equality rather than inferiority. From the child's perspective, reward is a right, and punishment necessitates retaliation. Communication patterns are viewed by the child in much the same way. Parents continue speaking to children from a position of authority and superiority without realizing that children are listening from a position of equality. "Talking down" to children results in children who in turn talk down to parents. This kind of interactional pattern can be seen in family after family, in varying degrees of intensity.

The purpose of parent education is to assist parents and children to discover more appropriate patterns of interaction based on an assumption of equality between adults and children. But here again confusion reigns, for the most frequent misconception of social equality is when equality is believed to be an expression of "sameness": To be equal means to be the same.

It is no wonder that adults are threatened by the idea of the equality of children and endorse a return to "the good old days" and "get tough" policies for home and school. Children are not as well educated as adults, do not have as much information or experience, and are not as big as adults. Certainly children are not as old as adults, but they *are equal*—if social equality, rather than implying sameness, *implies equality in terms of value or worth.* If the concept of equal value rather than sameness is accepted, then differences can exist in an equal social setting. Different roles for parent and child, for teacher and pupil, are possible as long as the interaction is based on an assumption of equal value and mutual respect. The parent education approach is designed primarily to teach methods of parenting to parents, as well as to other adults, that are consistent with the concept of equality. For example, rather than employing punishment as a disciplinary measure, which implies superiority of one person over another, parents are taught other corrective procedures. The development of logical consequences, adequately described by Dreikurs and Grey (1968), is one such technique.

The use of encouragement (Dinkmeyer & Dreikurs, 1963) is another approach designed to develop positive behavior in youngsters. The critical point here is that whatever training methods are employed, they must be consistent with the concept of mutual respect and equal treatment inherent in a democratic setting. The concept of equality is frequently misinterpreted as "permissiveness." However it is defined, permissive childrearing is not an expression of democracy; it is in fact an expression of anarchy. While autocracy may be defined as *order without freedom,* anarchy may be defined as *freedom without order.* Democracy is best characterized as *freedom with order.* For this reason children are educated toward democracy, which implies limits within which they experience freedom. Their right to choose, for example, is limited to those areas of life where age, experience, and readiness permit them to be at least minimally successful in making responsible choices. Therefore, it is essential to provide parents with a frame of reference to utilize to generate learning experiences for children within a margin of safety and responsible parenting.

An additional consideration is the need to provide parents with understanding of behavior in terms of dynamics rather than the traditional causal notions. Labeling behavior as "cute," "nasty," "mean," "bad," and "good" are considered impediments to understanding and change. Only in a society of equals are methods of understanding, encouraging, or motivating appropriate behavior a necessity. In the traditional autocratic family, one simply did as he or she was told. In a family of equals, motivation is important. Since autocracy implies external controls, no understanding is necessary. In the democratic family, where the goal of childrearing is internal control, attention must be paid to motivation if the child is to be trained toward self-control and self-sufficiency.

The Basis for Understanding Children's Behavior

In order to understand as well as effectively relate to and guide children, we have to become aware of their private logic—what they think of themselves, others, and life—the goals they set for themselves. We also have to observe them living according to this logic, regardless of how little they may be aware that they are doing so. It is in this connection that we find the four goals of misbehavior: (a) attention or service; (b) power or defiance; (c) revenge or retaliation; and (d) inadequacy or deficiency (Dreikurs, 1967).

Dreikurs first cited his discovery of the four goals of misbehavior in 1940. In the years that followed, he developed and elaborated his findings and formulated a detailed explanation of how these goals operated and could be corrected (Terner & Pew, 1978). Dreikurs often stated that he never met a "youngster"—a preadolescent—whose faulty behavior could not be conceptualized in one of these four mistaken goal patterns, although the particular behavior might be displayed in some slightly different variation (Dreikurs, 1947). When questioned about the universality of his findings or asked if there were not goals of misbehavior other than those he listed, Dreikurs stated, "I have no scientific proof, but I have found it empirically true in all my clinical work. If someone can ever demonstrate a fifth or sixth goal, I will be happy to incorporate it into my system [in Terner & Pew, 1978, p. 15]." Dreikurs also pointed out that these four goals could be found in Adler's writings about children (e.g., Adler, 1930) and that he merely identified and formulated them into a systematic scheme.

The concept of the four goals is based on the Adlerian assumption that human beings are social creatures whose behavior is purposeful and whose basic desire is to belong. Starting with this assumption, it logically follows that the primary goal of all human beings is to establish a place of belonging and a sense of social acceptance and usefulness. This goal is formulated in infancy as children seek a place in the family circle of adults and siblings, then it is directed to peer relationships outside the family unit during the school years, and it finally embraces the community at large when the growing child enters adolescence and then adulthood. Dreikurs (Dreikurs *et al.*, 1964) described the development of this goal as follows:

> In his formative years within the family, each child develops, by trial and error, certain ideas about himself, about others and about the possibility of finding a place for himself, first in his family and then in life in general. Very definite convictions are usually established within the first three to four years of the child's life. Neither he nor the people around him are aware of the means he has chosen to put them into practice. All his actions and attitudes are only facets of his general style of life, based on his central evaluation of himself and his abilities. Generally, dangers and disappointments play an important part in the formation of the life style that includes a scheme of action by which the child hopes to avoid future humiliation, setting up a fictitious goal of assumed security. The goals are fictitious because it is not true that only under specific conditions can he be worthwhile and have a place. It is our neurotic culture which denies anyone the feeling of being worthwhile and belong-

ing as he is, regardless of his failures or achievements; this insecurity drives people to set up a fictitious goal of assumed security [p. 44].

The four goals of misbehavior are mistaken approaches by which children, regardless of how varied their personality or background, attempt to find and secure a place of belonging, security, and acceptance within the family or group. These goals are mistaken because, although children can keenly, accurately, and carefully observe what goes on around them, they often misinterpret these events, draw mistaken conclusions, and make faulty decisions and generalizations. Thus, children who conclude that they do not belong or cannot make a significant contribution, develop the first mistaken goal and decide that they *only* have a secure place as long as they can get *attention or service* from others. So, as a result of this mistaken interpretation, they demand undue attention or service, in active or passive, useful or useless ways, and disturb in order to keep others busy with them. Their behavior is designed to get the attention or service that they prefer in a pleasant way, but they do not mind experiencing negative consequences if that is the only way that they can be noticed.

When pressure from others becomes so strong that the children do more for themselves and stop soliciting or demanding undue attention or service, or if adults become more forceful in thwarting these efforts, they may switch to the second mistaken goal of *power or defiance,* where they mistakenly conclude that they have a place *only* if they can do as they please. If asked to do something, they refuse to do it; if asked not to do something, they do it. These children try to show their parents and teachers, "I won't give in—I won't be bossed around—I'm the boss," which is equivalent to an invitation for a power contest. "I'll show you I can do what I want, and you can't stop me!" Most adults do not know how to respond to power struggles with children and intensify such conflicts in their best efforts to correct the situation.

When children no longer believe that they can get attention or display power, they seek the third mistaken goal of *revenge or retaliation* after deciding that the *only* way they can belong and feel significant is if they can hurt others as they feel hurt by others. Revenge is literally *vengeance* for perceived lack of significance and is the most vicious of the four goals. Finally, when children are unable to get attention, power, or revenge, they are likely to arrive at the fourth mistaken goal of *inadequacy or deficiency,* where they display real or imagined disabilities, give up in discouragement, and withdraw from social interaction or responsibility after concluding that this is the *only* way that they can have a place. "If you don't test me, you won't know how inadequate I really am—that I'm really no good." These are the four mistaken goals (Dreikurs, 1967, p. 138).

The four goals of attention, power, revenge, and inadequacy are *immediate goals* and are to be distinguished from *intermediate goals* (referred to as personality priorities in the Adlerian literature), such as psychological and physical comfort, pleasing others, controlling others, superiority to others, and meaningfulness in life (Pew, 1976), and *long-range goals* or *final fictional goals* (the life-style), such as trying always to be good, trying to be in control or the center of attention in all situations (Shulman, 1973). All of these goals are attempts to establish a place. But despite longer range goals, children respond to their immediate situation with shorter range, immediate goals in an attempt to find a place of security, adaptation, and orientation.

If children are sure of their place and feel they belong, they do not seek a place, but *have* it. As long as children have a feeling of belonging, security, and acceptance within the group, they behave in line with the requirements of the situation. But if they become discouraged, are not sure of their place, doubt their adequacy, or do not believe that they can have a place through what *they* can do, they are likely to develop one or more of the four goals in an attempt to establish their place through what *we*—the adults—can do (provide attention, service, etc.). When children become discouraged and do not believe they can find a place through useful cooperation and contribution, they almost inevitably try to feel significant or important by either demanding undue attention, trying to get their own way, attempting to get even, or displaying deficiency in order to be left alone (Dreikurs, 1967).

However, as Dreikurs has pointed out, even children who misbehave and defy the requirements, demands, and necessities of the situation still believe that their behavior will provide social status. They may attempt to get attention, prove their power, seek revenge, or display deficiency. Whichever of these four goals they adopt, their actions are based on the conviction that *only* in this way can they belong within the group. Their goals may occasionally change with the circumstances; they may attempt to attract attention at one moment, assert power, seek revenge, or display inadequacy at another (Dreikurs, 1950). Therefore, when children misbehave we should not label them as immature, lazy, aggressive, or whatever, which is descriptive rather than explanatory, but we should attempt to understand the purpose of their behavior and find one or more of the four goals (Dreikurs, 1967).

In helping people understand and put these concepts into practice,

Dreikurs made some important distinctions between children, adolescents, and adults. According to Dreikurs, the four mistaken goals can be easily recognized in children up to the age of 10. During this period, as hard as it may be for parents and teachers to admit, children's misbehavior is mostly directed toward or against them. This is because children's status in early childhood largely depends on the impression they make on adults. Later in adolescence they may develop many different goals in addition to the four faulty goals, such as constantly seeking excitement, entertainment, and fun in order to achieve social significance in their peer group. In adulthood, the additional mistaken goals of seeking money, power, and many others are found. As Dreikurs stated, "These original four goals can still be observed in people of every age and period of life; only then, they are not all-inclusive [Dreikurs *et al.*, 1971, p. 18]." Unfortunately, status and prestige can more frequently and easily be attained through useless, destructive behavior than through useful, constructive behavior.

Even though adults' goals are more complicated than those of children and adolescents, what really distinguishes adults from children and adolescents is merely that adults have learned to hide more effectively what they really think and feel—which may be considered beneficial because it helps them mask their antisocial attitudes and feelings. However, since adults are not really much different in their basic personalities from what they were as children, they often attempt to give the outward appearance of being something better than children, and then define themselves as "mature." And at a time when adults are becoming more and more threatened by children and know less and less about what to do with them, it is naturally easier and easier for adults to try to build up their own egos by looking down on children and defining them as "immature" (Dreikurs, 1967). Indeed, adults basically have the same attitudes as adults that they had as children; but during adolescence they learned, for appearance's sake, to subordinate these attitudes to the demands and expectations of society. Successfully covering up one's real motives and intentions then becomes a sign of "maturity." Children or adolescents who have not yet reached this level of "maturity" openly display their attitudes, and their goals are quite obvious; therefore, it is possible to easily recognize their goals by mere observation (Dreikurs, 1947).

In addition to observation, however, children's mistaken goals can be recognized by the effects these goals have on others—the immediate, impulsive reaction of other people. Whatever one is inclined to do in response to children's behavior is generally consistent with their goals and expectations. Giving undue attention, engaging in power struggles, seeking retaliation, or giving up in despair, are adult reactions that correspond to and reflect children's goals. This insight reveals, in the many transactions between adults and children, how and when the children's faulty behavior is reinforced by the adults' reactions (Terner & Pew, 1978).

The concept of utilizing one's own reaction to determine another person's goal is based on the innerconnectedness of interpersonal behavior and the Adlerian assumption that human beings are active, evaluating, interpreting, and decision-making social beings. For all practical purposes, it is assumed that no individual's behavior occurs in isolation, but takes place in relation to other people. We act, react, and interact with one another, and we think about those actions, reactions, and interactions. However, we tend to underestimate the influence we have on others and mostly think in terms of the influence others have on us. This is simply because we can more easily observe what others do and how we are affected by their behavior than what we do and how others are affected by our behavior. We are often oblivious of the fact that we elicit or evoke certain behaviors from other people and that the behavior we get from others has as much as or more to do with our own personal characteristics and provocations than those of the persons from whom we elicit the response. Competitive people, for example, are often totally unaware of their own contribution to their experience of the competitiveness of others but tend to conclude that the world is just that way; they expect competitiveness from others and that is what they get (Carson, in press).

As Willard and Marguerite Beecher (1966) stated, "The person who sees life as a competition and the world as a competitive place is astonished when anyone suggests that the world is not a competitive place, but that there are many competitive people who make it appear that way to those who are themselves competitive. Reality is what it is and in itself is neither competitive nor noncompetitive [p. 41]." Another example is that of people who anticipate punishment, become overly appeasing, and elicit abuse by their apologies. We can also observe that people who fear rejection tend to get rejected; defensive and suspicious people tend to evoke aggressive, retaliatory behavior; submissive people tend to elicit domineering, arrogant behavior; domineering people tend to elicit submissive or passive resistant behavior, etc. (Carson, in press). We subtly, and not so subtly, communicate to others what we expect—what we want, fear, etc.—and that is often what we get in return. As Dreikurs stated, "We are moving ourselves in line with what we anticipate [in Soltz, 1975, p. 10]."

The Social Context of Behavior

Each individual's behavior may vary greatly across different situations and social settings, depending on the expectations of the individual and the expectations inherent in the situation. Therefore, if we are truly to understand and appropriately modify faulty human behavior, we must view it in terms of the social context in which it occurs—the context in which we live and function. We must also learn to observe the behavioral sequence in which social interactions take place and become aware of how we prompt, draw out, elicit, evoke, provoke, or solicit specific responses from others and how they evoke such responses from us. We must become aware of how we carry out our self-fulfilling prophecies—how we get from others and life what we expect from and attribute to them—and how we help others carry out their prophecies. We can then fully realize that most human problems are basically public and social in nature. And we will be able to take appropriate developmental, preventative, or remedial approaches based on constructive alternative goals, strategies, and interactional patterns rather than on traditional, moralistic, or medical model approaches. Thus, we can avoid labeling people who display faulty behavior as sick, diseased, crazy, lazy, or bad.

Interpersonal behavior may be more specifically defined as what one person overtly or covertly does in relationship to another person who, in some respect, is the object of the particular behavior (Leary, 1957, p. 4). Interpersonal behavior can be characterized as being complementary or noncomplementary in nature (McLemore & Benjamin, 1979). *Complementary behaviors* are characterized by corresponding, harmonizing, or matching behaviors that tend to elicit, draw out, accompany, or complement each other. Complementary behaviors can be negative or positive, constructive or destructive; they are complementary as long as they tend to go together, as long as they consist of a mutual exchange. Thus, behavioral complementarity basically takes two forms: positive behavioral reciprocity and negative behavioral reciprocity.

Noncomplementary behaviors are characterized by oppositional, antithetical, or diametrical behaviors that tend to elicit the opposite of the behavior at hand, specifically the opposite of the particular behavior's expected complement. Complementary and noncomplementary behaviors can be observed in any human interaction. For example, if children learn to submit to and accept parental power, authority, and control, the relationship can be considered a complementary one based on *positive reciprocity*—each person is in agreement in terms of the roles and behaviors expected and responds with positive cooperation accordingly. However, one or the other, most often the child, becomes dissatisfied with this arrangement.

This shift often occurs as children reach adolescence and discover that in order to become autonomous they need to learn to be more independent, to think for themselves more, and to be themselves instead of a reflection of their parents. As a result they often conclude that they must resist parental control if they are to become autonomous. Their behavior is in turn defined and interpreted by their parents—not as a normal, healthy struggle for autonomy—but as defiance, disrespect, and a personal affront to the parents' integrity. At this point the parents often exert countermeasures of increased control, which only intensify the child's behavior.

Thus, a shift has been made to complementary behavior based on *negative reciprocity*—each person is still in agreement in terms of the roles and behaviors expected and responds with negative cooperation accordingly. The interaction is still complementary, but in a negative sense rather than in a positive one—both parents and children cooperate in maintaining the relationship. In trying to break the dependency bond, the children strive for total independence rather than the more realistic ideal of mutual interdependence appropriate to the human condition and necessary for effective human functioning. The more the parents use counter-control measures, the more the children feel they have to be totally independent. The children say, "You can't make me," and the parents say, "Oh, yes we can," and the war goes on. These behaviors are obviously mutually reinforcing. Both parties to the conflict try to force their definitions of the situation on the other, and no one gets anywhere. The parents have long forgotten the struggle for equality and respect with their own parents. They have also forgotten the sacred vows they made as children never to repeat their parents' mistakes with their own children.

Often underlying the anger, resentment, and hostility of each looms unavowed fear. Children fear losing or not developing an individual identity—and they fear losing the esteem of their peers for allowing themselves to be dominated by their parents. Parents fear that the worst will happen to their children; they do not trust the parenting job they have done, and fear losing the esteem of other parents and adults for not having more control over their children. Both parents and children define and interpret the behavior of the other personally as a devaluation of themselves rather than what it really is. This occurs easily when they have too much of their personal worth tied up in the roles they play as parents and children rather than in their intrinsic qualities. Both parents and children are struggling within themselves to define who they are and to safeguard a sense of belonging, security, and self-esteem. In order to change the faulty interactional pattern and develop a new pattern based on a new agreement and a more constructive relationship—one of mutual equality where children have more room to become autonomous and responsible and where parents feel more secure in relaxing some of their overprotectiveness and over-responsibility—the pattern of *complementary negative reciprocity* has to be broken.

In order to bring about this change, one or the other or both parties have to make certain changes. For example, this change may take place when children feel secure enough in themselves not to overreact to parental control (which is unlikely to happen) or when parents change their reactions to the children's behavior (give them more room for decision making and for becoming responsible, etc.) or when both parties make changes at the same time. In other words, noncomplementary behaviors are called for—doing the opposite of what is expected. Doing the unexpected makes it possible to establish a new relationship. Once this can be accomplished, an interaction of *complementary positive reciprocity* can be reached and a more secure and solid foundation for a constructive relationship can be developed. However, it must be added that although these changes are necessary, they are not necessarily sufficient. Other changes also have to be made, but one is well on the road toward a healthy relationship once these basic changes have occurred. The concept of complementary behaviors, doing the opposite, or doing the unexpected, is similar to the concept of "antissuggestion" (Terner & Pew, 1978), paradoxical intention (Frankl, 1963), or paradoxical communication (Adler, 1978; Fay, 1978; Haley, 1963).

Changing Faulty Goals

Behind every action is a hidden goal of which we are generally unaware. And, as we have seen, the immediate goals of children are based on their attitudes toward their parents, teachers, and society (Dreikurs *et al.*, 1971). Therefore, if the faulty goals of children are to change, adults must take the initiative to modify their own patterns of reacting to those goals. When adults change their responses to provocation, children are stimulated to seek new ways of gaining social recognition. If, at the same time, adults genuinely encourage children, they are on their way to a new, cooperative, and constructive relationship. The adults' reactions to the children's provocative behavior also offers a definite clue for determining which mistaken goal the children are

pursuing. Many different faulty behaviors—underachievenent, lazi-
ness, bedwetting, lying, stealing—can be an expression of any one of
the four goals. Knowing which goal is operating in conjunction with the
particular behavior is important, since it provides immediate insight
into the seriousness of the misbehavior and gives clues for how to
handle it (Terner & Pew, 1978).

After discovering children's particular mistaken goals, it is possible
to disclose these goals to the children in a hypothetical, nonaccusatory,
nonjudgmental manner, at a nonconflict time. When this approach is
taken, children often become intrigued to follow along with the line of
reasoning in order to become aware of and understand their goals. For
example, consider a parent who continually complains about having to
intercede in fights between siblings. We might guess from the parent's
annoyance that the purpose of the child's behavior is to gain undue
attention through keeping the parent busy getting involved in the
fights. Dreikurs would ask such a child, "Could it be that you fight with
your brother just to keep your mother busy with you?" The child's
immediate reaction is of utmost importance. If the guess is correct, the
child will "impulsively say yes or show his affirmation by a curious
roguish grin that Dreikurs termed 'the recognition reflex' . . . the
child's spontaneous reaction to the sudden feeling of being understood
[Terner & Pew, 1978, p. 157]." If the guess is incorrrect, there is no such
response from the child, and another guess must be made in order to
discover the correct goal of the behavior. The *recognition reflex* is more
precisely defined as follows:

> The recognition reflex is a peculiar smile and glint in the eyes indicating that the
> child has suddenly become aware of his goal, and is beginning to understand why
> he is acting in a certain way [Dreikurs, 1971, p. 42].

> In a sense . . . the "recognition reflex" is a gestalt phenomenon—a sudden insight
> or solution of a problem by recognition of its unitary pattern [Terner & Pew, 1978,
> p. 355].

> [Heinz] Ansbacher [Dreikurs, 1967] . . . pointed out the significance of the recogni-
> tion reflex and noted its intrinsic relationship to the "aha!" experience, first de-
> scribed by Karl Buhler. "The recognition reflex," he wrote, embodies the "flashlike
> expression which accompanies the joyful experience of a sudden insight into, and
> solution of a problem . . . which is defined by the therapist and which the coun-
> selee accepts with astonishment about the excellent fit of the interpretation. . . .
> The recognition reflex shows that Adlerian therapy provides a sudden, insightful
> learning in accordance with its general kinship to Gestalt psychology" [Terner &
> Pew, 1978, p. 365].

The recognition reflex and the adult's immediate, impulsive reactions
to children's behavior are the best tools for understanding children's

goals. However, as indicated previously, this is only strictly true for younger children (Dreikurs *et al.*, 1971). Since adolescents are in the process of adopting the facade of adulthood—defense mechanisms, safeguarding devices, rationalizations, putting up a front, etc.—neither they nor adults can be confronted with their underlying goals as directly, easily, or successfully as children (Terner & Pew, 1978). Although each of the four goals are discernible at any age, many other goals lend themselves as a means of finding a place in the peer group during adolescence, some of which are likely to develop in response to adult demands and authority. Teenagers often show their independence, autonomy, and identity by whatever means of dress, language, music, and so on, that adults dislike or find objectionable. More serious behaviors such as drug abuse, delinquency, and drag racing, also become methods of finding anti-adult satisfaction, pleasure, and excitement. In order to understand teenagers, therefore, one cannot rely solely on the four goals as observed in younger children. We have to become familiar with teenagers' private logic and observe the direction of their goals in relationship to their peer group as well as to adults and society in general if we are to guide them effectively (Dreikurs *et al.*, 1971).

The concepts of the four goals and the recognition reflex are two of Dreikurs' most significant contributions for understanding, correcting, and preventing children's faulty behavior. Numerous therapists, counselors, teachers, and parents have benefited from employing them in their relationship with children (Terner & Pew, 1978).

Parent Study Groups

Basically there are two components to the Adlerian model of parent education. One is the parent study group movement, which is based on parent leadership, study, and group discussion of Adlerian concepts of childrearing. The other is the Parent–Teacher Education Center movement, which is based on a model for counseling parents, children, and teachers.

At the present time, Adlerian parent study groups are being conducted in almost every section of the United States and Canada. The basic goals of these study groups include clarification of the fundamental requirements of living together as social equals with the democratic family unit; understanding that behavior has purpose and is movement toward a goal; and identifying and encouraging behavior appropriate for the development of responsible and interdependent individuals capable of cooperating and contributing to the family. Parents learn to guide their children, being neither permissive nor autocratic but truly democratic. According to Buckland (1971), the Adlerian approach is one of the parent education models that focuses on the family as an integrated social system and includes the opportunity for each family member to examine his or her interactions with other members of the family.

Parent study groups are based on Adlerian principles essentially as outlined by Dreikurs and Soltz (1964), Dinkmeyer and McKay (1973), Corsini and Painter (1975), or Gould (1977). The Dreikurs model, following *Children: The Challenge* (Dreikurs & Soltz, 1964), is the most widely used and also includes a study group leader's guide (Soltz, 1967). A comparable text and leader's guide is also available for teacher study groups (Asselin, Nelson, & Platt, 1975; Dreikurs *et al.*, 1971). Parent study groups are based on the following psychological principles (McKelvie, Elliaton, Dodson, Gillow, & Graftow, 1977, pp. 30–31).

1. Democratic relations between parents and children are based on mutual respect with an attitude of kindness and firmness. Kindness is expressed respect for the child; firmness is reflected in respect for one's self.
2. The ability to identify the child's mistaken immediate goals and the understanding of the social consequences of these behaviors enables parents to gain psychological understanding of children.
3. Since reward and punishment have no place in a truly democratic society where all are social equals, natural and logical consequences replace the authority of a person with the authority of reality and the social needs of the situation.
4. Encouragement that communicates respect, love, support, and valuing of the child as a person becomes the major tool for helping the child to feel a more positive sense of self-worth. Misbehavior is viewed as indicative of discouragement. Through building on a child's strengths and through parental warmth, acceptance, and love, a cooperative relationship is established. From this friendly relationship the parent is able to influence the child to more constructive and socially useful attitudes and behaviors. Adlerian parent education groups, then, would differ from the behavioral model on this point: the purpose of their child-rearing methods is not simply to modify a child's behavior, but more importantly, to modify his motivation. Changing behavior is of secondary importance, for the building of self-esteem, self-sufficiency, responsibility, cooperation, and social interest are the major goals.

Adlerian parent study groups typically consist of 8 to 12 members, ideally couples. These groups usually meet for approximately 2 hours, once each week for 8 to 12 weeks. The group leaders are usually parents who are familiar with the basic principles in *Children: The Challenge* (Dreikurs & Soltz, 1964), and have attended a previous study group. The leaders serve as moderators or facilitators, rather than as professional experts. Specific childrearing topics are discussed at each meeting, and time is allotted to discuss individual problems of the participants. A systematic format for leading groups is outlined in *Study Group*

Leader's Manual for Children: The Challenge (Soltz, 1967). Handouts and homework assignments are typically used to reinforce the concepts and topics that are covered during the meetings. Other Adlerian books and materials are also suggested for study (e.g., Dreikurs & Cassel, 1972; Dreikurs, Corsini, & Gould, 1975; Dreikurs & Goldman, 1972; Dreikurs & Grey, 1972; Soltz, 1970, 1975). McKelvie and his colleagues also conducted a survey of parent education research that was reported at the North American Society of Adlerian Psychology meeting in Minneapolis in 1977 (McKelvie, 1977). In their review of research to date, they reported that several general types of studies were being conducted. The most numerous were those that attempted to measure attitudinal changes. The most frequent population investigated regarding attitudinal changes was parents, followed by teachers and children. The second most frequently attempted studies dealt with behavior changes, equally divided between parents and children. The least frequently attempted were studies comparing Adlerian models with other theoretical models.

Related Research

In reviewing the outcomes of current studies it would appear that Adlerian study group research has produced rather encouraging but mixed findings, as indicated by the sample of studies that follows.

Studies by Orr (1974), Berrett (1975), and Downing (1971) found that there were significant positive changes in parental attitudes and behavior and increased knowledge of Adlerian childrearing principles. Although Croake and Burness (1976) found no statistically significant difference between the experimental and control groups in parents' perception of their children's disturbing behavior, parents who participated in the study groups reported fewer occurrences of children's bothersome behavior than parents in the control groups (Berrett, 1975).

Fears (1976) reported that the results of her study indicated that parents' attitudes and behavior were effectively changed after four Adlerian study group sessions.

Downing (1971) developed a training program for parents, drawn primarily from Adlerian, Rogerian, and behavioral approaches to human development. The data he collected indicated that parents who participated in the program showed a significant increase in the expression of trust and respect for their children.

Thorn (1974) investigated the long-term effects on parents of the childrearing principles presented in Adlerian parent study groups. His conclusions, based on a 40% return of questionnaires, were that after 2 years:

1. Eighty percent of the participants were still using methods they had learned in the study group.
2. Ninety-four percent reported that the study group had helped them resolve problems with their children.
3. Seventy-six percent were able to list specifically the methods they were still using.

The Thorn study points out the need to further evaluate the continuing influence that Adlerian parent education may have on parents and children (pp. 31–32).

Summary

The traditional autocratic methods of childrearing are no longer effective in societies that have become increasingly democratic. The emerging ideas about the equality of children demand appropriate methods of child guidance, consistent with self-discipline and individual responsibility.

Rudolf Dreikurs is to be given credit for bringing Alfred Adler's individual psychology to the attention of parents in many parts of the world. The approaches for educating parents in the principles of democratic childrearing presented in this chapter are based on parent study group and open-center family counseling models.

While there is a paucity of controlled experimental research, the descriptive literature abounds (e.g., Croake & Glover, 1977). Perhaps this is appropriate to the state of the art, since the task of reeducating an entire generation of parents has only recently been recognized as a legitimate role for those in the helping professions. This is reflected in the increase in parenting programs that are being offered in communities around the country. In the initial stages of development, it is only natural that the focus would be on technique and practice. For the time being we may have to be satisfied mainly with the research generated by those who are themselves involved in parent education and family counseling.

References

Adler, A. *Understanding human nature*. New York: Greenberg Publishing, 1927.(a)
Adler, A. A doctor remakes education. *Survey Graphic*, 1927, *58*, 490–491.(b)
Adler, A. *The education of children*. New York: Greenberg Publishing, 1930.
Adler, A. *Co-operation between the sexes: Writings on women, love, and marriage, sexuality*

and its disorders (Edited and translated by H. L. Ansbacher and R. R. Ansbacher). Garden City, N.Y.: Doubleday, 1978.

Adler, K. A. Philosophical and sociological concepts in Adlerian psychology. *Proceedings of the symposium: The Individual Psychology of Alfred Adler.* Eugene, Ore.: 1977.

Ansbacher, R. R. *The encyclopedia of world biography.* New York: McGraw-Hill, 1973.

Asselin, C., Nelson, T., & Platt, J. M. *Teacher study group leader's manual for maintaining sanity in the classroom.* Chicago: Alfred Adler Institute, 1975.

Beecher, W., & Beecher, M. *Beyond success and failure: Ways to self-reliance and maturity.* New York: Pocket Books, 1966.

Berrett, R. D. Adlerian mother study groups: An evaluation. *Journal of Individual Psychology,* 1975, *31,* 179–182.

Buckland, C. M. Toward a theory of parent education: Family learning centers in post-industrial society. *The Family Coordinator,* 1971, *21,* 151–162.

Carson, R. C. Personality and exchange in developing relationships. In T. L. Huston & R. L. Burgess (Eds.), *Social exchange in developing relationships.* New York: Academic Press, in press.

Christensen, O. C. A model for counseling. *Elementary School Guidance and Counseling,* 1969, *4*(1), 12–19.

Corsini, R., & Painter, G. *The practical parent.* New York: Harper & Row, 1975.

Croake, J. W., & Burness, M. R. Parent study group effectiveness after four and six weeks. *Journal of Individual Psychology,* 1976, *32*(1), 108–111.

Croake, J. W., & Glover, K. E. A history and evaluation of parent education. *The Family Coordinator,* 1977, *26*(2), 11–17.

Dinkmeyer, D., & Dreikurs, R. *Encouraging children to learn: The encouragement process.* Englewood Cliffs, N.J.: Prentice-Hall, 1963.

Dinkmeyer, D. C., & McKay, G. D. *Raising a responsible child.* New York: Simon and Schuster, 1973.

Downing, C. J. *The development and evaluation of a program for parent training in family relationship and management skill.* Unpublished doctoral dissertation, Indiana University, 1971. (University Microfilms No. 72-1541)

Dreikurs, R. The four goals of the maladjusted child. *Nervous Child,* 1947, *6,* 321–328.

Dreikurs, R. The immediate purpose of children's misbehavior, its recognition and correction. *Internationale Zeitschrift für Individualpsychologie,* 1950, *19,* 70–79.

Dreikurs, R. Adlerian analysis of interation. *Group Psychotherapy,* 1955, *8*(4), 298–307.

Dreikurs, R. *Adult–Child relations: A workshop on group discussion with adolescents.* Chicago: Alfred Adler Institute, 1967.

Dreikurs, R. *Rudolf Dreikurs papers* (Report No. 9). Washington, D.C.: Manuscript Division, Library of Congress, January 27, 1970.

Dreikurs, R. Technology of conflict resolution. *Journal of Individual Psychology,* 1972, *28*(2), 203–206.(a)

Dreikurs, R. Toward a techology of human relationship. *Journal of Individual Psychology,* 1972, *28*(2), 127–136.(b)

Dreikurs, R., & Cassel, P. *Discipline without tears.* Toronto: Alfred Adler Institute, 1972.

Dreikurs, R., Corsini, R., & Gould, S. *How to stop fighting with your kids.* New York: ACE Books, 1975.

Dreikurs, R., Corsini, R., Lowe, R., & Sonstegard, M . (Eds.). *Adlerian family counseling: A manual for counseling centers.* Eugene: University of Oregon Press, 1959.

Dreikurs, R., & Goldman, M. *The ABC's of guiding the child.* Morton, Ill.: Rudolf Dreikurs Unit of Family Education Association, 1972.

Dreikurs, R., & Grey, L. *A new approach to discipline: Logical consequences.* New York: W. Clement Stone, 1968.

Dreikurs, R., & Grey, L. *A parent's guide to child discipline*. New York: Hawthorn Books, 1972.

Dreikurs, R., Grunwald, B., & Pepper, F. C. *Maintaining sanity in the classroom: Illustrated teaching techniques*. New York: Harper & Row, 1971.

Dreikurs, R., & Soltz, V. *Children: The challenge*. New York: Meredith Press, 1964.

Fay, A. *Making things better by making them worse*. New York: Hawthorn Books, 1978.

Fears, S. Adlerian parent study groups. *The School Counselor*, 1976, *23*(5), 320–329.

Frankl, V. *Man's search for meaning*. Boston: Beacon Press, 1963.

Gould, S. *Teenagers: The continuing challenge*. New York: Hawthorn Books, 1977.

Haley, J. *Strategies in psychotherapy*. New York: Grune & Stratton, 1963.

Leary, T. *Interpersonal diagnosis of personality: A functional theory and methodology for personality evaluation*. New York: Ronald Press, 1957.

Lowe, R. N. *Dreikursian principles of child guidance*. Eugene: University of Oregon Press, 1974.

McKelvie, W., Elliaton, D., Dodson, R., Gillow, D., & Graftow, H. *Survey of parent education literature*. Unpublished paper presented at the North American Society of Adlerian Psychology meeting, Minneapolis, Minn., October 1977.

McLemore, C. W., & Benjamin, L. S. Whatever happened to interpersonal diagnosis? A psychosocial alternative to DSM-III. *American Psychologist*, 1979, *34*(1), 17–34.

Orr, D. *The effects of Adlerian parent study groups and the knowledge of Adlerian principles on the frequency of common family conflicts*. Unpublished master's thesis, Bowie State College, Md., 1974.

Pew, W. L. The number one priority. *International Association of Individual Psychology*. Munich, Germany, August 1, 1976.

Rom, P. Alfred Adler's individual psychology and its history. *Individual Psychology Pamphlets* (No. 1). London: The Adlerian Society of Great Britain, 1976.

Shulman, B. H. *Contributions to individual psychology*. Chicago: Alfred Adler Institute, 1973.

Soltz, V. *Study group leader's manual for children: The challenge*. Chicago: Alfred Adler Institute, 1967.

Soltz, V. *Articles of supplementary reading for teachers and counselors*. Chicago: Alfred Adler Institute, 1970.

Soltz, V. *Articles of supplementary readings for parents*. Chicago: Alfred Adler Institute, 1975.

Terner, J., & Pew, W. L. *The courage to be imperfect: The life and work of Rudolf Dreikurs*. New York: Hawthorn Books, 1978.

Thorn, P. *An evaluation of the long-term effectiveness of Adlerian study groups*. Unpublished master's thesis, Bowie State College, Md., 1974.

Chapter 4

Haim Ginott's Approach to Parent Education

ARTHUR R. ORGEL

In the era when psychoanalytic theory dominated the child guidance movement, most clinicians saw an inexorable relationship between behavioral disturbances in children and the personality problems of the important adults in a child's life (Orgel, in preparation). Ineffective or faulty parenting tended to be viewed as a derivative of psychopathology rather than ignorance or lack of skill; intervention, therefore, focused as much on psychological treatment of the adult as on treatment of the problem child. Some workers, in fact, maintained that children could not be helped or could not sustain emotional growth unless their parents were emotionally "reeducated" (Durkin, 1965). Implicit in this view is a value judgment about parents, their attitudes, motivation, and maturity, for it assumes that parents are not capable of becoming more effective, unless they are first liberated from the "dark recesses" of their own emotional conflicts. Even more important is the essential pessimism of such an approach, since it implies that one cannot significantly help troubled families, unless the parents are motivated for personal treatment. Thus, the distressed parent's request for help in coping, for advice, or for information is basically viewed as suspect—as a shallow and transparent detour around the real source of difficulty.

When parents seeking advice and assistance from professional experts are treated as though they were patients rather than "students,"

75

HANDBOOK ON
PARENT EDUCATION

the result is often less than productive. Resentment, resistance, and retreat are frequently the outcome when questions go unanswered and the counselor's responses focus on parental motivation, conflicts, and problems rather than on the child's behavior (Ginott, 1961).

Haim Ginott brought a different and more optimistic perspective to working with the parents of emotionally disturbed children. He believed that poor parenting often reflects lack of experience, misinformation, or exposure to poor parental models rather than sick attitudes or personal problems (Ginott, 1957a). Thus, in the early 1950s, he began experimenting with parent education and guidance groups as an alternative to traditional counseling and/or psychotherapy for parents of clinic-referred children (Ginott, 1957b), basing his work on the assumption that psychopathology is not necessarily the source of all parenting difficulties. He came to view parent guidance and parent education as parts of the clinical arsenal of tools, along with more traditional parental intervention techniques, such as counseling and psychotherapy. For Ginott, the use of any particular technique must depend on a prior and careful appraisal of the individual parent, his or her needs and condition, rather than on a broad prescriptive assumption about the necessity for or effectiveness of a single approach. Moreover, Ginott believed that the majority of parents, even among a population of referred families, are able to benefit from child-centered guidance and education rather than parent-centered psychotherapy or counseling.

Ultimately, Ginott's positive experience with the effectiveness of parent guidance groups led him to expand his work beyond the population of referred, clinic families. Like most of us who have experienced parenthood or observed parent–child interactions among our friends and relatives, Ginott was aware of the conflict, failures in communication, anger, and clumsiness that so often abide in the parenting role in our society. He felt that even the parents of "normal" and relatively problem-free children experience unnecessary distress and discomfort because of their lack of preparation for parenthood, and that this distress can seriously erode the self-confidence, self-respect, and thus the effectiveness of even the most conscientious and dedicated "ordinary" parents. He also believed that advances in our understanding of child development and childrearing techniques can and should be shared with the public, rather than remaining the exclusive province of the "expert" professional. Ginott saw no reason, for example, why effective techniques of setting limits, developed by the child psychotherapist, should not be adapted for the everyday problems of child discipline that confront all parents, or why techniques for communicating empathy to children could not be learned by any well-intentioned and reasonably intelligent adult.

At the same time, Ginott recognized the enormous wastefulness involved in the traditional roles of mental health professionals who apply their costly knowledge and expertise only to the relatively small numbers of families who seek professional help. Ginott came to believe, as have others (Cowen, Trost, Lorion, Dorr, Izzo, & Isaacson, 1975), that the most meaningful use of professional knowledge and its greatest potential for good lay in communicating it to a broad rather than a narrow spectrum of the population. Accordingly, in the last decade of his life, Ginott devoted himself almost exclusively to the education of adults rather than to the treatment of disturbed families. He extended his work to include education groups for nonreferred parents and the training of parents to work with other parents (Faber & Mazlish, 1974); in addition, he wrote and lectured profusely for parents of young children (Ginott, 1965), parents of teenagers, (Ginott, 1969), teachers (Ginott, 1972b), and others. His views of parent education, therefore, extended far beyond the consultation room into the popular literature and media; his views extended even beyond parents to other groups of adults who have significant roles to play in the development and education of children and youth. Thus, well before the current "vogue," Ginott's interests shifted from traditional clinical work into community and preventive psychology.

In the remainder of this chapter, I will present a basic outline of the Ginottian approach to parent education, its philosophical and theoretical premises, and its methodology. For the inevitable errors of omission and commission that are inherent in any "interpretation" of another's work, I take full responsibility.

The Ginottian Philosophy

Ginott's approach to parent education, unorthodox for its time, evolved from a varied and rather unique professional and educational career, one that provided him with opportunities to experience adult–child interactions from several vantage points rather than one. Originally trained in a school of education, he spent the first several years of his career as an elementary school teacher in Israel. He found his teaching role, however, singularly unrewarding (Ginott, 1972a), basically because of a felt discrepancy between the ideals, enthusiasms, and values that led him to prepare for a teaching career and the impotence and frustration that he experienced in trying to manage, educate, and inspire the young children in his classroom. He soon became profoundly disillusioned and developed a strong conviction that there was precious little relationship between his educational preparation and the job that he was supposed to fulfill in the classroom. This disillusionment, experienced by so many young educators, is poignantly described in the first chapter of his book *Between Teacher and Child* (Ginott, 1972a).

Ginott became convinced that he understood very little about children and that his "book knowledge" about child development did not translate into practical techniques and methods for effective classroom teaching. Accordingly, he emigrated to the United States, where he completed the undergraduate and graduate training programs in clinical psychology at Columbia University. His early experience as a teacher, however, profoundly affected his subsequent development as a child clinician and parent counselor, for it left him with a deep appreciation of the problems that confront the well-intentioned adult who exists on the "front lines" of interaction with children. The seeds of Ginott's skepticism about traditional approaches to parents and traditional formulations about the etiology of behavioral disturbances in children were planted at this time. So, too, was the abiding compassion and empathy for adults that pervaded his subsequent career as an educator, whether in the classical role of clinical teacher and supervisor (Orgel, 1975) or in his later role as community and preventive psychologist-educator.

Perhaps more important, Ginott's experience as a teacher imbued him with a profound distaste for the platitudes that often permeate professional efforts to educate adults who must work with children. He attributed his own "failure" as a teacher to a lack of skill and understanding rather than to personal "hang-ups," and ultimately he extended the courtesy of this self-evaluation to others who are clumsy, inept, and ineffective in dealing with children. For Ginott, troubled adults need help in coping—in the development of skills for communicating with and managing children. To respond to their needs with truisms, such as, "Be more understanding" or "One must be sensitive to the child's needs" or "One must be more attentive," is an anathema that leads, more often than not, to increased guilt, anxiety, and self-denigration rather than to the enhancement of skills. Thus, Ginott's stance as a parent educator was always problem oriented, directed toward the learning of better techniques for coping instead of learning trite and specious "theory."

The combination of empathy for the adult and appreciation of the need for practical help permeates all of Ginott's subsequent work. For him, the parent or teacher counselor provides an "empathic cradle" that helps to sustain the best learning "set" in the adult. Within this context, Ginott then provides instruction and supervision in techniques for more effective coping.

Ginott's empathic and practical set potentiated him to benefit from the two most influential teachers in his career: Virginia Axline and S. R. Slavson. As a graduate student assistant to Axline, Ginott "discovered" the significance of children's affective experience and the beneficial and growth-inducing effects that occur when the adult responds to these experiences with sensitivity and compassion. Even more, he learned a technique for communicating empathy, a technique that could be practiced and learned, and even taught to others—a technique that could be used in relationships with adults as well as children—to promote the kind of relationship within which positive change is most likely to occur. For Ginott as well as others (Gordon, 1970), this technique—the reflection of feelings—is at the core of all effective interventions. He employed it in his work as a psychotherapist and parent counselor and even in his role as a writer, where his "advice" is always embedded in a framework of prose that describes and accepts the pain, hurt, and anger associated with unrewarded effort:

> No parent wakes up in the morning planning to make his child's life miserable. No mother says to herself, "Today I'll yell, nag, and humiliate my child whenever possible." On the contrary. In the morning many mothers resolve: "This is going to be a peaceful day. No yelling, no arguing, and no fighting." Yet, in spite of good intentions, the unwanted war breaks out again. Once more we find ourselves saying things we do not mean, in a tone we do not like [Ginott, 1965, p. 11].

Later, as a psychological intern working under the supervision of Slavson, Ginott acquired his in-depth understanding of psychodynamic theory and of the intricate interactions between developmental levels and parent–child relationships, as they affect the emergence of normal or psychopathological behavior. This understanding provided Ginott with a theoretical framework for developing his skills as a clinician and a parent educator. Within this framework, he was able to direct himself to issues of parenting that are relevant and cogent both to the distressed parent and to the hierarchy of theoretical issues important in child development and personality formation. Thus, in teaching techniques for limit-setting and discipline, Ginott was able to direct himself in a practical and helpful manner to an issue of overriding concern to parents, while at the same time recasting the psychoanalytic concept of sublimation into a teachable (and learnable) communication skill (Orgel, in preparation).

From Slavson, Ginott also developed his predilection for group intervention techniques. Where clinically appropriate and feasible, Ginott preferred the group format, because it enable the trained professional to "spread his wealth" farther and also because he believed that, properly conducted, group encounters facilitate direct and vicarious learning (Ginott, 1961). Ultimately, Ginott's preference for group work extended from the activities therapy of Slavson and the group play therapy of Axline to parent education, where members share similar concerns and problems (but not necessarily similar techniques for problem solving).

Having worked with both Slavson and Axline, Ginott was confirmed in his belief that adults do not always have to undergo a psychological "overhaul" in order to deal more effectively with their children. To differing degrees, both of these great teachers shunned the traditional view of parents-as-culprits; both felt that the alleviation of children's symptoms alone could often improve the overall atmosphere and functioning within a family. Also, both believed that many parents are poor at their jobs because they are misguided rather than warped.

After attending Columbia, Ginott became the chief psychologist at the Jacksonville, Florida Child Guidance Clinic, where for 9 years he worked as a psychotherapist with emotionally disturbed children and adolescents. As a child psychotherapist he saw children of many different backgrounds and all levels of emotional disturbance, and he employed both individual and group formats for treatment. This intensive experience with troubled children honed his sensitivity to children's emotional needs and his skill in "deciphering" the language—"childrenese"—that children use to communicate their feelings. The concept of "congruent conversation"—the adult's use of words to describe affective experiences accurately—also developed during these years. So, too, did his technique of limit-setting, later so important in educating parents and teachers about issues of discipline.

During these years, Ginott also spent significant amounts of time working with the parents of clinic children and experimenting with different techniques of parent intervention. Starting with his refinement of group screening procedures for clinic parents (Ginott, 1956), he became increasingly interested in the use of group techniques, feeling that the classical model of individual treatment, unless clinically necessary, was a less efficient and often less effective use of the professional's skills. Ultimately, he developed a graded series of parent intervention techniques geared to theoretical considerations about the sources and seriousness of parenting problems (Ginott, 1957a).

During his time in Jacksonville, Ginott was also active as a clinical teacher of student psychologists, social workers, psychiatrists, and speech therapists. As a clinical supervisor, he took particular pride in turning "sow's ears," would-be therapists, into "silk purses." As with his work with parents, his clinical supervision tended to be problem-centered rather than personality-directed instruction in technique, "cradled" in an empathic appreciation of the novice's distress. In all probability, Ginott's positive experiences with students tended to confirm his beliefs about the possibility of teaching clinically derived knowledge and skills to a wider audience of nonprofessional adults. So far as I know, he never encountered any compelling evidence that his professional students were less disturbed, disturbing, or personally conflicted than the average parent or teacher (Orgel, 1975).

Thus, Ginott's background included experience as a classroom teacher, as a child psychotherapist, as a parent counselor and educator, and finally as a clinical teacher of young professionals. This varied career resulted in a deeply felt appreciation for both sides of the adult–child interaction and a conviction that the solutions for problems of parenting (or teaching, or child psychotherapy) must take into account the feelings and welfare of both participants. For Ginott, the primary purpose of parenting is the education of children, over time, in the business of effective coping. Whether functioning as a model or as a skilled shaper of behavior, the parents' effectiveness as teachers depend upon their ability to provide the child with a safe and accepting relationship. The parents' ability to do this, however, depends in turn upon their own feelings of comfort, safety, and self-confidence, which enable them to behave as mature models and permit them to attend to, guide, and shape the emotional, intellectual, and social development of the child. The goal of all parent intervention techniques, therefore, is to enhance feelings of competence and confidence by providing the sensitive emotional support, knowledge, and skills that result in sound teaching practices.

Theory and Technique

Like Slavson (1947a), Ginott accepted the premise that techniques of intervention should be employed differentially, depending upon the needs and characteristics of the people for whom they are used. For

Ginott, no one method of helping is universally applicable, but rather must be employed on the assumption that "different folks need different strokes." With respect to parent work, therefore, he felt that the professional helper needs an armamentarium of techniques at her or his command in order to deal meaningfully with different kinds of parents with different kinds of problems. The use of any particular intervention strategy is geared to an accurate study and appraisal of the individual parent, who, for Ginott, is always the focus of concern.

Originally, Ginott formulated his approaches to parent intervention in terms of a referred, clinic population. His primary goal was to develop intervention strategies for the parents of children who were themselves in treatment for identified problems. His approach to parent education, an intervention that is not usually "clinical" in conception, developed as a natural extension of his "clinically derived" thinking. It can best be understood in terms of the theoretical framework that Ginott used for his earlier clinical work.

Like most child clinicians, Ginott accepted the almost universally held belief that the treatment of disturbed children is facilitated if their parents can also be helped to change. But Ginott did not believe that all parents of disturbed children needed to change to the same degree or that all required the same kind of help. In his clinical work with children and parents, he perceived that there are varying degrees of relationship between parent values, attitudes, and psychopathology on the one hand and the etiology and perpetuation of a child's disturbance on the other. Thus, some parents precipitate and sustain their children's emotional problems because their own emotional disturbances discolor and distort their perceptions of and reactions to others. These parents can be powerfully threatened by perfectly "normal" child behavior, such as sibling jealousy or adolescent strivings for autonomy, because such behavior activates the parent's unresolved conflicts and evokes psychologically harmful parenting behavior. Thus, a sexually disturbed mother might become so upset by and anxious about her child's sexual curiosity, that she would respond with rejection and condemnation, ultimately leading to the development of pathological self-perceptions and responses in the child.

But other parents can evoke even equally "severe" problems because they are misinformed, naive, or model their parenting behavior after faulty examples. Such parents, for example, might overstimulate their children sexually by constantly inviting them into the parental bed, not because there is a "hidden agenda" of unresolved sexual conflict in the adult, but because the parents believe that shared beds provide a vehicle for cozy communication. Or a parent who is misinformed about issues of nutrition or ignorant of effective methods for ensuring a balanced diet might generate eating problems by being overly intrusive or demanding in this important area.

The degree to which poor parenting is tied to the personal, intrapsychic, disturbance of the parent, therefore, is the key to planning and implementing an intervention strategy. Thus, Ginott conceptualized his clinical work with parents on a continuum from parent-centered to child-centered intervention. At one end of this continuum lie problems that primarily derive from and are sustained by parental psychopathology. The intervention technique of choice with such problems is directed toward effecting fundamental changes in the intrapsychic functioning of the parent. At the other end are problems associated with poor parenting skills that derive from faulty learning rather than parental psychopathology. Such problems require child-centered approaches whose goal is to increase parent effectiveness but not to effect basic changes in parental personality structure. Thus, a correlation is implied between the level and goals of intervention on the one hand and the "parent-centeredness" of the problem on the other.

Within this theoretical framework, Ginott (1957a) described three different group treatments for the parents of referred children: psychotherapy, counseling, and guidance. All have in common a focus upon helping the individual participants to achieve therapeutic change. And all emphasize the importance of empathy as a vehicle for promoting change—that is, the premise that individuals are most likely to grow and to be receptive to new learning when they experience an atmosphere of acceptance, nonjudgment, and positive regard. But the three modalities are differentiated from one another in the degree of their propinquity to depth psychotherapy.

Group Psychotherapy

The goal of group psychotherapy, like the goal of individual psychotherapy, is to effect relatively permanent changes in the personality structure of the participants, that is, to rework "the balance of intrapsychic forces." The participants tend to be people with significant emotional disturbances that are associated with personal distress, ineffective coping (parenting or otherwise), and other symptoms of psychopathology. Participants are selected on the basis of thorough diagnostic study, and they are grouped according to a careful matching of levels of disturbance, similarity of symptoms, and other theoretical criteria that have to do with the relationship between type of pathology and symptom manifestation and potential for relating meaningfully within a group format (Slavson, 1947b).

As with individual psychotherapy, the group psychotherapy sessions are directed toward the working through of personal conflicts, catharsis associated with autobiographical memories, and exploration of "private" feelings toward the self and others. Development and exploration of the transference relationship is deliberately promoted as a means of encouraging emotional insight and (hopefully) changes in perception, symptom manifestation, ambivalence, and self-acceptance. Children and their impact upon parents are considered only in a secondary sense—for example, the degree to which the participants' experiences with their children relate to and facilitate the development of insight into their own difficulties. The "payoff" for improved parenting, therefore, is indirect and presumably takes a long time.

Details of the group psychotherapy technique have been described elsewhere (Slavson, 1947b). The technique itself has limited direct relevance for the topic of parent education since it is most distant from it in terms of child-centeredness. But Ginott's description of and use of the psychotherapy model clearly indicates that he recognized that some parents, hopefully a minority, are incapable of benefiting from parent education because their perceptions, values, and attitudes are too distorted to permit changes in parenting behavior without prior changes in their own feelings about and understanding of themselves. Examples would be parents who consciously or unconsciously express unresolved sexual, hostile, or dependent needs in their interactions with their children, or parents who, because of personal problems, behave in consistently rejecting, sadistic, overprotective, or neglectful ways.

For Ginott, moreover, the use of the parent education technique with such parents is not only ineffective, but may also be a disservice, either in the sense of increasing feelings of guilt and impotence in people who sense that they are not able to change and to learn, or in the sense of failing to guide such parents to the kind of help that they really need. This points up one of Ginott's major criteria for the effective and professionally competent parent educator, that she or he have enough clinical skill and judgment to know when *not* to employ the parent education technique.

Group Parent Counseling

Group parent counseling is analogous in scope to individual case work. It is an effort to help parents to increase their coping abilities and to become more comfortable in their relationships, particularly their relationships with other members of their families. The goals of counseling are more limited than those of psychotherapy; the counselor does not aim to achieve basic personality changes but rather to reduce situationally induced stress, conflict, and maladjustment so that coping is enhanced. Accordingly, he or she focuses discussions on the problems of adjustment and the conflcits and distresses associated with these problems but shuns the historical, highly personal, and dynamically fraught material that is evoked and explored in psychotherapy. By the same token, the transference aspects of the relationships between participants and counselor (or among participants) are neither encouraged nor examined in depth. The counselor avoids discussions that focus on intrapsychic conflict, and when such issues surface, she or he relates them to current coping difficulties rather than to autobiographical exploration.

Thus, the group counselor, like the skilled psychotherapist, must have a keen understanding of the dynamic significance of the participants' behavior, but she or he uses this knowledge to carefully control the depth of the group's discussions. The discussion topics in group counseling can be characterized as associative rather than free associative in content. The counselor imposes a structure on discussion by consistently guiding it in the direction of concrete problems that the participants encounter in their daily lives. Free associative aspects have only to do with the participants' emotional responses to these concrete issues. The group members' affective experiences, of course, are responded to with the same sensitivity, acceptance, and empathy that characterize any helping relationship.

In theory, the reduction of guilt and anxiety associated with this experience leads to a reduction in defensiveness and therefore to greater receptiveness to the development of new and better coping habits. Poor parenting behavior, even though it may be dynamically or historically derived, becomes less rigid and less perseverated, because the members become more accepting of their own feelings and more confident of their own abilities. In the group setting, this process of reducing defensiveness and enhancing self-image is facilitated by the vicarious experience of other people's problems ("I am not alone"), and by the empathy that participants eventually learn to provide to each other. The model provided by the confident, accepting, warm, and sensitive counselor is a major instrument for promoting such change.

One of the major goals of this process is to promote greater objectivity in the participants' relationships with their children and to inject a degree of "dispassion" into parental behavior based on a shared experience in the exploration of interpersonal distress within a problem-solving context.

All of this indicates that the selection of parents for a group counseling experience is of overriding importance. For the counselor to be able to control carefully and monitor the level of discussion, participants must be able to achieve a problem-oriented "set." Hence, in spite of the potential "push" of their own internal conflicts, the members' reality testing must be sufficiently intact that they can accept the guidance of the counselor, that they can listen to (and hear) each other most of the time, and are able to respond to the empathic qualities of the therapist with feelings of trust and confidence. They must also demonstrate some basic potential for coping, as evidenced in areas of objective accomplishment, even though their accomplishments are not always fully satisfying or rewarding. Such a parent, for example, takes the parenting role seriously and is fundamentally concerned with the child's welfare. He or she tries to be more effective as a parent, accepts responsibility for the physical and psychological care of the children, and at least most of the time recognizes that his or her difficulties in childrearing stem as much from his or her own inadequacies as from the behavior, "deficiencies," or "badness" of the child. In general, such parents tend to be moderately rather than severely neurotic or immature, and they tend not to be characterologically or psychotically impaired. They are people who rely on intropunitive defenses to a greater degree than projection or displacement. These parents, when they are not enmeshed in their own anxiety and anger, are capable of giving to and caring for others.

Parent education is not the treatment of choice for people who need group counseling, at least initially. Such people are too involved in their own anxieties and defensiveness to be able to attend in a sustained way to their children's feelings; their "understanding" of their children's behavior is too distorted and discolored by the threat that adheres to their parenting role. They are also limited in their ability to learn about and practice new skills, because the effectiveness of learning such skills depends upon an ability to bring some degree of objectivity to parenting problems and upon a reasonable ability to adopt a child-centered set. For such parents, parent education is effective only after a more intensive experience in counseling, which presumably has reduced the anxiety and defensiveness associated with their experiences as parents.

Group Guidance and Parent Education

Parent guidance groups were also designed for use with the parents of clinic-referred children. These groups represent the most child-centered of Ginott's *clinical* approaches. However, it was largely as a result of his experience with parent guidance groups that Ginott developed his interest in parent education, a modality usually employed with nonreferred people. His approach to parent education, therefore, is most similar, both theoretically and methodologically, to the parent guidance technique. Thus a description of the parent guidance format is directly relevant to an understanding of his approach to parent education. As stated earlier, Ginott's approach to parent education really represents an extension of the parent guidance technique to nonclinic parents or to clinic parents who present problems that are clearly a function of faulty knowledge and lack of skill and experience rather than parental psychodynamics.

SELECTION OF CANDIDATES

Group guidance is the treatment of choice for parents who are not themselves seriously disturbed but who have disturbed relationships with their children. Their childrearing efforts are impaired primarily because they lack skill and understanding as a result of having been poorly prepared for the demands of parenting. Their "failings" as parents, however, often generate significant disruptions in the parent–child relationship. On the one hand they feel inadequate, unrewarded, and unhappy about their parenting role and, on the other hand, they are easily intimidated by their children, who respond to parental indecisiveness with attention-getting, manipulative, and/or immature behaviors. Thus, such parents are often enmeshed in a "vicious circle" relationship with their children, even to the extent that their children may exhibit "clinical" symptoms.

As an example, consider the young mother who is intellectually and emotionally unprepared for the development of negativism in her young child. Let us also assume that she misconstrues the concept of permissiveness; she believes, like so many young, modern parents, that children thrive in a "laissez faire" environment and that a "good mother," therefore, must always be accepting of her child's behavior. Such a mother is in for trouble, because she increasingly feels impotent as her 2-year-old becomes increasingly resistive and provocative. Moreover, she cannot accept her own feelings of distaste and/or anger that are generated by her child's behavior, because such feelings do not jibe with her beliefs and values about what good parents should be. As she experiences the increasing anxiety and guilt associated with her unrewarded effort, her child also becomes more anxious and increasingly likely to behave in a defensive and/or symptomatic way, for example, by developing temper tantrums or excessive soiling or some other manifestation of distress. Even though such "symptoms" do not derive from maternal personality problems or serious rejection, their effect, as with all symptoms, may be to erode the quality of the parent–child relationship, the tranquility of the home, and even the marital relationship. Ultimately, mother herself may also manifest symptoms, such as headaches, depression, and sleeplessness, although these are clearly associated with situational stress rather than a history of emotional disturbance.

Obviously, such difficulties are often stage related, in the sense that deficiences in parental understanding or coping may not impact in such a harmful manner at all developmental levels. Thus, overly permissive mothers may be quite adequate and feel quite rewarded in their relationships with infants; they encounter problems only when the child begins to ambulate. Or a mother who has had a sound and satisfying relationship with her latency-age child may falter in trying to understand and deal with the strivings for autonomy and separation that suddenly increase at puberty. In fact, one of the hallmarks of parents who can benefit from guidance or parent education is that their problems are not chronic and therefore tend not to be described by the parent in "univalent" terms. Statements like, "That one was a problem from the day he was born," are counterindications for parent guidance or education. Statements like, "He was a wonderful baby, so happy and delightful; I don't know what happened," are positive indications for parent guidance or education.

Therefore, the skilled counselor attends carefully to the history provided by candidates for guidance or education groups, in order to discern implied correlations between problem onset and developmental levels or the emergence of new developmental tasks. When there is a clear relationship between these two, it is quite likely that the parent is in need of guidance and education rather than personality transformation. Particularly "susceptible" times are (a) the onset of walking; (b) the task of toilet training; (c) the start of school (especially first grade); (d) pubescence; and (e) the transition to high school.

Other criteria for selecting parents for guidance and education have to do with an appraisal of their functioning in areas other than parenting. Such people function in a relatively ego-syntonic manner in important areas of their lives—for example, social relationships, vocation, community and civic affairs, and marriage (except where the husband–wife relationship is being eroded by increasing problems in coping with the child). They are also relatively free of disabling symptoms and anxiety. Furthermore, they recognize their ineffectuality in parental coping, and they are generally highly motivated to learn new and better ways, provided they are responded to as people who need help with a problem rather than as people in need of treatment (Ginott, 1961).

GOALS AND LEADER

The goal of group parent guidance is more limited and discrete than the goal of therapy or counseling; it is to enhance the everyday functioning of parents in relation to their children, by sensitizing them to children's feelings, by providing them with a basic understanding of children's needs and behavior, and by helping them to develop better skills for communicating with, disciplining, and guiding their offspring.

The leader of parent guidance groups must also have a high level of clinical skill and insight. Like all therapists, his or her goal is to create an empathic atmosphere that reduces guilt and anxiety and thus the defensiveness and/or combativeness that interfere with learning. But the group leader must also guide discussions into child-centered issues, avoiding the digressive pitfalls that often arise in affectively laden group discussions. As a psychologically sophisticated thinker, the leader must shun the temptation to engage in academic discussion about theory; as a sensitive clinician, she or he must avoid delving into personal problems that come to the fore but that cannot be dealt with meaningfully in a child-centered format. Thus, the group leader must be very adept at retaining the practical, problem-centered focus of discussions, constantly relating the participants' personal "revelations" to current childrearing tactics and difficulties. Ginott felt that in many respects, the group guidance leader is effective because she or he models good parenting behavior (Ginott, 1961); that is, she or he listens with understanding and empathy, provides the words that describe feelings accurately, is kind but firm in her or his leadership, and strives to enhance rather than reduce feelings of self-esteem and self-confidence.

FORMAT

Ginott paid particular attention to the technique of group guidance, because he felt that its format could be used to emphasize its implicit qualities of shared experience, child-centeredness, problem solving, and nonjudgment. Typically, his guidance groups consisted of 10 or 12 parents who met for 15 weekly sessions, each session lasting 90 rather than the usual 50 minutes. This amount of time ensured that all of the members had ample opportunity to express themselves. Group members sat at a round table, to minimize the authoritarian or "me to thou" aspects of the leadership role. In front of each participant was a card with his or her child's first name, to highlight the child-centered nature of the discussions.

Ginott grouped parents homogeneously according to the age levels of their children—preschool, latency, adolescents, etc. This was to ensure that the members were dealing with developmentally similar issues and similar problems. Feelings of shared distress, common goals, and group cohesiveness are enhanced when members are talking about the same variety of subject matter. At the same time, Ginott felt that homogeneity of parental practice (or malpractice) was not desirable. He believed it important for members to experience vicariously the problems associated with several rather than one technique of childrearing. Thus, it is helpful for mothers who see themselves as "too permissive" to hear the distress experienced by mothers who see themselves as "too strict." This experience tends to reduce self-blame and to lead to increasing awareness of the futility of trying to describe, understand, and solve individual problems with generalized formulas or labels.

PROCESS

Ginott described several phases in the development of the successful group guidance or parent education process. The initial phase is one of *recitation*, during which the leader encourages the members to describe the problems that they are encountering with their children and the methods that they have employed to deal with these problems. As the litany of complaints, guilt, anger, and confusion unfolds, the leader responds with the attention, understanding, and acceptance that should characterize all helping people. This phase of the group discussion has several purposes. First, it is designed to provide the participants with an experience of empathy for their distress and thus to establish the leader as a safe, sensitive, and attentive person. Second, it is designed to point up the child-centered nature of the discussions that will follow. The leader constantly guides the subject matter to a description of parent–child problems, gently "extinguishing" tendencies to explore other, irrelevant materials. Third, its goal is to increase the members' feelings of a shared experience by exposing them, in a safe atmosphere, to the trials and tribulations of other people. Last, its purpose is to provide the leader with a "check" on the appropriateness of the guidance modality for each member. When a parent describes material that suggests the psychopathology-derived problems described previously or the kind of overly intrusive and demanding behavior that would be harmful to the group, he or she is met with privately and encouraged to accept another kind of help.

As phase one unfolds, group members experience a degree of relief and increasing comfort, perceiving that they are not alone and that their problems are not unique. These feelings are reinforced by their increasing awareness that the leader does not "point the finger of blame" or respond with lectures, chastisement, or the trite platitudes and guilt-provoking clichés that they have heard a million times before. As a result, the members feel increasingly safe, a development that relates to one of Ginott's fundamental theoretical premises, that people are receptive to new learning and capable of adopting a problem-centered set only when they are not personally threatened.

Ironically, as the participants feel increasingly comfortable in expressing themselves, they also experience some dissonance and discomfort in hearing the descriptions of failure provided by other parents who are using different techniques than themselves and who "explain" their problems in very different ways. Members begin to feel that the solutions to their problems are even more obscure than they had thought, and they tend to demand answers and "recipes" from the leader. This push for solutions initiates phase two, a period of *sensitization*. The effort here is to expand and enhance the members' attention to the feeling aspects of their children's behavior.

During this second phase, the skilled leader resists the parents' demands for easy formulas, postponing such "teaching" until the members have had ample opportunity to describe their experiences and to come to grips with the inadequacies of their own explanations for and understanding of their children's problem behaviors. The leader does use every opportunity, however, to point up the importance of children's feelings, emphasizing the cause and effect relationship between feelings and acts. When exasperated parents ask *why* their children behave so badly and why they seem to be unable to get them to behave in better ways, Ginott furnishes the general formula that children act mean "because they feel mean." His purpose here is to help parents realize that coping efforts that focus only on behavior, while ignoring feelings, are doomed to failure, and to focus parental attention on the affective messages inherent in their children's misbehavior. A second purpose is to promote the concept that feelings cannot be changed or "unlearned" so long as they are a hidden agenda in the parent–child dialogue, that new learning can only occur when all of the subject matter—feelings and behavior—is public. Therefore, as the group discussions continue, Ginott helps each member (and encourages the participants to help each other) to think about and explore the affective components of their child's behavior.

Ginott used two techniques to encourage parents to begin this process of emotional exploration. The first consisted of gentle but pointed questioning about the way that a child may feel during difficult parent–child interactions. Thus, when a member describes incidents of defiance or misbehavior, the leader asks, "How do you think John was feeling then?" thereby focusing the discussion on this "new" issue.

A second technique involves using examples related to the everyday emotional experiences of the members. The leader constructs scenarios: "Suppose you have spent hours cleaning the kitchen and your mother says nothing about your effort but instead manages to find and wipe up a tiny smudge on the refrigerator?" or "Suppose you have burned the pot roast, and your husband says: 'When are you going to learn to cook right?'." The group then explores its affective and coping responses to each imaginary episode, with the leader guiding them toward an appreciation of harmful and helpful responses to feelings. As the members develop awareness of the value of noncritical listening and empathic acceptance, the leader then encourages them to provide analogous examples from their parenting experience, gradually focusing discussions on the child's reactions when parents ignore, condemn, or belittle his or her affective experience.

In this teaching by example, Ginott was quite capable of "hamming it up," but his histrionics were always clothed in empathy and directed toward increasing the members' sensitivity to feelings. When feasible, he also encouraged role playing among the members in order to involve as many participants as possible in the experience.

For Ginott, this "sensitivity training" is the groundwork for all effective parent guidance. He believed that failures in parenting are almost always a result of failures in the way adults respond to children's feelings. He also believed that our society is particularly prone to reinforce a posture of "affective disregard," representing perhaps its greatest failure in preparing people for the parenting role. Accordingly, he used every opportunity to increase parents' sensitivity to feelings and to reinforce the "new" idea that a child's feelings are always involved in his or her problem behavior.

As the members become sensitized to the importance of feelings, they also become more dissatisfied with and critical of their own parenting behavior. But their dissatisfaction is now tied to an awareness of what has been missing from their efforts rather than an amorphous feeling of failure and incompetence. It is this self-dissatisfaction that provides the motivation for change, for increased understanding, and for the learning of new and more effective skills.

Ginott was sometimes accused of being too technique oriented, but it is clear that the skill-teaching aspects of his approach rest on a prior *learning of concepts*, phase three of the group guidance process. The leader does not "promulgate" these concepts, however, or present them as complicated or intellectualized theory. Rather, he or she offers them as simplified summary statements and conclusions, in response to the members' continuing descriptions of their failures and successes with their children. The members' increased sensitivity to the importance of feelings, their perception of the leader as an empathic and understanding person, and their dissatisfaction with their past behavior enable them to develop a new and better understanding of their children's behavior.

During this phase, the leader uses an active technique of questioning, aimed at helping parents to develop better insight into parent–child exchanges. He or she encourages parents to formulate reasons for their failures, and when they cannot quite generalize a principle for understanding, the leader provides the generalization for them (Ginott, 1961, pp. 183–184):

> Mrs. B: My son came home crying. The teacher yelled at him and belittled him in front of the whole class.
> Leader: What is the usual response of parents in such a case?
> Mrs. A: I would ask him what he did to make the teacher mad at him. "If the teacher yelled at you, you *must* have deserved it."
> Leader: How do such words affect the child?
> Mrs. A: He gets even more upset.
> Leader: Suppose we want to show him that we understand what he feels. How would we accomplish that?
> Mrs. C: After listening to him, we could say, "It must have hurt your feelings."
> Mrs. B: You hate people yelling at you.
> Mrs. D: You didn't like being yelled at in front of the whole class. Your feelings were hurt.
> Leader: What do we accomplish by this approach?
> Mrs. C: We show the child that we understand him.
> Leader: And that his feelings are important to us.

A major theme of phase three is to reinforce the distinction between feelings and acts and to encourage the belief that it is healthy for children to be able to experience and explore their feelings without guilt or fear. In addition, the leader emphasizes the concept that parents must assist in the development of such self-acceptance by describing and accepting their children's emotional experience. This distinction is refined further in a redefinition of the concept of permissiveness. Parents are helped to see that feelings should always be permitted but that behavior does not require unconditional acceptance. This conceptual distinction is the groundwork for the later learning of techniques of setting limits and discipline.

Another important goal is to develop an understanding of the role of ambivalence in human affairs. Through exploration of their own responses, the parents are led to realize that emotional experiences are neither logical nor reasonable in nature and that the coexistence of seemingly contradictory feelings is a normal rather than an undesirable fact of human life. The leader helps parents to see that children need to feel comfortable with their own ambivalence, and that they achieve such comfort in response to parents' reactions to their feelings. In this regard, the leader does not disparage or fault the members' differing moral and ethical values; rather, she or he tries to recast them as parents' judgments about *behavior* rather than person. As a matter of fact, the members are encouraged to expect reasonable standards of conduct in their children, and they are permitted to explore and ventilate their own feelings of anger and distress when these standards are violated.

A spin off of the parents' appreciation of ambivalence is the development of new concepts about the meaning of symptoms. Parents come to understand their children's behavior as it relates to fear and guilt about hateful and angry feelings that cannot be said in words. Within this context, parents are asked to formulate reasons for their children's nightmares, stomach aches, or enuresis, and to suggest new and better ways of reducing symptoms by encouraging children to express their fearsome experiences in words or other symbols.

The purpose of phase three is to provide the group members with a conceptual framework within which they can analyze and improve their parenting behavior. The insights that they develop serve as guidelines for evaluating their past failures and for developing better parenting habits. Parents begin to behave in more thoughtful ways; their descriptions of their problems now include a sensitive concern with the child's inner life, and their discussions are oriented more toward finding solutions than expressing guilt, impotence, or displaced anger toward the leader. Toward the end of this phase of guidance, the leader provides for further practice and for reinforcement of the members' new knowledge. He or she presents the group with additional childrearing "concepts" and asks members to illustrate each concept with examples from their own experiences (Ginott, 1961, p. 85): ·

If a child lives with criticism, he learns to condemn.
If a child lives with security, he learns to have faith in himself.
If a child lives with hostility, he learns to fight.
If a child lives with acceptance, he learns to love.
If a child lives with fear, he learns to be apprehensive.
If a child lives with recognition, he learns to have a goal.
If a child lives with pity, he learns to be sorry for himself.
If a child lives with approval, he learns to like himself.
If a child lives with jealousy, he learns to feel guilty.
If a child lives with friendliness, he learns that the world is a nice place in which to live.

The final phase of group guidance involves the *teaching and practice of better coping skills*. The leader does not advocate blanket methods but suggests techniques that are appropriate to and potentially helpful for the particular experiences described by the members. He or she also encourages the members to apply their new knowledge to helping each other find new and better ways of coping with problems, relying on the fact that the group members can often bring greater objectivity and insight to another person's problems than to their own. The participants are asked to try out their new skills and to bring their experiences, successes and failures, back to the group for further discussion. Thus, phase four is the laboratory part of the guidance process, somewhat analogous to the practicum aspects of clinical teaching.

One goal of phase four is to improve the affective vocabulary of the members, to provide them with more and better words for the accurate description and reflection of feelings. Through the group discussions and their experience with the empathic stance of the leader, they develop a richer repertoire for responding to the nuances of their children's feelings. The aim is to hone and sharpen communication skills by substituting specific for general and emotionally cogent for intellectualized responses.

A second goal is to provide parents with safe outlets for the expression of their own angry and resentful feelings. Ginott recognized that even the most competent parent will sometimes become emotionally upset by a child's behavior, but unlike the child therapist, parents are not protected by a clock that limits exposure to the more irritating and fatiguing aspects of children's behavior. Ginott felt that such feelings are both inevitable and legitimate, and he believed that parents must be helped to express and accept such feelings, when they occur, for two important reasons: (*a*) the bottling up of parental affect serves to increase defensiveness and avoidance rather than to enhance coping efforts; and (*b*) appropriate expression of parental feelings serves as an important modeling experience for the child. Ginott therefore encouraged parents to be open and frank about their own feelings, teaching them, however, to direct their expressions toward behavior and events rather than toward the child's feelings or personality: "When I see hitting, it makes me furious! Right now I am so enraged and discombobulated I can only yell! Hitting is not allowed in this house, and I will not tolerate it!"

This "practice in healthy hollering" serves several additional purposes. It provides parents with a safe substitute for past, more harmful habits; it sensitizes children to the fact that their behavior affects the way other people feel; sometimes it even helps to expand a child's vocabulary.

The major focus of phase four, however, is to teach parents effective techniques of discipline. For the most part, parents want and need help in dealing with their children's misbehavior, with situations in which children inappropriately express their negative feelings toward other people. The issues of setting limits and of guiding children to civilized ways of responding are therefore paramount to all parents. The Ginottian technique of discipline is described more fully elsewhere (Ginott, 1961; Orgel, in preparation). It can be summarized here as a four-step method of intervention that is built upon the concepts learned in phase three: (a) the accurate reflection of the child's angry and destructive feelings; (b) a passive-voice statement of the rule or principle that is being violated; (c) the provision of symbolic (subliminatory) substitutes for affective expression; and (d) reflection of the feelings that have been generated or exaggerated by the act of limit setting itself.

OVERVIEW

The stages described previously are the author's device rather than Ginott's and are simply a contrivance for examining and analyzing the Ginottian technique. In practice, parent guidance is a unified process in which the stages overlap with and meld into each other. Thus, some concept formation (stage three) certainly occurs during stages one and two, and some skills (stage four) are taught and learned as early as stage one. The timing of each development depends upon the composition of the group, the relative child-centeredness of the problems presented, and the rapidity with which the members learn.

By the same token, Ginott's distinction between parent therapy, counseling, guidance, and education groups is also relative. The parent-centered versus child-centered formulation implies a continuum rather than a typology. Ginott recognized this continuum by using all four approaches in a "sliding scale," reversible way at the Jacksonville Clinic. Parents were assigned to a modality on the basis of a tentative evaluation, but the clinic was always prepared to alter its plan as a function of the leader's increasing experience with each group member. And people often "graduated" from one modality to another, as a function of their changing needs and perceptions. Thus, parents who benefited significantly from a counseling experience might "top off" their experience in a parent guidance or education group. Sometimes, the parent education format was used for in-depth screening purposes; where parents were not able to benefit much from an educational group, they were invited to accept more intensive help.

It is particularly difficult to distinguish clearly between parent guidance and parent education, since both represent the child-centered end of the continuum. Originally, parent guidance was designed for clinic-referred parents, but obviously there are many nonreferred parents who are fully enmeshed in vicious circle relationships with their children; and by the same token, some clinic parents have "jumped the gun" in asking for clinical help with their problems. The distinction between guidance and education, therefore, is one of degree rather than kind. The amount of time spent on each stage, the amount of emotional and conceptual reeducation, the focus on understanding symptoms, the need for personal "catharsis" about childrearing difficulties, and the amount of practice in techniques will all vary according to the needs and experiences of the individual participants. Thus, where members are not yet severely distressed about their problems, a group can comfortably absorb more than 10 or 12 members, and discussions may emphasize the sharing of information about child development and behavior to a greater degree than usual. Or, in a "preventive" education group for expecting parents, stage one would be drastically attenuated, since the members have not yet experienced parenting problems and since the empathic qualities of the leader can be established with greater ease and in less time than is the case with parents who are experiencing acute distress.

Effectiveness of the Approach

An evaluation of parent education techniques is difficult, to say the least. Although there is now an extensive body of literature about parent education outcomes, few studies are specific enough to permit replications, comparisons of different approaches, or dependable conclusions about the effectiveness of a specific technique, such as Ginott's. Cobb and Medway (1978, pp. 235–236) describe the state of the field as follows:

> Research on correlates of successful parent consultation consists of a conglomerate of isolated findings with few studies building cumulatively on one another. Current knowledge is woefully deficient regarding functional relationships among consultant, consultee, client, process, and system variables and the outcomes of parent consultation.

The usefulness of the Ginottian approach is suggested, of course, by subjective impressions of parent educators who use it and by the approval of the parent participants. With some reservations, Ginott reported positive results based on his clinical evaluation of increases in the effectiveness and personal growth of people in his groups (Ginott, 1961), and he also reported positive feedback from most participants. Perhaps a bit more convincing is the report of Faber and Mazlish (1974), two mothers who attended one of Ginott's workshops and wrote about the experience from the parent's standpoint:

> The results of this experience were far-reaching. As we struggled to shape theory into practice, and practice into personal interpretation, we became aware of changes in ourselves, in our families, and in the members of our group [p. ix].

Clinical or parental testimonials aside, most of the research literature is hard to evaluate because of a lack of standardization of outcome measures, failures to specify the educational techniques used, wide variations in parent sample characteristics, and equally wide variation in the ages and problems of the participants' children.

Tavormina (1975) reports a study comparing a specifically Ginottian approach with behavioral techniques. Although the Ginottian method resulted in significant improvement over a control (no training) group, the results also indicated that behaviorally trained groups performed significantly better than the Ginottian groups. Since the children of the participants were all significantly retarded, however, the results are not unexpected. Children with IQs below 50 are probably not the best candidates for responding to parental training in reflective skills.

A more relevant and convincing study is reported by Gabel (1972), who examined the separate and combined effects of parent group education and group play therapy on maternal childrearing attitudes. Some 98 mothers were assigned to parent education groups (12 weekly sessions) or to no-treatment, control groups; their kindergarten children were seen in either group play therapy (12 sessions), placebo control (12 sessions of recreational play), or no treatment. The theoretical orientation of parent education and child psychotherapy were both specifically Ginottian.

The experimental group of parents showed a significant increase in their emphasis on parent–child understanding and positive but non-significant changes in four other childrearing attitude domains. Interestingly, the role of corollary, short-term, Ginottian group play therapy did not clearly contribute to improvements in parenting attitudes.

Gabel's results are probably somewhat diluted by the fact that all of the subjects were normal volunteers whose children were neither referred nor identified as having significant problems. In fact, children identified as potentially hyperactive (N = 10) were specifically excluded. Presumably, such a population is more limited in the degree to which it can improve than is a referred sample.

Two recent studies provide indirect support for the Ginottian technique, although the subjects are mental health aides rather than parents. Gesten, Cowen, Orgel, and Schwartz (1979) report significant improvements in the attitudes and effectiveness of mental health aides specifically trained in the Ginottian technique of limit setting, whereas Cowen, Gesten, Orgel, and Wilson (1979) found that the disturbed children seen by these aides showed improvements on a variety of measures. Although the paradigm here is closer to clinical supervision than parent education, the technique was specifically Ginottian and was described in sufficient detail to permit replication. Moreover, the aides are subprofessionals who are trained to relate to children in warm and empathic ways but who do not function as psychotherapists. In these two studies, pre–post measures of aide and children characteristics were also extensive and based on measures of demonstrated reliability, thus they are also replicable. The results, therefore, provide considerable support for the effectiveness of an "indirect," systematic educational effort, even though the effort was not specifically parent education. Considering that the aides see targeted children only once a week, the impact of the training is even more surprising. A replication of these studies with parents of targeted, problem children would go a long way toward evaluating the effectiveness of Ginott's approach.

Summary

Ginott's approach to parent education developed out of his varied experience as a teacher, child psychotherapist, parent counselor, and clinical supervisor. It is based on his conviction that the empathic relationship is a prerequisite for effective interpersonal learning and his recognition that appropriate modeling is the major tool of the parent educator.

The parent education technique is an extension or derivative of the treatment modalities that Ginott used for helping the parents of clinic-referred children: group psychotherapy, group counseling, and group guidance. These three techniques were employed according to theoretical considerations about the child versus parent-centeredness of children's presenting problems. Parent education occupies the most child-centered end of this continuum.

Ginottian technique is described in four stages: (a) recitation; (b) sensitization; (c) concept formation; and (d) skill learning. The relative importance and duration of each stage, however, varies greatly according to goal and subject variables.

Subjective and experimental studies of the effectiveness of the technique, while far from definitive, offer support for the efficacy of Ginott's approach to parent education.

References

Cobb, D. E., & Medway, F. J. Determinants in parent consultation. *Journal of Community Psychology*, 1978, 6, 229–240.

Cowen, E. L., Orgel, A. R., Geston, E. L. & Wilson, A. B. The evaluation of an intervention program for young schoolchildren with acting-out problems. *Journal of Abnormal Child Psychology*, 1979, 7, 381–396.

Cowen, E., Trost, M. A., Lorion, R. P., Dorr, E., Izzo, L. D., & Isaacson, R. *New ways in school mental health*. New York: Human Sciences Press, 1975.

Durkin, H. Mothers. In S. R. Slavson (Ed.), *The fields of group psychotherapy*. New York: International Universities Press, 1965.

Faber, A., & Mazlish, E. *Liberated parents, liberated children*. New York: Grosset & Dunlap, 1974.

Gabel, H. D. *Effects of parent group education and group play psychotherapy on maternal child-rearing attitudes*. Unpublished doctoral dissertation, University of Rochester, 1972.

Ginott, H. G. Group screening of parents in a child guidance setting. *International Journal of Group Psychotherapy*, 1956, 6, 405–409.

Ginott, H. G. Differential treatment groups in guidance, counseling, psychotherapy, and psychoanalysis. *International Journal of Social Psychiatry*, 1957, 3, 231–35.(a)

Ginott, H. G. Parent education groups in a child guidance clinic. *Mental Hygiene*, 1957, 41, 82–86.(b)

Ginott, H. G. *Group psychotherapy with children*. New York: McGraw-Hill, 1961.

Ginott, H. G. *Between parent and child*. New York: Macmillan, 1965.

Ginott, H. G. *Between parent and teenager*. New York: Macmillan, 1969.

Ginott, H. G. Personal communication, August 1972.(a)

Ginott, H. G. *Between teacher and child*. New York: Macmillan, 1972.(b)

Gordon, T. *Parent effectiveness training*. New York: Peter H. Wyden, 1970.

Orgel, A. R. Haim was my teacher, too. *Florida Psychologist*, May 1975, 25(4), 24–29.

Orgel, A. R. Haim Ginott's approach to discipline. In D. Dorr & M. Zax (Eds.), *Comparative approaches to discipline for children and youth*. New York: Springer, in preparation.

Slavson, S. R. *Child-centered group guidance for parents*. New York: International Universities Press, 1947. (a)

Slavson, S. R. (Ed.). *The practice of group therapy*. New York: International Universities Press, 1947. (b)

Tavormina, J. B. Relative effectiveness of behavioral group counseling with parents of mentally retarded children. *Journal of Consulting and Clinical Psychology*, 1975, 43, 22–31.

Chapter 5

Parent Effectiveness Training:
A Preventive Program and
Its Effects on Families

THOMAS GORDON

Parent Effectiveness Training was an idea conceived out of my growing dissatisfaction with the appropriateness of the medical model I
utilized in my professional work as a clinical psychologist in private
practice. I held myself out to the public as a "therapist" who treated
people with "emotional," "mental," or "psychological" problems.
While rejecting some of the symbolic trappings of medical practitioners
(wearing the white coat, calling people "patients"), I accepted others: I
introduced myself as "Doctor," I described my treatment method as
"psychotherapy" (or, for children, "play therapy"), and I sent out
monthly bills for my "consultation fees."

Incongruities in this treatment approach did not greatly trouble me
until parents began consulting me with hopes and expectations that I
work with a youngster they labeled a "problem child" or a child they
had diagnosed as having an "emotional problem."

Eager to apply the psychotherapy skills I had learned, I was unprepared for the discovery that these children seldom saw themselves as
having any kind of emotional problem. The initial conversation with
these youngsters typically followed this pattern:

Therapist: Would you like to tell me about your problem? Start wherever you'd like.
    Child: I don't have any problem.
Therapist: Well, your parents thought it might be helpful for you to talk about

101

HANDBOOK ON
PARENT EDUCATION

whatever is troubling you. That's my job to help kids solve their prob-
lems. You can talk to me.
Child: I don't have anything to talk about.
Therapist: You *must* have some problem that is troubling you. Perhaps I can help.
Child: You can help change my parents. They're the ones with the problem.
Therapist: You wish you could change your parents.
Child: Boy, do I.

From this point on, the youngsters began talking freely about their family life—the squabbles and conflicts, times when they felt treated unfairly, how their parents talked to them, how they disciplined, their disappointments and frustrations, their bitterness and anger, and so on. And although each of these youngsters was quite different from all the others, their descriptions of their parents and their family life were amazingly similar. I could not escape the conclusion that the parents were cut from the same cloth: While they were well intentioned about being good parents and having "good" kids, they ignored or dis-counted their children's feelings; they criticized and berated their opin-ions; they accorded them the status of secondary citizens in the family; their method of shaping or controlling the behavior of their youngsters consisted of administering rewards or punishment (the common model for disciplining dogs and training circus animals to perform); and the conflicts they got into were handled in such a way that the parent ended up as either a dictator (authoritarianism) or a doormat (permissiveness).

Understandably, my original view of the child as the one needing psychotherapy was replaced by the conviction that it was the parents who really needed my help. So my treatment strategy shifted to suggest-ing that the parents schedule therapeutic sessions with me. It was then I learned my second lesson: These parents did not appear to be emotion-ally disturbed, neurotic, or crippled by "psychological" problems; and they, too, resisted "entering into therapy" with me. Like their children, they were simply unhappy with their relationships in the family; they were disappointed in their children and dissatisfied with the way they were handling problems; they felt ineffective and inadequate as parents.

Clearly, my earlier picture of disturbed children in need of personal psychotherapy had not been accurate, and now I had to discard my conception of their parents as the ones who needed individual psy-chotherapy. It finally dawned on me that these parents and their chil-dren were having difficulties in their *relationships*—they were experienc-ing many problems in living together peacefully and happily, and they lacked the skills and methods for successfully resolving those problems. While most of the parents in these families were no more psy-chologically unhealthy than I, they were amazingly misinformed about what goes on in human relationships. In their formal education—as physicians, engineers, lawyers, teachers, accountants, business persons, and so on—these people had been offered next to nothing in the way of knowledge from the field of human relations. They were as uneducated in this field as were the managers, executives, and administrators in business and industrial organizations for whom I had been teaching human relations training programs of my own design for more than a decade. Such experience made me confident that I could design a similar training program for parents, incorporating the features that had made the other programs effective:

1. Training is best done in a group.
2. Theory is not enough—trainees need specific skills and methods.
3. Skill-practice in the class is required to give trainees the confidence to apply the methods "at-home."
4. A competent instructor is required to model the skills, to coach the trainees, and to handle their resistance to change.
5. The classroom climate must be free of the threat of evaluation and criticism.
6. The training must deal directly with the critical issue of power and authority in human relationships, so often ignored in human relations training.

The Design of Parent Effectiveness Training

From my first experiences teaching several pilot programs to parents in and around Pasadena, California, during the years of 1962 and 1963, I acquired additional ideas and insights that led to incorporating other critical features into the design of the parent program:

1. The course should be divorced completely from the medical model, with its distinctive language (group therapy, patients, doctor, psychological problems, sickness, treatment, professional fees, etc.). Instead, the course must be presented as an educational model in which the language of education is utilized (a course, training, class, students, instructor, textbook, assignments, tuition). Its name was carefully chosen to fit the educational model: Parent Effectiveness Training, now most often referred to as P.E.T.

2. The course should be much less expensive than psychotherapy (with most therapist fees at that time ranging from $25–$75 per hour) to permit delivery of the parent program to a much larger segment of the population. Tuition for Parent Effectiveness Training (covering books

and materials) now ranges from $35–$65 for the 24-hour course (from $1.50–$2.70 per instructional hour).

3. The course should involve both mothers and fathers, in marked contrast to traditional parent education in this country. Hence, Parent Effectiveness Training is almost always given in the evening.

4. The course should be easily transportable to any community. Consequently, it was designed so that other professionals could be trained as instructors. At present over 1000 new instructors are trained each year in week-long Instructor Training Workshops. This cadre of instructors has taught over 600,000 parents in Parent Effectiveness Training, in many hundreds of communities in every state and in a growing number of foreign countries.

5. In order to make Parent Effectiveness Training both broadly available and geographically accessible to parents, classes are sponsored by and conducted in many different kinds of organizations—for example, churches, synagogues, social service agencies, schools, YMCAs, counseling centers, adult education centers, community mental health centers, and so on.

6. In order to ensure the continued existence and nationwide growth of Parent Effectiveness Training, I developed a financial design that would make the program self-supporting rather than dependent on subsidies from foundations or governmental agencies, whose funding all too often is undependable and time limited. Consequently, the tuition parents pay provides revenue that covers the cost of the course material they receive, the fee for the instructor, the room rental, and a small fee to pay the national headquarters for the professional services and marketing support it provides instructors in the field. The national headquarters is an organization (a group of 33 full-time employees) called Effectiveness Training, Incorporated. Its services and support include the following: a newsletter for instructors, brochures and reprints, national advertising and publicity, a library of research on Parent Effectiveness Training, a national parents' referral system, film rentals, upgrading of course content and materials, and so on.

The Recruitment and Training of Instructors

Initially, I felt that instructors of Parent Effectiveness Training had to be licensed clinical psychologists like myself. I soon discovered, however, that very few of my colleagues were interested. They wanted to be therapists; many were getting involved in growth centers just springing up at that time; some did not feel there was sufficient financial return;

most were very skeptical about such training producing change in parents' behavior; they balked at doing the kind of work required to attract parents into the course (giving speeches, calling on ministers, pediatricians, or agencies); or they felt incompetent as teachers.

In contrast, it was not difficult to recruit instructors from other professional groups. Requests for instructor training came frequently from ministers, school counselors, marriage and family counselors, school psychologists, nursery school teachers, parent education specialists, youth workers, social workers, and many women who, after taking the course as parents, saw instructing as an opportunity for rewarding and valuable work outside the home.

By and large, the instructors we have recruited are people who first took the course as parents and discovered rewarding changes in their own families. Many instructors saw in P.E.T. an opportunity to enlarge and enrich their professional roles, which for them had become nonproductive or stultifying. Others were disenchanted, as I had been, with the diagnostic/treatment model and welcomed the chance to do preventive work with families. Very few who were trained as instructors had the expectation of great financial reward, inasmuch as the instructional fees are not high enough to support a person full-time. Most of our instructors already have full-time jobs.

The actual training for instructors contains the following components:

1. Enrollment in the Parent Effectiveness Training course (not required but strongly recommended).
2. Completion of a week-long Instructor Training Workshop, taught by one of our six national trainers.
3. Becoming familiar with the contents of a very comprehensive Instructor Guide (lesson plans for each of the eight sessions of the parent course).
4. Becoming familiar with the contents of the course textbook: *P.E.T.: Parent Effectiveness Training* (Gordon, 1970).
5. Instructors are encouraged to co-teach with an experienced instructor where such a person exists in the new instructors' community.
6. Practice teaching (an option): offering the course to a group of no more than 10 neighbors, friends, or relatives, who pay only a token tuition (to cover cost of materials).
7. All instructors receive feedback on the quality of their instruction from an evaluation form filled out anonymously by every participant at the end of the course.

8. In some communities, instructors form an association, one of the functions of which is the continuous upgrading of the instructional skills of its members.
9. Every instructor may attend, at no cost, a second Instructor Training Workshop as a refresher or retraining experience.
10. The national office organizes an annual convention for instructors, which provides them with continuing education both from invited speakers who have done outstanding work in the human relations field and from workshops in which instructors share (*a*) their experiences with special P.E.T. classes (low-income parents, day-care workers, parents of retarded children, foster parents, parents in foreign countries); (*b*) their instructional innovations; (*c*) their research; and (*d*) their ideas for improvements in the P.E.T. course content, and so on.

Over 15,000 instructors have been trained and authorized to teach P.E.T. They have come from all 50 states and from 15 foreign countries. Not all of them end up teaching P.E.T., but those who do universally find it to be one of the most rewarding and fulfilling experiences in their lives.

What Parents Learn in P.E.T.

The P.E.T. course is not unlike other programs involving skill training (such as piano lessons, tennis lessons, courses in painting or sculpting). In class, participants are shown specific skills through demonstration and modeling by the instructor, and they are given the opportunity to practice those skills under controlled conditions (role playing) and with coaching. However, the P.E.T. course itself merely starts a process—an ongoing and never-ending process of developing increased competence in applying the skills learned in the classroom to the real problems parents encounter in the home. Consequently, it can never be said that P.E.T. "trains" parents nor that it makes parents "effective." A more modest claim would be that in P.E.T. parents are shown a particular model for the parent–child relationship and taught the various interpersonal skills required to implement that model. Then it is up to each parent to apply those skills, practice them, and develop increased competence over time.

Seldom do any parents in P.E.T. fail to understand intellectually either the model or the skills, because incorporated in the course are experiences in which parents actually perform in class all of the skills they have been taught. Consequently, we know with a high degree of certainty *what* parents learn:

1. Parents learn to think and talk about their children in terms of their discrete existential behaviors (what they are saying or what they are doing) rather than in terms of abstract personality traits or characteristics, ordinarily accompanied by judgments or evaluations.

"Jimmy did not say hello to my friend."
versus
"Jimmy is shy and impolite."
or
"Kathy left her clothes in the living room."
versus
"Kathy is sloppy and inconsiderate."

2. Parents learn the importance of their behaving toward the child's behavior consistently or congruently with their feelings—whether their feelings are acceptance or nonacceptance; and they learn how to determine which of the two feelings they are actually experiencing. In short, parents learn that honesty is the best policy in human relationships.

3. Parents acquire a reasonable level of competence in using facilitative communications skills in responding to messages that children send when they share problems with parents. Drawing from my training as a Rogerian therapist, we teach parents to rely heavily on these three skills of the professional counselor: (*a*) silence; (*b*) door-openers or *open-ended questions;* and (*c*) active listening (*reflective listening*).

4. Parents acquire an effective level of competence in confronting children whose behavior is unacceptable to them by sending statements limited only to their own feelings (leveling, being congruent or transparent), as opposed to blaming, preaching, ordering, warning, and the like.

"I am too tired to play with you."
versus
"You are being a pest."
or
"I need more quiet to read my book."
versus
"You stop that yelling or you'll go to your room."

5. Parents learn a great deal about parental authority—the difference between authority derived from knowledge and experience (being an "authority") and authority derived from using rewards and punish-

ment (being an "authoritarian"). They learn about the various coping mechanisms children use in response to parental power (rebellion, retaliation, aggression, withdrawing, anger, submission, apple polishing, lying, tattling, bullying, forming alliances, noncommunication, avoidance, etc.).

6. Parents also learn the pitfalls of being permissive (giving in to the child, handling conflicts so the child wins and the parent loses). They come to understand the destructive effects on the relationship when children get their needs met at the expense of the parent having unmet needs.

7. Parents learn the pitfalls of being authoritarian (using power to make the child give in to the parent, so the parent wins and the child loses). They learn the price that they must pay when children's needs are frustrated by coercive power—that is, having to deal with the child's coping mechanisms as well as a deteriorating relationship.

8. Parents learn an alternative to the two win–lose methods of resolving conflicts—what we call the "no-lose" method by which parent and child employ a six-step problem-solving process to reach a mutually acceptable solution that will allow both to get their needs met (parent wins, child wins; or nobody loses).

9. Parents learn how they can enhance their influence over their children's values and beliefs by using the methods of an effective consultant—that is, getting "hired" by the client (child); listening to the problems of the client; *offering* knowledge and experience as opposed to imposing it; leaving the responsibility with the client to choose whether to accept or reject the consultant's knowledge and experience; and teaching by modeling.

Using language at a much higher level of abstraction than the language actually used with parents in the class, I could say that the P.E.T. course offers parents a particular model of interpersonal relationships that has been described by other social scientists with such terms as: reciprocal relationships; relationships in which there is social equity; relationships in which there is mutual need satisfaction; collaborative relationships; humanistic relationships; relationships in which there is mutual respect for the rights of each; and therapeutic relationships (facilitative of mutual growth).

While I have used each of those terms from time to time, I prefer describing what we teach in P.E.T. as *a model of democratic relationships.* I have attempted to express this model in the form of a credo, which is given out to each participant in P.E.T. with the suggestion that they have it framed and hung on a wall, as it is in our house.

A CREDO
For My Relationships with Others

You and I are in a relationship that I value and want to keep. Yet each of us is a separate person with unique needs and the right to meet those needs.

When you are having problems meeting your needs I will try to listen with genuine acceptance in order to facilitate your finding your own solutions instead of depending on mine. I also will respect your right to choose your own beliefs and develop your own values, different though they may be from mine.

However, when your behavior interferes with what I must do to get my own needs met, I will tell you openly and honestly how your behavior affects me, trusting that you respect my needs and feelings enough to try to change the behavior that is unacceptable to me. Also, whenever some behavior of mine is unacceptable to you, I hope you will tell me openly and honestly so I can try to change my behavior.

At those times when we find that either of us cannot change to meet the other's needs, let us acknowledge that we have a conflict and commit ourselves to resolve each such conflict without either of us resorting to the use of power or authority to win at the expense of the other's losing. I respect your needs, but I also must respect my own. So let us always strive to search for a solution that will be acceptable to both of us. Your needs will be met, and so will mine—neither will lose, both will win.

In this way, you can continue to develop as a person through satisfying your needs, and so can I. Thus, ours can be a healthy relationship in which both of us can strive to become what we are capable of being. And we can continue to relate to each other with mutual respect, love, and peace.

What Happens to Parents and Their Families ?

In order to find out what happens after the P.E.T. class is over and the parents try to apply their new skills, we have relied primarily on the reports of those parents who continue meeting with an instructor in post-course sessions (usually called continuation classes) and on the results of a study done by my daughter, Judy Gordon Sands. She conducted in-depth interviews with a sample of 92 P.E.T. graduates. Within the sample were parents who had taken P.E.T. for as long as 10 years prior to the interview, and as recently as a few months. The results from this study provided all the material for the book I later wrote with Judy called *P.E.T. in Action: Inside P.E.T. Families* (Gordon, 1976).

The content analysis of the transcripts of these tape-recorded interviews revealed a wide range of reported changes in both parents and their families. These included: (*a*) redefinitions of the parent role; (*b*) new insights about themselves as parents; (*c*) new insights about their children; (*d*) increased trust in the creative capacities of their children; (*e*) more confidence as parents; (*f*) deeper and more intimate relations with their children; (e) more responsibility and self-direction shown by children; (h) increased ability of children to solve their problems themselves; (i) more consideration by children of parents' needs; (j) more honest and open communication; (k) more willingness by children to negotiate conflicts; (l) more respect on the parents' part for their own rights and needs; and (m) the parents' use of less control and domination of children.

A small sample of verbatim parent comments classified within the categories preceding shows both the wide range of changes reported as well as the flavor of their responses to the course:

- "I'm more in control of myself."
- "I am more relaxed, less uptight, less inclined to come unglued."
- "I feel I know what is going on in each specific interaction with the children."
- "We've learned to trust each other and appreciate each other's needs."
- "I'm more nonjudgmental."
- "It has changed my focus from the child as a problem to me and what I'm doing."
- "We simply never think of using punishment, of any kind."
- "I'm more aware of how important it is to be in touch with my own needs."
- "P.E.T. changed my whole outlook—I see our relationships all different now."
- "I now feel confident to assert my own needs—to take care of myself, not live my life for my kids or let them walk over me—and all this without guilt."
- "We're not afraid any more to talk about feelings."
- "I have a new awareness that parents don't necessarily have all the answers—the kids can be creative and come up with answers."
- "I'm aware now that nobody has to be in control and calling the shots."
- "Now kids can blast at me and I can see that they have a reason to."
- "Now we honestly love each other."
- "Since experiencing that I have rights and feelings worthy of respect, I have pursued a career, taught P.E.T., got an advanced degree . . . I, who was terrified to speak out loud in an audience, am now giving lectures, teaching classes, doing counseling. Before P.E.T., I really didn't trust myself, my ideas, or even my own judgment of whom I could trust."
- "Since P.E.T. training, I am closer to my sons in an intimate way I would never have dreamed of, and at the same time I am happier about their independence."
- "The greatest effect in our relationship was having my son come to us and say, 'I really think you love me more than you used to.'"

From the same study we also obtained evidence that some parents (a small percentage of our sample) found it quite difficult to use some of the skills they learned in the P.E.T. class. Some admitted failing to apply the skills; others experienced attrition in their use of the skills; some just couldn't find the time. One parent was still convinced P.E.T. methods would never work when parents and children collide over value differences. And a number of parents felt they needed more training because of their low level of competence in using the skills.

Findings from Research Studies

The effects of P.E.T. have been evaluated in 25 separate research studies, copies of which are on file in the research library of Effectiveness Training Incorporated. The quality of these studies varies considerably with respect to the kinds of instruments used, the size of the samples employed, the degree to which other variables are controlled, and the statistical techniques chosen by the experimenters. Nevertheless, all of them found changes that were statistically significant. The specific findings from these studies are briefly stated in the following section.

Changes in the Parents after P.E.T.

1. Parents showed increased confidence in themselves in the role of parent (Aldassy, 1977; Andelin, 1975; Garcia, 1971; Larson, 1972; Lillibridge, 1971; Miles, 1974).
2. Parents showed increased acceptance of their children (Lillibridge, 1971; Mee, 1977; Peterson, 1970; Schofield, 1976; Williams & Sanders, 1973).
3. Parents showed increased trust in their children (Aldassy, 1977; Garcia, 1971; Geffen, 1977; Hanley, 1973; Larson, 1972; Lillibridge, 1971; Schmitz, 1975).
4. Parents showed increased understanding of their children's behavior (Aldassy, 1977; Garcia, 1971; Geffen, 1977; Hanley, 1973; Knowles, 1970; Larson, 1972; Schofield, 1976).
5. Parents showed an increase in democratic attitudes and a decrease in authoritarian attitudes and practices (Knowles, 1970; Mee, 1977; Peterson, 1970; Pieper, 1977; Piercy & Brush, 1971; Stearn, 1970).
6. Parents showed improvement in overall parental attitudes and/or childrearing behaviors, as measured by such tests as Child Management Inventory, Parent Attitude Survey Scales, and Hereford Parent Attitude Scale (Aldassy, 1977; Haynes, 1972; Larson, 1972; Williams & Sanders, 1973).
7. Parents showed improvements in their self-esteem (Larson, 1972; Stearn, 1970; Williams & Sanders, 1973).
8. Parents showed a reduction in the number of problems with their children (Larson, 1972).
9. Parents showed a reduction in anxiety (Williams & Sanders, 1973).

10. Parents showed an increase in the use of progressive educational practices (Schofield, 1976).
11. Parents improved their scores on tests of empathy, understanding, positive regard, congruence, and acceptance (Mee, 1977; Piercy & Brush, 1971).
12. Mothers and fathers made equal gains in overall positive parental attitudes (Aldassy, 1977).
13. Parents showed more willingness to accept children's right to hold beliefs different from parents' (Peterson, 1970).
14. Parents and their children showed no significant decrease in "interpersonal distance" (Knight, 1974).

Changes in the Children of P.E.T. Parents

1. Children who participated with their parents in P.E.T. showed a progressive increase in the level of moral reasoning on Kohlberg's Scale (Stanley, 1978).
2. Children of P.E.T. parents designated as underachievers gained an average of one full grade point in school (Larson, 1972).
3. Children of P.E.T. parents perceived them as having increased their acceptance of them as persons (fewer rejections) (Lillibridge, 1971).
4. Children of P.E.T. parents showed a decrease in inappropriate and disruptive behaviors (children were potential dropouts) (Miles, 1974).
5. Children of P.E.T. parents showed increase in self-esteem (Schofield, 1976; Stearn, 1970).

Others

1. Hospital staff who were taught P.E.T. showed reduction of use of nonfacilitative, nontherapeutic communication with patients (Kilburn, Gerard, & Ray, 1971).
2. Undergraduate students who took listening training from P.E.T. showed increase in use of empathic verbal responses (Moritz, 1976).
3. Staff of mentally retarded hospital who took P.E.T. showed decrease in tension and irritation with each other (Willenson & Bisgaard, 1970).
4. Girl Scout leaders who took P.E.T. showed an increase in how much they valued freedom of choice for troop members (Aunkst-Dewald, 1976).

In the preceding summary of research findings, note that the first seven parent variables were found to change significantly in *three or more* independent studies. Such consistency is impressive, and it cannot help but increase our confidence in P.E.T. as a program that produces important changes in parents. In addition, the five studies in which statistically significant changes were found in the *children* of P.E.T. parents strengthen our conviction that the skills parents learn in P.E.T. subsequently bring about positive effects on their children.

Additional support for this claim is presented by Martin (1975), who wrote:

> *Parent Effectiveness Training* by Gordon and *Between Parent and Child* by Ginott derive from a more traditional therapeutic orientation that emphasizes the way feeling expressions are interchanged between parents and children and conflicts are verbally resolved. These books were not considered in the research review because they are not research. . . . Nevertheless it is of interest that the themes emphasized [therein] find a rough parallel in the research literature. . . . Sensitivity in responding to the child's needs and the honest expression of the parents' feelings without continual nagging and criticism, as emphasized in the approaches of Gordon and Ginott, are supported by the almost universally found correlation of parental acceptance with the child's general adjustment. It is reassuring to see a growing congruence between research findings and popular, contemporary child-rearing literature [p. 529].

P.E.T. in Practice

As part of our follow-up study of 92 P.E.T. graduates mentioned previously, we asked the parents if they might be willing to write a personal document in which they described in some detail how they put P.E.T. in practice and how their families changed over a period of time. Thirty-four such personal documents were submitted, each quite personal and different, yet all very moving and informative.

Each of these personal stories confirmed that the P.E.T. course merely provided parents with the skills to begin a *process*. No one leaves P.E.T. an effective parent, yet parents do become motivated to start using their skills—to begin somewhere. In each of these families, a process of change was started, and not always a smooth process. Some took two steps forward and one backward. It was apparent, too, that none of these parents ever *arrived*. Even after many years of applying the P.E.T. skills, all of these parents were still growing, still improving and, sometimes, still groping.

I have selected one of these personal documents for inclusion in this chapter because it illustrates so well the difficulties and disappointments parents encounter in putting P.E.T. into practice, as well as the successes and rewards.

A Family Turns Around*

My story begins four years ago. It was a few weeks before Halloween, a cold damp night with the feel of winter in it. I had been to a Cub Scout Den Mothers' meeting and when I arrived home, I found my husband, two of our older sons, Steve and Mike, and our fourteen-year-old daughter, Lisa, at the kitchen table, with the tension so thick it was suffocating.

The boys were so concerned about Lisa that they had decided to tell us that she and her friends were into drugs—pot, speed, and LSD, primarily. We felt sick, yet it only confirmed the gnawing suspicions we had had for nearly a year. Lisa was an attractive girl with long shiny brown hair and dark brown eyes. She was a good student, played several musical instruments, and had always seemed well liked by her friends. She had been school captain of her elementary school. When a girl with so much to give begins having trouble at school and flying into a rage at the slightest criticism at home, there is something terribly wrong. We told her how worried we were, and Jim, my husband, insisted she stop seeing her crowd of recent friends completely. Seething with resentment and rage, she announced that we were not going to tell her who her friends should be, left the house, and disappeared.

The next day we tried to locate her, but without any results. We had figured she would probably stay at the home of a friend. But when phone calls to most of the logical places failed to turn up a lead, we were worried sick, wondering where she was, whether she was safe.

The second night she called us to ask our permission for her to stay in a house for runaways in the inner city. We said no and begged her to come home. She hung up and disappeared again.

A few days later, a member of the staff at her school called to say that she had gotten in touch with him. He was the one person she seemed to feel she could trust not to force her to do anything. He had made arrangements for her to stay in a private home and said she would be willing to enter family counseling if we would. We agreed and during the next two weeks had several sessions with a psychologist.

Jim and I finally reached the point where we felt we were doing all the giving and we resented Lisa's continued refusal to come home. In addition, we could ill afford the cost of the counseling. So she moved home and an uneasy truce was established. We had little reason to trust her. One morning I saw her heading away from school, so I got out the car and drove her there—only to find out later that she had immediately left school by another door and spent the day at a friend's house. Not long after that a counselor brought her home from school suffering from an overdose of speed. There were few days without crises.

While this alone would have been enough to worry us sick, our sixteen-year-old son, Bill, was also having problems. He was sick much of the time, probably from drugs and from not eating right, and was finally hospitalized and treated for a possible ulcer, although the tests were negative.

Back in school, he dropped further and further behind in his work. He cut classes frequently or fell asleep in them. Eventually he got caught smoking and was sus-

* From *P.E.T. in Action*, T. Gordon, New York: Wyden Books, 1976. Permission granted to reprint here.

pended for the next two weeks. His behavior was erratic and he tended to disappear for a day or two at a time, telling us ridiculous stories about his whereabouts when he wandered home.

Bill was a gentle person, timid as a small child and sensitive. He had many fears. I had worried about his ability to cope with school, but he seemed to do well enough if the pressure wasn't too great. He had grown into a tall, good-looking youth with light hair and cornflower blue eyes. He loved music, but not the discipline of practice or being in a band. He was not a person who would hurt others deliberately, but he was certainly destroying himself.

My frustration and feeling of helplessness had my stomach tied up in knots, my head throbbing, and my heart breaking. My depression was so overwhelming that I did not want to talk to anyone, even to reach out for help. Our family doctor suggested P.E.T., but I could not believe a course could help my needs. So things continued through a shaky Christmas and then, the week after New Year's Eve, the nightmare resumed. Bill took an overdose of LSD. He couldn't stop hallucinating and finally came to me for help.

Jim was out of town, so Mike and I drove him to the hospital, where he was admitted to the security end of the psychiatric ward. I will never forget the sound of the metal door being bolted behind us.

In the next two weeks he began to see the hospital as his escape. All the pressures were off, he was being waited on, he had a private room, his own stereo and snacks any time he wanted them. But his doctor told us he was completely uncooperative and recommended having him declared incorrigible and sent to a state school. Somehow, we didn't see how that would do anything but increase the problem. So at the end of the second week we brought him home.

The stage was set for the final act. Jim had gone back to work, after driving us home from the hospital. Bill and I were in the kitchen, having some soup, and I told him I'd take him to school after lunch to find out where he stood and what he would have to do to catch up. But he wouldn't buy that idea. He became hostile and incoherent and said he was leaving. With that, Lisa appeared and said she'd go with him. She had cut school and was sulking because, the night before, we had told her she would have to wait until summer to take Drivers' Education. The two of them packed a duffel bag, being careful to include only the belongings they felt were really theirs. Before they left, I said, "Are you sure you know what you're doing?"

Lisa replied, "I know we may be making a mistake, but we have to find that out for ourselves." And off they trudged across the ice and snow of the park behind our house. It must have been ten degrees that day and my insides felt almost that cold and numb with fear for them.

This time there were no phone calls, nothing. Even their friends were frightened. There was no sign of either one after they left the house, although I did find out they had withdrawn Bill's savings from the bank. The days stretched into a week and, on the tenth day, we received a letter from Lisa telling us they were in California living on a farm and would like us to send Bill's driver's license and their social security cards. We did.

A few weeks later, about the time we were beginning to get used to the situation, an earthquake hit southern California in the area where we knew they were living. They had no phone. We were frantic! That afternoon I received a call from our local police asking if we had a son, Bill, sixteen, and a daughter, Lisa, fourteen, in California. My insides contracted with terror! But the terror quickly gave way to relief as the officer explained that they were all right and were being held in a detention center near where they had been living. The night before, Bill had been discovered by the police wandering in the sheriff's parking lot. He had sent the police to the commune where Lisa was. Apparently, he couldn't stomach the situation any longer. Their money and most of their belongings had been confiscated and they weren't eating very regularly. The house was dirty and in poor repair and there was no plumbing. The detention center must have been something of a relief, but the two of them were kept separated and neither knew where the other one was until after the earthquake. The detention center was damaged but Bill and Lisa were not hurt and were later transferred to Los Angeles.

My husband got into the car almost immediately and drove the two thousand miles to L.A., stopping only once, briefly, for Coke and gas. Bill and Lisa were relieved to see him and must have realized how very much he cared about them to have put aside everything else to make that long, arduous trip. The journey home was surprisingly tranquil, the conversation relaxed and quite normal. Back home, they both seemed somewhat subdued and more willing to live within our regulations.

Bill was so far behind at school that he dropped out and went to work full time as a bag boy. I was glad he had something constructive to do, but wondered how long he would keep his job, because he was late for work frequently or didn't show up at all. We were not letting him use the car very often because we knew he was drinking, but he was riding with friends who were equally irresponsible and that was a worry.

Lisa went back to school and quickly made up the work she had missed. But she was restless and ill at ease. She was cutting school a lot and turning in most of her work late, and we were concerned about what she and her friends were doing during all those hours they weren't in school. If we questioned her about the slightest thing, she'd fly into a rage, and we were afraid we were making things worse. In a sense, we were letting her blackmail us into staying out of her affairs completely. The tensions began to build up again. Somehow we survived that spring, but we recognized our need for help. Our doctor continued to urge us to take P.E.T., and in May I found a class and we got started.

My climb up out of the depths of despair began. I began to grow as new insights and understandings tumbled in on me with each week of classes. I felt as though I was slowly emerging from a closed-in shell into a beautiful sunlit world full of color and music.

What did I actually learn that could cause such a transformation? The first startling discovery was that I did not have to "own" my children's problems. I did not have to find solutions for all the problems of all my seven children. Secondly, I learned how to develop a separateness from my husband and children. Until this time, I had been upset if any of them were upset and, with such a large family, it wasn't very often that somebody wasn't upset.

With me, being upset meant feeling cold and clammy, having stomach cramps and diarrhea, not wanting to move. Fixing meals and caring for the children took a tremendous act of will. Nothing seemed worth the effort of doing it. I learned about my need to have everybody in the family happy and productive to feel good about myself, and I suppose that was the key to freeing myself from it; to learning how to feel "OK" about myself so that I could help the others when they were feeling "not OK."

It didn't happen overnight. Earlier I described the situation with Bill and Lisa when we began P.E.T. I suppose at first they suspected that we were learning some new way of controlling them. But when we began to tell them about what we were learning, they gradually came to see P.E.T. as a way of improving all the family relationships, reducing the tensions that had been upsetting them as much as us.

We began by talking about feelings, and I put one list of feeling words on the refrigerator door and one in my pocketbook. When somebody started talking about a problem or seemed upset in any way, I would quickly refer to the list and say, "You're resentful." "You're disappointed!" "You're furious!" or whatever seemed appropriate. This usually produced laughter and teasing, which is not the normal goal of Active Listening, but it succeeded in relieving the tension and making everyone feel better and that was a step in the right direction. Eventually, I managed to use AL with more skill and, once the children had experienced how nice it was to have me really hearing them, they felt less wary of it. It's become the most valuable skill I learned.

I remember before P.E.T. when Bill told me he'd been suspended from school. I hugged him and cried. I felt bad for him, but I felt just as bad for myself, as if I were to blame somehow. How much more helpful it would have been if I had let him know it was his problem and that I had confidence he'd be able to solve it himself; if I had Active-Listened to him, letting him know I would help in any way I could if he wanted me to. One night after I had learned about AL, he came into the kitchen seething with resentment because his father had not let him take my car because he got in too late the last time he'd had it. He exploded with, "I'd like to take the car and smash it into something!"

A year before I would have thought, "It'll be a long time before he gets his hands on my car again!" Instead, I said, "You're really mad!" and he began to pour out all his grievances. I continued to Active-Listen and within half an hour he was talking calmly and munching on a sandwich, the hostility completely dissipated.

With Lisa, Active Listening was quite threatening at first. There were a lot of things she did not want to reveal to us in those troubled days, but eventually she felt desperate enough to unload it all. By that time we were ready to handle it.

Our other children were also pleased with the changes that were taking place. You can't have so much tension in a family without everyone being affected by it to some degree. The older children were involved with school activities and part-time jobs and weren't home much except to eat and sleep. But I was very much concerned about the younger ones—Lanie, Rob, and Carol—feeling insecure and developing problems. So I made a special effort to Active-Listen to their feelings and to try to get in touch with their needs.

Our six-year-old daughter, Carol, was only two when I first used Active Listening with her. My husband had driven off with her two older sisters and she began to cry. I was going to suggest watching TV or something when I remembered AL. So I said, "You're upset because Daddy left you home." She stopped crying and looked up at me with such love that I was overwhelmed. She knew that I understood how she felt and that was her need, to have me know how she felt. She has become increasingly aware of her own feelings and the feelings of others. She will tell her friends and teachers when something makes her uncomfortable or shy or embarrassed. And sometimes she'll say to me, "You're upset" or "You're angry."

My efforts to Active-Listen had some very unexpected benefits. For instance, Steve, our oldest son, had never had any serious problems, but he had never talked to us much, either. So one day when he came in looking smugly pleased about something, I said, "You seem awfully happy today." To my amazement, he flopped down in a chair and spent the next half-hour telling me about how well things were going at work. He hadn't talked that much in years.

Mike, too, had needs I'd never thought about before. He was an excellent student and very much involved in band and student government and was extremely self-sufficient, so I'd never had any worries about him. But I suddenly realized that, operating under such tremendous pressure, he really appreciated an interested ear to help him unwind occasionally.

Lanie was concerned with fairly typical sixth-grade girl problems; too old for some things, not old enough for others. She was either very happy or very unhappy, and I probably got more practice using AL with her than any of the others. And it worked. The problems that upset her were her problems and AL let her keep the ownership of them and find solutions to them that really satisfied her. Naturally, she made mistakes, but she learned from them. For instance, she was a school patrol captain and didn't like telling the other patrol members when they weren't doing their jobs right. This reluctance got her in trouble with the advisor. By being allowed to keep the ownership of the problem, she was able to solve it herself. I was just there to listen while she talked it through.

The hardest skill for me to learn was sending "I-messages." I had always felt reluctant to complain about the annoying little things the kids did because I didn't like to nag. So I would let the little things build up until I finally erupted over something relatively unimportant, simply because I'd become saturated. There was no more room and the irritations wouldn't go away just because I ignored them. For example, one wet towel on the bathroom floor, one glass left in the living room, or one box of crayons left on the kitchen table right before dinner, were no great problem individually but after a whole day of silently taking care of such little things, I would have so much resentment built up that if anyone looked at me the wrong way during dinner, that's when I'd explode. Using "I-messages," I try to keep up with the little things so they don't build up and take control of me.

My husband had a problem with "I-messages," too. He was terribly frustrated by the idea that you could tell the kids how you felt—yet you had to let them decide what *they* were going to do about it. It was very hard for him to accept the fact that there was no way he could force his decisions on them short of escorting them everywhere and chaperoning them constantly. But he kept trying to avoid the Roadblocks and gradually his efforts were rewarded. We had problem-solved what hours our kids should be in at night, and they gradually became more cooperative about observing them. We limited ourselves to what our fears and worries were when they were out late—the accidents that could happen and the possibility they could be picked up by the police for violating the curfew—and what our legal responsibilities were. Or you might say we let them know what tangible effects their behavior could have on us.

Problem-solving by Method III also became a part of our "modus operandi." Lisa hated cleaning her room, but she liked to cook and didn't mind giving Sharon her bath, so we would trade jobs. Most of the things we use Method III for are little problems like Rob and Lanie and Carol deciding who is going to watch what on TV, or how we're going to get Lanie to work and Rob to his football practice at approximately the same time but in opposite directions. But we also used it to plan an unexpected vacation. We had not made any summer plans because we'd all been too busy with the daily routine and, one day in late July, we decided we needed a change. So Jim and I rounded up the family and began by telling them we wanted their ideas about where we should go and what we should do. We all entered into the discussion without any preformed decisions since it was such a sudden idea. We ended up spending a really memorable week in a spectacular area in northern Minnesota. We stayed in a cabin, but Bill, Mike, Lisa, and Lanie went on a three-day canoe trip, portaging between the lakes and camping in wilderness at night. It was a wonderful chance for them to strengthen the bonds between them.

I have recounted only a brief chapter in the lives of our family, but it was a period of dramatic change. The changes continue day after day.

Bill has grown a lot in four years. He decided to go back to high school the fall after he dropped out, and has since graduated. He has outgrown his need for drugs, has a responsible job, and is engaged to a girl we're very fond of. He stops in to see us often, and our relationship is full of love and warmth. He has returned to our church and wants to be married there. Most important, he's making value decisions as he runs into problems, and he is acting on them.

Lisa, too, has changed. I enjoy having her around now. I feel comfortable with her again. Gone are the tense, cold barriers that seemed to rise between us in the past, making conversations stilted and awkward, if possible at all. She is working in a state hospital for the retarded and plans to go into nursing. She, too, comes home often and expresses her love for us in many ways, doing things for us, bringing flowers or applesauce cake.

Perhaps the following will show how much P.E.T. has become a part of our everyday lives. A few days ago, Bill had to back out of a date to take Carol bowling, and she began to cry. So I said, "You're disappointed."

"Yes," she answered, "nobody ever wants to do anything with me."

"You feel left out of things," I replied.

"Maybe Daddy will take me," she said.

"Well," I answered, "Daddy has been out of town all week and got home very late last night, so he may not want to go out."

(More sobs.) "It's not fair! You get to spend more time with Daddy than I do, 'cause I have to go to bed early."

"You'd like to do more things with Daddy," I answered.

"Yes. I like to do things with Daddy. I miss him when he's gone."

"I think Daddy would like to have you tell him that," I said.

She had brightened up by this time and she heaved a sigh and said, "It sure feels good to get all that off my chest."

There is such joy and understanding in our relationship. I'm always comfortable with Carol, never afraid she won't understand me. How different things might have been if I had understood the skills and human psychology that P.E.T. has taught me before we had our older children. It would not have prevented problems; these seem to be part of our human condition. But perhaps we would all have suffered less.

References

Aldassy, M. C. *The relationship of P.E.T. to change in parent attitudes.* Unpublished master's thesis, California State University, Hayward, California, 1977.
Andelin, S. *The effects of concurrently teaching parents and then their children with learning*

adjustment problems the principles of P.E.T. Unpublished doctoral dissertation, Utah State University, 1975.

Aunkst-Dewald, M. *The impact of teaching P.E.T. to volunteer Girl Scout leaders.* Unpublished master's thesis, Seton Hall University, South Orange, N.J., 1976.

Garcia, J. *Preventive programs in parent education: A study of P.E.T.* Unpublished master's thesis, University of Southern California, 1971.

Geffen, M. *The value of a course in P.E.T. for single parents.* Unpublished doctoral dissertation, California School of Professional Psychology, Fresno, California, 1977.

Gordon, T. *P.E.T.: Parent effectiveness training.* New York: Wyden Books, 1970.

Gordon, T. *P.E.T.: Parent effectiveness training.* New York: New American Library, 1975.

Gordon, T. *P.E.T. in action.* New York: Wyden Books, 1976. (Also published by Bantam Books, 1978.)

Hanley, D. F. *Changes in parent attitude related to a parent effectiveness training and a family enrichment program.* Unpublished doctoral dissertation, United States International University, California, 1973.

Haynes, S. *Altering parental attitudes toward child-rearing practices using parent education groups.* Unpublished manuscript, Boston University, 1972.

Kilburn, K. L., Gerard, E., & Ray, E. *P.E.T. program evaluation.* Unpublished manuscript, Porterville State Hospital, California, 1971.

Knight, N. A. *The effects of changes in family interpersonal relationships on the behavior of enuretic children.* Unpublished doctoral dissertation, University of Hawaii, 1974.

Knowles, L. *Evaluation of P.E.T.: Does improved communication result in better understanding?* Unpublished manuscript, Chico State College, California, 1970.

Larson, R. S. Can parent classes affect family communications? *The School Counselor,* 1972, *19,* 261–270.

Lillibridge, M. *The relationship of a P.E.T. program to change in parents' self-assessed attitudes and children's perceptions of parents.* Unpublished doctoral dissertation, United States International University, California, 1971.

Martin, B. Parent–child relations. In F. D. Horowitz (Ed.), *Review of child development research.* Chicago: University of Chicago Press, 1975.

Mee, C. B. *P.E.T.: Assessment of the developmental gains in parents' capacity to counsel their children.* Unpublished doctoral dissertation, Catholic University of America, Washington, D.C., 1977.

Miles, J. M. *A comparative analysis of the effectiveness of verbal reinforcement, group counseling, and parent effectiveness training on certain behavioral aspects of potential dropouts.* Unpublished doctoral dissertation, Auburn University, N.Y., 1974.

Moritz, E. D. *The acquisition of empathic communication skills through the Active Listening training in Thomas Gordon's P.E.T.* Unpublished doctoral dissertation, University of Montana, 1976.

Peterson, B. *Parent effectiveness training and change in parental attitudes.* Unpublished manuscript, University of Santa Clara, 1970.

Pieper, A. G. *P.E.T. and parent attitudes about child rearing.* Unpublished master's thesis, California State University, Hayward, California, 1977.

Piercy, F., & Brush, D. *Effects of P.E.T. on empathy and self-disclosure.* Unpublished manuscript, Mental Hygiene Consultation Service, Ft. Benning, Georgia, 1971.

Schmitz, K. P. *A study of the relationship of parent effectiveness training to changes in parents' self-addressed attitudes and behavior in a rural population.* Unpublished doctoral dissertation, University of South Dakota, 1975.

Schofield, R. G. *A comparison of two parent education programs—P.E.T. and behavior modification—and their effects on the child's self-esteem.* Unpublished doctoral dissertation, University of Northern Colorado, Greeley, Colorado, 1976.

Stanley, S. F. Family education to enhance the moral atmosphere of the family and the moral development of adolescents. *Journal of Counseling Psychology,* 1978, *25,* 110–118.

Stearn, M. *The relationship of P.E.T. to parent attitudes, parent behavior, and child self-esteem.* Unpublished doctoral dissertation, United States International University, California, 1970.

Willenson, D., & Bisgaard, S. *P.E.T. for psychiatric technicians in state institutions for the mentally retarded.* Unpublished manuscript, Brainerd State Hospital, Minnesota, 1970.

Williams, B. F., & Sanders, B. *A comparative study of the relative effectiveness of P.E.T. and a program of behavior modification.* Unpublished manuscript, Alamance County, North Carolina, 1973.

Chapter 6

Transactional Analysis: Promoting OK'ness

STEPHEN T. SIRRIDGE

In the last half-century there has been a growing concern for the child in the context of his or her relationship with the family. Previously, most families were concerned with raising physically healthy children with a minimum of psychological problems, and providing offspring with sufficient skills and ethics "to make it" in the world. More recent assessments of raising children have defined that "parenting" is more than handing down information by word of mouth and behavioral example. This assessment has underscored the realization that good parent management skills are rarely an innate quality, but that in many instances, parents need help with and training for the demands of childrearing. The thrust, then, of more contemporary approaches to parent education is in the direction of incorporating the old values of skill and health with the new values of individuality and happiness for each young child.

Brief History of Parent Education

The generation of parents who labored through the 1940s were able to obtain carefully researched information from the writing of Arnold Gesell and his associates at the Yale Child Development Laboratory (Gesell, Halverson, Thompson, Ilg, Castner, Ames, & Amatruda, 1940;

123

HANDBOOK ON
PARENT EDUCATION

Gesell & Ilg, 1946). Gesell, writing for the medical, academic, and lay audiences, provided many details concerning the physical and motor, social and personality development of the growing child. In addition, millions of parents without sufficient backgrounds for raising babies found solace in Benjamin Spock's *Baby and Child Care* (Spock, 1945). Other significant information about children was less available to the general public because of its specialized or technical nature. Margaret Mead, Erik Erikson, and Jean Piaget all made unique and significant contributions to the understanding of child development and family relations. In the period of the late 1960s and early 1970s, a concerted effort was being made to adapt the scientific principles of Skinnerian operant conditioning to the area of parent education. For this purpose, semiprogrammed texts were written that presented, by didactic means, an excellent vehicle for conveying a functional analysis approach to human behavior (Becker, 1971; Patterson & Gullion, 1968; Smith & Smith, 1966). This shift in emphasis away from the laboratory to the level of the individuals who control the consequences in a child's environment (parents) was a logical progression of the application of behavior modification principles.

Gaining momentum at a similar period of time was the interpersonal theory of Eric Berne, called Transactional Analysis. Berne's *Games People Play* (1964) and Harris' *I'm OK—You're OK* (1969) presented a new theoretical frame of reference to explain behavior and feelings, and postulate a pattern of growth of the human personality. As Transactional Analysis theory was elaborated, the need for specific approaches to direct themselves to the topic of growth and development and raising children became apparent. The aim of this chapter is to present to parents or professionals several of the more well-known and functional approaches of Transactional Analysis as they relate to parents "promoting the OK'ness" of their children.

Basic Transactional Analysis Theory

Transactional Analysis (TA) is an interpersonal theory; that is, it is a theory that defines as its primary focus the social relations between people and the development of personality within a social environment. As the name implies, TA is the complex analysis or study of transactions and how these social interchanges shape an individual's personality and determine an overall pattern or style of life.

TA, as a theory of personality, contains an organized and integrated set of assumptions, and a series of concepts to more specifically define these conjectures of how the world works. Thus, the goal of this section is to define the major concepts of TA and provide the reader with an appropriate background for evaluating more individual departures from the general theory.

Human Needs

One basic need of all human beings is the need for stimulation. It was Eric Berne (1973) who stated that "far from trying to avoid stimulating situations, most organisms, including human beings, seek them out [p. 21]." He acknowledged this "hunger" for stimulus or sensation early in his writings and defined "strokes" as the basic unit of recognition between people. He noted that Harry Harlow's (1959) research with infant monkeys demonstrates the existence of a social drive (in addition to biological drives) that necessitates a level of contact-comfort for successful adjustment. Likewise, Rene Spitz's (Spitz, 1945) research clearly identifies that infants who are not handled and/or stimulated develop a condition called "marasmus" where they fail to thrive. The result from the lack of stimulation often eventually leads to the death of the infant. In addition, case studies of stimulation- or stroke-deprived adults and elderly persons has shown the slow and incipient development of temporary emotional disturbances (often marked by withdrawal and depression) and rapid physical decline. Thus, stimulation, especially physical touching, is an important component in the survival of all human beings.

Recognition hunger is an extension of stimulus hunger in that it applies to the symbolic (use of language) way that people receive strokes. As children grow into adults, the number of physical strokes diminishes and is replaced by verbal recognition. The need for contact and stimulation remains; however, the avenue for meeting these needs changes from physical to verbal.

Another hunger that needs to be resolved each day is "how will a person fill his or her time." Each person has learned preferred ways of enjoying, using, wasting, and frittering away time. A person learns ways to fill time according to what is acceptable in his or her family and society. Time structure not only helps plan what a person does with time, but minimizes or maximizes the amount of strokes that can be obtained from others.

Strokes

The concept in TA that embodies or defines the need for stimulation is "strokes." A stroke, in its broadest context, is a unit of recognition. A stroke is a pat on the back or a word of recognition. A verbal insult or a kick in the shins is also a stroke. The stroke that feels good and helps a person feel OK about himself or herself is called a positive stroke. The other type of recognition that is painful or leaves a person feeling bad and not-OK is labeled a negative stroke. As mentioned previously, each person needs strokes to survive, whether the strokes are pleasant or unpleasant. A child who does not obtain the necessary positive strokes he or she needs, will set it up to acquire negative strokes rather than receive no attention at all.

Positive and negative strokes come in all shapes, sizes, and intensities. Basically, they fall into two broad catagories: recognition based on "doing," and recognition based on "being." A stroke given to a person for what he or she does and how that person performs is called a conditional stroke. For example, when a mother says to a child, "I like you when you make your bed and clean up your room," she is paying attention to him or her based on the condition that something is done in return (i.e., the child makes the bed and cleans up the room).

A stroke given to a person for "being" has been named an "unconditional" stroke. This recognition is based on the person being alive and existing, and not on any act or performance. For example, when a father says to his daughter, "I like you and I care for you because you are you," he is telling her that she is liked because she exists. Unconditional strokes are given with no strings attached.

Both types of strokes are necessary for developing positive feelings about self and appropriate social skills for adjusting to a world with other people. Conditional strokes, positive and negative, label for the child the things he or she must do to get attention from significant adult figures. This process earmarks to the child the things other people like and do not like. Alternately, positive, unconditional strokes help the child to define his or her sense of self, the internal boundary, that allows the child to perform with the certainty that he or she is good and important. A balance in the child's stroke economy is necessary so that the child does not define feelings about self based on doing and achieving, nor should the child be overwhelmed with suffocating strokes for being, which neglect to define what the child does that is important.

Basic Life Position

The dynamic interplay of giving and getting strokes defines for children their feelings about themselves and other people in the world. How a person feels about himself or herself and others is called a basic position. There are four basic life positions that denote the relationship of self to the world.

1. *I'm OK—You're OK.* This is a healthy position that says that "on the whole" the person is satisfied with himself or herself and comfortable with other people. The statement implies that the person can feel all feelings and be OK in being aware and expressing them. This position is a winning position, and motivates the person to "moving on" and "growing."

2. *I'm Not OK—You're OK.* This is a position of the person who feels inadequate and inferior in comparison to others. The person's sense of self lies in the hands of others who must bestow the gift of OK'ness to them. It is a depressed and unworthy position.

3. *I'm OK—You're Not OK.* This is a position of a person who defines others as inadequate and unworthy. Although the person is scared, insecure, and distrustful of others, the basic life stance is being one-up on other people. It is an angry, ignoring, condescending position.

4. *I'm Not OK—You're Not OK.* This is the "nowhere" position because the person does not trust anyone, including himself or herself. It is a position of someone who feels he or she cannot win, and life is bleak and not worth it.

The life positions of people are in part determined by the strokes they give and receive. If children feel OK about themselves and others, then they will probably draw upon reserves of positive strokes, enabling them to give and enjoy themselves. A winning person has the energy and stroke support to carry out the activities of a fully functioning personality structure—the functions of feeling, thinking, and doing.

Personality Structure

The personality of each individual is composed of several parts called ego states. "Ego states are organized ways of defining reality, processing information, and reacting to the world [Babcock & Keepers, 1976, p. 30]." Stated in another way, ego states are a definable collection of behaviors, values and feelings that are visible and focused in conscious awareness. The building blocks of TA are three observable ego states: the Parent, the Adult, and the Child.

A person operates in one of three distinct ego states at any one time. The diagnosis of ego states is made by observing visible and audible characteristics of a person's appearance. The ego states are distinguishable on the basis of body movement, paraverbal voice features, and the content of verbal utterances.

The three ego states can be diagrammed by three circles (see Figure 6.1). The three circles signify that each of the three ego states is separate

FIGURE 6.1. Ego states.

and discrete and can be identified by different contents and actions. The Child ego state is present from birth (probably is functioning prenatally); the Parent and the Adult ego states are adaptations to a social world that requires each person to think and take care of himself or herself.

CHILD EGO STATE

Eric Berne (1964) states that "the Child is in many ways the most valuable part of the personality and contributes to the individual's life exactly what an actual child contributes to family life: charm, pleasure and creativity. In the child reside intuition, creativity and spontaneous drive and enjoyment [p. 25]."

The Child ego state is the repository of the person's biological needs and basic feelings. It provides for the person a sense of who he or she is and, as such, is often experienced as the most real part of the person. The Child part of each person has recorded all the significant emotional events of a person's life, even from infancy. Thus, the Child ego state in an adult has the same feelings and ways of behaving that he or she had as a child. The Child can be natural; that is, act on its own, connected only to internal needs and wants. The Child can also be adapted, which is the response of a person in a pleasing or rebellious fashion.

The Child ego state tends to make fleeting appearances in grownups because of sanctions against acting "childish or childlike." Situations of great pain or joy and less inhibited activities (sporting events or playing with children) allow for the spontaneous emission of childlike expressions of delight, anger, fear, and sadness. The childlike behavior also is accompanied by the corresponding perceptions, thoughts, and feelings of a 3- to 5-year-old.

ADULT EGO STATE

The Adult part of the personality gathers and processes data, follows the rules of logic, and arrives at conclusions. The Adult is considered an impassionate organ, computer-like in the absence of feeling because of its function of observation and prediction of external reality.

The Adult ego state is first operative in the infant at a sensorimotor level, and moves to a more symbolic level with the child's use of word combinations at 2 years of age. Throughout the development of the individual child, his or her information levels increase and the structure of cognitions become more complex and mature. The Adult's most mature level of functioning begins at the age of 12 and rounds out more fully at 16, with the onset of a child's ability to deal with abstract, hypothetico-deductive ideas. Each person possesses a functional Adult ego state, but it may vary in level of sophistication.

PARENT EGO STATE

The Parent ego state is the part of us that has recorded the behavior of significant others in a person's life. It contains the rules a person has learned about things he or she should or should not do, manners, traditions, values, and what is important. Thus, the Parent ego state is a videotape of instructions about all the things a person needs to know to get along in the society and culture in which he or she lives. The Parent ego state, because it is a copy of the behavior of the mother and the father, can be critical and controlling, or helping and nurturing.

The Parent ego state of the child will reflect the values and how-to's of the parents. No one set of parents has all the needed information to get along in the world. In addition, the parents' perspectives of the world are limited and distorted by prejudice and singular experiences being generalized to "that is the way things are." As the child acquires more data about the world and attaches to other significant authority figures, he or she updates (adds and subtracts) the Parent ego state repertoire.

EXCLUSIONS AND CONTAMINATIONS

Appropriate use of the three ego states requires flexibility and fluid-ity so that the person can respond to the external world with a full complement of feeling, thinking, and doing parts. A person who shuts off the functioning of one or more ego states is involved in a process called exclusion (see Figure 6.2). The person is excluding from his or her awareness a significant part of the ability to adapt, get personal needs met, and solve problems. As a result, a person who successfully shuts off basic personality functions will probably experience problems in living.

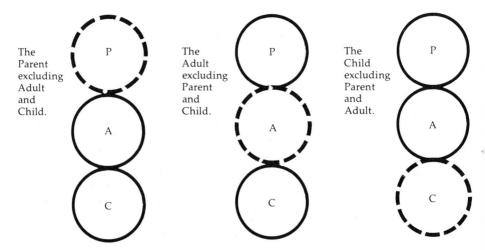

The Parent excluding Adult and Child.

The Adult excluding Parent and Child.

The Child excluding Parent and Adult.

FIGURE 6.2. Exclusions.

The ego state diagram of the circles does not ensure the distinct separation of feeling, thinking, and doing. In the human personality, overlap arises between what is fact and opinion, and what is thinking and feeling. This phenomenon is characterized by the Adult ego state holding as fact certain ideas stemming from the Parent or the Child (Steiner, 1974). The process leads to a blending of fact and fiction, and is appropriately named "contamination" (see Figure 6.3). For instance, a

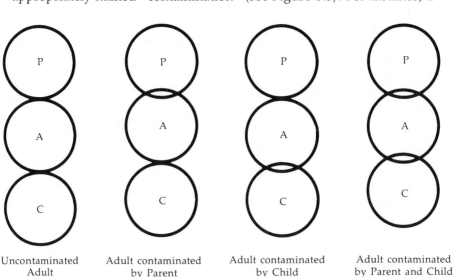

Uncontaminated Adult

Adult contaminated by Parent

Adult contaminated by Child

Adult contaminated by Parent and Child

FIGURE 6.3. Contaminations.

parental idea such as "sex is evil and bad," or "work before play," may become a part of the person's adult ego state.

Transactions

A transaction is an exchange of strokes between two people. Each transaction combines a stimulus from one party and a response by another party. The response may then serve as a stimulus for a response and that would constitute another transaction. In an ordinary conversation about the weather, there are a series of small transactions, each with a stroke. The number of transactions experienced by an individual is an index of his or her stroke economy (the accepting, giving, and trading of strokes).

When a person transacts with another person, he or she uses the various ego states. The way the ego states are utilized in relating to others results in definable patterns of communication. There are three basic types, or rules, of communication:

1. If the ego state addressed is the one that responds, communication can proceed indefinitely. This type of transaction is called a complementary transaction (see Figure 6.4).

A person who is engaging in complementary transactions can exchange strokes from a variety of ego states. He or she can be engaged in conversation about how disrespectful kids are today (Parent-to-Parent transaction), solving a problem (Adult-to-Adult transaction), playing

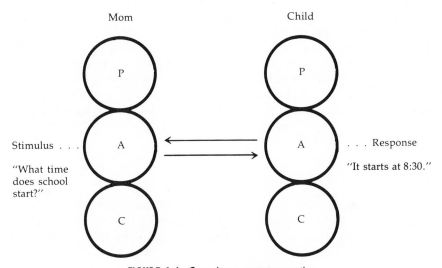

FIGURE 6.4. Complementary transaction.

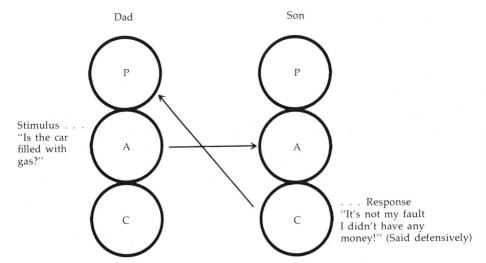

Dad   Son

Stimulus . . .
"Is the car
filled with
gas?"

. . . Response
"It's not my fault
I didn't have any
money!" (Said defensively)

FIGURE 6.5. Crossed transaction.

together and having fun (Child-to-Child), or nurturing or reprimanding another person (Parent-to-Child transaction).

2. If the ego state that a person responds with is not the one the other person intends, communication breaks down or off. This communication that is fractured and cut off is called a crossed transaction (see Figure 6.5). In a crossed transaction, the initial subject is lost unless the topic is reintroduced (this constitutes a recrossing). Arguments are typical examples of how transactions get crossed as initial topics get lost in the shuffle.

3. The third type of communication involves a hidden agenda, and this type of transaction is called ulterior (see Figure 6.6). Along with the overt message, there is a covert psychological communication, and the enticement is to recognize and respond to the hidden message. The opening moves to a game are made with an ulterior transaction. The overt message is communicated by the verbal message, while the hidden agenda is carried by word connotations, voice inflection, and gestures.

Games

A game is an "ongoing series of complementary ulterior transactions progressing to a well-defined, predictable outcome [Berne, 1964, p. 48]." Clearly, a game includes three important elements: (a) a behavioral sequence with a defined beginning and end; (b) an ulterior motive; and

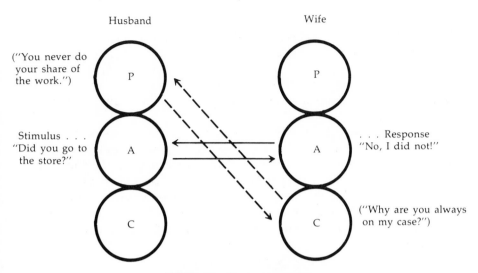

Husband   Wife

("You never do
your share of   P   P
the work.")

Stimulus . . .   . . . Response
"Did you go to   A   A   "No, I did not!"
the store?"

                                                                   ("Why are you always
                  C   C   on my case?")

FIGURE 6.6. Ulterior transaction.

(c) a payoff for the players involved. According to Berne, every game is basically dishonest and the outcome has a dramatic, exciting quality. Although the game seems to move in a predictable direction and apparently has been repeated on other occasions, a person will generally experience a lack of awareness that he or she is involved in a game.

The motivation for playing games comes from a person's payoff. "To understand why people transact with each other at all, some driving force has to be postulated; and this explanation is found in the motivational concepts of stimulus hunger, structure hunger, and position hunger [Steiner, 1974, p. 74]." Games provide satisfaction for all three of these hungers, and this satisfaction is referred to as the advantage, or payoff, of the game.

The essence of stimulus hunger is the exchange of strokes. As previously mentioned, each person has a basic and innate need for stimulation and contact with other people. Through the vehicle of games, a rich source of strokes, the needs for excitement, stimulation, and recognition are met. A person who cannot obtain strokes in a straightforward manner will play games to acquire strokes in a devious and ulterior way. A game of "wooden leg," played by a sorrowful and pitiful little child, will attract a lot of time, attention, and encouragement. The child learns to use the handicap to get others to do his or her work and thinking.

Structure hunger defines in what way a person spends his or her time. To satisfy structure hunger, an individual seeks social situations within which time is structured, or organized, for the purpose of obtaining strokes. Thus, a person has a need to establish social relations in order to transact with other people. The structuring of time can be in long, complex blocks of time or short, terse transactions. A game of "Ain't it awful" regarding the weather, requires an endless stream of "awfulisms" and quite adequately fills in the time with another person while waiting for a bus.

Position hunger relates to the person's feeling of OK'ness as it reflects upon himself or herself and other people. Decisions about OK'ness are based on transactions between people that occur in early childhood. In order to prove to the feeling (Child) part of the person that those old decisions are right, the person engages in games to reinforce that position. There is some comfortableness in knowing that perceptions made by the self are accurate and enduring, even if the games lead to bad feelings and self-defeating behavior.

Here is a list of common games:

Ain't It Awful	Kick Me
Schlemiel	Stupid
See What You Made Me Do	Do Me Something
Cops and Robbers	Wooden Leg
If It Weren't for You	Harried
Rapo	Let's You and Him Fight
Debtor	Blemish
Courtroom	Uproar
Now I've Got You Son of	Poor Me
a Bitch (NIGYSOB)	Addict
Yes, But . . .	

In general, there are two types of games: NIGYSOB and Kick Me. The former usually entails a persecuting position with the objective of one person winning and the other person losing. When people feel put down, but sense that they asked for it, they know they are playing a self-defeating (victim) game like Kick Me.

Games are played at varying degrees of intensity or hardness. A first-degree game involves a payoff of hurt feelings, so the payoff will generally occur at the psychological level. Second-degree games receive some sort of social payoff or consequences, as when the student gets suspended or dismissed from school for selling drugs or stealing. Some games, however, are dangerous and the outcomes result in physical damage. A real-life game of Cops and Robbers may result in a shootout where the person is killed or injured.

A game of NIGYSOB ends with a feeling of winning or putting down the other person. A game of Kick Me may end with the feeling of being victimized. Players can switch places, or roles, while playing games; however, each person plays the games that best fit his or her life decisions, and that person plays them from a favorite position. The positions in a game, and the switches that may occur in a series of transactions, can best be understood in a schematic called the Karpman Drama Triangle (Karpman, 1968; see Figure 6.7).

The NIGYSOB player plays the Persecutor (P) when feeling superior and criticizing the Victim (V). The Victim may unwittingly play the patsy for this righteous individual. However, when the Persecutor, in a state of guilt over his insulting treatment shifts to Rescuer and attempts to mollify and comfort the Victim, he may end up the Victim if he is told by the other player "to forget it." The switches go in either direction around the triangle, and a player may find himself playing as many as three positions in a full-handed game.

Related to the payoff in games is the concept known colloquially as "stamp collecting." Collecting or trading stamps is the process whereby feelings are saved up by a person who plays games so when enough stamps are accumulated they can be "traded in." That is, an individual does not deal with his or her feelings in the situation, sits on them or continues to collect more feelings, then figures he or she is entitled to dump these feelings all at one time. "Cashing in" may be accumulated for a blow-up, a drug binge, a suicide attempt, or some other pathological outcome.

A "racket" is the individual's basis for collecting trading stamps, and it is a feeling that is used in the home as a substitute for adult action. Rackets are taught by parents and represent what happens when mom and dad get uptight. A person will play games and continue to store up and collect feelings to reinforce his or her existential position. A NIGYSOB player can support his or her "you're no good" position and collect anger stamps in an anger racket modeled from a nervous, anx-

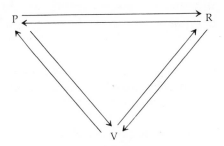

FIGURE 6.7. Karpman Drama Triangle.

ious parent. Likewise, an "I'm not OK" player may continue to play the victim position and gather sad/lonely stamps to support the suffering racket observed by the child long ago in childhood.

Script

The way an individual lives life and how it turns out is his or her script. It is a pattern, theme, or Story line that threads its way in repetitive form throughout a person's lifetime. When a person makes a life script, he or she incorporates present and future events with previous life experience. The script includes all that a person has learned about acquiring strokes in the family, preferred ways of transacting, the psychological games that he or she has learned, the chosen basic life position, and the cultural and historical influences that he or she has experienced. Babcock and Keepers (1976) state that script decisions are often phrased like resolutions—"Well, if this is the way things are, then from now on I'll (or never) do . . . ." For example, an individual makes decisions about getting close to others, whether men or women are trustworthy, and adequacy and trust in self, and the individual then sets out in life to collect data to support these script decisions, which were made early in childhood with limited information about the world. By updating these early decisions and by obtaining additional new information about intimacy, trust, and adequacy, the person can change the course or theme of his or her life.

Scripts can be catagorized according to their course and outcome. Some scripts are tragic (also called *hamartic*), and their course is characterized by a string of third-degree games, ending in injury, illness, imprisonment, disgrace, or death. Other scripts call for a person to be a "loser" by setting goals and never reaching them. The course of the latter life pattern is a series of setbacks and disappointments, ending with the person "not making it." Another series of life patterns, although not as destructive and disappointing, are dull and humdrum, without much happening or going on. These scripts are called "banal scripts," and refer to a drab story line where a person never reaches his or her potential.

Some scripts call for the person "to make it" and be a "winner." This story line contains many chapters where goals are set and achieved. The winner sees himself or herself as OK, and thrives on interacting with an OK world.

Everyone has a life script. A person can determine what many of his or her script decisions are by examining parent messages and child feelings. Some messages from parents are spoken and are out front;

these give the child directions as to what is expected if he or she is going to make it in the world and get strokes in the family. The messages that emanate from the Parent ego state of the parents are called counter-injunctions or attributions, and they inform the child what he or she must do to remain in the favor of the parents.

Another series of messages, largely nonverbal and unspoken, spring from the Child ego states of the parents and dictate a heavy dose of "don'ts" on the child. Some injunctions may be alluded to verbally and may include only simple restrictions on the free behavior of the child (don't sing, don't laugh too loudly), whereas other injunctions can be passed on with great intensity, which can bring on severe repercussions. Thus, an injunction of "don't think or be adequate" from a smothering mother who does everything for her child, severely cripples the child's ability to master important developmental tasks and the satisfaction that accompanies success.

The script matrix (see Figure 6.8) shows how the script may be formed. The Parent ego states of both biological parents feed "do" messages to the Parent ego state of the child. At a different level,

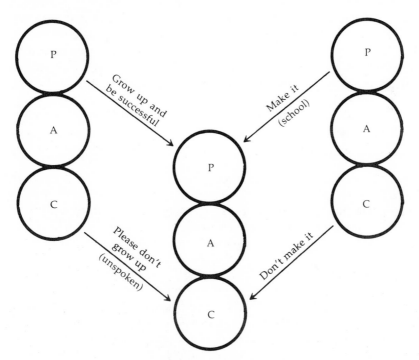

FIGURE 6.8. Script matrix.

unhealthy injunctions from the Child ego states of the parents contaminate the Child ego state of the child, discount his or her importance, and advise the child on how to develop a harmful script. At times, the Child injunctions of the parents seek to undermine the verbal prescriptions from their Parent ego states. This creates confusion in the child, who cannot ascertain which part of the message he or she should respond to—the "do" or the "don't." For example, the parents may have told the child to get as much education as possible, while the Child part of them is bragging about how well they did without finishing school. The Child ego state in the parent may be jealous of the child having the opportunity for school, or of the son or daughter doing better than they did in school. Invariably, the power of the injunction is enough to override the spoken or surface request and set the tone for the child's life program.

Transactional Analysis Approaches to Parent Education

An inevitable extension of basic Transactional Analysis theory is the structuring of theoretical concepts in an attractive package for parents. Such a package needs to relate to how parents "got to be where *they* are," as well as "now that they have children, *how to raise* them in a healthy and growth-oriented fashion." The purpose of this section is to survey several of the more popular approaches that provide parents with information regarding TA and parenting.

Traditional Approaches

Leaders of parent education groups in the early 1970s were aware that the published writings of Eric Berne, in their original form, were not appropriate for their purposes. Berne's style of writing was complex, and his approach was oriented toward theory and its application to psychotherapy. Two books used extensively to fill this gap were *I'm OK—You're OK* (Harris, 1969) and *Born to Win* (James & Jongeward, 1971). Although neither book is specifically addressed to parent education, they do present for the lay audience the major principles of Transactional Analysis. The traditional approach is concerned with the four basic levels of analyses: (*a*) structural analysis, which is the analysis of the individual personality; (*b*) transactional analysis, which is the analysis of what people do and say to one another; (*c*) game analysis, which is the analysis of ulterior transactions leading to a payoff; and (*d*) script analysis, which is the analysis of life positions that a person plays out in life. Thus, the traditional approach presents a perspective based on the writings of Eric Berne, an approach that deals with the essential concepts and processes of TA.

Thomas Harris' book, *I'm OK—You're OK*, was, along with Eric Berne's *Games People Play* (Berne, 1964), one of the first presentations of TA theory to the general public. Both books were tremendous commercial successes and subject to widespread use and discussion. In surveying the contents of Harris' book, it appears that he is primarily concerned with structural analysis (ego states) and transactional analysis (rules of communication). He looks at the composition of the three ego states (Parent, Adult, Child), the distortions of ego state boundaries (exclusion and contamination), and presents the various types or levels of transactions between people.

As indicated by the title, *I'm OK—You're OK*, Harris' book treats the concept of the "basic life position" as fundamental to the study of interpersonal relationships. Throughout the book, references are made to the maintenance of each individual's essential reference to himself or herself and the outside environment. Harris postulates that the child records all early experiences, even those events that occur during birth. Near the end of the infant's second year of life, using his or her newly found language and conceptualization abilities and pulling on the backlog of recorded events, the infant makes a primitive, rational decision about himself or herself and the world outside. Harris (1969) states in his book, "I believe this state of equilibrium, evident at the end of the second year or during the third year, is the product of the child's conclusion about himself and others: his life position [p. 42]." Thus, in this state of equilibrium, the little child makes the first attempts at making sense out of life and providing a basis for predictability. The life position predicates all future transactions with others; games, strokes, time structure, and life theme.

Harris directs several parts of his book to speaking about children and adolescents. Three important statements are made in these chapters with regard to solving problems with children. First, children do not experience problems in isolation from the family. In order to solve difficulties, both "junior" and the parents must be "redone." Harris believes that therapy without parents being involved simultaneously is a waste of time, energy, and money. Second, he believes that improvement in parental relationships with preadolescents and adolescents can be enhanced through the use of contracts. A contract is defined as a "statement of mutual expectations, drawn, discussed and restated from time to time at the Adult–Adult level" (Harris, 1967, p. 162). Based on his own experience with children's groups, Harris believes that the combination of total family involvement, in addition to the use of contracts, significantly alters behavior in children and improves family communication. Third, Harris is convinced that teaching the language of TA to all ranges of children can help them extend their awareness of what they are thinking and feeling and strengthen their position for evaluating reality and solving problems. He gives several examples of teaching TA concepts to the retarded and to adolescents, and having them use the system to structure reality in a new and more efficient manner.

Born to Win (James & Jongeward, 1971) has been an inmensely popular (1,500,000 copies sold) introduction to the theory of Transactional Analysis. It covers many of the same concepts as *I'm OK—You're OK*, with the addition of several other fundamental components on TA, namely, script and game analysis. Also, a chapter on basic needs (called human hungers), and a chapter on personal and sexual identity are important contributions to the text. The authors are oriented toward the application of TA to the daily life of the average person. The writing style is characterized by thoroughness and clarity. In addition, the book is sprinkled throughout with relevant and helpful examples, thereby meeting the needs of the casual reader and student alike.

An important departure of *Born to Win* from any of its predecessors is the unique combination of two approaches to understanding people: Transactional Analysis as developed by Eric Berne, and Gestalt theory as interpreted by Fritz Perls. Gestalt-oriented experiments are added at the end of each chapter to supplement the TA theory. The purpose of these experiments is to offer to the reader an avenue for discovering the fragmented parts of the personality and integrating them into an understandable whole. The exercises provide the avenue for gaining awareness of each person's feeling, thinking, and doing in the "now."

Born to Win offers to the parent several valuable perspectives that facilitate the understanding of self and the passage of appropriate permissions to children. The whole concept of "winners and losers" permeates the book; that is, the development of a life-style based on achievement and authenticity is systematically organized and presented to parents as the model for healthy living. James and Jongeward stress all the qualities that make a "winner a winner" (namely those qualities of flexibility, spontaneity, thinking, and timing), and facilitates the journey toward discovery of who the person is, what he or she is passing on to another generation, and how a person changes to a winning position.

The Gestalt exercises are an important process in defining what are the person's own values, feelings, and thinking positions, and what belongs to his or her parents. This process is enormously important because it forces the parents to separate themselves out from their parents and their own growing up, and it prevents the passage of unhealthy and prejudicial messages to the children. This process of separating out the worthwhile experiences and dispensing with the unusable is personally gratifying and important for future interactions in the family.

The chapter on "Personal and Sexual Identity" is an integral chapter to parents (especially those who are thinking about being parents), because it stresses two basic issues in interpersonal functioning: personal identity and sex identification. The issues include a discussion covering the link between a child's name and his or her script (e.g., a child named junior or "III" assumes he should follow in his father's footsteps), and how a child begins to establish life-long identifications through early play experiences. Another primary identification is made early in life, and James and Jongeward take time to discuss the OK'ness or not OK'ness as a person of a particular sex. Modeling of appropriate sex behaviors and the stroking of whatever sex the child may be are listed as essentials for the parent in developing a secure sense of maleness or femaleness in a child.

In summary, the traditional approaches filled a noticeable educational gap by presenting to the lay public an understandable approach to basic TA theory. The leading texts, *I'm OK—You're OK* and *Born to Win*, cover the major principles and concepts of Transactional Analysis, each with variations that add to the strength of their presentations. Although both books were not specifically aimed at parent education, they have been used in this context with success.

Developmental Approaches

The developmental approaches to Transactional Analysis are based upon an emphasis on the growth and development of the child. This frame of reference states that the child not only moves through the stages of physical, cognitive, and motor development, but also progresses through a series of recognizable and predictable stages in the development of his or her personality. Each of these stages is characterized by certain developmental issues that must be experienced and worked through. For example, children establish a trust relationship with parents around them meeting their physical and emotional needs, and this trust in significant others is a natural and necessary event in the development of healthy personality functioning. The developmental approach, then, offers to parents a breakdown by ages and stages of the important components of the developing child.

Becoming the Way We Are (Levin, 1974), and *Raising Kids OK* (Babcock & Keepers, 1976) are the most representative approaches to instructing parents on childrearing. Both of these books introduce basic TA concepts in the early chapters and cover the highlights of each significant growth stage. Of the two, *Raising Kids OK*, is far more comprehensive in its treatment of growth and development material, and it has received far greater attention in the area of parent education.

Parent, Adult, and Child, as diagrammatically presented in the three circles in Figure 6.9, are the basic schematic representatives of the personality. Developmental theorists break down the development of the Child ego state into three component parts, establishing a time period around which each part develops and the specific functions adopted by each structure. This additional study of ego states is referred to as second-order structural analysis, or the analysis of the structure of the Child. Figure 6.9 represents the developmental pictures of the child.

The Natural Child (C_1) is operative when a person is born (probably has functioned at some level through prenatal development). This is the part of the person that is most in touch with internal physical and emotional needs. The Natural Child is hooked to the survival of the organism and is operative until the person dies. The Natural Child part of a person feels hunger, pain, fear, anger, and joy, and is the essence of a person's wants, needs, and desires. The Natural Child is pleasure oriented and "wants what it wants, when it wants it."

The Primitive Adult in the Child (A_1) is called the "little professor." The "little professor" is creative and intuitive, and it formulates basic

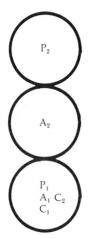

FIGURE 6.9. Second-order structural analysis. Key: P_2 = Parent ego state (6 to 12 years); A_2 = Adult ego state (18 months to 3 years); C_2 = Child ego state; P_1 = Primitive Parent (3 to 6 years); A_1 = Primitive Adult (6 months to 18 months); C_1 = Natural Child (birth to 6 months).

ideas about the workings of the world. These ideas about the world develop as the infant seeks out new situations and conducts many experiments in physics and psychology. The infant checks out what happens to objects if they break or bounce, and what people do. Babcock and Keepers state succinctly the basic function of the "little professor" when they say that A_1 seeks to answer the question, "What do I need to do to survive around here?" (Babcock & Keepers, 1976, p. 33).

The Primitive Parent part of the Child ego state (P_1) has been referred to by many names: "electrode," "supernatural child" (Levin, 1974), and "pig parent." The Primitive Parent takes in the major events of the child in his or her third to sixth years. It is the part of the person that adapts to the demands of the grownups in his or her life. It helps children to fit into the family and helps them compromise their own needs with the demands of society. In the process of recording events and responding to the demands of the social structure, the child takes in much information that is prejudicial and contaminated. In addition, the P_1, in attempting to fit, may make adaptations that are not positive and satisfying for the child, and that are maladaptive to the society as a whole (e.g., the child in an abusing home).

C_2 is a composite of all the parts of the child, Natural Child, Little Professor, and Primitive Parent. It represents the Child functions that exist in the person from roughly birth to 6 years old. The Adult ego state (A_2) is the part of the personality that thinks logically. It begins functioning at about 18 months and becomes considerably more functional at 3 years of age, when the system of using language is more fully developed. The A_2 of an adult is the repository of a whole lifetime of gathering facts about life and the world. The Parent ego state (P_2) is the part of the person that begins to incorporate a value system and valuable how-to's about making it in society (i.e., social relations). The Parent begins its usefulness to the person at age 6, reaches a more potent stage by 9 years, and reaches a significant level of sophistication during adolescence.

One of the significant aspects of looking at personality development from a growth-oriented, ages and stages frame of reference is that it is easy to underline the major issues of each period. Although events in one period will continue to be important in following stages (e.g., thinking will be important in a person's entire life), each developmental period has a central task for the child to work through and assimilate.

The central developmental task in the birth to 6 months period is to receive the necessary feeding and stroking to establish a trust relationship with the world. This trust works both ways, for it involves the trust that infants develop in knowing when they need something and getting it effectively (crying), and the trust infants have in the parenting figures to ascertain what is the need and to fulfill the request. The essence of a trust relationship is the development of a special attachment to one parenting figure (usually the mother), called "symbiosis." The symbiosis is a natural and necessary phenomenon for the baby. This process allows the child to make his or her first social contact in the world, a contact with someone who cares about the child's needs. An infant who does not form an attachment (for reasons such as abandonment or inconsistent and abusive parenting), increases the probability of maladjustment as he or she progresses through childhood into adulthood.

In contrast to the position put forth by Harris about the infant's entrance into the world in a Not-OK position, the developmental approach says that the infant feels OK about himself or herself. As such, there is a naturalness about having needs and wants and having someone bigger and more able to take care of them. The OK'ness is a part of the infant being who he or she is, a helpless organism that expresses what he or she needs in a spontaneous fashion. The destructive interaction of the parent may corrupt this state, but the initial position is one of health and naturalness.

All the infant needs of the previous period (birth to 6 months) remain, but the dominant expression of the 6- to 18-month period is the energy of the "little professor" as it pushes the infant to discover his or her environment. Exploring, then, is the prominent developmental issue. The child begins to break part of the symbiotic attachment with the mother and moves out to discover the physical world alone. Against a firm backdrop of limits and protection, the child develops the basic constructions of physics (position in space, gravity, etc.) from which the symbolic world of words is based.

The world of sensorimotor sensations gives way to the onset of symbolic function. In the period of 18 months to 3 years of age, the child begins to acquire an increasing spoken and understanding vocabulary. This vehicle allows the child to think about things when they are not present and recreates scenes while in play (practice shaving at nursery school). Children begin to think about feelings, what they are, what labels belong to what feelings, and how a person solves problems around feelings.

A critical issue in the 3- to 6-year period is the defining of what is real and what is fantasy. The name "supernatural child" fits very closely the development of magical thinking in children and the need for children to separate out the real from the unreal, or magical. In addition, the development of appropriate social skills in order for the child to fit in the family and school occurs at this time. The child is beginning to put together the first draft of a script and how it works with different people in different situations.

The latency period of 6 to 12 years of age is important because at that time children are asked to take over some caretaking functions for themselves and to develop value systems to guide and direct them. Children in grade school adopt a whole host of new skills and incorporate a moral and ethical value system from a variety of parent figures. The value system of the latency-age child is a fundamental building block for adolescence, because it offers the child a framework within which to shape his or her thinking and direct behavior.

Adolescence is viewed by the developmentalists as more than a period of identity search, but a recycling of all developmental issues. The dynamics of adolescence, then, are the reemergence of prior developmental issues against a new backdrop of abstract thinking and sexuality. The tasks of adolescence are to define oneself, find adequate identification and expression of sexual needs, and gradually separate from the family with a secure sense of independence.

The concept of symbiosis is a particularly important dynamic within the developmental framework because it describes a very natural process on the part of the child, both in the establishment and gradual resolution from the mother. Problems arise when the symbiosis breakage is not complete at each major juncture, and the residual affects each succeeding stage. The nature of these problems lies in the fact that individuals (infants, children, and adults) seek out relationships where the full complement of ego states (Parent, Adult, and Child) is not utilized by either individual, and a person does not reach his or her full potential of feeling, thinking, and doing when the situation demands it. An intensely symbiotic relationship cripples the growth process and creates a dependent relationship where one party provides for the other a function they should and can perform. For example, a child needs to learn to ask for the things he or she needs and wants without the parents figuring it out and moving in to provide it.

There are several processes that keep the unhealthy symbiosis active and ongoing. The means by which people undermine themselves is called passive thinking and passive behavior (Schiff & Schiff, 1971). When people think passively, they do not use information that is available about themselves, others, and the situation. Passive thinking is called "discounting," because people disregard, minimize, or ignore information that they have or can obtain. Discounting may occur with the denial of the very existence of a problem, minimizing the significance of a problem, excluding the possibility of solving a problem, and discounting one's ability to solve an identified problem.

While using some level of passive thinking to avoid problem solving, an individual may compel other persons to be more uncomfortable about the problem than he or she is; that is, the person attempts to get someone else to take over the job of problem solving. As a result, an unhealthy symbiotic relationship is set up where one party has abdicated the responsibility for problem solving and another party has taken it over. *Passive behaviors* are used to maintain the symbiosis that prevents the person from developing skills to meet personal needs and solve difficulties. There are four kinds of passive behavior (Schiff & Schiff, 1971); these include doing nothing, overadapting, agitating, and incapacitating or moving into violence.

The view of the developmentalist is that children will conduct experiments in passive thinking and passive behavior to see whether others will support their lack of responsibility. Teachers and parents who support passive thinking and behavior in children are doing them a disservice; they undermine the child's ability to develop a full complement of flexible and potent problem-solving skills.

Other Approaches

A BOOK FOR PARENTS

Muriel James wrote another book specifically directed toward parents, which is aimed at helping parents integrate the content of TA into solving everyday concerns. *Transactional Analysis for Moms and Dads* (James, 1974) is characterized by much of the simplicity and readability enjoyed in her previous work (James & Jongeward, 1971). Although the format of her book is quite different, her approach is still traditional; that is, she focuses almost exclusively upon transactional, structural, game, and script analysis.

The style of the book is question and answer. It surpasses some of the earlier efforts in the behavioral field because it takes the form of parents in a long chat with the author. The rigidity of question–answer is not a problem, as James seeks to answer questions that naturally evolve from previous ones.

James' book is marked by several key components, not the least of which is her approach to parents as a parent herself. This lends credibility to her writing and allows her to integrate many personal experiences to explain concepts and to offer examples of how problems can be solved. This approach tells parents that she has the same problems as other parents and offers an appropriate model for solving difficulties under stress.

In her book James addresses common problems faced by parents. In this way she meets the needs of parents who are looking for a book that relates to the average family (not to an extraordinary therapeutic situation). Situations involving information about sex, death and divorce, losing tempers and yelling at kids, family squabbles, childhood illness, etc., are covered with frankness and honesty.

James also offers to parents some cookbook advice and techniques to go along with that advice. Rather than presenting only problems, she introduces some simple solutions. For example, a family meeting could be arranged for the purpose of dumping stamps and giving strokes, thus creating a situation where people get in touch with feelings and deal with them.

Finally, an important accent to James' book is her approach to children as frogs and princes/princesses. She says that every child is born to be a little prince or princess, but childhood experiences may cast a spell and make them feel like frogs instead. This analogy illustrates the importance of parental stroking for children and highlights the fact that moms and dads and kids can throw their froggy skin off and be what they were meant to be—healthy, happy human beings.

TEACHING TA TO KIDS

One question that invariably arises in parent education groups is how TA concepts can be taught to children. Alvyn Freed, in his book *TA for Kids* (1971), has addressed this task of explaining TA concepts in a readable and understandable way for elementary school children (optimal age for reading is 7 to 11 years of age). His text draws on the work of Eric Berne and Thomas Harris, thus promoting a more traditional TA approach to instructing children. The basic concepts of ego states, transactions, strokes, basic life positions, and stamp collecting are presented in an organized and sequential fashion.

The goal of *TA for Kids* is for children to be able to *understand and apply* the concepts of TA. To ensure application, Freed concretizes his presentation with many pictures, and he places at the end of each chapter a list of exercises. The exercises review material specific to that chapter and ask the child to relate to the questions with his or her own personal frame of reference. For example, the concept of strokes is presented and the child is invited to think about what kind of strokes he or she likes and dislikes. In addition, the text may be read by children, with both the content and the exercises providing an excellent vehicle for discussion.

A particularly interesting component in Freed's book is his use of analogy, that is, finding a concrete metaphor or image to portray a concept. One specific analogy is his notation of "parent poison" and

"Not OK disease" as descriptive terms for the concept of life script. The child who reads this chapter understands that the script is something that gets passed along from parents to children (parents learned it from their parents) without anyone being aware of it, and the disease can get worse if the messages keep coming at a faster and more intense rate. Such use of concrete analogies facilitates the understanding of one of the most global and complex concepts of TA.

Similar to Harris' book, *I'm OK—You're OK*, Freed introduces the idea of contracts. He sees contracts as necessary for the successful and smooth running of a home, but he also sees a contract as a promise. A promise is a basis for establishing and maintaining trust, and keeping a promise is important if a person wants to be believed. No one can keep all their promises (nobody is perfect), but this does not mean that just because a person has disappointed us once we should conclude that he or she can never be trusted again. Freed merely says that people make mistakes and what makes the difference is that they are generally trustworthy.

In summary, *TA for Kids* is certainly a viable approach for parents and children learning TA together. By developing the book into discrete units, a parcel of time can be set aside to work on a unit and the family may pick it up again at another time. It offers an approach for the family to become involved in learning more about themselves in a creative and fun way.

Freed has also published *TA for Tots* (1973), a simpler version of *TA for Kids*. The former book is offered as part of a comprehensive package including leader's manual, records, film strips, cassettes, posters, and warm fuzzies. The material seems to have a lot of appeal to the younger child and involves the parent interacting with the child with a variety of audiovisual materials.

A PARENT PROGRAM

S. O. Hesterly has written a guide to the study of TA as it applies to the raising of children. The name of his monograph is *The Parent Package* (1974a), and this booklet is oriented toward the parents being actively involved in study or educational group experience. Hesterly's parent package is designed to be used in connection with the James and Jongeward book, *Born to Win*, but it may be utilized independently. Together with the parent package, a *Leader's Guide to the Parent Package* (Hesterly, 1974b) is available and includes detailed instructions for organizing and leading a short-term parent education group. The leader's package includes 36 small-group exercises and activities to assist the participants in applying the concepts of TA to their own life experiences.

The Structure and Process of TA Groups for Parents

Each theoretical frame of reference, each group leader, and each set of group participants add to the diversity and individuality of a parent education course. Groups vary in how much didactic and experiential learning takes place; they also vary depending on the level of control and direction exerted by the leader. The structure and process of the group, then, is dictated in large part by the content of the material, the style of the leader, and the needs of the parents. Parent education groups operating from a TA point of view, like other content-oriented groups, function according to the fundamental rules of structure, process, and leadership.

What is an educational TA group like? What are the goals of the group, and what kinds of activities are parents involved in? Granting the fact that all groups are distinct and different, there are some general components likely to be implemented in the structuring of a TA group. First, an assumption is usually made that parents will make changes in their own behavior and grow in their ability to understand themselves and their children. As such, specific concerns that each parent has about his or her children will be addressed, as well as how the parents can obtain a series of insights about themselves for their own personal growth.

Stroking, as a basic process in transacting and relating with people, is generally introduced as a concept and implemented as an ongoing part of the group process. Strokes will be given and received on an informal basis (talking before and after group), and often integrated as a formal part of each group meeting. For example, the last 5 to 10 minutes of the group may be set aside for giving strokes and dumping stamps. This process allows for the modeling of appropriate behavior, provides a vehicle for people to relate to others in a straightforward manner, and reinforces each person's needs for learning and for being.

Most TA groups are structured around a balance of didactic presentation and experiential learning. Because of the many concepts and specific jargoning in TA, presentation of basic material (in combination with reading assignments) is important in the overall structuring of the group. At the same time, the integration of exercises to facilitate the assimilation of material at all levels of the personality (feeling, thinking, and doing) is equally necessary. Exercises may be included that are oriented toward examining a person's values and standards, the kinds of strokes that feel best to a person, or a short sketch (art or writing) of who a person is, and how his or her life has turned out. In both the books, *Born to Win* and the *Parent Package,* exercises for the group process facilitate the learning of material and the addition of a new perspective of looking at oneself and others.

A good leader responds to the specific needs of her or his group. Many parents will be seeking answers to ongoing family situations (with both spouse and children) that are negative and stressful. Their goals in group are to learn more about themselves, as well as to solve immediate problems. These problem situations are generally dealt with by a combination of group sharing, leader input, and individual parent analysis of the situation. The input of others is necessary because the group process is built on the interaction of participating members. The "Parent" position of the leader is essential to establish her or his potency and position in the group, and parents who present problems must be actively involved in the solution of their own problems.

Analysis of each problem situation generally centers around the basic TA processes of strokes, transactions, games, payoffs, and script decisions. The analysis of these areas is directed toward identifying what is going on in the situation, what people are getting out of the situation, and how the problem can be changed so that everyone can get the things they need and want.

In summary, a TA parent group involves a great deal of learning about oneself: the values, beliefs, feelings, needs, and thinking/remembering that make a person who he or she is. It is a situation that promotes sharing, making contact with others, and experiencing parts of oneself that are shut off from awareness. In the end, it provides parents with a model to structure (analyze and solve problems) reality, and an avenue to identify personal needs and the needs of others.

Summary

Interest in parent education has grown considerably in the last generation. Information about raising children began with data about ages and stages, and has developed into a framework for conveying to parents the important aspects of facilitating healthy and happy growth in children. The Transactional Analysis philosophy of personality has provided an important frame of reference for analyzing how people relate and how that applies to raising children.

Transactional Analysis is an interpersonal theory that focuses upon relationships between people. The theory outlines several processes that are important to personality development and transactions between people. As a social being, people have a need to be stimulated and seek out contact with other people. This need underscores the efforts of each individual to achieve necessary levels of recognition and the structuring of time to elicit this recognition.

The concept of "strokes" is basic to the understanding of how and why people relate to each other. A stroke is a unit of recognition and embodies both positive and negative words, gestures, or actions.

Some strokes are given to people for doing (conditional) and other strokes are given for being (unconditional), and each person needs a balance of doing and being strokes to feel good about himself or herself and other people.

The way parents stroke a child defines in large part his or her basic life position. The life position of a child embodies his or her feelings about self and the world. Along with a basic orientation to the world, the child develops a distinct and individual personality. The content of that person is different, but each person is made up of a feeling, thinking, and doing part. The part of the personality that has wants, needs, and feeling is called the Child. The Adult ego state is the part of the personality that thinks and assesses the reality situation. The part of the personality that has values and many behavioral how-to's is the Parent ego state. Although each of us has three ego states, people ignore or use each ego state to a greater or lesser extent. Some people have inconsistencies in their personality functioning that are called contaminations, whereas other people choose not to use one or two personality functions. By choosing not to use one or more of the components of personality, the person excludes that function in adjusting to the demands of the external world.

When a person gives strokes, he or she is using the ego states to transact with another person. Transactions can be complementary, crossed, or duplex in nature. The duplex transaction is the basis for a primary vehicle for structuring time called games. A game is a nonstraightforward way to relate to others, but offers a high level of stroking and a format to reinforce a person's basic life position.

A person's life theme is his or her script. Some scripts are positive and winning; other scripts are losers. Of the losing scripts, an individual may choose a dull approach to life or a tragic course that may lead to injury or death.

Of the popular approaches to Transactional Analysis, some are more traditional and offer to parents an emphasis on structural, transactional, game, and script analysis. The traditional approaches to TA copy the basic tenets established by Eric Berne. A developmental approach favors an emphasis on the various stages of personality development and the issues predominant in each stage. The developmental approach also focuses on how children learn to solve problems and on specific behaviors that block finding solutions for problems. Other more general approaches to parent education offer parents their own style of relating TA to raising children.

The final section of the chapter dealt with the structure and process of an educational TA group for parents. Although there is a wide variation in the presentation of course content and the style of leadership, most TA groups include a balance of concepts and experiential learning. In addition, the needs of individual parents are addressed through group discussion. The ultimate goals of such groups are increased parental awareness of their own issues and the presentation of a workable system for structuring reality and solving problems.

References

Babcock, D. E., & Keepers, T. D. *Raising kids OK*. New York: Grove Press, 1976.

Becker, W. C. *Parents are children*. Champaign, Ill.: Research Press, 1971.

Berne, E. *Games people play*. New York: Grove Press, 1964.

Berne, E. *What do you say after you say hello?* New York: Bantam Books, 1973.

Freed, A. M. *TA for kids*. Los Angeles: Jalmar Press, 1971.

Freed, A. M. *TA for tots*. Los Angeles: Jalmar Press, 1973.

Gesell, A., & Ilg, F. L. *The child from five to ten*. New York: Harper & Brothers, 1946.

Gesell, A., Halverson, H. M., Thompson, H., Ilg, F. L., Castner, B. M., Ames, L. B., & Amatruda, C. S. *The first five years of your life; A guide to the study of the preschool child*. New York: Harper, 1940.

Harris, T. A. *I'm OK—You're OK*. New York: Harper & Row, 1969.

Hesterly, S. O. *The parent package*. Berkeley, Calif.: Transactional Publications, 1974.(a)

Hesterley, S. O. *Leader's guide to the parent package*. Berkeley, Calif.: Transactional Publications, 1974.(b)

James, M. *Transactional Analysis for moms and dads*. Reading, Mass.: Addison-Wesley, 1974.

James, M., & Jongeward, D. *Born to win*. Reading, Mass.: Addison-Wesley, 1971.

Karpman, S. Script drama analysis. *Transactional Analysis Bulletin*, 1968, 7(26), 39–43.

Levin, P. *Becoming the way we are*. Berkeley, Calif.: Transactional Publications, 1974.

Patterson, G. R., & Gullion, M. E. *Living with children: New methods for parents and teachers*. Champaign, Ill.: Research Press, 1968.

Schiff, A. W., & Schiff, J. L. Passivity. *Transactional Analysis Journal*, 1971, 1, 78–89.

Smith, J. M., & Smith, D. E. P. *Child management*. Ann Arbor, Mich.: Ann Arbor Publishers, 1966.

Spitz, R. Hospitalism, genesis of psychiatric conditions in early childhood. *Psychoanalytic Study of the Child*, 1945, 1, 53–74.

Spock, B. *Baby and child care*. New York: Simon & Schuster, 1945.

Steiner, C. M. *Scripts people live*. New York: Bantam Books, 1974.

Chapter 7

Behavior Modification and Child Management

RICHARD L. SIMPSON

Although it is often difficult to obtain agreement among professionals in the various helping and child development professions on virtually any matter of importance, there is general agreement that a child's parents are probably the most significant individuals in his or her life, especially during the formative years. Long before Sigmund Freud (1938) dared to suggest in a formal manner the influence of parent–child interactions on behavior, professionals and nonprofessionals alike seemed to acknowledge the vital role that parents played in the development of their offspring. Accordingly, even though on occasion it has been suggested that a paucity of attention has been given to the significance of parent–child relationships and childrearing advice, one need only review the religious, social, cultural, or educational history of this or any other society to acknowledge that parents have historically been recognized as one of the primary determinants of a child's behavior. In addition, the same perusal of history will convince even the most stubborn individual that parents have historically been provided more than ample advice on conducting their childrearing and other family affairs.

There is an obvious historical precedent for providing parents with advice on the various components of childrearing. But even though a great deal of child development and childrearing information has been disseminated to the family in the past, most of this information would

HANDBOOK ON
PARENT EDUCATION

fail to qualify as formal counseling or professional consultation. While one could hardly argue that certain elements of motherly (or fatherly, grandmotherly, etc.) counseling have not measured up to relatively high standards and have passed the rigid tests of time, one must also acknowledge that these informal processes generally have not been based on professional knowledge and training nor on an orderly and tested body of knowledge. Thus, for example, mothers might be instructed in procedures for disciplining their children by their own parents, who may actually have a very limited knowledge of child growth and development and the empirical laws upon which sound disciplining techniques should be based. However, even though the difference between informal childrearing advice and professional consultation is ostensibly based on the skills and training of the counselor and the orderliness and validity of the body of knowledge that is being applied, there is at least some evidence to suggest that in many instances professionals have not been particularly effective in disseminating childrearing and parenting skill information.

Although the reasons for this failure are numerous and varied, one important factor is that many professionals in the "helping" disciplines have not perceived their role as that of parent trainer. That is, many professionals have not attempted to train the parents with whom they come into contact in specific skills that are associated with becoming a better parent. Consequently, rather than being considered participants in the treatment program, parents have been considered the objects of treatment by a closed society of professionals who ostensibly have possession of skills far beyond the comprehension level of the parents.

In almost every instance, treatment procedures have been designed to uncover the variables associated with personality development through analyzing the parent–child interaction process. It is evident from these strategies that the parents themselves become the objects of treatment or are the means to the treatment of the child rather than partners in the change or development process. It is also evident that these strategies are often not designed to disseminate skills that can be applied across a number of environments with a child. Finally, since parents, teachers, and other pragmatic evaluators tend to emphasize a child's developmental and overt behavior gains as the primary measures of progress, it is obvious that the previously discussed strategies would not be associated with overwhelming success.

One approach that has been associated with relatively impressive results and that has managed to circumvent at least some of the previously discussed problems has been behavior modification. This approach, which entails the application of an experimental analysis strategy to specific human behaviors, is based on the assumption that parents should be given the opportunity of assuming an active role in the change process rather than being relegated to the position of a passive recipient of the intervention.

The behavioral approach focuses on observable and measurable behaviors. Behavior, as used in the model, refers to any observable and external response (Sulzer & Mayer, 1972). In addition, the model is based on the assumption that the overt behavior of an individual can be controlled through the systematic application of learning theory principles. Finally, since the model assumes that the application of these principles is a learnable skill and that "problem behaviors" represent inadequate or incorrect learning, rather than evidence of underlying pathology on the part of the parent or child, parents can logically be instructed in procedures for training their offspring to make more appropriate and developmentally mature responses.

The Behavioral Approach

As early as the 1940s, B. F. Skinner (1948), among the most renowned of all psychologists and social planners, suggested the use of a scientifically determined procedure based on the concepts of behavioral technology as a means of enhancing the family and social structure system. Among the concepts presented in his book *Walden Two* were principles for developing and augmenting the quantity and quality of parent–child interactions.

Although one does not have to accept all, or for that matter any, of the novelistic propositions put forth in Skinner's "Good Life" (1948), one should be aware enough to recognize that since the publication of *Walden Two*, a behaviorally based technology capable of facilitating child development, developing more appropriate parent–child relationships, and training functional parenting skills has been developed. This technology now exists for parenting both the "normal" and the exceptional child. In fact, more and more parents are being trained in procedures for bringing about planned changes in the behavior of their own children through the use of a behavioral model. As noted by Berkowitz and Graziano (1972), "This entire development provides a new framework for clinical intervention, which, in addition to therapeutic value, has important implications for future use in a systematic and prevention-oriented model of mental health intervention [p. 315]."

The behavioral model, as applied to the parenting process, implies that the parent or guardian will actually carry out specific behavioral procedures that are designed to accomplish and evaluate preestablished goals. Thus, the model implies that the parents will function in a training role with their own children.

The process of behavior modification is designed to modify the frequency, rate, duration, or intensity of some observable behavior through the systematic application of learning theory principles. The selection of observable and overt behaviors is a salient and basic concept in behavior modification because only with such behaviors can appropriate evaluation techniques be applied. For example, if the parents of an adolescent were allowed to apply behavioral principles to increase their offspring's "happiness" behavior, great difficulty would undoubtedly be experienced in obtaining agreement not only among independent observers on the frequency, rate, intensity, or duration of the behavior, but also about the effectiveness of any intervention procedure that might be devised. However, even though "happiness" is very difficult to define and measure, the parents could be instructed in precisely determining the duration with which their child interacted with a peer or the frequency and duration of his or her crying episodes. Only with such precision can the techniques associated with behavior modification be effectively utilized.

It is conceptually significant to also note that the strategy of focusing on overt behaviors enables the behavioral engineer to eliminate from consideration not only unobservable behaviors and processes, but also indirect intervention approaches. Thus, a behavioralist would, for example, argue that a child's inability to effectively relate to his or her parents and peers does not necessarily indicate a "lack of ego strength" or other equally unobservable explanation. In addition, any intervention procedure that might be implemented would be designed to train the subject in more appropriate and useful interpersonal skills rather than attempting to manipulate the strength of the ego. Thus, even though a child's "ego strength" might improve as a function of behavioral manipulation, the intervention technique would be designed to directly remediate some observable and measurable deficiency.

Notwithstanding arguments to the contrary, most behavioralists would acknowledge that human behavior is probably caused by both observable and unobservable factors. Nonetheless, behavioralists are concerned only with those overt variables that are directly measurable. Specifically, behavior is assumed to be primarily a function of observable antecedent and consequent events. That is, behavioral principles are structured in such a way as to assume that observable environmental events that precede and follow a behavior under focus are of greatest significance in determining and maintaining the behavior. In addition, primary attention is given antecedent and consequent environmental events because of the behavioralists' ability to clearly understand and manipulate these factors, which theoretically will be associated with predictable changes in overt behavior.

Finally, the behavioralists' emphasis on observable and measurable behaviors and environmental events creates a situation conducive to employing nonprofessional individuals, such as parents, as extensions of the treatment process. That is, the procedures are such that parents can be instructed in applying them with their own children and in thus extending the treatment process to natural and everyday environments and for extended periods of time. More traditional therapies, on the other hand, focus on more unobservable factors and esoteric intervention techniques which, in addition to being difficult to evaluate, are not amenable to transmission and application by nonprofessional individuals who have extensive contact with the individual of concern in the natural environment.

One additional benefit to the behavioral approach, and an inherent principle in the model, is the wide applicability of the procedures. While as many as 8–10% of school-age children may be considered exceptional in some way, that incidence figure does not imply that the remaining 90–92% of the "normal" population do not have problems. Obviously any parent of even the most adjusted and developmentally mature child would acknowledge that challenges and problems are a constant element in the childrearing process. Consequently, because of the complexity of child development and childrearing, and because few parents are trained to be parents, even the most dedicated and conscientious will be faced with a difficult task for which they have little or no preparation.

The techniques associated with behavior modification become applicable and appealing to all parents because of the precision, efficacy, and transmittability of the procedures, and because virtually every parent of every child will find the techniques useful. In addition, behavior modification is one of the few effective intervention procedures that does not assume "sickness" or abnormality and that therefore carries the virtue of not "labeling" individuals with whom it is used. Probably parents of all but the most troubled children would be reluctant to consider seeking psychiatric or psychological counseling because of the stigma associated with such consultation. However, since behavioral principles view all maladaptive behaviors to be governed by the same laws, no attempt is made to differentiate between "normality" and "abnormality." Rather, behaviors are evaluated relative to their individual adaptiveness and techniques are provided for retraining specific behaviors that are considered to be maladaptive.

Involving Parents in the Modification Process

Obviously a question that must be addressed relative to the use of parents as planned facilitators of change—regardless of the technology employed or the orientation favored—is the rationale for such a procedure. Since historically parents have neither been recognized nor employed as professional trainers in the educational and developmental processes of their children, a strategy that relies on parents as a treatment resource must be evaluated and justified.

Perhaps the question of why professionals should involve parents in the intervention and relearning process can best be answered by recognizing that during a child's formative years the parents or guardians are the most significant adults in his or her life. Consequently, since a positive relationship has been established between the influence of the parent or guardian and a child's development, it would seem beneficial to not only the parent and child, but also society in general, to implement procedures associated with facilitating the process. O'Dell (1974) suggested that there are not only obvious advantages to utilizing parent resources, but that parents should specifically be encouraged to use a behavior modification approach. O'Dell noted a number of advantages to this strategy:

1. Behavior modification techniques have been transmitted to individuals with little or no knowledge of traditional therapy procedures.
2. Behavior modification is a consistent and empirically based model.
3. Groups of individuals can be instructed in the technology of behavior modification simultaneously.
4. The time required to train individuals in the use of the procedures is relatively short.
5. The procedures are extremely parsimonious and allow for maximum use of professional staff talent.
6. The model does not assume "sickness" as the basis for the problem behavior.
7. A majority of childhood behavior problems are responsive to a behavioral approach.

8. A behavioral approach allows for treatment in the natural environment by the individuals who routinely experience the problem.

As a further argument for the promulgation of parent-implemented behavioral programs, O'Dell (1974) noted that

> Parent training is vitally important if effective preventive mental health programs hope to meet the demand for professional services. Also, parent training follows the growing trend toward working in the natural environment and behavior modification offers a relatively easily learned and empirically derived set of concepts for such a parent training model [p. 419].

Williams (1959) was among the first to report the use of a simple extinction procedure by parents to eliminate bedtime tantruming in a 21-month-old child. Williams reported that the parents were able to achieve cessation of bedtime crying in a relatively short period of time and that the problem behavior did not reappear at a later date. Although not spectacular in its methodology or results, this study demonstrated that parents could be taught to effectively utilize behavior modification procedures in a natural environment. Thus, in essence, this study initiated a new era of parent participation in the training of their own children.

In an effort to apply the technology of behavior modification with a handicapped child through the use of parent participation, Wolf, Risley, and Mees (1964) designed intervention procedures for a severely emotionally disturbed preschool child. The subject, who was institutionalized at the time the study began, exhibited a number of severe behavioral excesses and deficits. During the initial phases of the program, institutional staff used time-out procedures and differential reinforcement to decrease aberrant behaviors and to increase appropriate responses.

After the child's behavior had been significantly modified and control had been established, the parents were phased into the modification process. Initially, the parents were trained to interact with the child for short periods of time. In later sessions, the parents were permitted to take their son home where, again, they were prompted in applying behavior modification procedures. Gradually, the parents assumed greater responsibility for their child's behavior and required less assistance from the institutional staff in correctly carrying out the procedures. Within the period of a few months, the boy was sufficiently improved to remain at home several nights per week. Eventually, the child was able to leave the institutional setting and live with his parents on a full-time basis. Follow-up evaluations several years later indicated that the subject had maintained the gains previously made and that he was progressing satisfactorily at school.

In an application of behavioral techniques with more "normal" children, Wahler, Winkel, Peterson, and Morrison (1965) effectively instructed the mothers of three preschool boys in the techniques of extinction, differential reinforcement, and time-out. In a similar study, Allen and Harris (1966) trained the mother of a 5-year-old girl to use a token economy system to eliminate self-scratching.

Although historically behavior modification programs implemented by parents have focused on decreasing aberrant or inappropriate behaviors, other child and adolescent developmental concerns have also been dealt with through the use of the technology. For example, Aragona, Cassady, and Drabman (1975) arranged for the parents of 15 overweight girls to use a behaviorally based reduction program. The subjects, aged 5 through 11, were exposed to one of two experimental conditions or a control condition. One experimental condition involved having the parents reinforce their daughters for losing weight, while the parents themselves were fined portions of an enrollment fee for failing to attend sessions or failing to meet weight-loss criteria. The second experimental group was exposed to only the response cost procedure (i.e., parents were fined if they failed to attend meetings or if their children failed to lose a predetermined amount of weight). After 12 weeks of the respective treatments, the results indicated that the children in the two experimental groups had lost significantly more weight than those exposed to the control condition. However, after a 9-month period, there were no weight differences among the subjects assigned to the various groups.

The principles upon which the concepts of behavior modification are based have been empirically derived, and although the technology has been found to have tremendous utility and efficacy (even when applied by nonprofessionals in the natural environment) the ultimate success of any program will be a function of the skill of the individual using it. Thus, even the most efficient and well-planned strategy must be correctly implemented if it is to produce change. In an effort to determine variables in parents that may be correlated with the successful application of behavior modification techniques in the natural environment, several researchers have attempted to evaluate the parents with whom they have worked. Mira (1970) failed to find a relationship between the intellectual abilities, education, and socioeconomic status of parents and their ability to benefit from training. However, Mira tended to employ a system that emphasized direct teaching rather than a lecture or reading format. Others (Patterson, Cobb, & Ray, 1972) have reported that parents who fall into the lower socioeconomic category and who lack formal education are difficult to train. Furthermore, it has been found that families lacking integration and cooperation and individuals evidencing pathology are poor candidates for the role of therapeutic intervener (Bernal, Williams, Miller, & Reagor, 1972; Patterson, 1965).

Obviously, there are problems in the application of behavioral procedures by parents. The data so far strongly suggest that when correctly equipped with the technology of behavior modification, parents are able to become more effective in their role and are most able to provide their offspring with the training needed to function in society. Reports of parental success in using behavior modification with a variety of children and youth serve to demonstrate the efficacy and adaptiveness of the behavioral strategy. In addition, it appears logical that when parents are trained in procedures for managing behaviors of concern in the environment in which the behavior is manifested, the greatest degree of success and generalization will be realized. As noted by Ross (1972):

> If behavior is to be modified, the modification must take place when and where the behavior manifests itself. This is rarely the therapist's consulting room, and as a consequence, behavior therapists working with children frequently find themselves working through the adults who are in a position to be present when the target behavior takes place, and who have control over the contingencies of reinforcement [p. 919].

The Methodology of Behavior Modification

As indicated previously, behavioral principles are only applicable with observable and measurable responses. Furthermore, the target behavior must be reliably defined in such a manner as to allow the various individuals who are in contact with the subject to perceive the behavior in the same way. For example, to one parent a tantrum may consist of crying and screaming while to another it may take the form of headbanging. Therefore, it is essential in using a behavior modification approach that each individual observing the behavior perceive it in the same way. This principle is especially true when the model is to be applied by parents with their own children in the natural environment.

The behavioral engineer who attempts to establish a program to be implemented by parents with their own children—in addition to determining that the target behavior is observable, measurable, and defined in such a manner as to allow for reliability—must solicit other basic information from the parents. First, the program manager must determine whether the pinpointed behavior is under the child's control. Behaviors such as playing cooperatively, saying "thank you," and screaming are responses typically under a child's control, whereas sweating, breathing, and salivating are usually beyond an individual's authority. Although not an infallible rule, the process of determining whether a behavior is under a child's control, and consequently the type of intervention procedure to be employed, usually consists of determining whether the target behavior is a function of an environmental stimulus that occurs prior to or after the response. Respondent behavior, or learning based on classical conditioning, is a response elicited by a stimulus.

According to Hall (1970), respondent behavior is usually involuntary and involves the smooth muscles or glands of the body. An example of a respondent behavior would be heart palpitations in a child following an announcement by his or her teacher that oral reading will be the next scheduled activity. In virtually every instance, a respondent behavior is caused by a stimulus occurring prior to the manifestation of the target behavior. Operant behaviors, on the other hand, are affected, and thus they are a function of the stimuli that follow them. Operant responses are therefore not only under an individual's control, but are also maintained by the environmental events that follow them.

It should be graphically apparent that the behavioral engineer must be in a position to determine whether a behavior is controlled by an antecedent or consequence, since the manipulation of the incorrect variable may not only be ineffective, but may also have the potential to create additional problems. Although the major thrust of this chapter will be on the manipulation of consequences, and thus on operant behaviors, appropriate diagnostic attention must be given the target behavior and its controlling stimuli to assure that correct procedures are employed.

In addition to categorizing the response as respondent or operant, the behavioral engineer must determine, either through interviewing the parents or observing the child, whether or not the behavior identified by the parents to be modified contains movement. Behavior modification procedures are most applicable with operant behaviors that contain movements that are amenable to observation and recording procedures. For example, parents can be trained to see a child pick up his or her toys or hear a "please" or "thank you." On the other hand, behaviors that contain little or no movement are difficult to evaluate. Lying down, or the absence of movement, for example, in most instances would not be as appropriate a target behavior choice as a response containing movement.

Prior to establishing a problem-solving program, the behavioral engineer should also determine whether or not the target behavior chosen by the parents is repeatable. Even though the parents of a child who engages in a severe temper tantrum approximately every 6 months might desperately want to modify the response, it would be a poor choice of behaviors, since it occurs so infrequently.

Prior to implementing a parent-operated behavior modification program, it should be determined whether or not the target behavior has a definite starting and stopping point. It should be determined that the operant behavior has a definite cycle of repeatable movement. For measurement procedures to be most accurate and functional, the behavior should consist of a relatively short cycle that contains both a definite starting and stopping point. Saying words or refusing to comply with a parental request, for example, both have these cyclical characteristics. Sleeping, on the other hand, not only has relatively vague starting and stopping points, but also involves a cycle that is somewhat lengthy in duration for most parent-directed programs.

Parents must also be aided in selecting a target behavior that can be modified. Especially with developmentally delayed children, at least initially, behaviors that have been totally unresponsive to other treatments should not be selected. For example, although most behavioral engineers should be responsive to the needs and motivations of the individuals with whom they are working, allowing parents to select talking in sentences as the behavioral goal for a 9-year-old severely retarded nonverbal child would not be wise. Rather, selecting a behavior that can be changed would be more appropriate. After the behavioral engineer has established his or her own validity and the validity of the technology used, and after the parents have established their own capabilities, more difficult targets can be considered.

Once the behavioral engineer has been satisfied that the parents have selected an appropriate target behavior that contains the basic characteristics needed for the employment of a behavioral model, procedures for measuring the behavior must be established. Although parents may appear somewhat overwhelmed and threatened by what may seem to be an extremely esoteric task, the behavioral engineer can usually dispel these feelings by engaging in two basic activities. First, parents should be apprised of the importance of accurate behavioral measurements and informed that this component of the behavioral model is an integral and basic element of using the system (Phillips, 1978). Parents who wish to use the behavior modification system can usually be motivated to participate in the measurement process if they are told that only through measurement can a thorough understanding of the target behavior and its antecedent and consequent events be obtained and that without measurement activities, no objective determination can be made regarding whether or not the intervention program is achieving the desired results.

The second, and perhaps the most important, consideration associated with achieving reliable parent data and successfully initiating the strategy is to program the parents for measurement success. Because professionals frequently perceive the measurement process to be so simplistic that it requires no explanation, or because incorrect assumptions of competence are made, the process may be misunderstood or the parents may feel ill equipped to engage in what they perceive to be an overwhelming task. Consequently, it is absolutely essential that, regardless of the measurement procedure being considered, careful explanation, programming, and modeling methodology be employed. When provided the proper instruction and materials, parents are usually able to accomplish this basic step in using behavior modification. Since without success in this area the actual intervention program cannot be applied, it is essential that appropriate attention be given this task.

The actual measurement process will probably involve the use of one of three types of procedures. According to Hall (1970), these include automatic recording, direct measurement, and observational recording. Since parents typically obtain behavior measures in the home or other natural environment, they are usually directed in obtaining observational recordings. For that reason, the present discussion will focus on observational procedures. Hall specifically listed five types of observational recordings that can be made. These include continuous, event, duration, interval, and time sample recording techniques.

As implied in the name, continuous measurements or anecdotal records involve an attempt at recording each behavior manifested by a child over a given period of time. Although this procedure allows for the recording of a variety of behaviors, it both tends to lack reliability and requires a relatively lengthy observation period.

One of the observational procedures most amenable to parental participation in behavior modification programs is event recording. This observational procedure consists of making a cumulative record of behavioral events. Thus, for example, parents could be trained to record the number of words a child verbalizes or the frequency of one child hitting another. Event recording is typically quite usable by parents. In addition, it has the advantages of being adaptable to the behavior being observed and the individual observing.

Duration recordings involve determining the amount of time an individual engages in a target behavior during a specified period of time. This recording procedure is most preferable when the length of time the behavior occurs is considered to be more significant than the frequency. For example, the duration of a temper tantrum may more accurately describe the behavior than an event record.

In interval recording, an observation period is divided into equal time segments. The parent using this procedure would then note whether the target behavior occurs during each interval. Although the procedure requires the undivided attention of the parent conducting the observations, it has the advantages of accommodating more than a single target behavior and potentially evaluating both the frequency and the duration of the behavior.

Even though time sampling is similar to interval recording, it does not require continuous observations. Rather, the individual observing determines whether or not the child being observed is engaging in the target behavior at the end of each interval. For example, a child's cooperative play behavior might be observed by the parents for 1 hour, with recordings made at the end of each 5-minute period. Thus, every 5 minutes the parent would observe whether or not the child was playing cooperatively. This procedure has the advantage of providing adequate behavioral measures without monopolizing a parent's time.

The previously described measurement procedures are employed to aid the parents and the behavioral engineer in assessing the frequency, rate, duration, or intensity of the target behavior. These preintervention measures or baselines make it possible both to evaluate the target response and later to determine whether or not attempts to modify the response were successful. Although this phase of the intervention procedure is sometimes perceived as a preliminary activity to the actual program, its importance cannot be underestimated. Only when parents complete baseline activities can the next phase of the program be undertaken. Thus, the integrity of any parent implemental intervention program will be only as valid as the initial measurement strategy.

Basically, parents who are interested in obtaining child or youth development information or management strategies are confronted with problems that can be classified into two groups. In the parents' estimation, their offspring manifests either a behavioral excess or a behavioral deficit. For example, the parents may perceive their offspring to be lacking in some basic response, such as the ability to eat correctly, complete school tasks, or interact with peers and siblings. Or, the parents may perceive their child to be exhibiting too much of some behavior. For example, parents may consider their child to talk excessively, get into too many fights, or manifest an excess of other behavioral patterns. Consequently, because of the nature of the model and the manner in which patterns of concern are operationally defined, behavioral principles are designed either to increase or decrease the probability of occurrence of some specific response under specific conditions.

This task is carried out through the systematic manipulation of reinforcers and punishers. Operationally, a reinforcer, at least as applied with operant responses, is any environmental event that strengthens a behavior it follows (Skinner, 1953). A punisher (or aversive consequence), on the other hand, is an environmental event that weakens the future probability of the behavior it follows (Millenson, 1967). Thus, a concept that must be communicated to parents is that if an environmental event does not change the behavior that was intended, then it does not operationally qualify as a meaningful consequence, regardless of whether the parents or the behavioral engineer perceive it to be a reinforcer or a punisher. In addition, this concept implies that the only valid strategy for determining whether a potential consequence will be effective is to observe its influence on the behavior it follows. For that reason, parents must again be reminded that effective measurement techniques are mandatory, since without this procedure it is difficult to determine the value of most consequences.

Research Findings on the Efficacy of Using Parents as Agents of Change

A number of researchers have demonstrated that parents can effectively manage the behavior of their own children through the use of positive reinforcement programs. Risley and Wolf (1966), for example, used shaping and reinforcement procedures to teach adaptive behaviors to an institutionalized autistic child. After successful laboratory results had been achieved, the child was returned to the natural home environment where the mother was instructed in applying the same techniques. Specifically, this home-implemented intervention procedure resulted in a significant increase in puzzle assembly and picture naming and generally in more adaptive behavior.

Hawkins, Peterson, Schweid, and Bijou (1966) provided mothers with instructions on how and when to interact with their own children in the natural environment. The results indicated that providing parents with procedures for applying behavior management techniques was associated with improved interactions and child behavior.

Others (Haring & Phillips, 1962; Reith & Hall, 1974) have conducted programs that have used reinforcement in the home environment to increase desirable school behavior. Edlund (1969), for example, demonstrated that parents could be trained in basic behavior modification principles and reinforcement procedures so that they were able to promote desirable school behaviors through reinforcing their offspring for completing assignments and engaging in acceptable social behavior. Kroth, Whelan, and Stables (1970) also reported that they were able to accelerate academic and behavioral growth in school through the use of behavior change techniques applied by parents in the home. In this study, parents were able to promote desired school-related growth through the use of graphing and reinforcement procedures.

Token reinforcement programs have also been successfully implemented by parents in the natural environment with their own children. A token reinforcement program makes use of an intermediate reinforcer that is exchangeable at a later time for a more desired reinforcer (Becker, 1971). Parents have been instructed in techniques for rewarding desired behaviors with tokens, which can be exchanged at a later time for an agreed upon reinforcer. O'Leary, O'Leary, and Becker (1967), for example, reported that they were able to train the parents of a 6-year-old aggressive child in effective behavior modification procedures, which included the use of a token economy system. Initially, the parents were provided a demonstration of methods for providing verbal praise and food reinforcement when the subject and his brother were involved in cooperative and appropriate play activities. Tokens, which were exchangeable for various reinforcers, were next phased into the program. Gradually, the parents were able to employ all of the procedures originally developed by the behavioral engineer and eventually were able successfully to gain and maintain control over the child's behavior. Finally, the parents reported that the child began to emit more cooperative play behaviors with children in his neighborhood and that his other social skills began to improve.

Extinction procedures, or the withholding of reinforcement that has previously been provided following a response, has also been widely applied by parents with their own children (Russo, 1964; Williams, 1959). However, parents, as well as other individuals contemplating the use of extinction or differential reinforcement techniques, should be apprised that extinction techniques will only be effective when the parents and others in the natural environment are totally consistent in their use of this technique. Thus, if the parents intermittently respond to the target behavior or if other individuals in the environment continue to reinforce the behavior, extinction may not occur. Moreover, the successful use of extinction requires that all reinforcing stimuli maintaining a behavior be identified and eliminated, which may be impossible under some circumstances. Although the time-tested technique of ignoring a child when he or she misbehaves and attending to the child when he or she acts in an appropriate manner has obvious validity, it must be precisely applied in order to have the desired effect.

While it would be good if parents were able to manage and modify the behavior of their children via the exclusive use of positive consequences, indications are that, at least with some children, this is not possible or practical. Especially with regard to the education and management of handicapped children, punishment contingencies must be considered as a viable part of the behavioral engineer's repertoire. Because of recent legislation requiring a free and public education for all children and youth, and specifically because of the concept of the least restrictive environment, parents are being given the option of maintaining even severely handicapped children in the home and mildly handicapped children in the regular classroom.

In conjunction with these developments, it should be realized that the techniques employed by parents to manage their children's behavior must coincide with the strengths and weaknesses of the child. If parents are to be effective in their role as implementers of treatment, they must have the flexibility of employing a number of proven techniques, including punishers. Although positively oriented techniques must be the basic foundation of any program, it must be recognized that parents, as well as professionals, may prove to be ineffective with some students if they are required to rely totally on these procedures. Negative consequences, when employed judiciously and with appropriate supervision, can be very effective.

As noted previously, punishment contingencies seem to be most effective when applied in conjunction with a routine of positive consequences. Since an effective punishing consequence serves to decrease the probability of an inappropriate behavior at the same time that a positive consequence strengthens a desirable response, optimum results can frequently be achieved with the simultaneous use of both procedures. Nonetheless, even in view of the potential that punishers offer, behavior engineers would probably be wise to exhaust their repertoire of positive reinforcers and extinction techniques before considering punishers. If a punishment consequence is selected, it is suggested that a reinforcing consequence that can be withdrawn from the child be selected instead of a physical punisher.

One procedure that has been widely used with good results by both parents and professionals is time-out from reinforcement. Time-out involves removing a child from a reinforcing environment for a short, specified period of time contingent upon her or his emitting a given inappropriate behavior. For example, if a child engages in a maladaptive behavior, he or she might be required to quietly spend a short period of time in an isolated area. The effective use of time-out requires that the subject normally be exposed to a reinforcing environment and that the time-out area be a sterile, albeit humane, environment.

Wahler (1969) reported that the parents of two young boys who displayed persistent oppositional and disruptive behaviors were able to use time-out as an effective intervention procedure. Five-minute time-out periods for noncompliance were employed, whereas parental approval and physical praise were provided for compliant responses. The results indicated that the experimental procedures were effective and that the parents became more effective in their administration of reinforcers during the course of the study.

In another study, Zeilberger, Sampen, and Sloane (1968) taught a parent to apply effectively differential consequences to a 4½-year-old boy's behavior. At home, and in several nursery schools, the subject had exhibited high rates of screaming, fighting, disobeying, and other maladaptive behaviors. The parent used 2-minute time-out periods to decrease physical aggression, screaming, and bossing, whereas verbal praise and special treats were contingently used to increase significantly compliance and cooperative play.

Response cost systems have also been effectively applied by parents with their own children. This procedure, often used in conjunction with a token economy program, involves a "fine" system or point penalty for certain types of maladaptive behaviors. Thus, parents might not only allow a child to earn tokens for engaging in previously identified adaptive and appropriate behaviors, but also fine the child for maladaptive responses. O'Leary et al. (1967), for example, trained parents to remove tokens following the observation of an inappropriate behavior. This procedure, in conjunction with a time-out and token economy program, were effective in decreasing disruptive behaviors and increasing cooperative sibling behavior in the home and other environments.

Other more powerful punishing contingencies have also been reported in the literature. For example, Risley (1968) employed electric shock with a 6-year-old female subject to eliminate autistic behaviors. This treatment procedure was employed only after time-out, extinction, and reinforcement of incompatible behavior techniques were unsuccessfully used. Later, the electric shock procedures were effectively transferred to the home setting. Positive side effects, such as increased eye contact and in-seat behavior, were also reported along with a decrease in autistic behaviors following the parents' use of this program.

Even though strong or moderately strong punishment contingencies have been associated with some success, these procedures have also been heavily criticized. Rightly or wrongly, society in general has failed to accept the use of strongly aversive procedures with children (Anderson & King, 1974). In addition, it has been suggested that the benefits derived from the use of these procedures are outweighed by the negative emotional reactions that are frequently evoked (Bucher & Lovaas, 1968).

As an alternative to more intensive punishment procedures, Foxx (1971) developed a procedure known as "overcorrection." This procedure consists of two procedures; the first is to correct the environmental effects of an inappropriate act, and the second is to require the individual to practice a relevant and appropriate behavior that is incompatible with the disruptive behavior.

The method for achieving the first objective, "restitutional overcorrection," requires "the disruptor to correct the consequences of his misbehavior by having him restore the situation to a state vastly improved from that which existed before the disruption [Foxx & Azrin, 1973, p. 2]." For example, a child who throws food on the floor would be required to wash, clean, and then wax the floor. A method known as "positive practice overcorrection" is used to achieve the second objective. Continuing with the same example, the child who throws food might be required to set the table and aid with the proper placement of food for a given period of time.

Barnard, Christophersen, Altman, and Wolf (1974) were successfully able to train the parents of four handicapped children in overcorrection procedures that led to the elimination of hand biting and head banging. The overcorrection procedure for hand biting involved requiring the child to brush her teeth with an oral antiseptic for 2 minutes each time she engaged in the target behavior. She was then required to wash the affected area of the hand for 2 minutes and then to apply hand cream to the area. Head banging was eliminated by first applying an ice pack to the child's head for 3 minutes each time he engaged in the behavior. This was followed by washing the bumped area of the head with a mild soap for 2 minutes and then brushing the child's hair for 1 minute. As noted previously, both techniques were very effective in eliminating the deviant behaviors.

As suggested from the previous discussion, behavioral engineers are in a position to counsel parents in the use of a number of different and effective procedures. The actual success of any program and intervention variable, however, will be determined by whether or not the program manager is able to promote the use of behavior management techniques and later to program the parents for success. This will probably be contingent upon the establishment of the designer's own validity and the validity of the philosophy initially, and then the careful attention to the details involved in successfully applying the technology. Specifically, the behavioral engineer must be able to counsel parents in pinpointing, operationally defining, and measuring the behavior. Later, the engineer must be able to devise practical, economical, realistic, and effective intervention plans and performance expectations. The program manager must not only be in a position to aid the parents in applying the procedures in a consistent, constant, and immediate fashion, but must also be sensitive enough to know when it is appropriate to suggest modifications for program maintenance or change.

Parent Training Programs

A number of training programs have been developed to train parents in applying the principles of behavior modification with their own children. As with other models of parent education, behavioral parent training typically uses a group format. Since the focus is on parents mastering and applying specific behavioral techniques, these groups are usually quite instructor oriented. Some programs involve workbook activities, short quizzes, and the week-by-week sharing of parental experiences in applying behavioral techniques. In some cases the instructor is the main source of information; in other instances self-instructional or programmed materials are extensively used. In this section, a representative sample of these programs are described and discussed.

READ, Parent Education Project

Project READ (Baker, Brightman, Heifetz, & Murphy, 1973) was designed to assess the efficacy of implementing a behaviorally oriented parent training program that relied on a minimal amount of professional involvement. With the support of a grant from the National Institute of Child Health and Human Development, a series of instructional materials were developed for use by parents of mentally retarded children and youth. The materials were designed to train parents, without the aid of professional input, in procedures to instruct their own children in self-help, social, and language skills. The materials were also designed to train parents to modify problem behaviors with their own children, although the major emphasis was on procedures for remediating skill deficits. Each of the training packets provided instructions in selecting a skill or behavior for modification, applying consequences and evaluating the influence of the intervention.

An analysis of the effectiveness of the training materials and procedures revealed that the parents were effective in applying behavioral principles with their own children in the absence of professional consultation. In fact, the data indicated that best results were obtained when mothers used the behavioral training materials in the absence of professional assistance, especially in self-help training.

On the basis of the data generated, it was concluded that motivated parents could be trained to function independently and effectively as behavior change agents with their own children.

Parents Are Teachers

Parents Are Teachers (Becker, 1971), a programmed text based on behavioral principles, is designed to train parents in systematically applying consequences in order to achieve planned behavioral changes with their own children. The program, based on several behaviorally oriented parent training projects, accentuates the use of consequences applied by parents with their own children. The author suggests that the program is appropriate for parents of typical and atypical children and youth and paraprofessionals. The consumers of the program are provided immediate feedback through written "exercises" that follow each training unit.

The program specifically focuses on the nature and application of reinforcers and punishers and common problems experienced by parents relative to applying management procedures. This program is not only comprehensive, well programmed, and motivating, but it is also written in such a fashion as to maintain the interest of most parents without being threatening to them.

Responsive Parenting Program

The Responsive Parenting Program (Hall, 1976) was developed to train parents in using behavior management techniques. The program, based on a cooperative agreement between a public school district and a state university, was originally offered to parents in the cooperative school district through a grant from the National Institute of Mental Health. This "preventive mental health training program" was developed as a means of responding to consumer (parent) needs and as a way of circumventing professional manpower shortages. In addition, the program was developed to aid parents, who are assigned the primary task of implementing preventive and remedial mental health procedures, in functioning more effectively with their children. Specifically, the program was developed to: (a) train parents in the basic concepts of applied behavior analysis; (b) modify behaviors selected for change; and (c) train parents to teach other parents applied behavior analysis procedures.

Parents involved in the program attend 2-hour weekly sessions over a period of 12 weeks. The first 10 sessions are devoted to training the participants in some aspect of behavior management, whereas the last 2 sessions are used for maintenance and follow-up. Specifically, the parents are exposed to lectures, demonstrations, and role-playing sessions on: (a) the concept of respondent and operant behavior; (b) procedures for operationally defining and measuring a behavior; (c) charting techniques; and (d) behavioral research designs and strategies and reinforcement, extinction, and punishment procedures. A manual developed through the Responsive Parenting Program is used in conjunction with the training program.

Evaluation efforts have indicated that the program is quite effective in its methodology and structure. Assessment data have included examination reports of parents over the basic materials presented in the program, child data reports, pre–post child management surveys, and surveys of consumer satisfaction.

One novel approach to this program is that parents who complete the program are entitled to participate in training other parents.

For Love of Children: Behavioral Psychology for Parents

The book *For Love of Children* (McIntire, 1970) is designed to train parents of children and youth in the principles and application of behavior modification. The first section of the book, "Parenthood by Design," discusses behavioral principles related to normal child development. Included in this first section is the role of such concepts as rewards, punishers, and consequences in the development of behavior. The second section, "Blueprints for Change," is concerned with the application of behavior modification procedures to a variety of common problem behaviors. Special attention is given to the use of behavioral principles in dealing with the problems of teenagers. The final chapter in the book provides an analysis of the manner in which reinforcement can be used as a major underpinning to successful family living.

Living with Children

G. R. Patterson and M. E. Gullion (1971) employ a programmed, behaviorally oriented textbook to train parents in procedures for promoting appropriate behavior and decreasing inappropriate behavior in their own children. The book is based on the behavioral assumption that both parental and child behaviors are learned and specifically that parents can teach their children adaptive as well as maladaptive responses. In the same fashion, Patterson and Gullion describe the manner in which children can train their parents to respond in a less than adequate fashion, creating an atmosphere of conflict and tension in the home. Using the concept of "social learning" (behavior is most often learned by our interactions with others), parents are trained in using a behavioral strategy both to interpret the behavior of their children and to modify those responses that are maladaptive. The authors describe the program as applicable for parents with children who manifest "problem behaviors" as well as with children who are more adaptive. However, the authors suggest that for parents applying the principles with "problem children" it should be used in conjunction with professional guidance (Patterson & Gullion, 1971).

The format of the programmed text requires that parents actively respond to the concepts presented by selecting an appropriate word or concept to complete a series of sentences and paragraphs. This format, and the constant and immediate feedback provided through it, is used for both of the major sections, training parents in social learning concepts and applying the principles to modify severe behavior problems. The social learning concepts include an overview of basic behavioral information, the nature and use of social and nonsocial reinforcers, the manner in which children shape the behavior of their parents, observation and recording procedures, and techniques for weakening undesirable behaviors and strengthening desirable responses.

The second section of the text focuses on behavioral principles that can be used by parents, with the aid of professional assistance, to modify "extreme" behavior problems. Included are a series of descriptions of behavior problems encountered by families and a treatment program used to bring about more adaptive behavior.

Parenting the Exceptional Child

The Severe Personal Adjustment Project (Simpson, 1978) developed and implemented as part of its program a parent training model based on learning theory principles. Although this U.S. Office of Education demonstration project focused on education and training procedures for autistic and autistic-like children and youth and their families, the parent training component is described as "applicable for both typical and atypical populations between the ages of 3 and 18."

The program requires the direction of a professional experienced in both parent counseling and behavior modification procedures. These training coordinators make use of three sequentially arranged, professionally developed audiovisual presentations and a workshop manual that are designed to instruct parents in the various concepts of using behavior modification with their own children. The workshop manual provides step-by-step directions for individuals coordinating the training sessions. Also included are feedback exams to determine the level of understanding of the participants following each session and small-group activities for allowing the parents to implement the program with their own children or adolescents. The first slide and tape presentation provides an overview of the behavior management process and procedures for selecting and operationally defining a behavior for modification. The second program details procedures for observing and measuring the behavior under scrutiny. The final audiovisual segment provides information on charting and graphing the data generated through the observation process and procedures for applying consequences to modify the behavior of concern. Procedures for conducting follow-up sessions are also provided.

Efficacy data presented suggest that training procedures are associated with high levels of parental success. Specifically, data available reveal that approximately 85–90% of the parents using the program under controlled conditions were able to effect the behavior changes with their own children that they initially identified.

Child Management

Employing a self-instruction format, Smith and Smith (1966) developed a program to train parents in using the technology of behavior modification. In addition, their book, *Child Management*, was written for the purpose of establishing a procedure for "interpreting behavior, so that they [parents] can create a healthy learning environment [p. i]."

Through the program, parents are instructed, via the use of behavior management procedures, in techniques for training their own children. Included in the program is an analysis of contingencies that may perpetuate an operant response, procedures for developing consistency in parental responses, establishing and enforcing rules, and employing the parent as a model. The program not only provides understandable, practical suggestions for parents, but also contains a special section on two of the most common problem areas experienced by parents—eating and bedtime compliance. In addition, the book facilitates the parental comprehension process through the use of a programmed format and constant feedback.

Although only subjective data were presented, this documentation did serve to establish the efficacy of the training procedures. Both changes in parent responses on childrearing instruments and parent ratings of behavior change in their own children supported the utility of the training program.

Summary

This chapter has focused on the use of behavior modification procedures by parents with their own children. Without question, it has been shown that parents are effective agents of behavior change with their own children when given appropriate guidance. Thus the issues faced by professionals who are charged with "working with parents" is not whether the approach is effective, but rather how to make a valid method functional. In addition, it appears that the professional community has begun to recognize that parents are a valuable resource and that only through the establishment of a therapeutic alliance can this resource be utilized.

Although this chapter has dealt with a number of issues in the area of parent-applied behavior modification programs, because of limited space it has provided only an overview of the subject. Consequently, individuals who wish to develop and implement behavior management programs for parents to apply with their own children should consult appropriate resources for specific direction.

References

Allen, K. E., & Harris, F. R. Elimination of a child's excessive scratching by training the mother in reinforcement procedures. *Behavior Research and Therapy*, 1966, 4, 79–84.

Anderson, K. A., & King, H. E. Time-out reconsidered. *Instructional Psychology*, 1974, *1*, 11–17.

Aragona, J., Cassady, J., & Drabman, R. S. Treating overweight children through parental training and contingency contracting. *Journal of Applied Behavior Analysis*, 1975, *8*, 269–278.

Baker, B. L., Brightman, A. S., Heifetz, L. J., & Murphy, D. M. *The READ Project Series*. Cambridge, Mass.: Behavioral Education Projects, 1973.

Barnard, J. B., Christophersen, E. R., Altman, K., & Wolf, M. M. *Parent-mediated treatment of self-injurious behavior using overcorrection*. Paper presented at the 82nd Annual Convention of the American Psychological Association, New Orleans, 1974.

Becker, W. C. *Parents are teachers*. Champaign, Ill.: Research Press, 1971.

Berkowitz, B. P., & Graziano, A. M. Training parents as behavior therapists: A review. *Behavior Research and Therapy*, 1972, *10*, 297–317.

Bernal, M. E., Williams, D. E., Miller, W. H., & Reagor, P. A. The use of videotape feedback and operant learning principles in training parents in management of deviant children. In R. D. Rubin, H. Festerheim, J. D. Henderson, & L. P. Ullman (Eds.), *Advances in behavior therapy*. New York: Academic Press, 1972.

Bucher, B., & Lovaas, O. I. Use of aversive stimulation in behavior modification. In M. R. Jones (Ed.)., *Miami symposium on the prediction of behavior, 1967: Aversive stimulation*. Coral Gables, Fla.: University of Miami Press, 1968.

Edlund, C. V. Rewards at home to promote desirable school behavior. *Teaching Exceptional Children*, 1969, *1*, 121–127.

Foxx, R. M. *The use of overcorrection procedures in eliminating self-stimulatory behavior in a classroom for retarded children*. Unpublished doctoral dissertation, Southern Illinois University, 1971.

Foxx, R. M., & Azrin, N. H. The elimination of autistic self-stimulatory behavior by overcorrection. *Journal of Applied Behavior Analysis*, 1973, *6*, 1–14.

Freud, S. The psychopathology of everyday life (Translated by A. A. Brill). In *The basic writings of Sigmund Freud*. New York: Modern Library, 1938.

Hall, R. V. Behavior Modification. *The Measurement of Behavior*. Merriam, Kans.: H & H Enterprises, 1970.

Hall, R. V. *Parent Training: A preventive mental health program*. National Institute of Mental Health Grant, University of Kansas, 1976.

Haring, N. G., & Phillips, E. L. *Educating emotionally disturbed children*. New York: McGraw-Hill, 1962.

Hawkins, R. P., Peterson, R. F., Schweid, E., & Bijou, S. W. Behavior therapy in the home: Amelioration of problem parent–child relations with the parent in a therapeutic role. *Journal of Experimental Child Psychology*, 1966, *4*, 99–107.

Kroth, R. L., Whelan, R. J., & Stables, J. M. Teacher application of behavior principles in home and classroom environments. *Focus on Exceptional Children*, 1970, *3*, 1–10.

McIntire, R. W. *For love of children: Behavioral psychology for parents*. Del Mar, Calif.: C.R.M. Books, 1970.

Millenson, J. R. *Principles of behavior analysis*. New York: Macmillan, 1967.

Mira, M. Results of a behavior modifications training program for parents and teachers. *Behavior Research and Therapy*, 1970, *8*, 309–311.

O'Dell, S. Training parents in behavior modification: A review. *Psychological Bulletin*, 1974, *81*, 418–433.

O'Leary, K. D., O'Leary, S., & Becker, W. C. Modification of deviant sibling interaction patterns in the home. *Behavior Research and Therapy*, 1967, *5*, 113–120.

Patterson, G. R. A learning theory approach to the treatment of the school phobic child. In L. P. Ullman & L. Krasner (Eds.), *Case studies in behavior modification*. New York: Holt, Rinehart, and Winston, 1965.

Patterson, G. R., Cobb, J. A., & Ray, R. S. A social engineering technology for retraining aggressive boys. In H. Adams & L. Unikel (Eds.), *Georgia symposium in experimental clinical psychology* (Vol. 2). Springfield, Ill.: Charles C Thomas, 1972.

Patterson, G. R., & Gullion, M. E. *Living with children*. Champaign, Ill.: Research Press, 1971.

Phillips, L. W. The soft underbelly of behavior therapy: Pop behavior Mod. *Journal of Behavior Therapy and Experimental Psychiatry*, 1978, 2, 139–140.

Reith, H. J., & Hall, R. V. *Responsive teaching model readings in applied behavior analysis*. Lawrence, Kans.: H & H Enterprises, 1974.

Risley, T. R. The effects and side-effects of punishing the autistic behaviors of a deviant child. *Journal of Applied Behavior Analysis*, 1968, 1, 21–34.

Risley, T. R., & Wolf, M. M. Experimental manipulation of autistic behaviors and generalization into the home. In R. Ulrich, T. Stachnik, & J. Mabry (Eds.), *Control of human behavior*. Glenview, Ill.: Scott, Foresman, & Co., 1966.

Ross, A. O. Behavioral therapy. In B. B. Wolman (Ed.), *Manual of child psycho-pathology*. New York: McGraw-Hill, 1972.

Russo, S. Adaptations in behavioral therapy with children. *Behavior Research and Therapy*, 1964, 2, 43–47.

Simpson, R. L. *Parenting the exceptional child*. (Developed under Federal Contract 300-75-0309, Bureau of Education for the Handicapped, Department of Health, Education and Welfare). Kansas: University of Kansas Press, 1978.

Skinner, B. F. *Walden Two*. New York: Macmillan, 1948.

Skinner, B. F. *Science and human behavior*. New York: Macmillan, 1953.

Smith, J. M., & Smith, E. P. *Child management*. Ann Arbor, Mich.: Ann Arbor Publishers, 1966.

Sulzer, B., & Mayer, G. R. *Behavior modification procedures for school personnel*. Hinsdale, Ill.: Dryden Press, 1972.

Wahler, R. G. Oppositional children: A quest for parental reinforcement control. *Journal of Applied Behavior Analysis*, 1969, 2, 159–170.

Wahler, R. G., Winkel, G. H., Peterson, R. F., & Morrison, D. C. Mothers as behavior therapists for their own children. *Behavior Research and Therapy*, 1965, 3, 113–124.

Williams, C. D. The elimination of tantrum behavior by extinction procedures. *Journal of Abnormal and Social Psychology*, 1959, 59, 269.

Wolf, M. M., Risley, T., & Mees, H. Application of operant conditioning procedures to the behavior problems of an autistic child. *Behavior Research and Therapy*, 1964, 1, 305–312.

Zeilberger, J., Sampen, S. E., & Sloane, H. M. Modification of a child's problem behavior in the home with the mother as therapist. *Journal of Applied Behavior Analysis*, 1968, 1, 47–53.

PART III

APPLICATION TO VARIED GROUPS

Chapter 8

Parenting Atypical Families

PAMELA C. MARR
C. E. KENNEDY

Forty-nine out of every 50 American children live in families (Kenis-ton, 1977). However, there is considerable variety in the types of families: two-parent families; single-parent families; reconstituted families; adoptive families; foster families; communal families. What used to be thought of as the "typical" family—husband breadwinner, wife homemaker—is now the "atypical" family. Only one-third of the husband–wife families have the husband as sole breadwinner. Four out of every 10 children spend a part of their childhood in a one-parent family, usually with the mother as head of household. Most of these children therefore will also spend some of their childhood in reconsti-tuted families.

A wide range of social changes have contributed to changing families patterns. There has been a 700% increase in the divorce rate since the turn of the century. In the last two decades the percentage of the first born babies that belong to unwed mothers has more than doubled, from 5% to 11%.

As we consider the concerns and many of the developmental experi-ences of these atypical families, we find a great deal of similarity with parenting concerns of foster parents. In single-parent families, adoptive families, and reconstituted families the children experience separation from natural parents, and in the case of adoptive and reconstituted families they have to adjust to new family patterns and new family

181

HANDBOOK ON
PARENT EDUCATION

members. Often the parents need to share their parental identity and role with parents from other periods of the child's life. Parents and children frequently have difficulty relating their atypicality to the stereotypes and social expectations of their community.

Blending the legal commitment of child to his or her family with the emotional, attitudinal, and identity relationships may pose as special tasks in atypical families. Some examples are the child's relating to a diseased or divorced parent or to the multiple grandparents in the divorced family.

Because of limited space and because the authors' research and experience have been primarily in the realm of foster parent activities, we have chosen to devote the major portion of this chapter to a presentation of parenting within the foster care system. Therefore, we will offer only a thumbnail sketch of parenting concerns in the various forms of atypical family life and then move to a consideration of some of these concerns as experienced in foster parenting.

Single-Parent Families

The incidence of persons choosing the role of single parent via pregnancy outside of marriage, adoption, or foster care seems to be increasing in frequency and popularity (Klein, 1973). However, most persons become single parents as a consequence of family crisis and the resultant disorganization, such as the illness or death of a spouse, desertion, separation, or divorce. Thus, a single parent may need skills in dealing with separation trauma and grief, both that of his or her own self-process and that of the children. Change from two-parent to single-parent status may be accompanied by change in living accommodations, change in employment, or change of school (Glasser, 1970).

The single parent is faced with the tremendous responsibility of childrearing without the support system that was built into the more traditional (nuclear or extended) family forms. Arranging appropriate child care is a concern, since the single parent does not have the usually established spouse relationship to share decision making. She or he needs skills also to gain access to a network of community resources such as school or mental health counselors and community recreation programs.

The single parent is faced with the task of adjusting to multiple changes in her or his own life and patterns of relating while trying to be a relatively stable socializing force in the child's life. Skills for coping with stress, modeling a coherent value system, the ability to remain flexible in adjusting to changes are all necessary for the single parent to learn. The single parent and child are in the process of establishing new relationships and new identities.

Maintaining the child's relationship with the absent parent and other relatives from the absent parent's side of the family may be a difficult task for the single parent, requiring special skill. Also, a concern most single parents face is that of providing adequate relationship experience with persons of the opposite sex (sex of the absent parent) that will aid the child in learning male–female roles and behavior acceptable to the normative society.

In addition to other concerns, the single parent needs skills for helping the child cope with attitudes of friends, relatives, and the community. Although new family forms are gaining wider acceptance, the single-parent family will need to contend with a society that is still oriented toward the traditional nuclear family: father–mother–children (Geddes, 1974).

Adoptive Families

The roles of adoptive parenting would seemingly be similar to that of natural parenthood, especially when it is an infant adoption. However, there are some parenting skills that are unique to the adoptive setting. Adoptive parents need skills for accessing and relating to the adoptive agency. They also need to have skills for relating to the legal system in the adoption process (Carrieri, 1977).

The adoptive parent will need skills for creating a family identity for the child (McNamara, 1975). This means skill not only in helping the child adapt to and feel a part of the adoptive family, but also in helping the child to understand and relate to his or her biological family. Although little or no information may be available about the biological parents, it is most often helpful for children to at least know that they do have a set of biological parents as a part of their self-identity.

Adoptive parents may need skills in relating to the needs of the older adopted child. The older child who is adopted has often lived in institutions or foster homes until the adoption, which gives him or her a unique personal and family history. The child may have developed special emotional problems related to life experiences thus far that will require special parenting skills. There may be racial and ethnic differences between the adoptive child and parents. The adoptive parent may need skills for helping the older children with feelings of separation and loss from relationships in his or her previous living situation.

The older adoptive child may have mental, physical, or emotional handicaps for which the adoptive parent will need special parenting skills.

Reconstituted Families

The percentage of persons experiencing divorce is increasing rapidly. However, age for age, the remarriage rate for divorced persons is higher than for single persons. Therefore, there is a rapidly increasing number of families with stepchildren. In some instances this may include children from the previous marriages of each spouse.

While the majority of reconstituted families are successful, there are special considerations that can be noted regarding stepparenting relationships. These concerns include a tendency for stepchildren to: (*a*) have a strong preference for one of their parents; (*b*) feel discrimination; or (*c*) desire to emulate a biological rather than stepparent. Stepparents sometimes have an exceptional tendency to feel that problems with their stepchildren are due to their own parenting shortcomings (Stinnett & Walters, 1977).

It is virtually impossible for the stepparent to assume the parent role completely. That role must be shared with previous parents. The children often have unrealistic expectations fostered by their anxieties, needs, and social pressures. Greater competition among stepchildren is a frequent stress factor in reconstituted families.

Stepparents and stepchildren who are able to recognize the new nature of the relationships they are entering will be more likely to participate in ongoing planning and review of the parenting experiences. Thus they will be more likely to achieve creative and successful family lives.

Communal Families

An alternative form of family life that has some similarity to the traditional family, with its extended family members, is the communal family. In these families, parenting is often provided for children-in-general by adults-in-general. While some communal groups assign parenting responsibilities to a few adults, in most communities children tend to go to different adults for different needs.

There are many pros and cons currently being expressed regarding communal childrearing (Stinnett & Walters, 1977). The advantages include an increased sense of belonging and exposure to many adult role models. Transition to adulthood is easier because children learn early to take responsibilities in the community. While communal children are believed to grow up with fewer feelings of alienation from adults, there is some criticism of overpermissiveness in children's discipline. Some observers also criticize communal families for neglecting or tending to consider children as miniature adults.

Foster Families

Helping children adjust to new living arrangements, to separation and pain of past family relationships, and to the varied kinds of support and constraints from the community are some of the challenges that parents of all atypical families face in common. We will look at these in more detail in this section as we consider foster parenting.

Characteristics of Children in Foster Care

In 1977, there were nearly 400,000 children in foster care in the United States. Three-fourths of these foster children were being cared for in foster family homes, as distinguished from institutional care.

More than half of the children in foster care remain in foster care from 4 to 6 years. Until the early 1900s many of the children who came into foster care were orphans. Today most children in foster care have one or both parents living. For example, parents sometimes place a child in foster care when they decide to relinquish parental rights (as in the case of an unwed mother). Sometimes parents voluntarily place a child in foster care because of a temporary crisis in the family. If the child's needs are not being met in the family, the courts may remove the custody or guardianship of the child from the parents and place the child in foster care. Sometimes parental mistreatment of the child may bring his or her removal into foster care. Whether the child is placed voluntarily by the parents or involuntarily through the courts, the need for foster care is most often the result of family stress and disruption.

Needs of Foster Children

In this section we will describe briefly some of the factors that lead to placement of children in foster care. These form the psychosocial background of the children foster parents are caring for. The need for foster care placement is usually the interaction of several stress factors present in the family situation. However, a helpful way to understand the variety of factors is to look at them individually.

Physical illness in the family is often a factor. Physical illness of a parent or a member of the family may come as it usually does, unexpectedly and at a time when the family is not able to deal effectively with the stress it brings. Quite often, doctor or hospital expenses place too great a burden on a family's exhausted budget. Physical illness that requires hospitalization of a parent may leave no one at home to care for the child. Even hospitalization of one child in the family may leave the other children without adequate care in the home. Such physical problems as a stroke, multiple sclerosis, or a debilitating accident may leave a parent unable to care for the child for an extended period of time.

The mental illness of a parent may cause him or her to behave in ways that are harmful to the health and safety of the child; for this reason the child may require foster care placement. Such behaviors as carelessness that cause the child to be exposed to serious accidents or violent conflicts with a spouse or neighbors that cause the child to be in physical, mental, or emotional danger may be manifestations of mental illness and require separation of the parent from the family.

A parent who is an alcoholic or drug addict may neglect the needs of the child and even endanger the child's health and safety. The alcoholic or drug addict parent may not be able to hold a job, and this may put the family under financial stress.

When a parent is arrested for criminal behavior, the child may be placed in foster care. This is especially true if the other parent is no longer living, has deserted the family, or is unable to manage a family alone. Many times while a parent is in prison, the child remains in foster care until he or she reaches the age of majority.

Marital conflict that results in physical violence and agression can create an extremely dangerous environment for a child. Aggression may turn toward the child, or the child may become an accidental victim of the violence. Often a child will be removed from the home until the parents learn better methods of resolving conflicts. Marital conflicts that result in the separation or divorce of parents or the desertion of one parent may be a factor in the decision to place a child in foster care. This is especially true if the remaining parent is unable to manage the family alone.

Child abuse and neglect rank high on the list of reasons for the decision to place a child in foster care. While "child neglect" is a rather broad term that probably results from many of the situations already described, it is sometimes difficult to separate child neglect from child abuse. There are some clear-cut cases of physical abuse to the child, such as excessive beating, but the lines between the two are thin and often tragically interwoven. Therefore, they are considered together in this discussion.

When discussing child abuse and neglect, it is best to recognize that there are three factors involved in each case: the child + the parent + the situation = child abuse and neglect. Research has shown that it is an interaction of these factors, rather than only one factor, that causes child abuse. That is, the characteristics of the child may elicit a set of responses (perhaps anger and frustration) from the parent within the confines of a particular situation that causes the parent to become violent and aggressive toward the child. With another child or in a different situation, the parent might respond in a more appropriate way.

Child abuse and neglect may occur when the parent is too emotionally immature to cope with the difficult tasks of childrearing, especially if the child is particularly difficult to manage. Some parents may abuse and neglect their children simply because they lack knowledge and understanding of normal child development and lack skills for dealing effectively with the developmental stages their child is passing through. Or parents may abuse their child in an overzealous attempt to discipline the child and manage his or her behavior. Lack of knowledge, inability to cope, and overzealousness are characteristics that are particularly true of parents who are mentally deficient. A parent may have a neurotic or psychotic personality problem. The personality problem may be so severe that the act of child abuse and neglect may be considered sadistic or criminal.

A child may also come into foster care because of his or her own behavior problems or conflict with other members of the family. Often a child's behavior is so much in conflict with the parents or other family members that it seems best for all concerned that the child be placed in foster care. This in no way implies that the conflict is the child's fault or that he or she is "bad." It simply means that there does not seem to be any possible resolution for the conflict within the family. In most cases, both parents and child need to learn better methods of communication and conflict resolution.

Sometimes a child's behavior brings her or him into conflict with the law. When a child's behavior is antisocial to the extent of breaking the community's laws and regulations, the child may be placed in foster care.

When a child has a mental or physical handicap that requires special care and treatment, the parents may not be able to care for him or her within the family. When there are several other children and the family is experiencing other stresses, the parents may not have the emotional or physical resources necessary to deal with the child's special needs.

A teenage girl who is pregnant out of wedlock may be placed in foster care if the pregnancy causes too much stress and anxiety in the family. If the baby is placed for adoption, the girl may return home, but in such cases special care is taken that the return is in the interest of her welfare. If the girl chooses to keep her baby, the infant, and sometimes both the infant and the teenage mother may be placed in foster care. Foster parents can ensure proper care is given to the infant and can provide nurturance and child-care training for the teenage girl.

Only a small number of children are in foster care because of the death of both parents. There are fewer orphans today than in the past, and they are more readily adopted. But the death of one parent may be a factor in placement if the remaining parent is unable to support and care for the child. When there are several children in the family, it may be especially difficult for the remaining parent to meet the needs of the children.

Financial burdens of the family are often a factor in the need to place a child in foster care. Although it is not usually the only reason, financial stresses are quite often an integral part of the situation that requires the child's being placed in foster care. Sometimes the family budget has been stretched to its maximum when an unexpected crisis makes it impossible to meet the needs of the child adequately.

NATIONAL CONCERNS

Foster care programs have been the focus of national attention through legislative and advocacy documents such as Kenneth Wooden's book *Weeping in the Playtime of Others* (1976). The National Foster Parent Association, National Council on Adoptable Children, National Action for Foster Children, and other advocacy groups have brought to national attention such needs and rights as rights of the foster child to permanency in family life.

Also, court suits by foster children against social service agencies have brought national attention to the foster child's rights to participate in decision making about his or her family life. Public policy, which emphasizes keeping the family's ties together whenever possible, has raised awareness of the need to reduce foster care placements through supportive services to the family and by training foster parents to work more closely with natural parents.

Foster parents are key members in a team of human service specialists who are working together to create physical resources and helping relationships to rehabilitate the foster child and facilitate his or her normal development. The services that foster parents render include the extensive range of physical, social, and psychosocial care required for children's survival and nurture, such as the kind of care that usually is provided by natural parents. In addition to this child-maintenance care, foster parents provide the special attention and rehabilitation services required by children experiencing special stress.

NORMAL MAINTENANCE AND NURTURANCE CARE

Let us first consider individual maintenance, the services that provide for a child the fundamental necessities of food, shelter, health, socialization, and personal nurturance. To provide such services the foster parent first needs competence in budgeting and purchasing. She or he needs skills in food preparation and the maintenance of housing. These skills must include an understanding of basic nutrition and other fundamentals of health. The foster parent needs to recognize and treat minor illnesses and must be referred to and work with medical personnel in case of severe sickness or handicaps.

Work habits, attitudes toward community, and social values, which will determine an individual's ability to become a self-sustaining and contributing member of society, are developed during the childhood and adolescent years. How well this is done by the foster child will depend on the helping-relationship skills of the foster parent. Major responsibility for the socialization processes and the personal and psychological nurturance of the foster child resides with the foster parent.

Approaches to Foster Parent Education

At the present time the status of training for foster parents is considerably in flux as the profession moves from a voluntary to a paraprofessional or professional career status. Therefore, the parent educator who elects to work with foster parent education may in one situation contract with a foster parent association, in another with a social service agency, and in another with a community college or adult education program.

The authors have recently completed a national survey of foster parent education programs and materials (Kennedy, Marr, Passmark, & Parker, 1978). In our survey we found a consistent pattern that distinguishes between the content of preservice (preplacement) training and ongoing or in-service training.

Preservice Training

Preservice training is the time for providing the overview of what is to be expected in the foster care placement. It usually focuses on the agency–foster parent relationship, separation and grieving processes of the child, and dealing with natural parents. Preservice training is often used as a self-selection process for foster parents in which they have an opportunity to decide if foster parenting is for them.

In-Service Training

In-service training focuses on child development, discipline and behavior management techniques, communication skills, and special behavior problems. A likely reason for this difference in focus of training between preservice and in-service is the experiencing of day-to-day living with a foster child. Caring for a child who is experiencing a variety of stresses develops a readiness for more specific information and skills. Foster parents are more likely to understand and utilize the information when they can apply the information directly to their current placement situations. Thus, most in-service training is likely to include time for problem solving for foster parents.

Another aspect of in-service training is that of specialization. Many in-service courses are offered with the idea that foster parents who have an understanding of the basic processes of foster care placement, either through preservice training or experience, need and want training that focuses on specialized concerns in foster care. Some examples of specialized concerns in foster care include training parents to deal with children who have emotional, physical, or mental handicaps; children with learning disabilities; adolescents, especially those who have come before the court; infants; unwed mothers; or abused and neglected children.

Another aspect of in-service training is development of advanced professional identity and skills. Experienced foster parents, those who have stayed with the system long enough to "know the ropes," are often in a position to take leadership roles. It seems important that foster parents not only are given the opportunity to take leadership roles, but also are provided with training for professional leadership skills. Courses in teamwork, legal aspects of foster care, and child advocacy become an important part of the development of this professional identity.

Foster Parent as Adult Learner

Foster parents come from a wide range of educational and socioeconomic backgrounds. Some have graduate degrees and full-time positions as professionals, others have elementary or some high school work and are employed in labor and skilled trades. At this time, the majority of foster parents provide foster parent services in addition to other employment being performed by at least one of the parents. However, this is changing rather rapidly as foster parenting is increasingly being viewed as a full-time professional commitment. Nevertheless, most persons now serving as foster parents view foster parent education as something that must be worked in "on the side."

Experienced foster parents approach the in-service aspects of foster parent education as something that needs to be brief and immediately practical. They want to be treated as experienced adults who come to class with information to share and with problems to solve. Often the class becomes a support group as the foster parents share with one another the special situation they are working through with their children.

Many aspects of parent education are adaptable to foster parent education through drawing upon the real-life situation of foster homes. However, there are some special topics that pertain primarily to the unique circumstances of foster parents. The following sections present a brief overview of four topics in a parent education program that would be specifically oriented to foster parenting. In these sections we present the ideas somewhat in the form that they might be used in an actual parent education class for foster parents. These topics are The Foster Parent as a Member of a Foster Care Team; Separation and Grieving; Natural Parents; and Foster Family Relationships.

The Foster Parent as a Member of the Foster Care Team

Attitudes about Working with the Agency

It is important for the foster parent to know that she or he is viewed as a responsible member of a team and that the information concerning the child is confidential material. The foster parent also needs to recognize that in the final analysis the child, having been taken temporarily from the natural parents, "belongs" to the state and not to the foster parent, or even to the agency. Both the agency and the foster parent are caring for the child in behalf of the state. The state has designated the primary responsibility for the child to the agency, and the agency in turn "hires" the foster parent to care for the child. Thus, there is an employer–employee relationship in which both the agency (employer) and foster parent (employee) have certain expectations of each other. In some instances the relationship between foster parents and agency staff is viewed as colleaguial rather than employer–employee.

The foster parent must approach the acceptance of a foster child into the home with the understanding that she or he will need to share the experience with other responsible persons. Not only will the foster parents provide information to the agency about the child's daily growth and development, but they may also need to be willing to share information and assistance with court persons and police. Foster parents also need to be able to work with counselors, therapists, and teachers in planning for the needs of the child.

RECORD KEEPING

Foster parenting involves a great deal of paper work. Initially, the foster parents need to complete applications necessary for licensing, which usually include information about themselves as individuals and information about their family life-style, family income, decision-making processes, family needs, and goals. This is extremely important to all foster care team members, because the agency needs to have an accurate understanding of the foster family in order to make a placement that will provide for the optimum growth and development of the child as well as the satisfaction of the foster family.

Maintaining health records and financial reports of expenditures for the foster child are also an important, although at times frustrating, activity in foster parenting. Keeping daily records for the child is extremely important in providing the agency with information about the child's progress. It is also important in providing information that can be kept with the agency's file so that should the child be moved or returned home and need foster care at a later time, there will be some information about the history of the child. Notes about his or her progress in adjusting to the foster family, school, friends, and relationships with his or her own family will be important to the caseworker. It is especially important to the *natural* family to have up-to-date and accurate information about their child's progress on file with the agency.

Record keeping may include writing anecdotes about special events in the child's life such as birthday parties or school activities. It may involve keeping pictures or mementoes in a scrapbook for the child. The foster parents and foster child are responsible for putting together information about the child's history. There is a real need for foster children not to "lose" themselves and their childhood through the foster care placement. Having an accurate concept of the past can help the child adjust to foster care and have an understanding and acceptance of herself or himself.

OTHER AGENCY STAFF

Although the linkage between the various personnel in the agency is probably different with each agency, there are some persons that foster parents almost always need to know about. The first person with whom potential foster parents may come in contact is often called the "homefinder." This person is responsible for recruiting foster parents. Most often this person doubles as the licensing worker or the foster care caseworker. The foster care caseworker is probably the one person who is most concerned with placing the child in the foster home, maintaining contact with the foster parents and the foster child during placement, and preparing the child to leave foster care. The caseworker usually has some responsibility for working with the natural family in changing their situation so that the child can return to his or her natural home.

Other agency staff associated with foster care may include the caseworker's supervisor, the finance worker, and a protective caseworker. The protective caseworker is especially concerned with getting assistance for the natural family to strengthen the home so that the child can return. There may also be a separate licensing worker who is responsible for evaluating the physical and psychosocial aspects of the foster home and for the training and qualifications of the foster parents.

Separation and Grieving

Foster children come into placement for a variety of reasons. Their life experiences have been different, and each of them has unique needs. However, the trauma of separation from family is a common experience for children placed in foster care. When children are placed in foster care, they are separated from the persons they know and trust and on whom they have learned to depend. The environment in which they are placed is different and strange to them.

How the child deals with separation will be influenced by his or her early "attachment" experiences. Between the ages of 6 months to 2 years (usually at 6 to 8 months), the child forms an "attachment" to the mother or to the person in his or her environment who is most stimulating and most responsive in meeting his or her needs. Usually this person is the mother because she is most often responsible for feeding, clothing, and caring for the child. However, the meeting of the child's physical needs does not seem to be the characteristic that will cause the child to form an attachment. Stimulating children by looking at them, smiling at them, and talking to them seems to be the characteristic that is most important.

The closer the child comes to being 2 years old without having formed an attachment, the less likely it becomes that he or she will ever form an attachment successfully. It is possible for a child to form an attachment after 2 years of age, but the prospect becomes very slim.

If the foster child has never formed an attachment, he or she may show little reaction to being separated from the parents. However, the child who has formed normal attachments with members of his or her family is likely to display a variety of reactions to separation. The child may go through a period of mourning; this process will be unique to each child. It will be important for the foster parents to anticipate and be sensitive to the child's reactions to separation.

The foster parents can help children with the feelings they experience by displaying acceptance and helping them to verbalize their feelings. This means the foster parent must be able to pick up cues from the child. For example, when a young boy says "My old man is a drunken bum," he may be expressing more than a description of his parent. Under that description lie the feelings of affection for his father and the disappointment he feels because his father's drinking problem has caused him to live with another family instead of with the parents he loves.

He may also have the feeling that "My old man is a drunken bum so that's why I am no good." The foster parent can help the hidden feelings come out by reflective comments such as "You're disappointed with your father," "You are feeling hurt because you have to live with us instead of with your parents," or "You're angry when you see that your father's drinking has caused you to be separated."

Foster children may not know how to relate to foster parents because of poor relationships they have had with their own parents. They may expect to be punished severely for minor transgressions or may expect that adults don't care what they do as long as they don't get in the way. Some children may feel hostile toward the foster parents because they feel the foster parents are in conspiracy to keep them from their family or because they cannot deal with the anger, fear, and hurt feelings they have toward their own parents. Or, children may turn feelings of hostility and frustration toward themselves and do things that are self-defeating or self-destructive. They may try to hide or deny the feelings by becoming withdrawn from or overplacating toward the foster parents.

The confusion children feel between loving and missing their family on one hand, and hating the parents and themselves for what they think or imagine they have done is terribly painful. Because of this pain, children often strike out at the foster parents.

Natural Parents

The Foster Parent's Relationship with the Natural Parent

Often natural parents have unresolved conflicts and needs that are a part of the reason for their child's placement, and they may need "parenting" as much as the child. For this reason, the foster parent needs to be a patient teacher of the natural parent as well as of the child.

Parenting is a skill that needs to be learned, and it is possible that circumstances in the life of the natural parents have interfered with their learning these skills. Also, there may be factors of health or other matters that have made it impossible for them to perform the parenting responsibilities in the way they would have liked. Thus, one of the foster parent's tasks is to patiently help the natural parents resolve these conflicts and learn constructive parenting skills.

In some cases, the natural parents see the child as the cause of their problems or as a threat to unresolved feelings that they, the parents, have. They may cast the child into the role of perpetrator of evil or evil in itself. They may identify the child with the spouse or other person who has caused them pain and may feel a need to punish the child because of feelings about the other person. In other cases, the natural parents may overindulge the child on a visitation because they feel guilty. Can you imagine what it would feel like to have someone else taking care of your child because you were not able to do it?

Foster–Natural Parent Communication

Meetings with the natural parents are an important part of foster care for two reasons: (a) the child needs to have clarity about the relationship with both sets of parents; and (b) the foster parent and the agency personnel need to help the natural home be able to care once again for the foster child.

Foster parents need to be aware of their own feelings about the natural parents and the child. It is easy to fall into the trap of saying "I could understand this or I could understand that, but I just can't understand why Jimmy's father is this way." Foster parents have to be constantly forgiving, not only to keep their sanity, but also to provide a model for the child as he or she works out feelings about his or her parents. Perfection is not the answer, but honest awareness of your feelings may be; willingness to communicate your awareness and acceptance of the situation is what is important for the child.

The foster parents' relationship with the child's natural parents involves helping the child deal with feelings about his or her natural parents. The child will often have considerably mixed feelings toward both the natural parents and the foster parents. He or she may be confused about whom to identify with.

Often children come into foster care without knowing or understanding how or why they are in placement. Even if they know some of the outward manifestations or circumstances, they may not understand or be aware of the undercurrents of what has happened. The child may then fantasize or invent reasons for placement that are destructive. Foster children almost always feel that they are in some way to blame for the events that lead to placement.

The child's conflict of identity between the foster parents and the natural parents may be so great that the child may not be able to commit himself or herself to either. This may also inhibit the child from committing himself or herself to other persons in the environment. Assisting the foster child to explore his or her feelings of conflict will be helpful to the child.

It is not necessary for the foster parents to "whitewash" the situation with "It'll be all right," or "Don't worry about it," or by ignoring the child's feelings. It is not necessary for the foster parent to invent solutions or give advice like "When you get home you'll be so busy you won't worry about us." It is far better to allow foster children to arrive at their own solutions by becoming aware of their feelings and the possibilities that might occur.

The foster parent must be accepting of whatever the child says he or she is feeling in order to help the child in exploring feelings and in order to keep communications open.

Foster Family Relationships

Like a person in a foreign country, it may take the foster child time to learn the routines, activities, values, goals and systems of communication within the foster family. Foster children need some clear guidelines about what happens in the family, without being overwhelmed with rules and regulations. The foster parents and their biological children also need time to adapt to the customs, habits, and routines of the foster child. Neither the foster family nor the foster child should be required to make all the adjustments. Accommodations need to be made by both parties.

A time should be planned for the child to talk privately with the foster parents. A conference time in which the child has the full attention and interest of the foster parents might make the foster child feel like an accepted and special part of the family. It might also provide an opportunity for the child to express his or her needs and concerns. The foster parents would then be able to have a clear understanding of what the child is experiencing and gain insights into improving the quality of the relationship.

Foster parents need to be aware of the feelings of competition and rivalry that foster children may feel with natural children. It is easy for foster children to feel that they are outsiders and that the natural children are favored. It is also dangerous to play favorites and to make too many allowances for the foster child's behavior.

Role of the Natural Children

Natural children need to be protected from having their needs and rights abused. The relationship between a foster child and other foster family children works best when they have a voice in the decision to bring a foster child into the home. The foster family children can be a tremendous asset in ministering to the needs of the foster child when they understand the importance of their role and know that their place in the structure of the family is secure. Often the foster family children can help foster children learn the family routines, express their feelings, and introduce them to the community better than the foster parents can. Foster family children can also set an example of how to relate to the foster parents, particularly if the foster children have had poor relationships with adults in their home environments.

Preparing for Separation

Knowing that the child will be in foster care temporarily, foster parents need to have some skill in preparing themselves, their children, and the foster child for separation that comes when placement ends. Foster parents need to be persons who are emotionally mature enough to give affection and emotional support to the child during his or her time of placement and yet not become so attached and dependent as to hamper readjustment to his or her own family, to an adoptive family, or to a permanent foster home or institution. Clearly, it is difficult to balance among the feelings of affection for the foster child and the realistic needs of the foster child to grow in independence. Foster parents express their love while also helping the child to keep the contact with his or her family and while facilitating the child's preparation for living with his or her own family again, living with an adoptive family, or living alone as an adult.

Fear and Hesitation in Returning Home

Part of the work of being a foster parent is to prepare the child to leave foster care. Children may have realistic fears about returning to their own families. The foster parent can best help by providing continued contact with or information about the foster child's natural family during placement and explain how the parents' lives are changing too because of their experiences. If the child is having difficulty establishing communication, the foster parents can be helpful in easing the child's fears by setting an example of how to interact with his or her natural family. The foster parents may be helpful in providing the natural parent with information about the foster family's routine and especially about what has been happening to the child while in the foster home.

Termination of placement may involve one of several alternatives. Foster children may return to their natural homes; they may be moved into child-care institutions; they may be placed in adoption; or they may have reached age 18 and elect to live as independent adults. Each of these alternatives will have different levels of attractiveness, varying with the specific situation. Foster parents have an important task of guidance in helping the foster child prepare for the next step in life.

In the ideal situation, the agency takes into careful consideration the foster parent's, natural parent's, and foster child's feelings and thoughts as they make a new placement decision or return decision. It is important that all persons involved feel that they have had input in determining the decision.

Conclusion

Parenting in atypical families offers the joys and satisfactions experienced in parenting in typical families. It also includes the typical responsibilities and stresses. In addition, parenting in atypical families brings unique challenges because of the special circumstances of these relationships and often because of prior family conditions. Therefore, the guidance and support of parent education programs, prepared especially for the different kinds of atypical families, is vitally important. Persons wishing further background on research and training in foster care may want to examine the writing of Fanshel (1975), Felker (1974), Geiser (1973), Gruber (1978), Goldstein, Freud, and Solmit (1973), Jurich (1979), Reistroffer (1974), Stone and Hunzeker (1974), Panitch (1977), Guerney (1976), Rutter (1978), Sarason (1976) and McFadden (1978).

References

Carrieri, J. E. *The foster child: From abandonment to adoption.* New York: Practicing Law Institute, 1977.

Fanshel, D. *Toward more understanding of foster parents.* San Francisco: R & E Research Associates, 1975.

Felker, E. H. *Foster parenting young children: Guidelines from a foster parent.* New York: Child Welfare League of America, 1974.

Geddes, J. B. *How to parent alone: A guide for single parents.* New York: Seabury Press, 1974.

Geiser, R. L. *The illusion of caring: Children in foster care.* Boston: Beacon Press, 1973.

Glasser, P. H., & Glasser, L. N. *Families in crisis.* New York: Harper & Row, 1970.

Goldstein, J., Freud, A., & Solnit, A. J. *Beyond the best interests of the child.* New York: Free Press, 1973.

Gruber, A. *Children in foster care: Destitute, neglected . . . betrayed.* New York: Human Sciences Press, 1978.

Guerney, L. A program for training agency personnel as foster parent trainers. *Child Welfare,* November 1976, *55*(9), 652–660.

Jurich, A. P. Coping with moral problems of adolescents in foster care. *Child Welfare.* March 1979, *68*(3), 187–195.

Keniston, K., & the Carnegie Council on Children. *All our children: The American family under pressure.* New York: Harvest/HBJ, 1977.

Kennedy, C. E., Marr, P. C., Passmark, L. C., & Parker, C. J. *Resource catalogue for foster parent education.* Manhattan, Kan.: Kansas State University, 1978.

Klein, C. *The single parent experience.* New York: Avon Books, 1973.

McFadden, E. J. *Fostering the Battered and Abused Child.* Ypsilanti, Michigan: Eastern Michigan University, 1978.

McNamara, J. *Adoption advisor.* New York: Hawthorne Books, 1975.

Panitch, A. *Comparative approaches in foster care training.* Boise, Idaho: Boise State University, 1977.

Reistroffer, M. *Foster parents and social workers: On the job together.* New York: Child Welfare League of America, 1974.

Rutter, B. A. *The parent's guide to foster family care.* New York: Child Welfare League of America, 1978.

Sarason, I., Linder K., & Crnic, K. *A guide for foster parents.* New York: Human Science Press, 1976.

Stinnett, N., & Walters, J. *Relationships in marriage and family*. New York: MacMillan, 1977.

Stone, H., & Hunzeker, J. *Education for foster family care: Models and methods for foster parents and social workers*. New York: Child Welfare League of America, 1974.

Wooden, K. *Weeping in the playtime of others*. New York: McGraw-Hill, 1976.

Chapter 9

Involving Parents in the Education of Their Handicapped Children: An Essential Component of an Exemplary Program

MERLE B. KARNES
RICHARD C. LEE

In recent years, parental involvement in programs for handicapped children has undergone a significant change. Until recently, parents were only minimally involved in educational programs for their handicapped children; essentially parents were viewed by teachers as disinterested and/or not having the skills or background necessary to contribute to their special child's education (Kroth, 1975). Today, however, as a function of PL 94-142, parents are becoming involved not only in writing but also, whenever possible, in implementing individualized educational plans (IEPs) for their handicapped children. Given this changing role for parents, there is now a need to restructure educational programs for the handicapped to reflect increased levels of parent involvement.

In this chapter, a number of concepts, guidelines, and strategies for increasing parental involvement in programs for their handicapped children are explored. The intent is to familiarize students and teachers with this information in order to aid them in designing and implementing an effective parent involvement program. First, a rationale for parent involvement is presented. Next, some basic considerations in planning a parent involvement program are presented. The third section provides a brief review of programs for parents of the handicapped, and finally, conclusions are drawn concerning programs for parents of handicapped children.

201

HANDBOOK ON
PARENT EDUCATION

Rationale for Parent Involvement

There are several reasons, other than legislative mandates, for involving parents in their handicapped child's education. One of the most compelling of these is the fact that parents, when properly trained, are extremely effective teachers of their exceptional children. Numerous studies and intervention programs, for example, have shown that parents of the handicapped can be effective training agents for the children (Berkowitz & Graziano, 1972; Karnes & Lee, 1978; O'Dell, 1974).

Many of these parent training studies have relied on behavior modification techniques. Typically, parents are trained to identify their child's problem behavior, to collect data on the behavior, and to implement a consistent intervention procedure. Using a behavioral approach, parents of the handicapped have been trained to successfully modify a wide range of difficult behaviors exhibited by their children, including oppositional behavior (Wahler, 1969), violent tantrums (Straughan, 1964), isolate behavior (Wagner, 1968), excessive crying (Williams, 1959), and a variety of self-help behaviors, (Graziano, 1971; Nolan & Pence, 1970).

Several "nonbehavioral" intervention programs have also successfully trained parents to teach their exceptional children (Karnes, Teska, Hodgins, & Badger, 1970; Patterson, 1971; Walder, Cohen, Daston, Breiter, & Hirsch, 1967; Weikart & Lambie, 1970). One example of such a program is reported by Karnes and her associates (Karnes et al., 1970). These researchers trained economically disadvantaged mothers to stimulate the intellectual development of their high-risk infants. Half of the meeting time was devoted to discussion of personal and community problems, and mothers shared ideas, solutions, and generally provided support for each other. Monthly home visits were made by the two staff members to observe the mothers working with their infants and to reinforce what had been taught at the meetings. Significant increases in the level of intellectual functioning of the children were noted. Corresponding positive changes were found in the attitudes and self-concepts of the mothers in their relationships with their children.

In addition to the research evidence on the effectiveness of parent intervention, numerous other reasons, advanced by several authors, justify developing effective parent involvement programs. Among them are the following:

1. Knowledgeable parents can be the strongest advocates for program continuation and extension. In several cases parent advocacy has been directly responsible for altering the policies and laws of

school boards, advisory councils, and state and federal legislatures (Karnes, Zehrbach, & Teska, 1972).

2. Parents are consumers who pay either directly or indirectly for the program their child is receiving. As a result, they have a right to have a voice in what and how their child is taught (Karnes *et al.*, 1972).

3. Parents of a handicapped child will continue to have more responsibility for their child over a significantly longer period of time than parents of a normal child. They need parenting and teaching skills above and beyond those needed by parents of a normal child (Shearer & Shearer, 1972).

4. Using parents as instructional aides is an effective way of implementing the concept of individualized instruction. When parents are employed as teachers or aides, the classroom teacher will be able to spend more time collecting data or working with a particularly difficult child on a one-to-one basis.

5. Involvement of parents in the education of their child can have a positive effect on other siblings in the family. Studies have shown, for example, that parent training during the preschool years was beneficial not only to the target child, but also to his or her siblings (e.g., Gray & Klaus, 1970). Parents are thus able to generalize skills, making for better teaching of all their children.

6. The presence of parents working in the classroom provides children with opportunities to learn to relate to many different adults. These kinds of experiences are important in preparing children for interpersonal relationships in future adult roles (Karnes *et al.*, 1972).

7. Parents can serve as effective agents in generalizing or transferring learning from the classroom to the home as well as to other settings. Numerous studies, for example, have documented that parents are effective generalization facilitating agents (Marholin, Siegel, & Phillips, 1975; Stokes & Baer, 1978).

8. Parents know their children better than anyone else; thus, they can serve as critical resources to program staff in developing instructional objectives for their children. This is, in fact, the logic underlying parent involvement in IEP conferences mandated by the new law.

9. Parents can help establish a link between school and home. Communication between home and school is necessary for creating environments where the needs of handicapped children are consistently met (Kroth, 1975).

10. Parents can serve as valuable curriculum resources to a program.

Each group of parents represents an untapped pool of talent, each with special knowledge that can be shared. It may be unnecessary to purchase elaborate materials when parents can share their materials and experiences.

11. Parent involvement can greatly accelerate children's learning.

Schools or centers working with children without benefit of parent involvement cannot begin to accomplish alone what staff and parents can accomplish together. Fredericks, Baldwin, and Grove (1974), for example, have demonstrated that a parent program in conjunction with a school program, will almost double the rate of acquisition of a particular skill. Similarly, Bronfenbrenner (1974), after an in-depth survey of the effects of a variety of intervention programs—some with and some without parent involvement—concluded:

> The evidence indicates that the family is the most effective and economical system for fostering and sustaining the development of the child. The evidence indicates further that the involvement of the child's family as an active participant is critical to the success of any intervention program. Without such family involvement, any effects of intervention, at least in the cognitive sphere, are likely to be ephemeral, to appear to erode rapidly once the program ends. In contrast, the involvement of the parents as partners in the enterprise provides an ongoing system which can reinforce the effects of the program while it is in operation and help to sustain them after the program ends [p.55].

The preceding rationale indicates that parent involvement is beneficial to both the exceptional child and his or her educational program. It is thus incumbent upon special educators to assure that all parents become involved in a meaningful way in their handicapped child's program.

Basic Considerations in Planning a Parent Involvement Program

Programs for parents of handicapped children have developed in highly individual ways. In part, this is due to the need for teachers to develop programs to meet the unique needs of parents in their community or school. But despite the individualized nature of these programs, there are several basic considerations that serve to ensure a quality parent involvement program. In this section, such considerations of an exemplary parent involvement program will be discussed.

Establish a Program on a Set of Basic Assumptions

A first essential consideration in planning a quality parent involvement program is to delineate a set of assumptions on which the program should be established. These assumptions, some of which have
been identified by Karnes, Zehrbach, and Teska, (1972), concern the
relationship of parents both to their handicapped child and to his or her
educational program. According to these assumptions:

1. *Parents are interested in the growth of their handicapped child and
want to acquire new and improved skills in order to promote the child's
growth.* This point assumes that it is important for professionals to
approach parents in a positive manner, conveying to them the belief
that teachers are sincerely interested in involving parents in a partnership to promote the growth of their handicapped child. It is also important for teachers to communicate a willingness to give time and energy
to helping parents learn more effective techniques for interacting with
their child.

2. *Parents are willing and able to learn improved skills for working with
their handicapped child.* Research findings cited earlier suggest that parents can improve their parenting skills and that this will be reflected in
improved progress of their child.

3. *Parents are able to effectively work in a classroom setting including one
where their own child is enrolled.* Although educators were once reluctant
to have parents working in their child's classroom, experience has
shown that in such settings parents can teach other children as well as
their own without interfering with the teaching–learning process. In
fact, research suggests that this process can be enhanced. To work
effectively as teachers, parents must first have acquired some basic
teaching skills and must be ready emotionally to undertake this type of
participation. It is the role of the professional staff, together with the
parents, to determine if he or she is prepared for direct teaching in the
classroom.

4. *Parents will find time to become involved in their child's program if the
involvement makes sense to them.* To ensure parent involvement, parents
must feel that participation is worthwhile, both from the standpoint
of meeting their own needs, interests, and desires, and from the
standpoint of the growth of the child. Having family members engage
in meaningless activities like cleaning up spilled milk, dusting books,
straightening chairs, or putting toys away is unlikely to lead parents to
believe they are making a meaningful contribution. On the other hand,
if parents are involved in playing games that enhance language and/or

academic development, they will be more likely to view their contribution as important and find time to engage in such activities.

5. *Parents will involve themselves most when their training is specific and when they can see some direct applications.* If teachers expect parents to follow through in the home with a suggestion, the suggestion must be specific. For example, telling parents that they should stimulate their delayed child's language is far too global a suggestion. In contrast, if parents are given specific suggestions to teach their child to label or match objects, the parent will be more likely to implement the suggestion. Teachers should also remember that parents are often reluctant to teach some tasks because of fear of not doing something right. Professionals can allay these fears by being more specific.

6. *Parents are easiest to involve when their goals and values are compatible with those of the school.* Teachers find that parents who share the same values and standards as the school are often willing and eager to involve themselves in various facets of the educational program. In contrast, when parents do not value education, have difficulty following through on responsibilities, or promote dependence of their handicapped child, they will be reluctant to become involved because of differences with the school in value systems. It is the role of school personnel to assure the parents that in time their goals and those of the school will become more compatible, particularly if parents attempt to involve themselves in the educational progress of their child.

7. *Parents will require the greatest flexibility in programming when there is a wide discrepancy between the goals and values of the school and home.* As mentioned, family members whose goals and values correspond with those of the school are more likely to become involved in the educational program. On the other hand, because differences in values and goals may arise, parents may feel uncomfortable engaging in activities appropriate for their child's growth. Therefore, teachers should conduct a needs assessment to determine the entry level of parents in the involvement program. Such an assessment will enable the teacher to recognize individual differences among parents and program accordingly for them.

8. *Parents will become involved to the extent that they participate in decision making.* Parents, like anyone else, want a voice in what they do, how they do it, and when they do it relating to their child's program. Experience has taught us that if parents play a part in decision making, they will show a greater commitment to involving themselves in the various activities of the parent involvement program.

9. *Parents will involve themselves most when informed of the progress of their efforts.* It is discouraging for parents to work day after day and

never receive feedback on their efforts. Such feedback is essential if parents are to continue to put forth an effort. At the same time, teachers should remember to make the feedback instructive and, as often as possible, positive. Remember that negative feedback or feelings of failure can cause family members to become discouraged and disinterested.

10. *Parents will involve themselves when professionals show respect for them as individuals.* It is fundamental that teachers approach each parent with genuine respect. No matter how contrary the parents' goals, values, and practices are from the school's, teachers must respect the right of the individual to feel and act the way he or she does. When teachers convey respect, parents will feel more comfortable and willing to involve themselves in the program. Good rapport is based on mutual respect, and when parents feel respected they will become open to learning new and better ways of fostering their child's development.

11. *Parents will involve themselves most when served by professionals who have been trained specially to work with parents in divergent, appropriate ways.* The more skills teachers acquire through formal preservice and in-service training and experience, the better able they will be not only to evoke confidence in parents, but also to involve them in flexible ways in the educational program. In addition, when teachers are more skilled, they are more able to help parents to determine their appropriate entry level of involvement.

12. *Parents will involve themselves most when the approach is individualized.* Parents, like children, have individual needs, interests, and skills. An approach that attempts to match an involvement activity with parents' interests and skills will encourage parent involvement. For example, to expect all parents to attend a group meeting on a subject not relevant to all their needs is not an appropriate procedure for individualizing family involvement.

13. *Parents will develop more positive attitudes when involvement is successful.* In a previous assumption, the importance of feedback to parents for continued enthusiasm and effort in involvement was stressed. The point to be emphasized here is that the more successful a parent is in a given involvement activity, the more he or she is likely to become involved in that activity and other activities as well.

14. *Parents will need less help and support from professional staff as they acquire more effective knowledge and skills.* The most important goal of a parent education program is to help parents become self-sufficient in terms of working with the handicapped child and in making decisions regarding his or her welfare. Program activities should reflect a gradual movement toward this independent behavior on the part of the parents.

15. *Parents will acquire sufficient skills to instruct other parents.* In a good parent involvement program, parents of handicapped children will eventually become very effective in working with other parents of handicapped children. Generally, teachers should view this as a positive occurrence, since it is often more meaningful for parents to provide information and share solutions to certain problems with each other than to call on the aid of the teacher.

Be Sensitive to Stages of Parental Reaction

To work effectively with parents of handicapped children, teachers must understand the emotional climate in the home. Because parental attitudes largely determine the home atmosphere, teachers are to be aware of what happens to parents when they learn that their child is handicapped. Thus, a second consideration in planning parent programs is to be sensitive to stages of parental reaction and to attempt to counsel parents through each stage of adjustment.

Numerous writers have identified different stages of parental reaction to the realization that a serious problem exists in their child's development (Baroff, 1974; Bryant, 1971; Keith, 1973; Kessler, 1966). Some of the more common stages of parental reaction are discussed here briefly.

Denial. A common parental reaction to the diagnosis of a handicap is simply not to believe the problem exists. Families may doubt the diagnostician's competence and seek the opinions of several different experts. Underlying this behavior is the desperate hope that the initial diagnosis is wrong. There is little professionals can do for families at this stage except to understand their feelings. At the same time, it should be remembered that prolonged delay in accepting the diagnosis may deprive the child of treatment and intervention at critical times, and thus teachers must do their best to help families gradually accept their child's handicapping condition.

Anger. According to Gardner (1973), anger is also a common parental reaction in the early stages of accepting their child's condition. Generally it stems from feelings of helplessness and frustration toward both the child and themselves. In some instances parental anger is justified, especially if parents have been dealing with professionals who have been providing them with false hope and have been less than honest about their child's condition. On the other hand, the anger reaction is abnormal if it is prolonged or if it is directed inappropriately toward the child. In dealing with parental anger, the best strategy for teachers is to attempt to direct it into useful channels, such as working for organizations to benefit children with similar handicapping conditions.

Guilt. Inappropriate guilt is a common reaction when parents learn their child is handicapped. According to Gardner (1973), it often takes the form of preoccupation with parental transgressions or mistakes that the parents believe may have caused the problem. The parents who attribute the cause of the child's condition to themselves are attempting to control what is otherwise beyond their control. Teachers and other professionals must simply do their best to reason with the parents at this stage.

Shame. Often parents experience shame over the birth of an impaired child. They are concerned with the anticipated disapproval of others, and they believe their child will be judged as inferior. Parents in this stage are often helped by talking to parents of other handicapped children. Parents are more likely to accept the counsel of others who have experienced shame than the advice of a teacher who may not have an impaired child.

Blame. According to Gardner (1973), the blame reaction is an attempt by parents to place the responsibility for their child's condition on others in order to cushion their own feelings. Parents may blame the child's teacher and school for inappropriate education, the doctor for faulty prenatal care, or perhaps hereditary factors on "the other side of the family." This parental attitude can affect the child and undermine his or her acceptance of professional services. Once again parent-to-parent counseling may be the best strategy in helping to overcome parental blame.

Overprotection. This reaction is often characterized by parents' denying their child opportunities to play with other children. Parents use several excuses: "It's too cold, wet, or hot to allow the child to play," "The other boys play too rough," or perhaps "Other children will ridicule my child." By denying the child the right to be a child and interact with other children, the parent is further handicapping him or her. Numerous studies have documented the immense amount of teaching that takes place in child-to-child interactions (Hartup, 1970). Overprotection is perhaps best handled by convincing parents to involve their child in an educational program and extracurricular activities (Karnes *et al.*, 1972).

Emotional Adaptation. Emotional adaptation is the final stage of adjustment by parents. It is at this stage that parents have intellectually and emotionally accepted their child's handicapping condition. And while this stage is not free of difficult times or even crisis periods, parents have developed more positive attitudes toward themselves and their child that allow them to now acquire the skills necessary to make a significant contribution to their child's future.

Use Several Strategies for Involving Parents in the Program

Parents can be involved in almost every phase of their handicapped child's program. Their roles in these programs will vary both in terms of their responsibility and the extent of their involvement. The following is a list of roles that parents might fulfill within programs for their handicapped children.

1. *Serving on administrative or advisory councils.* Parents can and should, whenever possible, serve on a program's administrative or advisory council. In this capacity parents can advise on overall program goals and objectives and serve with other parents and school personnel on task forces that counsel administrators in the areas of fund raising, legislation, building improvements, employment of new personnel, and so on. It is at this level of involvement that parents can contribute to program decisions that will directly affect their child's educational program. Parents who are involved in decision making are generally effective supporters of those decisions.

2. *Program advocate.* In the role of program advocate, parents can assume responsibility for a program of public relations activities. They can talk to friends and other professionals within the community about the program in which they and their child are participating. Parents, as program advocates, can also write letters to officials at the local, state, and national levels and can attend local school board meetings to speak for the financial support necessary to assure program continuation. Most educators agree that, as program advocates, parents are extremely valuable in helping to ensure program acceptance and continuation.

3. *Staff member.* Parents can serve as volunteers or paid staff members within their child's program. Parents can be taught to aid teachers in a variety of ways within this role. They may be taught techniques to observe and record behavior in the classroom, to help teachers in making and organizing curriculum materials, to assist in teaching certain activities, or to provide extra help for special events, like field trips. When involving parents as staff members, it is important to recall

several of the basic assumptions cited earlier, especially: (*a*) that the involvement is meaningful; (*b*) that parents are included in making classroom decisions; (*c*) that parents receive feedback from the program staff; and (*d*) that the involvement program is individualized to meet parent needs.

4. *Teacher.* Whenever possible it is desirable to train parents to directly teach their own child. This training can occur either in the home or at school, or both. Although training parents to teach their children is sometimes difficult, it is, as research shows (e.g., Karnes & Lee, 1978), quite worthwhile. Teachers who wish to train parents as teachers are encouraged to refer to one of several good resources for training parents (Abraham, 1974; Becker, 1971; Becker & Becker, 1974; Gordon, Greenwood, Ware, & Olmsted, 1974). In addition to these resources, there are some general guidelines teachers should follow in training parents to teach their children. These include: (*a*) Training should be as direct and concise as possible; (*b*) training should take place in a practical setting with handicapped children either in the home or at school; (*c*) new teaching skills should be introduced gradually with ample opportunity to practice the skills; (*d*) parents should be assigned teaching tasks that are compatible with their level of competence; (*e*) teachers should employ a continuous system of feedback requiring them to monitor the parents' teaching; (*f*) teachers should adapt a simplified communication system that avoids educational jargon and provides concrete directions and demonstrations where possible; and (*g*) teachers should assist parents in acquiring skills to help their handicapped child generalize skills and concepts.

5. *Curriculum developer.* Suggestions from parents regarding curriculum should be actively sought by the staff of programs for handicapped children. Because parents know their children well, they can often suggest curriculum goals, teaching techniques, and reinforcers appropriate for their child. In addition, parents have special talents and can make invaluable contributions to the curriculum by designing activities and specialized materials.

6. *Counselor to other parents.* As mentioned earlier, parents will eventually become skillful enough to counsel other parents of handicapped children. In this role, parents can share solutions to mutual problems in dealing with children and offer each other emotional support. Such mutual support can significantly increase the impact of the program on child progress. Teachers can encourage parents to determine the content for discussion groups at parent meetings or perhaps by encouraging parent-to-parent partnerships. Finally, parents who work as counselors can be extremely effective in recruiting other parents into the program.

7. Evaluation. Several programs for exceptional children have given parents significant responsibility for assessing and evaluating their child's progress and the progress of the program in general. This information provides the staff with important feedback that is used in making program decisions. In this role, parents are trained to observe and collect data on their child's behavior at school, in the home and, when appropriate, in other settings as well. Parents can also be trained to provide careful narrative descriptions of their child's behavior to help teachers in identifying as yet undiagnosed problems. As evaluators of the overall program, parents can contribute by completing questionnaires, by participating in informal discussions with the teacher about the program, through structured interviews in which teachers ask questions to elicit specific information, and through structured observations of the classroom program.

The preceding roles indicate that parents can be involved in all phases of a program's operation. In fact, research suggests that the more directly involved parents are with their child, the better progress the child will make (Lillie, 1974). Thus, as mentioned earlier, it is mandatory that parents be trained to work with and teach their own child.

Structure the Program around Mutually Determined Goals

Effective parent involvement programs must be structured around goals determined by both parents and the professional staff. These goals will reflect the needs of parents, the staff and program and, of course, the needs of the child. To help determine goals, the teacher must identify the interests and needs of parents. This can be accomplished by preparing questionnaires to be sent home to the parents or through group meetings or interviews held at home or in school.

Some appropriate goals for a quality parent involvement program might include: (a) to aid parents in becoming effective teachers of their children; (b) to aid parents in understanding and supporting the school's educational program; (c) to help parents improve their ability to control their lives and those of their handicapped children; (d) to improve parent's self-concepts; and (e) to improve parent-to-parent relationships within the involvement group.

Develop Program Objectives

When general program goals have been determined by parents and staff, specific program objectives can be developed. These objectives, like the goals, should be mutually determined by parents and staff and represent their interests and needs.

An objective, according to Mager (1962), is simply a precisely phrased statement of what is to be achieved. As such, it makes it possible to determine whether a program has accomplished what it set out to do. Mager (1962) lists three characteristics of an effective instructional objective:

1. It is a statement that identifies in observable and measurable terms the behavioral act.
2. The statement specifies conditions under which the behavior is to occur.
3. The statement defines the criterion of acceptable performance.

An example of an objective used in the Precise Early Education for Children with Handicaps (PEECH) Project's parent involvement program that will help to illustrate Mager's principles is that by the end of the school year, at least 80% of parents who have attended discussion groups will be able to identify three alternate procedures for dealing with their child's tantrum behavior.

Develop an Activity Plan for Reaching Program Objectives

When program goals and objectives have been developed, the next step is to design activities to meet these goals and objectives. These activities should be organized into a comprehensive plan for meeting goals.

When designing activities, there are several general considerations to keep in mind. These include:

1. Decide how people will participate in an activity.
2. Prepare the environment for the activity.
3. Be certain that every detail of the activity is carefully planned, including what will be done, how it will be done, who will be responsible, and how much time will be needed.

The following is an example of a sample parent involvement activity used in the PEECH Project.

Topic   Dealing with behavioral problems.

Goal   To familiarize parents with child management techniques for dealing with problem behaviors exhibited by their children at home and at school.

Objectives Parents will be able to name and discuss five techniques for managing inappropriate child behaviors at home and in school. When given a card designating a problem behavior, each parent will be able to describe and role play an appropriate management technique.

Instructional Procedures

1. Introductory lecture given by teacher on techniques for working with children with behavior management problems.
2. Videotape of the teacher illustrating each of the following procedures for managing inappropriate child behavior:
   a. Pinpointing the problem behavior.
   b. Collecting a baseline on behavior.
   c. Using consistent intervention procedures like active ignoring, positive reinforcement for appropriate behaviors, time-out from positive reinforcement, modeling appropriate behaviors, and, when necessary, establishing a token economy system.
   d. Maintaining the appropriate behavior.
   e. Enhancing generalization of appropriate behaviors to other settings.
3. Role-playing activities. Parents working in small groups will stimulate techniques for managing inappropriate behavior.
4. Wrap-up discussion, summary, and completing of evaluation forms.

Develop an Evaluation Plan

The final step in planning a parent involvement program involves using methods to determine whether or not program goals have been accomplished. When one considers all the time and effort that are involved in planning and implementing a good program, it is important to determine whether the program's goals and objectives have been achieved. This information is invaluable in helping to make future program decisions.

As mentioned earlier, there are several strategies for evaluating a parent involvement program. Parents can fill out questionnaires at the end of each activity and at the end of the year. Questions on these forms can relate to the effectiveness of the presentation, the relevance of the content, the usefulness of discussions or perhaps the effectiveness of the instructional materials and audiovisual aids that were employed.

Participating in informal discussions is another way for parents to aid in evaluation. They may also participate in structured interviews that are designed to gather specific information such as which ideas or techniques discussed in small group sessions do the parents find most useful in the home.

Consider Parents as Full Participating Members of the Educational Team

Recent laws, especially PL 94-142, have made the involvement of parents in the decision-making process mandatory. Parents are a much needed source of information to every member of the multidisciplinary team, and therefore their position on the team is unique. The contributions of parents to these deliberations should be considered priority information and respected; this is a main prerequisite for working successfully with children.

It is a well accepted fact that working with parents involves more than attending conferences and writing reports. Rather, it should be a long-term working relationship that encourages confidence and freedom to discuss problems and plans pertaining to the child and the family.

Teachers should expect some disagreement in working with parents. Generally, these differences arise because of different values or different views on other factors relative to programming. It is a sound idea for teachers to determine parental expectations early in the program and to work out any differences. As with any good relationship, compromise is often essential.

Share All Relevant Information with Parents

Federal and state legislation supports the rights of parents to information concerning their child. Moreover, it seems a matter of common sense that such information be made available to parents, since they must make the critical decisions about their child's future. Certainly professionals recognize the need for complete information to make intelligent educational decisions, and it is unrealistic to expect parents to make similar decisions with limited information.

Professionals also have responsibility for interpreting the information in terms parents will understand. This is particularly important in view of the fact that parents will need to work with a new set of professionals sometime in the future, and may be called upon to recall accurately what has been explained to them about their child in the past.

Build on the Parents' Strengths

Of all the considerations in planning that have been mentioned, building on parents' strengths is perhaps the most important. Parents, like their children, have different strengths and weaknesses. It is incumbent upon professionals to identify the positive aspects of parents and build on these as the program is developed.

Programs for Parents of Handicapped Children

Scattered throughout the special education literature are descriptions of programs that have successfully involved parents in the education of their handicapped children. The overwhelming majority of the well-developed parent involvement programs have been developed for parents of handicapped infants and preschool-aged children. This section briefly reviews some of the more prominent parent involvement programs, grouping them into two categories: (*a*) home-based programs; and (*b*) school- or center-based programs.

Home-Based Programs

The first major type of parent involvement program is that which is based in the home. Typically, in these programs parents are trained by professionals—parent educators, home teachers, or home visitors—to provide direct instruction to their child. Home-based programs offer several advantages, including the facts that: (*a*) the school is extending to the home; (*b*) parents will directly work with their child; (*c*) programs can be individualized more easily to meet the needs of each family; and (*d*) the program is beneficial to all family members.

A typical example of a home-based program is the Portage Project. The major intent of the Portage approach is to train parents to use behavior modification techniques with their children; that is, parents are trained to arrange contingencies for effective learning and to observe and record behaviors. Instruction of parents takes place in the home and is conducted by teachers trained in an applied behavior analysis of child development and in assessment techniques. The children range in age from birth to 6 years and have been diagnosed as behavior problems, emotionally disturbed, mentally retarded, physically handicapped, or economically deprived.

When a child is referred to the project, a teacher visits the home to conduct an assessment to determine whether the child is eligible for the program. After the initial assessment, the teacher visits the home each week with materials needed to carry out the teaching activities. The heart of the teaching program is the Curriculum Guide (Shearer, Billingsley, Frohman, Hilliard, Johnson & Shearer, 1970), which consists of: (*a*) a developmental sequence checklist with 450 behaviors from birth to 5 years of age in five developmental areas—cognitive, language, self-help, motor, and socialization; and (*b*) a set of curriculum cards that match each of the behaviors on the checklist. The checklist is used to determine the child's entry and subsequent progress throughout the program. In teaching sessions the teacher prescribes a behavior from the checklist that is to be achieved by the child within a week. As the parent gains experience and confidence in teaching and in recording the child's progress, the teacher increases the number of behaviors to be taught each week.

The teaching of a new task is first demonstrated by the teacher who then observes the parent working with the child. The teacher uses prompts, primes, and fading methods to help sharpen the parent's teaching skills. As an aid, an activity chart, which describes the goal to be achieved and how often the skill is to be reinforced, is left with the parent each week. The parent is then instructed to record on the chart the child's behavior each day for each prescription. When the teacher returns the following week, she or he checks the child's progress on the previous week's activity and discusses the findings with the parent, always reinforcing both parent and child for their efforts.

Evaluation of Portage rests on a pretest–posttest design and is based on the Developmental Profile and the Catell Infant Intelligence Scale as well as on other specific skills, including mother–child interaction and interaction and cooperation skills obtained through observation. Significant results have been reported in all of these areas.

Another home-based program was reported by Fraiberg, Smith, and Adelson (1969) at the University of Michigan. This program, serving blind infants, consisted of home visits made by clinical psychologists twice monthly to work with mother and child. Since the infants were blind, mothers were trained to develop a "tactile–auditory" language system that would permit interaction between infant and mother. Areas emphasized in working with the mothers included interpersonal response, prehension, object discovery, and locomotion. Although no formal evaluation of child progress was reported, parental response to the program was very positive.

Santostefano and Stayton (1967) reported on a home-based project in Massachusetts designed to train mothers to work with severely to moderately retarded children with mean chronological ages of 5 to 6.

Mothers who volunteered for the program were trained for 4 months in monthly meetings to use certain materials for 10 to 20 minutes daily and to keep a brief daily record. Materials consisted of black and white plywood cutouts of geometric shapes which, over the course of the program, the mother arranged in increasingly difficult combinations. The child responded to each task by removing a predetermined cutout. Using modeling and physical guidance, mothers were able to significantly increase their child's intelligence (as measured by the Stanford–Binet) over a comparable group of untreated control children.

Patt (1969) reported on a home-based program for the Spanish-speaking parents of blind–deaf children who were 2 years of age. A specially trained bilingual teacher visited each family once or twice a week to train parents to relate to their uniquely handicapped children. Mothers learned to provide clear physical signals to their deaf–blind children expressing pleasure by handling and caressing and disapproval by a firm handgrasp or a slap. Over a 1½-year period, mothers were successfully trained to teach their children to master such functional activities as taking solid food, asking for a drink, finding a toy, and learning to walk.

Another home-based program, the Telstar Project in Alpena, Michigan, serves moderately to severely handicapped children, from birth to 6 years. The intent of this project is to place one handicapped child with a normal child in a day-care home, which provides for the care of both. The children are placed in satellite homes, located near their usual place of residence, where a satellite worker agrees to take one nonhandicapped child in the home with the handicapped child and to participate in 90% of the required in-service training activities, which are based on the curriculum entitled *Meyer Children's Rehabilitation Institute Teaching Program for Young Child*, (1974). The curriculum, developed at Meyer Children's Rehabilitation Institute, emphasizes such areas as self-care, body usage, and language development. Each child is evaluated on a bimonthly basis by project staff.

A final home-based project reviewed here uses a multifaceted approach to parent training. This program, the Comprehensive Training Program: Infant and Young Cerebral Palsied Children, is located in Milwaukee, Wisconsin, and is designed to help cerebral palsied children from birth to 3 years old to develop skills in speech and language through direct intervention and intense parent participation. One area of emphasis is on prespeech development, which includes sucking, swallowing, and biting skills. Emphasis is also placed on experiential development of the child, since the opportunity for cerebral palsied children to learn by exploring their environment is limited.

Family participation begins in this program by asking parents to complete questionnaires designed to survey their knowledge about cerebral palsy, as well as their needs and fears. There are six aspects to the program, including: (a) active parent participation in the child's training program; (b) individual family counseling; (c) group conferences; (d) monthly evening meetings; (e) Saturday morning meetings called family affairs; and (f) parent advisory subcommittees. During the "Saturday morning affairs," parents and other adults are provided with demonstrations of specific techniques for working with cerebral palsied children.

School- and Center-Based Programs

The second major type of parent involvement program involves parents in their handicapped child's school or center. These include programs in community preschool, Head Start, day-care, kindergarten, or public school settings. Parent participation in schools offers a number of advantages. First, it expands the teacher's available human resources, thus permitting a more personalized and individualized program. Second, it brings about closer and more sustained contact between parents and teachers, which makes for a better parent program. And third, when parents work in the classroom it enables them to make a direct contribution to their child's progress.

A typical example of a school-based parent involvement program was developed at the University of Southern California (Bolen, 1973). The noncategorical program is designed to train parents to work with severely handicapped preschool children in the classroom setting. Training emphasizes the development of parent competencies in behavior modification principles, curriculum development, teaching competencies, and information on continuing educational programming. Data on program effects have not as yet been reported.

The University of Washington Child Development and Mental Retardation Center involves parents in the infant program segment of its preschool program (Hayden, 1975). In this program, parents are trained to stimulate their handicapped infants, to help them attend to sound, and to establish eye contact. This program offers parents an opportunity to work with their infants under teacher supervision right in the classroom.

The Preschooler's Workshop in Garden City, New York (Bloch, 1974), offers an individualized approach to working with parents of emotionally impaired preschool children. Parents participate in the initial assessment of their child's functioning and help in planning the nature of their involvement in the educational therapy of their child. One aspect of the program includes using mothers as classroom aides. Various other parent services include a traditional child-focused counseling service, a mother's discussion group, a parent group focusing on relations and feelings, and a home study program.

Another program promoting parent involvement in the classroom is the therapeutic preschool (Woodside, 1975), a community-based program affiliated with the University of North Carolina at Chapel Hill. This program, based on a psychoeducational model, contracts with parents to make weekly visits to the classroom for 1 hour, during which time teachers illustrate the use of behavior management techniques. Other supportive interventions in the parent program include assisting parents in contacting social welfare or public health agencies, arranging transportation, arranging speech therapy for the children, arranging therapy for personal problems, and making some home visits.

The Regional Intervention Program (RIP) in Nashville, Tennessee (Wiegernik & Parrish, 1975), uses parents to provide direct service in the classroom to their developmentally disabled and behaviorally disordered preschool children. This program is designed around three service modules implemented primarily by parents under the direction of professionals. First, the intake module is designed to familiarize families with the RIP approach. Second, the individual tutoring module trains parents to provide one-to-one classroom instruction in functional speech and adaptive behavior to their child. And third, the generalized training module aids parents in implementing child management procedures in several settings. Once parents demonstrate competence in the skills taught in each module, they serve as assistants in the module and thus train other parents.

A final example of a center-based parent involvement program is the PEECH (Precise Early Education for Children with Handicaps) approach, which serves parents of multiple handicapped children and which is under the direction of Merle B. Karnes at the University of Illinois. The PEECH approach to parent involvement is structured around the ATSEM (Karnes et al., 1972) model for parent education. ATSEM derives its label from the initials that stand for the five main areas: (A)cquaint, (T)each, (S)upport, (E)xpand, and (M)aintain.

During the "Acquaint" phase, teachers are educated in the process of involving the family member in activities for maximizing the growth of the child, both at home and at school. The end of the "Acquaint" phase is signaled when professionals working with the family are able to assure the family's commitment in working to maximize their child's growth. The attainment of this goal is often subtly indicated.

During the "Teach" phase, parents learn a set of techniques, skills, and attitudes that aid them in teaching their child new knowledge and behaviors. These skills are often attained by providing parents with concrete tasks to teach the child until the parent learns how to teach concepts without help. Parents are considered to have reached the end of the "Teach" phase when they have demonstrated the ability to approach the child and teach him or her new concepts and ideas with little direction from others. Since there are considerable individual differences among parents with regard to their ability to teach children, the goals of the "Teach" process differ.

The third phase of the model is "Support." It is defined as that time during which the family member requires special support of an emotional, social, or economic nature. During this phase, teachers may help parents learn how to obtain specialized services for their child, to finish high school, to seek additional help from Aid to Dependent Children, or perhaps to seek help from a mental health facility. Regardless of the parents' needs, teachers are encouraged to help parents seek individualized help during this phase. Termination of the "Support" phase occurs when the family indicates they can function independently of additional supportive help.

The "Expand" stage of the model is entered when the parents feel secure emotionally and socially and are able to expand their horizons with the child. Such growth may be indicated when the parent takes the child into the supermarket for the first time without fearing that the child will throw a temper tantrum or in some other way embarrass the family member. Termination of the "Expand" phase of the model is difficult to define because theoretically a parent should never cease to attempt to expand the child's development of knowledge. Yet, once a family demonstrates through day-to-day behavior that they consistently expand the child's knowledge and skills, it seem appropriate to go on to procedures that will maintain such behavior.

The "Maintain" phase of the model is multifaceted. Some individuals who reach this phase have made considerable progress in working with their child, but require continued reinforcement to maintain this higher level of functioning. Another aspect of the "Maintain" phase is that it is often used to help parents "Acquaint" other parents with the program. It would seem that providing family members with the opportunity to help others understand the program is one way of assisting the *helping* person learn and reinforce previous learnings. For example, if a parent has difficulty accepting fully the handicap of his or her child, then explicating this feeling to a newly entering parent may help parents to clarify their own feelings.

In summary, the ATSEM model is a process-oriented model that focuses on bringing parents into contact with the PEECH Project and then involving them actively in the program. At present, the ATSEM model is being disseminated nationwide as part of the PEECH approach.

There are, of course, other school- and home-based programs for parents of handicapped children too numerous to review here. Other sources reviewing such programs include Karnes and Lee, 1978; Karnes and Teska, 1975; and Karnes and Zehrbach, 1977.

Conclusions

Based on the concepts, guidelines, and strategies reviewed in this chapter, the following recommendations concerning parent involvement in programs for their handicapped children seem warranted:

1. Programs for handicapped children cannot be considered complete unless parents are actively involved in the education of their children.
2. Flexibility and individualization of parent involvement are of the utmost importance. Because parents, like children, are different, and their understanding and acceptance of their children differ, so does their readiness to involve themselves in the educational program of the child. Some parents may be ready to participate in directly teaching their children, while others are able only to help prepare program newsletters. As a result, professionals must be prepared to involve parents in different phases of the program.
3. Parents deserve a voice in determining their involvement in their child's program.
4. Parents have a right to expect professionals to provide them with training and information that will enable them to determine the handicapped child's stage of development. It is only then that parents can become active participants in developing, implementing, and assessing an individualized educational program for their child.
5. A needs assessment should be conducted to determine the content of an individual parent's involvement program. Such an assessment should examine both parental and program needs.
6. Research suggests that directly involving parents in the education of their handicapped child can have a positive effect on children in the family—handicapped and nonhandicapped alike.

7. Training of parents of handicapped children should ultimately focus on increasing their direct teaching skills with their children. Research has shown this to be the most profitable interaction for the child.
8. To work successfully with parents of the handicapped, teachers must develop skills not normally emphasized in their preservice training. Therefore, practicing teachers should receive skilled-oriented in-service training provided in the schools preferably by parent educators with experience in developing home- and school-based parent involvement programs.

As mentioned earlier, the question is no longer whether parents should be involved in programs for their handicapped children, but rather how such involvement should be facilitated. It is the opinion of these authors that the monumental task of providing training to parents of the handicapped must be approached with patience and with constant attention to quality of effort.

References

Abraham, W. *Parent talk*. Scottsdale, Ariz.: Sunshine Press, 1974.

Baroff, G. *Mental retardation: Nature, cause and management*. Washington, D.C.: Hemisphere Publishing, 1974.

Becker, W. C. *Parents are teachers: A child management program*. Champaign, Ill.: Research Press, 1971.

Becker, W. C., & Becker, J. W. *Successful parenthood*. Champaign, Ill.: Research Press, 1974.

Berkowitz, B., & Graziano, A. Training parents as behavior therapists: A Review. *Behavior Research and Theory*, 1972, 10, 297–317.

Bloch, J. *Developing early intervention programs for emotionally handicapped children*. New York: New York University, 1974. (ERIC Document Reproduction Service No. ED 104 107).

Bolen, J. M. *Noncategorical preschool model program*. Los Angeles: University of Southern California, Instructional Materials Center for Special Education, 1973.

Brofenbrenner, U. *A report on longitudinal evaluations of preschool programs. Is early intervention effective?* (Vol. 2). Washington, D.C.: U.S. Department of Health, Education and Welfare, 1974.

Bryant, J. Parent–child relationships: Their effect on rehabilitation. *Journal of Learning Disabilities*, 1971, 4(6), 40–44.

Fraiberg, S., Smith, N., & Adelson, E. An educational program for blind infants. *Journal of Special Education*, 1969, 3, 121–140.

Fredericks, H. D., Baldwin, V., & Grove, D. A home-center parent training model. In J. Grimm (Ed.), *Training parents to teach: Four models*. Chapel Hill, N.C.: Technical Assistance Development Systems, 1974.

Gardner, H. *The arts of human development*. New York: Wiley, 1973.

Gordon, I. J., Greenwood, G. E., Ware, W. B., & Olmsted, P. P. *The Florida parent education follow through program.* Gainesville: Institute for Development of Human Resources, University of Florida and the Florida Educational Research and Development Council, 1974.

Gray, S. W., & Klaus, R. A. The early training project: The seventh-year report. *Child Development,* 1970, *41,* 909–924.

Graziano, A. M. *Programmed therapy: The development of group behavior approaches to severely disturbed children.* New York: Pergamon Press, 1971.

Hartup, W. W. Peer interaction and social organization. In P. Mussen (Ed.), *Carmichael's manual of child psychology* (Vol. 2). New York: Wiley, 1970.

Hayden, A. H. A center-based parent training model. In J. Grimm (Ed.), *Training parents to teach: Four models.* Chapel Hill: University of North Carolina, 1975.

Karnes, M. B., & Lee, R. C. *Early childhood: What research and experience say to the teacher of exceptional children.* Reston, Va.: Council for Exceptional Children, 1978.

Karnes, M. B., & Teska, J. A. Children's response to intervention program. In J. J. Gallagher (Ed.), *The application of child development research to exceptional children.* Reston, Va.: Council for Exceptional Children, 1975.

Karnes, M. B., Teska, J. A., Hodgins, A. S., & Badger, E. D. Educational intervention at home by mothers of disadvantaged infants. *Child Development.* December 1970, *41,* 925–935.

Karnes, M. B., & Zehrbach, R. R. Alternative models for delivering services to young handicapped children. In J. B. Jordan, A. H. Hayden, M. B. Karnes, & M. W. Wood (Eds.), *Early childhood education for exceptional children.* Reston, Va.: Council for Exceptional Children, 1977.

Karnes, M. B., Zehrbach, R. R., & Teska, J. A. Involving families of handicapped children. *Theory into Practice,* June 1972, *11,* 150–156.

Keith, R. The feelings and behavior of parents of handicapped children. *Developmental medicine and child nemology,* 1973, *15,* 524–527.

Kessler, J. *Psychopathology of children.* Englewood Cliffs, N.J.: Prentice-Hall, 1966.

Kroth, R. Facilitating educational progress by improving parent conferences. In E. Meyer, G. Vergason, & R. Whelan (Eds.), *Alternatives for teaching exceptional children.* Denver: Love Publishing, 1975.

Lillie, D. Dimensions in parent programs: An overview. In J. Grimm (Ed.), *Training parents to teach: Four models.* Chapel Hill, N.C.: Technical Assistance Development System, 1974.

Mager, R. F. *Preparing instructional objectives.* San Francisco: Fearon Publishers, 1962.

Marholin, D., Siegel, L., & Phillips, D. *Treatment and transfer: A search for empirical procedures.* Paper submitted to *Psychological Bulletin,* 1975.

Meyers children's rehabilitation institute teaching program for young children No. 88, Omaha, Nebraska: Meyer Children's Rehabilitation Institute, 1974. (Available from the Council for Exceptional Children, 1920 Association Drive, Reston, Virginia).

Noland, J. D., & Pence, C. Operant conditioning principles in the treatment of a selectively mute child. *Journal of Consulting and Clinical Psychology,* 1970, *35,* 265–268.

O'Dell, S. Training parents in behavior modification: A Review. *Psychological Bulletin,* 1974, *81*(7), 418–433.

Patt, E. *Effects of pre-school service for deaf blind children.* Paper presented at Special Study Institute, San Francisco State College, June 1969.

Patterson, G. R. Behavioral intervention procedures in the classroom and in the home. In A. E. Bergin & S. L. Garfield (Eds.), *Handbook of psychotherapy and behavior change.* New York: John Wiley, 1971.

Shearer, D., Billingsley, J., Frohman, S., Hilliard, J., Johnson, F., & Shearer, M. *Developmental sequential checklist* (The Portage Project, No. 12). Unpublished manuscript, Cooperative Educational Agency, Portage, Wisconsin, 1970.

Shearer, M., & Shearer, D. The Portage Project: A model for early childhood education. *Exceptional Children*, 1972, *39*, 210–217.

Stantostefano, S., & Stayton, S. Training the preschool retarded child in focusing attention: A program for parents. *American Journal of Psychiatry*, 1967, *37*, 732–743.

Stokes, T., & Baer, D. M. An implicit technology of generalization. *Journal of Applied Behavior Analysis*, 1978, *11*, 590–620.

Straughan, J. H. Treatment with child and mother in the playroom. *Behavior Research and Therapy*, 1964, *2*, 37–41.

Wagner, M. K. Parent therapists: An operant conditioning model. *Mental Hygiene*, 1968, *52*, 452–455.

Wahler, R. G. Oppositional children: A quest for parental reinforcement control. *Journal of Applied Behavior Analysis*, 1969, *2*, 159–239.

Walder, L. O., Cohen, S. I., Daston, P. G., Breiter, D. E., & Hirsch, I. S. *Behavior therapy of children through their parents*. Paper presented at the annual meeting of the American Psychological Association, Washington, D.C., April 1967.

Weikart, D. P., & Lambie, D. Z. Ypsilanti-Carnegie Infant Education Project. In J. Hellmuth (Ed.), *Disadvantaged child 3—compensatory education: A national debate*. New York: Bruner Mazel, 1970.

Wiegernik, R., & Parrish, U. A parent-implemented preschool program. In J. Grimm (Ed.), *Training parents to teach: Four models*. Chapel Hill: University of North Carolina, 1975.

Williams, C. D. The elimination of tantrum behavior by extinction procedures. *Journal of Abnormal Social Psychology*, 1959, *59*, 269.

Woodside, R. U. *The therapeutic preschool: A service research and demonstration project*. Paper presented at the International Federation of Learning Disabilities, Belgium, January 1975.

Chapter 10

Working with Parents of Preschoolers

JOSEPH LAPIDES

The premises of this chapter are that parental involvement in the education of their children is a lifetime process that begins before the onset of formal education and continues beyond it; that the child is viewed as the same learner in both the school setting and at home, despite differences in content and response; that the parent is an instructional ally in the development of learning activities; and that if children are to reach their fullest potential, there must be opportunity for parents to influence the character of the programs affecting the development of their children. The reader will be provided with rational, empirical data and with descriptions of model preschool programs that involved parents of preschoolers, based on the author's experiences with Head Start families.

In primitive societies, as well as in more traditional cultures of the Far and Middle East, childrearing responsibilities are shared by large extended family groups. Children are the responsibility of grandparents, aunts, uncles, and cousins as much as of their own parents. Throughout the early part of this century, close family groups shared the burdens and joys of childrearing in America as well. But, today, parents function almost entirely alone until schools and other community agencies enter the scene.

It is the contention of Segal and Yahraes (1978), that "children today find considerably fewer sources of affection, guidance and support in

227

HANDBOOK ON
PARENT EDUCATION

the family than ever before. For the typical child, it is either from parents or from no one that he or she will receive psychological nurture [p. 168]." As a result, parenting classes for parents of preschoolers become increasingly crucial alternatives to the isolation of nuclear families.

Placing children in preschool programs helps the mother, in particular, to resolve her most typical conflict—wanting to be a good mother, yet craving time and opportunity to be a person in her own right. By participating in such a program the mother does not give up her parental responsibility, but shares it with teachers and with other mothers who help her in the childrearing process.

The major areas of concern in such programs are: direct parental involvement in decision making in program planning and operations; parental participation in educational and other program activities as volunteers, observers, or paid employees (e.g., Head Start); and parents working with their own children in cooperation with professional staff (e.g., Home Start).

The Head Start program was conceived as providing comprehensive educational, health, and social services to low-income children. It would do this in the context of the child's family, and would emphasize parent involvement and participation in all aspects of the program. Over 5 million children have been served by Head Start since 1965. There are currently approximately 400,000 children in over 1400 Head Start centers in America—with at least an equal number of parents. The program thus provides an effective model for working with parents of preschoolers.

Research supported by Head Start suggests that parent involvement does sustain developmental gains. Weickert and Lambie (1969) reported that children whose preschool experience had included a parent intervention component made significantly higher gains than those who attended preschools without this element. Among children whose preschool experience has *not* included parent involvement, experience in a center-based program did not produce additional gains. Children who had experienced no parent intervention either in preschool or school, but who spent a full day in kindergarten or in a special program, fell six IQ points. No such drop was seen in children who were enrolled in half-day kindergarten programs or by children whose parents participated in a biweekly intervention program.

Other findings suggest that although parent involvement in later preschool years does not produce large gains in cognitive development, it enhances the impact of the regular preschool program. In other words, parent involvement with a preschool classroom program is better than just a preschool classroom program. In contrast, absence of parent involvement in the preschool program reduces the impact of the early childhood education program (Schweinhart & Weikart, 1977).

Taking parents as decision makers and parents as childrearers as the two fundamental forces in the relationship of parents in early childhood education programs, working with parents in a preschool setting can be discussed in terms of a four-fold process: (*a*) direct involvement in decision making in program planning and operation; (*b*) participation in classroom and other program activities as volunteer observers or paid employees; (*c*) organizing activities in the areas of child management, child development, and parent effectiveness; and (*d*) working with their own children in cooperation with professional staff.

Decision Making

Parental involvement in programmatic decision-making roles has been rooted in social and political origins. One feature of the civil rights movement was bitter and articulate criticism of the public schools, especially in urban areas. This criticism focused upon the lack of relationship between the educational experiences offered by the schools and the local community's cultural experiences and needs, and created demands for community control over educational policy and decision making in the schools and other institutions that serve the local community. In addition, it was increasingly believed that people would not be committed to decisions in which they had no input and that the processes of considering information, decision making, and implementation are in themselves educational and aid in developing leadership skills.

Kinds of parent involvement depend on the program goals, on the developmental needs of children, on specific ethnic and cultural factors, and on the sociopolitical situation. In parent cooperative schools, for example, parents play various roles at different times. They are responsible for the administration of the school, they may be required to participate regularly as teacher assistants in the classroom, or to implement educational activities relating to all of the spheres of child development, school administration, and early childhood education activity.

What Do Parents as Decision Makers Do in an Early Childhood Education Program?

Parents and staff work together in determining the goals of the program and planning the day-to-day activities of their children. Parents contribute to this process knowledge of their own children's needs while the professional staff contributes its knowledge and experience about children, learning, and program operations, and assists the parents by offering alternatives from which the parents may choose. Parents in early childhood education programs are also active in community needs assessment, hiring of staff, and planning of health and nutrition services.

Involving parents as decision makers is fundamental in the Head Start program. A recent study by Stubbs, Godley, and Alexander done for Associate Control, Research, and Analysis (1978), which looked at opportunities for parent involvement in a nationally representative sample of Head Start programs, found that ideas and suggestions of parents were reflected in the work plans of 87% of the programs; in 58% of the programs parents helped conduct a community needs assessment; and in 80% parents assisted in hiring staff. Most programs (88%) reported that the parents helped in such functions as determining parent volunteer activities, deciding how parents' activity funds would be used, and selecting sites for field trips.

It is understandable that many parents may benefit from some training and support as they begin to function as advisers and decision makers. The staff of an early childhood education program should use its knowledge and training to help parents in the decision-making process. Intervention strategies that increase parents' decision-making effectiveness include counseling and outcome rehearsal. Moreover, parents must see concrete results from their efforts, or they will feel ineffective and lose interest.

Parent Participation in Classroom and Other Program Activities as Volunteers, Observers, or Paid Employees

Parent volunteering in early childhood education (ECE) programs includes assisting with children in the classroom, such as in the woodworking area, or playing a musical instrument; telling stories; accompanying children on field trips or to the dentist or physician; helping to prepare materials for activities; photographing important events. Volunteers can help at home by assuming administrative and support functions such as telephoning other parents for meetings, washing and repairing doll clothes, making curtains, babysitting for other parents who attend meetings, repairing books, toys, and equipment, and collecting and saving materials for use in the preschool program. This is by no means a complete list of activities.

The parents' interest in their own contribution to their child's education, and the positive experience gained by enhancing it, may be sufficient to maintain high levels of participation. However, in a successful program the motivation of parents to participate will be strengthened by feedback from the program staff about the progress of their child. Another incentive, aside from the child development aspect, is the possibility for developing new social relationships. Participation for this reason is especially important to single parents—the largest consumers of preschool programs. Lapides (1976) attributes an 80% attendance record to programs where the teacher showed persistent interest in having parents come to the class and work with her.

Attendance at meetings can be stimulated by teachers visiting homes to report events of missed meetings; or by participating mothers forming a support group that sustains group effort over time.

In most preschool settings parent volunteers make the difference that permits children to try out new activities—to paint when others play with blocks, to sing a new song, to converse. Working together with other children, and with other parents and teachers, parents acquire a common body of understandings and beliefs about child development that they can continually test in practice, enhancing their parenting skills.

Both parents and children gain with the utilization of parents in volunteer or paid staff positions. Parents discover a psychological closeness and intimacy like that in large extended families or kinship groups. Teachers' sensitivity to individual parents' attitudes, cognizance of their own input, as well as recognition of the importance of volunteer services, can facilitate this process. Thus, some of the sharpness of isolation and loneliness experienced by young nuclear families is ameliorated or transformed into positive action.

Activities for Parents in the Areas of Child Management, Child Development, and Parent Effectiveness

The generalization may be reiterated that parents remain the *primary* influences on their children's intellectual and emotional development. The paramount responsibility of early childhood education programs is to help parents to recognize this as a fact of life, and to provide basic assistance so that parents can comfortably function in this role long after the child leaves the early childhood education program. Over time, parents influence the child's use of mass media, social relationships, exposure to social/cultural institutions, to work and professions, and to much of the child's total experiences both inside and outside the home.

If childrearing practices differ from family to family and from culture to culture, this is compounded in America where parental care varies from the extremes of parental neglect and abuse to overinvolvement. The truth is that there is little preparation for the difficult tasks of parenting except by imitating our own parents' childrearing practices.

A further difficulty is that parents are besieged with advice and opinion from a wide variety of "experts" ranging from other parents, mothers-in-law, teachers, newspaper columnists, and the media, to national and international child development specialists.

It comes as no surprise that in the face of such authority parents feel insecure about their ability to rear their children. The advantage of effective parent education programs, however, is the extent to which they encourage parents to select the techniques that feel "right" to them. Programs must demonstrate awareness that parents are the prime educators of their children—that they possess individualized knowledge about their children and that they alone have the daily contact for making decisions concerning their children's well-being. Parents of children in preschool programs will gain the most from training sessions in which they are active participants and which provide them with materials that seem relevant to their daily lives and their own experiences.

In working with parents it should be borne in mind that adults must be viewed as being responsible, self-directed, and independent. They respond best in learning situations that allow them to explore alternatives and to test out the concepts in terms of their feelings and past experiences. Preschool programs will find that work with parents can be most effective in learning situations that include group discussions, case studies, observations and analysis of behavior, role playing, brainstorming, and skill practice. It is imperative that parents be involved in setting the goals for their learning experience.

In order to facilitate the role of parents as the primary educators and developers of their children, Head Start adopted the *Exploring Childhood Program* (Felt, 1973) for parents. (Film and other resource material for this program were developed by the Educational Development Center, Newton, Massachusetts through grants from the National Institute of Mental Health and support from the Office of Education, Department of Health, Education and Welfare.)

Exploring Parenting (Bruce, 1978) projected five goals for parents: (*a*) get to know yourself better; (*b*) learn more about children; (*c*) examine various approaches to childrearing; (*d*) recognize and improve your own parenting skills; and (*e*) examine how society influences families and children. The program was designed with the assumption that parents already possess a wealth of experiences, knowledge, and skills, and it addresses itself to enhancing existing competencies through a variety of activities.

The program is organized as a series of 20 3-hour sessions constructed to ensure the active involvement of parents. The sessions offer information and provide for exploration of personal values, feelings, and the testing of notions about parenting.

Sessions 1–4 explore the everyday problems in childrearing and introduce the learning processes that will be utilized throughout the program.

Session 5 introduces the concept of human development and the patterns children follow in growing and learning.

Session 6 focuses on understanding and responding to children who have special needs because of developmental differences or disabilities.

Session 7 examines play, its importance in people's lives, how it changes with maturity, and how parents can facilitate children's play.

Sessions 8 and 9 examine children's art, emphasizing what art means to a child, how to respond and support children's artistic expressions, how to look at children's art as indicators of development, temperament, and style.

Sessions 10–12 provide parents with opportunities to explore difficulties in dealing with emotions. The parents look at how reactions to strong feelings and coping mechanisms change over time and explore different ways in which children and adults deal with these feelings.

Session 13 helps parents to explore and understand their values and communicate them to their children.

Session 14 offers parents the opportunity to think about discipline so as to facilitate the imparting of values and shaping children's behaviors.

Session 15 provides parents with a forum for sharing their family with others through reports of mini-histories of their families, of the families they grew up in, and the families they are raising.

Session 16 examines some of the problems and possibilities for personal development encountered by the single parent.

Session 17 focuses on how adults and children react to and cope with changes and problems in their lives.

Session 18 examines stress-inducing factors in family relationships, ways in which stress interferes with parenting and care giving, and the support processes that can help parents cope with stress in their lives.

Session 19 provides information on contributing factors to accidents in the home and helps parents develop steps to prevent accidents and increase safety in the home.

Session 20 examines expectations that people outside of the family have for children and how these expectations affect the child and the family.

Exploring Parenting (Bruce, 1978) utilizes a multimedia approach, that is, it uses films, records, and printed materials. A preliminary report on the impact of this program indicates that there is enthusiastic acceptance of the training, and many users recommend that it be made available to all parents. *Exploring Parenting* is by no means the only training program for parents. Early childhood education programs can arrange for many derivations of parent effectiveness training.

Parent Conferences and Home Visits

The partnership between parents and teacher/workers that develops around improving the children's world is further enhanced through parent conferences and home visits by the teacher.

Through the parent conference, teachers and parents get together in pursuit of the same goals; that is, the best possible program for the child and the creation of a partnership to enhance the child's world. It is the time for talking together about the child. Teachers are provided the opportunity to share with the parents their observations of the child, report the child's accomplishments, ask questions and clarify issues; and parents can share their knowledge and experience of the child, respond to questions, and likewise clarify issues. If parents of preschoolers are hard to get along with or difficult, it is often because they are insecure. When workers understand this, they can—again through the conference—help by being friendly and nurturing the parent, just as they would with a "difficult child."

In the conference parents learn from their children's teacher what the child enjoys doing most among activities such as painting, singing, block building, digging, collecting, being with adults, being with children, being read to, doll play, dressing, clowning, or dealing with new experiences. Knowing that their only child hits, kicks, bites, scratches, or day dreams—or loses appetite when confronted with disappointment—can give parents valuable insight and a realistic perspective on the child's unique pattern of development. The converse is true as well: Teachers who get important feedback from parents about how the child reacts to anxiety, disappointment, or conflict will be in a better position to plan and assist in the coping processes of the children in their preschool program. Parents and teachers can also report how much guidance children need in accepting limits, new activities, sharing possessions and equipment, sharing adult attention, finishing projects, accepting differences, accepting friendliness and affection, solving problems, accepting criticism, and overcoming fears. The list of information shared is limited only by the imagination of those who share it.

The home visit by the teacher, although similar in content to the parent conference, introduces a highly essential dimension to the partnership and the sharing of information, goals, and objectives. The home is a vital center of human growth and development, and through the home visit the teacher learns to understand the context in which the child lives. At the same time, when they relate to the teacher at home, children learn to sense the depth of the partnership that has developed between their parents and the teacher.

Working with Their Own Children in Cooperation with Professional Staff

Accumulating evidence (documented in this section), suggests the enormous influence that parents have upon the behavior of their children, prticularly on their intellectual and academic achievement, and indicates that programs that teach parents skills in educating their children are effective alternatives for preschool education.

In one reported study (Schweinhart & Weikart, 1977), home visitors engaged parents in the education of their own children as a supplement to a preschool program; subsequently, significant differences were found in mental ability test scores between the control children and those who were involved in the preschool and home visitor programs. Although the differences between the experimental and control groups decreased after the termination of the program, group differences persisted during the first year of elementary school. There was evidence also of vertical diffusion, that is, the younger children in the experimental group families also showed more rapid development.

Gray (1970) contrasted a preschool program with a program that taught mothers to teach their children. The home program showed equal effectiveness in terms of lower cost as well as allowing for vertical diffusion to younger children in the family and some horizontal diffusion in the neighborhood. Gray's results suggest that a home program that teaches a mother to teach her child may be an alternative or a supplement for a preschool program.

In the study by Radin and Weikart (1967), the researchers utilized trained educators to teach parents how to support their child's education in conjunction with half-day preschool programs. The combined programs, after successive improvements and refinements, resulted in IQ gains of up to 30 points in low-IQ children.

Levenstein (1970), who conceptualized books and toys as "verbal interaction stimulus materials," had toy demonstrators use selected materials in home visits with mothers, had mothers use them under the supervision of the demonstrator, and encouraged mothers to use the toys and books that were left in the home. Two- and three-year-old subjects showed a mean IQ gain of approximately 17 points after 32 visits over a 7-month period. Levenstein also discovered that a child's IQ level can be maintained or increased by a reduced number of visits the following year. In previous studies Levenstein relied on professional social workers as toy demonstrators, but in recent studies paraprofessionals were trained for the role without depreciating the effectiveness of the interaction.

The promising results of these parent-based, home-based intervention programs show that working with mothers is an effective method for producing gains in intellectual development that is comparable to child-centered programs.

The major goals of a home-based program are to:

1. Involve parents directly in the full development of their own children.
2. Help strengthen in parents their capacity for facilitating the overall development of their children.
3. Provide children and families with comprehensive child development services for whom a center-based program is not feasible (O'Keefe, 1978, p. 17).

The linchpin of a home-based early childhood program is the home visitor, who visits weekly to assist parents in their parenting role. A typical home visitor makes 60- to 90-minute weekly home visits (A Guide for Planning and Operating Home-Based Child Development

Programs, 1974). They undertake many different activities in the following areas:

NUTRITION

1. Read and evaluate newspaper food ads with mothers to develop a shopping list.
2. Help prepare a snack with mothers and children as a means for increasing knowledge about nutrition.
3. Show mothers how involving children in meal preparation can be a learning experience for the children (e.g., noting colors, sizes, shapes, textures of food, counting eggs, spoons, and other items).
4. Arrange for local resource people (e.g., home economists) to demonstrate the preparation of nourishing but inexpensive meals to small groups of mothers.

HEALTH

1. Help mothers assess the health needs of their children.
2. Arrange first aid and home safety courses for parents and small groups of parents.
3. Provide parents with health information.
4. Show mothers how to keep home health records.
5. Show mothers how to assist and reinforce a child's hygiene activities.
6. Discuss child development issues.
7. Help mothers recognize the innate strengths and capabilities existing within their families and in their children as individuals, and offer ways to encourage those strengths and capabilities to promote mental health.

EDUCATION

1. Help mothers recognize "everyday living experiences" that can be capitalized upon to become effective learning experiences.
2. Encourage mothers and children to use the library and accompany them if needed.
3. Join mothers in reading stories to their children.
4. Identify materials in the home that can be used for toys and games—and for learning.
5. Operate a toy lending library; help mothers and fathers make toys and educational materials for their children.
6. Help parents reinforce their children's positive behavior.

7. Reinforce positive ways in which parents relate to their children.
8. Explain to parents what they are teaching as they involve their children in making beds, washing clothes, planting, repairing, etc.
9. Help parents learn ways of enhancing their children's language development.

Love (1976), who evaluated the home-based program for Head Start, offered evidence that mothers working at home to promote the education and development of their own children can, with the support of a home visitor, elicit outcomes comparable to those attained by children attending a center-based program. It was noted that, as an additional bonus, the mothers encouraged their children to help with household tasks and actively engaged in the education of their children by providing them with books and play things.

Hertz (1977) in his analysis of the impact of selected federal programs concluded that the impact on parent attitudes and behavior in Home Start followed the same lines as in Head Start, but appeared to be more positive and comprehensive.

Until a few generations ago, the educational function of the family was taken for granted. Families were deemed the educators of the young in the ways of the society in which they lived. In the complex, highly specialized society of today, however, the family's educational role has been more obscured, if not ignored. Studies about the relationship between the family and learning and education have focused on how well or poorly families prepare children for the educational system. In this outlook, socialization has been regarded as the family's function, and education as that of the school's. The relationship between the two, and the continuities and discontinuities between them, have been ignored until recently.

There now appears to be renewed recognition of the scope of learning that takes place within the context of the family. Leichter (1974) states:

> The family is an arena in which virtually the entire range of human experience can take place. Warfare, violence, love, tenderness, honesty, deceit, private property, communal sharing, power, manipulation, formal status hierarchies, egalitarian decision making—all can be found within the setting of the family. And so, also a variety of educational encounters, ranging from conscious, systematic instruction to repetitive moment to moment influences on the margins of awareness [p. 175].

There is no simple cause-and-effect relationship within families. Family members learn from each other. What is becoming abundantly clear, however, is that parents need to be involved in the education of their children—at multiple, complex, informal levels—in order to ensure the children's continued development and success.

Future Prospects

American society faces a crucial dilemma in how it views the family's role in the care and development of young children. This conflict stems from the contradiction that exists between a strong belief in the traditional values of motherhood and family-centered childrearing on the one hand, and the real world on the other hand, which precludes an increasing number of parents and families from fully carrying out the childrearing function they once had.

The literature and the media frequently underscore the changes occuring in the American family. Of note is Bronfenbrenner's (1975) report that the majority of mothers of school-aged children, namely 51%, now work. The trend is not confined to women with school-aged children; the proportion of mothers who participate in the labor force and have children under 6 has tripled since 1948; today, one in three mothers with children under 6 is working. More than one-sixth of all children in our country are living in single-parent families. The single parent is usually a woman, the head of an independent family, and she is almost always working full-time. In addition, despite birth control and sex education, the number of teenage parents is increasing.

Even among families that are intact and well off economically, it seems that parents spend less time in activity with their children. Many parents seem to have abdicated their educational responsibility to schools, not because they are irresponsible, but because they do not have time. Activities that once automatically brought parents and children together because of the necessity of physical and economic survival—for example, household industry, apprenticeships, and farming—are no longer a part of family life. Parents now and in the future must make conscious efforts to "spend more time with the kids," if they are in fact to become a vital part of each other's lives.

There are indications that parents will need assistance and specific help in fostering quality parent–child behaviors. Gordon (1977) identified family variables that influence scholastic achievement in children. These variables include whether,

(1) parents see themselves as teachers of their children; (2) talk with them and not at them; (3) they take them to libraries, or the museums or the parks; (4) they sit around the dinner table and share and plan; (5) they listen; (6) they display a child's work on the . . . wall; (7) they themselves read and talk about what they read.

Further to be noted are such variables as communication processes, values, sense of family and family pride; self-concept and a sense of potency of the family members, which also influence the child's development. [Gordon 1977, pp. 75–76].

The promotion of these family variables in our changing society will necessitate new and vigorous strategies for working with parents and prospective parents. Early childhood programs became fortuitous opportunities to implement such strategies.

The involvement of busy parents in the education of their children will require creative and innovative approaches just to get them to come to the child centers for conferences or classes. Administrators will have to develop flexible schedules for their staff to have the time to work with parents during their nonworking hours. Child-care workers will need to learn how to work with adults and keep them motivated and interested in the parent activities of their centers. Fathers, the often ignored parent, will have to be engaged and mobilized to provide emotional and positive experiences necessary for the development of their children.

When scheduling volunteers for various events, administrators and teachers ought to think of before-working hours, early evening, or even Saturday mornings for their activities. Use of facilities will have to be expanded to make it possible for parents to use them in their free time, for their own continued development and participation in center activities.

The keys to working with parents of preschoolers will continue to be the recognition that parents are the prime educators of their children, that parents know their children, and that, based on this knowledge, parents will work with care givers to the best advantage of their children. And finally, it is important for preschool personnel to recognize that the American family has changed and that flexible and innovative preschool programs need to be developed to involve and to meet the needs of children and their parents.

Summary

The trend toward working with parents in early childhood education is increasing and is based on six factors:

1. The increased demand for participation in all decisions by all sectors of society, including parents' demands for increased control over education.

2. Preliminary evidence that parents determine educational outcomes more than do schools as they are presently constituted, and that they are thus appropriately considered a central part of the educational process.
3. Increased concern for the first 5 years of life during which education traditionally has been the responsibility of parents.
4. The failure of school-based systems to deliver equality of educational outcomes.
5. Increased appreciation for what the schools can learn from parents as resources.
6. A rising awareness of the possible need for education for parenting in all sectors of society.

The increase of parent involvement in preschool settings as educators, as paid and volunteer staff, as decision makers, and as resources has been validated by evidence from experimental programs—especially parent involvement as educators. Many programs are now available as models for parent education, although there are few guidelines on how to develop parent/school partnerships and how to create effective parent decision-making bodies. The available studies, do, however, provide some limited guidance in these areas.

Extrapolating from current data warrants encouragement and expansion of a variety of programs that work with parents of preschoolers. Some notes of caution must be sounded. First, parent needs and desires must be better understood than they are at present. Second, differing expectations of kinds of parent involvement should be made explicit during planning, and ways for resolving possible conflicts should be built into the programs. Third, the programs must be viewed as part of a comprehensive strategy for early childhood education. In this way one may expect appropriate benefits from parent involvement, but not miracles.

References

Bronfenbrenner, U. Reality and research in ecology of human development. *Proceedings of the American Philosophical Association*, 1975, *119*, 439–469.
Bruce, K. U. *Exploring parenting—A leader's guide* (Department of Health, Education and Welfare Contract No. 105-76-1178). Washington, D. C.: Roy Littlejohn and Associates, 1978.
Felt, M. C. *Exploring childhood program.* Newton, Mass.: EDC School and Society Programs, 1973.
Gordon, I. J. Parent education and parent involvement: Retrospect and prospect. *Childhood Education*, November–December 1977, pp. 71–79.

Gray, S., & Klaus, R. The early training project: A seventh-year report. *Child Development*, 1970, *41*, 909–924.

A guide for planning and operating home-based child development programs (Department of Health, Education and Welfare Publication No. OHD 75-1080). Washington, D. C.: Office of Human Development, Head Start Bureau, 1974.

Hertz, T. *The impact of federal early childhood programs on children* (Report No. SA-11455-76). Paper prepared for the Office of the Assistant Secretary for Planning and Evaluation, Department of Health, Education and Welfare, Washington, D. C., July 1977.

Lapides, E. Parent involvement of former Head Start parents in the public schools. Unpublished masters thesis, Towson State College, 1976.

Leichter, H. J. Some perspectives on family as educator. *Teachers College Record*, 1974, *76*, 2.

Levenstein, P. Cognitive growth in preschoolers through verbal interaction with mothers. *American Journal of Orthopsychiatry*, 1970, *40*, 426–432.

Love, J. *National Home Start evaluation: Final report* (DHEW Contract No. HEW 105-72-1100). Cambridge, Mass.: High/Scope Education Research Foundation, March 1976.

O'Keefe, R. A. *What Head Start means to families.* A report to the Secretary of Health, Education and Welfare, unpublished manuscript, August 1978.

Radin, N., & Weikart, D. A home teaching program for disadvantaged preschool children. *Journal of Special Education*, 1967, *32*, 183–190.

Schweinhart, L., & Weikart, D. P. Research report—Can preschool education make a lasting difference? *Bulletin of the High/Scope Foundation*, 1977, *4*, 1–8.

Segal, J., & Yahraes, H. *A child's journey.* New York: McGraw-Hill, 1978.

Stubbs, J., Godley, C., & Alexander, L. *National Head Start parent involvement study, Part I: Opportunities for parent involvement* (OCD Contract). Washington, D. C.: Associate Control, Research & Analysis, April 1978.

Weikart, D. P., & Lambie, D. Z. *Ypsilanti-Carnegie infant education project progress report.* Ypsilanti, Mich.: Department of Research and Development, Ypsilanti Public Schools, 1969.

Additional Resources

Bronfenbrenner, U. *A report on longitudinal evaluations of preschool programs: Is early intervention effective?* (Vol. 2). (DHEW Publication No. OHD 75–25). Washington, D.C.: Department of Human Development, 1974.

Carson, J. C. *Parent power: Primary activities for the home.* Washington, D. C.: Washington Technical Institute, 1973. (ERIC No. ED 086 327).

Ellin-Data, L. *The effects of the Head Start classroom experience on some aspects of child development: A summary of national evaluations 1966–1969* (DHEW Publication No. OHD 76.30088). Washington, D. C.: Department of Human Development, 1976.

Gordon, I., & Guinaugh, B. *A home learning center approach to early stimulation* (Report No. NIMH-5-MHI6037-06). Gainesville Institute for Development of Human Resources, University of Florida, 1974.

Gordon, T. *P.E.T. Parent effectiveness training.* New York: Peter H. Wyden, 1972.

Gray, S., Ruttle, K., & Wyrick, M. *Home visiting with mothers of toddlers and their siblings: Interim report on second post-testing of waves I & II.* Report to the National Institute of Education on Contract No. NE-C-00-3-0261, 1975.

Hewett, K. D. *Partners with parents: Home start experience with preschoolers and their families* (DHEW Publication No. 78-31106). Washington, D. C.: U. S. Government Printing Office, 1978.

Radin, N. *Three degrees of parent involvement in a preschool program: Impact on mothers and children*. Paper presented at the annual meeting of the Midwestern Psychological Association, Detroit, May 1971. (ERIC No. ED 052 831).

Weikart, D. *Longitudinal results of the Ypsilanti Perry preschool project*. Ypsilanti, Mich.: High/Scope Educational Research Foundation, 1970.

Weikart, D. *Home teaching with mothers and infants*. Ypsilanti, Mich.: High/Scope Educational Research Foundation, 1974.

Chapter 11

Parent Education: One Strategy for the Prevention of Child Abuse

SUELLEN FRIED
PENNI HOLT

The mental hospitals, prisons, alcohol and drug abuse treatment centers, and juvenile institutions of this country are filled with those who were abused and neglected as children—and their numbers increase each year. Child abuse is a national epidemic. Each year the statistics of child abuse mount, and it is feared that a campaign to increase public awareness and alert people to recognize and report suspected abuse will only result in the presently burdened system being deluged with so many cases that it will not be able to respond.

The problem of child abuse begins in the family. The family is a crucial institution in our society, and no one wants to usurp the parents' traditional role of childrearing. At the same time, we are faced with the social consequences of many inadequate family systems. Parenting has become an increasingly stressful responsibility, with parents getting little or no training for the task. One hopeful solution to this growing concern is parent education.

The intent of this chapter is to look at some of the identified causes of child abuse and neglect and eight parent education programs that are being instituted to try to preempt the problems before they occur. All of these programs can be implemented in communities through the cooperative efforts of volunteers and professionals. The most positive aspect of this situation is that if we do indeed learn to prevent child

HANDBOOK ON
PARENT EDUCATION

abuse and neglect through parent education, we can prevent a host of other serious social problems as well.

Problem and History of Child Abuse and Neglect

Each year several thousand children are in danger of being killed—by their parents. This dramatic statement is well documented and underscores the severity of the child abuse problem.

In 1975, it was estimated that between 200,000 and 500,000 children are physically abused each year in the United States, and an additional 465,000 to 1,170,000 are severely neglected or sexually molested (Nagi, 1977). A 1978 study by Gelles estimated that between 1.4 and 1.9 million children were vulnerable to physical injury from their parents in that year. It should be noted that the study was concerned with only seven specific forms of parental violence and did not seek information about burnings, torturing, sexual abuse, or any forms of neglect. In addition, the children studied were only between the ages of 3 and 17. Previous research suggests that a great deal of child abuse occurs between the ages of 3 months and 3 years, and had this age group been included, the figures would certainly have been higher. Two other factors—the fact that the study was based on self-reports and that single-parent families were excluded—lead to the conclusion that the figures *underestimate* the true level of abuse. The Gelles study is extremely significant, however, because it estimates at least 1 million children higher than previous estimates of the incidence of physical abuse (Gelles, 1978).

If neglect is added to our statistical estimates of child abuse, the tally is much higher. Based on a survey of responses from child protection agencies in 1972–1973 in Florida, and applying this ratio to national projection yields, it can be estimated that for every case of reported abuse, there are approximately three cases of neglect (Nagi, 1977).

An important factor in the child abuse picture is that children have been considered the property of their parents since our earliest civilizations, and this deeply imbedded attitude still prevails. Infanticide was an accepted practice for many generations. Unwanted children and malformed babies were regularly abandoned in early Babylonian, Hebrew, Greek, and Roman cultures. Even early English law condoned infanticide, if it took place within the first few days of birth. Brian Fraser (1976) writes that in the sixteenth century in England, economic stress led to the apprenticeship of poor children, and by 1760, the Pauper Apprentice System was so badly abused, and the children so cruelly and inhumanely treated, that the system was outlawed. American patterns paralleled those in England, and until the early 1900s, American courts offered little protection for children who were cruelly treated by their parents (Fraser, 1976).

Most people are still horrified to learn that the first case of child abuse in this country, the famous Mary Ellen case, was tried under the law protecting prevention of cruelty to animals, as there were no laws to protect children in 1874 (Fontana & Besharov, 1977). Mary Ellen, a malnourished and physically abused child, became the center of legislative concern in New York when concerned individuals found themselves powerless to protect her rights as a child under law. Even that shocking case didn't mobilize us into national action. A few Societies for the Prevention of Cruelty to Children did spring up across the country, and in 1877, the American Humane Association formed to devote itself to the prevention of cruelty to children and animals (Brown, 1979).

The child abuse issue, as a major concern, however, remained sub-rosa until 1962, when Dr. C. Henry Kempe coined the term, "the battered child syndrome" (Kempe, Silverman, Steele, Droegemeuller, & Silver, 1962). His purpose was to grab the attention of both physicians and the public. The term has now been dropped and replaced with the more inclusive phrase, "child abuse and neglect" (Helfer & Kempe, 1976).

By 1966, every state enacted an abuse reporting law and acknowledged legally that child abuse is a serious social issue. Eventually, the federal government recognized the problem and in 1974, PL 93-247, the Child Abuse Prevention and Treatment Act was passed, establishing a United States National Center on Child Abuse and Neglect within the Department of Health, Education and Welfare (Fontana & Besharov, 1977).

Definition of Child Abuse

The Model Protection Services Act of 1975 provides the following definition: "An 'abused or neglected child' means a child whose physical or mental health or welfare is harmed or threatened with harm by the acts or omissions of his parent or other person responsible for his welfare." Harm is further defined as injuries sustained as a result of excessive corporal punishment, sexual abuse, failure to provide the basic necessities of life, abandonment, or failure to provide adequate care and supervision (Fontana & Besharov, 1977, p. 102). The vagueness of such criteria can obviously lead to legal dilemmas.

One of the obstacles in developing a comprehensive plan of attack against child abuse has been identified as the lack of a widely accepted definition (Zigler, 1978). Gelles' (1978) view is that "the definition of child abuse varies over time, across cultures and between social and cultural groups [p. 1]." There are some who believe that the issue is best served by taking a narrow view of abuse as serious physical injury (Uviller, 1978); others opt for a broader definition that includes physical and emotional abuse and neglect (Fontana & Besharov, 1977; Helfer & Kempe, 1976; Martin, 1976); and at the end of the continuum, there is the notion that any interference with the fulfillment of the child's developmental needs constitutes abuse (Albee, 1978).

Legal Implications

Within the last 15 years, every one of the 50 states and the District of Columbia has enacted a Reporting Act that mandates professionals to report suspected cases of abuse. Not all states include neglect and/or sexual abuse, but at least each state has determined a legal authority to investigate physical abuse when it is reported. Most states spell out mandated reporters, such as physicians, nurses, osteopaths, law enforcement personnel, teachers, dentists, and social workers (Fontana & Besharov, 1977). The majority of states provide a criminal penalty for failure to report a suspected incident; however, this penalty is seldom invoked, and most reporting comes from family members and neighbors who are not required by law to report (Nagi, 1977).

The Model Child Protection Act, upon which most state statutes are based, does not make provision for punishment of abusers, but rather attempts to assist and encourage parents to seek help in meeting their child-care responsibilities. Family services are first offered on a voluntary basis, and the authorized protective agency resorts to the court only if necessary. The emphasis is clearly on identification for the purpose of responding to the needs of the hurting family (Fontana & Besharov, 1977).

The Reporting Acts have been quite successful in validating the extent of the child abuse problem. The most dramatic example is Florida. As a result of updated statutes and 24-hour toll-free reporting line, reported cases increased from 17 to 19,120 in 1 year's time (Nagi, 1977).

As states have greater opportunity and responsibility to intervene in the protection of children, the issue of parents' rights versus children's rights will become more polarized, for in truth, their interests are not always compatible. The law is destined to play a major role in this struggle.

Who Are the Abusers?

Abusers are parents or guardians who perpetrate or allow abuse of their children. They are generally impulsive, dependent, isolated, depressed, vulnerable to criticism, and lack coping skills, self-esteem, and self-control (Fontana & Besharov, 1977). Abusers come from all educational, ethnic, religious, geographic, social, and economic backgrounds; however, Gelles (1978) indicated that abuse rates in urban areas are greater than in small cities, suburbs, or rural communities. Manual workers have rates of abusive violence that are 45% higher than those of white-collar workers. College graduates and those with less than an eighth grade education are less abusive than high school graduates. Also, there is no significant difference between blacks and whites in their abusive behavior, although families with incomes of less than $6000 per year are twice as likely to abuse as the most wealthy respondents (over $20,000). The Midwest is the region with the highest rate of abuse. Younger parents are the most violent and Jewish parents have the lowest rate of violence.

Abusers are so emotionally bereft that they are in no position to meet their children's needs. In many cases the profile of the abusive and/or neglectful parent comes into focus as a person who is not so much monstrous as misinformed, not so much pathological as pathetic, not so much hopeless as helpless.

Why Abuse?

There are many factors that contribute to the existence of child abuse and neglect:

1. There is often a "target" child in abusive families. One child is seen as special, different, too active, too passive, etc., and he or she becomes the target of family aggression. It might be that the child reminds the abuser of a hated stepparent, is the other parent's favorite, has a foible that the abuser despises, is considered to be evil, is handicapped, or was premature (Young, 1964).

2. A crisis or series of crises will often trigger abusive behavior. Examples would be such situations as loss of a job, separation from a loved one, a death, an unwanted pregnancy, an emotional defeat, or even a trivial event that may seem monumental to the adult who is in desperate need of nurturing (Kempe & Helfer, 1972).

3. Many parents are not emotionally prepared for the responsibilities of motherhood and fatherhood and frequently overact or withdraw from the frustrations of parenting. As children, they never learned

interpersonal skills. The emotional deficits of *their* critical developmental years have limited their ability to value themselves and interact with others (Helfer, 1978b).

4. Often it is a lack of basic information about child development that leads to abuse. Expecting a child to respond to discipline at the age of 2 months or demanding bladder and bowel control at the age of 6 months can cause parents to punish a child who cannot physiologically or psychologically perform. Malnutrition in infants, often leading to damage of the central nervous system or death, is the result of ignorance about basic nutritional needs in many cases (Kempe & Helfer, 1972).

5. Abuse is generally a pattern of behavior handed down from one generation to another. Severe forms of discipline are not usually recognized as abuse but merely repeated family traditions. From 80 to 90% of identified abusers care about their children but are limited in their parenting skills because of the model that they received (Kempe & Helfer, 1972).

6. Isolation is a common pattern among abusive families. Many do not have telephones. They are estranged from the rest of the community and cut off from any support networks. Their basic mistrust leads them to reject overtures from neighbors, social workers, and physicians (Helfer & Kempe, 1976).

7. Violence is a chronic condition for many families in our society. Slightly more than 1 out of 100 children are beaten up by a parent each year and 40% are beaten at least once while growing up. Some 3 children in 100 have grown up with parents who used a gun or knife on them (Gelles, 1978).

8. The problem of teenage pregnancy has significant consequences relating to our concern for children. Death occurs twice as much for babies born to teenagers under 18 as for babies born to women aged 20 to 29. One million teenagers become pregnant each year in the United States (National PTA, 1978). Many teenagers have babies for the wrong reasons. They want an excuse to leave home or drop out of school, or in their yearning to be loved and cherished, they expect that an infant will meet their needs for affection and support.

Educational and Therapeutic Intervention

The initial focus in the area of child abuse was to expose the medical, social, and legal perspectives of the problem (Helfer & Kempe, 1968).

More recent concerns have been to stimulate the transition from research in the field to therapeutic services (Kempe & Helfer, 1972), and then, most importantly, to move toward the preventive approach (Helfer & Kempe, 1976).

Helfer (1977) speaks eloquently about the potential of primary prevention. He even challenges the volunteer brigade to disregard the abused child and the anguished family. His logic is that we have never erased a social problem by treating it after the fact. He claims we will never have enough resources, manpower, or money to solve the agonies of alcoholism, poverty, crime, or child abuse. As an example, he cites the epidemics of cholera and polio. It was not the medicine and lung machines that corrected those diseases. Rather, it was a sewer system and a vaccine (preventive measures) that made it possible for those disorders to be eradicated. Unless we muster our energies to *prevent* the horrors of abuse, neglect, and sexual exploitation, Helfer believes that we are doomed to failure.

Prevention as a key concept is hard to define. As a general term it includes the theory of primary, secondary, and tertiary prevention. Primary prevention is defined in the *Interdisciplinary Glossary on Child Abuse and Neglect* as "Providing societal and community policies and programs which strengthen family functioning so that child abuse and neglect is less likely to occur." Secondary prevention is "intervention in the early signs of child abuse and neglect for treatment of the presenting problem and to prevent further problems from developing." Tertiary prevention is "treatment after child abuse and neglect has been confirmed" (National Center on Child Abuse and Neglect, 1978, p. 63).

If we examine the contributing factors of child abuse and neglect and commit ourselves to a primary prevention focus, it becomes obvious that the way to strengthen family functioning is through parent education programs.

Helfer, in his booklet published by the National Committee for Prevention of Child Abuse (1978a), calls for a comprehensive system of supports for parent–child interaction that begins at birth, follows through the preschool years, and continues into the school curriculum. There are several viable types of programs that impact these stages and speak directly to the abuse factors described previously.

In the following table, these eight abuse factors are listed along with a corresponding program that could be viewed as an intervention response. The rest of this chapter will be devoted to exploring these specific parent education programs.

Factor	Program
1. Target child	1. Bonding/attachment practices in maternity units of general hospitals
2. Family crises	2. Home visitor program
3. Emotional deficits and copelessness of parents	3. Crash course in parenting
4. Lack of basic information about child development	4. "Pierre the Pelican" Newsletter
5. Limited role models	5. "Footsteps"—a television series
6. Isolation	6. Drop-In Centers and Parents Anonymous
7. Violence	7. *People Are Not for Hitting* and "Some Wounds Never Heal"
8. Teenage pregnancy	8. Education for Parenthood curriculum

Parent Effectiveness Training (Gordon, 1970), Systematic Training for Effective Parenting (Dinkmeyer & McCay, 1976), and other such structured programs are being viewed in many communities as part of the child abuse prevention scheme.

Conclusive evidence that any of these programs, if implemented, would prevent child abuse and neglect does not exist. With a cautious, but hopeful perspective, let us look more closely at the programs that communities and states are launching. The National Committee for Prevention of Child Abuse is organizing a citizen's network of volunteer professionals and professional volunteers to coordinate community, state, and national efforts. At the present time they have state chapters in Kansas, Indiana, Illinois, Alaska, Massachusetts, Michigan, Minnesota, New Jersey, and North Carolina, and chapters are in formation in Wisconsin, Kentucky, Hawaii, Nebraska, and South Carolina. As the national organization offers materials, technical assistance, and consultation to each state chapter, each state in turn will provide similar services to community coalitions. Hopefully, the primary prevention programs described here will be initiated in every chapter and ultimately there will be a 50 state volunteer network to mobilize the enthusiastic energies of caring people all across the country.

The Bonding Attachment Program

The book, *Maternal Infant Bonding* (Klaus & Kennell, 1976), brought the use of the term "bonding" into common language, although the authors are now promoting the term, "attachment," in preference to bonding. The attachment process is described as follows:

Early in life the infant develops an attachment to one individual, most often the mother. Throughout his lifetime the strength and character of this attachment will influence the quality of all future bonds to other individuals. An attachment can be defined as an affectionate bond between two individuals that endures through time and space and serves to join them emotionally [Kennell, Voos, & Klaus, 1976, p. 25].

The original impetus of Kennell and Klaus to explore the attachment process came from their observations that premature infants returned as abused children with much greater frequency than full-term babies. They speculated that lack of contact between mother and the newborn, who was confined to an incubator, might be relevant to future abandonment or abuse.

Before conducting their own studies, they turned to research that had been accomplished in the animal kingdom. One such study described the consequences of bonding disruption between mother goats and their kids. If the newborn kid is removed from the mother and separated from her for the first 5 to 10 minutes after birth, the mother will reject the kid when they are reunited. However, if the mother is permitted to bond with her kid for the first 5 to 10 minutes, she will nurse and nurture the dependent offspring (Klaus & Kennell, 1976).

In research with infants, we now have information that a baby experiences six states of consciousness, from deep sleep to dreaming. The baby enters life in the fourth state and remains alert for about 45 minutes to 1 hour before falling into a deep sleep for the next 3 to 4 hours. Kennell and Klaus, based on their research, feel that contact between mother, father, and baby right after birth can have a significant effect on the developing attachment process (Klaus, 1978).

In an address delivered in Wichita, Kansas in June 1978, Dr. Klaus reported on a study conducted with an experimental and control group of new mothers. In the control group, the mothers had contact with their babies for feeding purposes only, following the traditional hospital procedures. In the experimental group, mothers and babies spent four additional hours together each day. The two groups were followed for 5 years by independent researchers. At the end of that time, several differences emerged between the two groups; one of which is relevant to child abuse. In the group where the mothers had prolonged contact with their infants, less battering of children was noted (Klaus, 1978).

Klaus and Kennell see the hospital as a major setting for early parent education, and their studies and innovative practices are having much influence throughout the country. An enlightened maternity unit today will offer a wide range of opportunities for parent–child interaction including the presence of the father in the delivery room; a birthing room that is furnished like a home setting; private, intimate time for mother, father, and baby to share the first 30 to 45 minutes of life;

rooming-in possibilities for mother and baby; encouragement for mothers to nurse, sometimes immediately after birth; "coaching" for new parents in regard to handling, cooing, and establishing eye and skin-to-skin contact; sibling visitation; and general contact with the new baby for extended periods of time before leaving the hospital.

The American Medical Association (AMA) and the American Nursing Association have both taken positions calling for bonding practices. The 249-member House of Delegates, the policymaking body of the AMA, adopted a statement on *Parent and Newborn Interaction,* urging enhancement and humanizing of the birth experience (American Medical Association, 1978). They recommend that hospital medical staffs review hospital practices covering delivery and encourage immediate bonding of mothers and fathers with their newborn infants.

Those intent on promoting primary prevention methods to ameliorate child abuse see professional and public awareness of bonding/attachment ideas as a major thrust of parent education. Medical professionals such as obstetricians, pediatricians, family physicians, obstetrical nurses, and hospital administrators need to acquaint themselves with the data that are emerging—especially that which concerns parents of premature babies and infants with birth defects. Consumer demand for such services, however, will hasten implementation of sensitive practices.

Home Visitor Program

The concept of the home health visitor, as proposed by Kempe, is to establish a strong link between the private and public health care system in our communities (Kempe & Helfer, 1972). Home health care service emphasizes prevention, using a skilled visitor who is able to counsel on a variety of family issues, from providing practical information to the detection of child maltreatment. This one-to-one relationship is a unique form of parent education.

The Home Visitor program has been in effect in European countries for many years, using nurses as the home visitor. A similar program is being piloted in the United States in Kansas (Dugan, 1979). The program is a collaborative effort by the State Department of Health and Environment Division of Maternal/Child Health, the Health Department in Junction City, Kansas, and the State Department of Social and Rehabilitation Services (SRS). In this program nurses are used to recruit, screen, and supervise the home visitors who are not professionals, but mothers themselves.

Eleven home visitors, working 20 hours a week for the minimum wage, have been calling on new mothers in five counties in central Kansas. The home visitor first sees the mother in the hospital and sets up an appointment for a follow-up visit at home within a week to 10 days. He or she brings pamphlets about nutrition, community resources, and welfare services, if needed, and, more importantly, a caring presence. The visitor encourages the family to maintain basic immunization standards and to have periodic examinations by a physician. The visitor is available to the mother for unlimited revisits, based on her needs and desires. From October 1, 1977, to September 30, 1978, there were 1912 births in the project area. Some 1250 mothers received a home visit and there were 589 revisits. Home visitors in Kansas have averted several family crises by testing well water, picking up on sibling illnesses, contacting the appropriate welfare agency, and in one dramatic instance, rescuing a wife from an abusive husband (Dugan, 1979).

The home visitor has three roles: teacher, friend, and community liaison. As teacher, the home visitor demonstrates basic infant care, such as feeding, bathing, diagnosing, and treating minor childhood illnesses. Infant nutrition, stimulation, and emotional needs are stressed and modeled. As friend, the home visitor provides a non-threatening, supportive relationship. In some instances she becomes a surrogate grandmother, a confidante, and a person to be trusted. As community liaison, the home visitor provides information regarding community services. She encourages the family to use available resources and assists in making those contacts.

The results of a year's experience are very encouraging. During the first year of the home visitor program in the communities receiving the service in Kansas, no deaths have occurred from child abuse and no children required hospitalization due to extreme battering or neglect. During the previous year, 3 children died and 11 children had been hospitalized in connection with abuse and neglect.

Crash Course in Parenting

What happens to people who missed out on the normal, loving experiences that most people receive from their parents? According to Kempe (1978), these persons frequently have difficulty in their friendships and marriages and even greater difficulties with parenting. They tend to choose partners who are equally deprived and unsupportive, and in spite of this barren background are somehow expected to offer tenderness, affection, and caring concern to their own children. Is it possible to replenish the void? Is there some way to make up for the missed nurturing and retrain the sensory responses from negative to positive experiences?

Helfer and his associate, Ruth Esba, have designed a "Crash Course in Childhood for Adults" (Helfer, 1978b). Using the book as a text, they have been training professionals to become "coaches" in parenting interaction skills. Following a systematic training and supervision experience, a trained "coach" can work with those who need to learn specific skills of interaction that were not learned, or were poorly learned, during the critical childhood period.

The training manual contains approximately 70 specific tasks to accomplish and 25 problems to solve during the process of taking the "Crash Course." The content of the course covers three basic areas of interaction:

1. Interacting with one's environment by making your senses (touching, looking, etc.) work for you rather than against you.
2. Interacting with one's self through building a positive self-image and gaining control over one's life. This includes sections on decision making, awareness of feelings, responsibility, guilt, actions, and trust.
3. Interacting with others, that is, acquaintances, close friends, dates, and mates. Considerable emphasis is placed on sexual interaction and its meaning for the student.

A student is any young adult (parent, nonparent, or older teenager), who feels that his or her interpersonal skills for getting along with others were not learned well enough during childhood. Helfer and Esba believe that weekly meetings with their coach, in individual sessions or in small groups, may only be necessary for 3 or 4 months to achieve the desired results. Other students may need 12 to 15 months to reach their goal.

The authors do not believe this course should be viewed as a course in parenting, but rather as a primer or prerequisite for a parenting course. Because there are so many abusive parents who could benefit from the "back to basics" approach, the program should be considered in the continuum of parent education resources. One of the criticisms of some of the more structured programs is that they work well for basically healthy families who want to become healthier, but they miss the mark for those who cannot enter parenting skill sessions at that level.

"Pierre the Pelican" Newsletter

A project used widely in Louisiana, Hawaii, Kansas, Mississippi, Massachusetts, North Dakota, Rhode Island, and Texas, is "Pierre the Pelican," a newsletter series created in 1947 by Lloyd Rowland (Rowland, 1947). The series was named for the pelican, which is the state bird of Louisiana.

The postnatal series begins at birth and continues monthly for the first year; it is received every two months the second year; three letters are sent during both the third and fourth years; and two letters arrive during both the fifth and sixth years. Each letter contains information about child development and guidance to new parents. For example, the letter that arrives when the baby is 3 months old discusses communication through sound, touch, and eye contact; it also deals with fears, chewing and biting, security and peacefulness, bottle feeding, involvement of father, baby sitters, and has an updated paragraph on single parenthood. The newsletter is a four-sided, folded pamphlet, complete with illustrations and composed of easy to read, brief paragraphs. The series was recently revised to take changing life-styles into consideration, such as greater responsibilities in the parenting role by fathers, alteration of all references to doctors as "he," and modernized illustrations (Rowland, 1977).

The first newsletter has been delivered in many ways. In the beginning, the first letter, like all the others, was mailed. In some cities today, nurses on the maternity floor introduce Pierre. In other communities, the first letter is part of a packet, prepared and hand delivered by volunteers who go to the hospital and welcome the new baby to the community. The volunteers offer linkage to new-mother support groups, useful community telephone numbers, a gift for other siblings, and appropriate pamphlets. With the new mother's consent, the volunteers see to it that her address is forwarded to the Health Department, Mental Health Association, or other community agency that is willing to handle the postage and subsequent mailing of the newsletter.

The Michigan Department of Mental Health (1952) conducted a major research project using the postnatal series and concluded that parents who used the "Pierre the Pelican" pamphlets showed significant differences in childrearing knowledge from those who had not. In part of a seven-point summary, the Michigan study states:

> The Pierre and control parents were compared in relation to their answers to the "concept" questions (i.e., questions involving understanding of child rearing practices, but not dependent on economic or other environmental situations). The Pierre group was significantly better informed than the controls on these items. This result is one of the most striking bits of evidence that the Pierre letters are an effective means of educating parents [p. 69].

A prenatal series was designed in 1950, 3 years after the postnatal letters were developed, at the suggestion of a psychiatrist who felt that much could be done to form positive attitudes about parenting before the baby arrives (Rowland, 1950). The prenatal pamphlets arrive monthly beginning with the second month of pregnancy, when the obstetrician requests the letters for his or her client. Each letter is aimed to make the expectant mother feel more comfortable about the emotional and physiological changes she is experiencing. The letters offer advice about positive health habits, reassurance that her feelings and thoughts are not uncommon, and preparation for the unexpected stages that come with pregnancy.

Rowland's original intent was to use Pierre as a mental health tool by providing new mothers with basic information about their babies and to relieve the stress that accompanies anxious parenting (Rowland, 1979). It is quickly being adopted by those concerned with the prevention of child abuse as a parent education strategy. Most children who are killed by their parents, die before they are 5 years old. Severity of abuse is a factor of age. The younger the child, the more severe the abuse. The first few years of a child's life are the most vulnerable and cause the greatest stress for parents (American Humane Association, 1979). Therefore, programs that can give parents and children the best start possible should have a top priority.

"Footsteps"—A Television Series

Another hope for reaching parents who may not have connected with a support network of any kind is the public media. If all other outreach efforts fail, one promising alternative remains in television. One such program was "Raised in Anger," aired on January 11, 1979, on National Public Service Television. The program was narrated by Ed Asner and funded by the 3M Corporation in the hope that viewers might empathize and possibly identify with the abusive parents depicted. It was effective, and in one city, 37 parents called the local crisis line following the program.

"Footsteps" is a new television series about parenting brought to Public Television by Kentucky Educational TV and funded by the U.S. Office of Education. The 20-episode series consists of dramatizations of five fictional families who face a particular problem in each segment. The five families are: the Sandburgs—white, middle-class, working parents with two children; the Marshalls—black, middle-class family with two children; the Hornbrenners—newly divorced parents with one child; the Rileys—rural, working-class, teenage expectant parents; and the Sanchezes—Mexican-American, working-class, extended family.

Each production explores a specific theme such as identity, individuality, early stimulation, prenatal preparation, learning through TV, death, attachment and independence, discipline, food habits, or play and fantasy. The program suggests alternatives and options open to parents in raising their children. Following the 20-minute dramatic presentation, series co-hosts, Rob Reiner and Penny Marshall, and Mike and Judy Farrell, introduce a short documentary that summarizes the essential point of the story.

Jerrold Sandler, "Footsteps" project director, noted,

> The series tries neither to preach at viewers nor offer them formula solutions. What we're pushing are positive attitudes. We want parents to know that they're not alone in dealing with the pleasures and problems they face in raising children; that it's not impossible to be a parent; and that there is no one answer to a particular problem [Sandler, 1979].

For example, in the eighth program, entitled "Spare the Rod," Sandy and Ted Sandburg disagree about the "right" way to train their children. Sandy thinks her children should learn to make their own decisions. Ted's family believes that permissiveness invites disaster and maintains that strict discipline is necessary to teach self-control and direction. A birthday party at grandma's brings the conflict to a head. The playlet demonstrates that threatening, scaring, or yelling is not the most effective method of discipline, and the show offers diversion as a positive alternative.

A discussion guide intended for leaders who work with parent groups, child-care workers, and students of child development is available, as is a teacher's manual and a student guide kit. The manuals and guides are filled with stimulating articles, activity suggestions, and a bibliography (*Footsteps: A Discussion Guide*, 1979).

In *Footsteps: A Publicity Resource Kit* (1979), Herman W. Land, President of the Association of Independent TV Stations, Inc., says about the series:

> "Footsteps" represents an advance in the use of TV as an educational instrument. It tackles a formidable problem: educating the young parent in the marvelous, difficult world of rearing the young. It does so on the basis of an unusual harnessing of creative talents and the hard-headed investigation and testing of research. It demonstrates the feasibility of bringing together creative practitioners and research experts and successfully uniting their skills to produce an entertainment that educates. In short, it works [Land, 1979].

Drop-In Centers and Parents Anonymous

The need for a support group and interaction with other parents is more than a pleasurable experience; it appears to be a social necessity. At the Yerkes Regional Primate Research Center in Atlanta, Georgia, mother–infant relationships among primates are being observed to discover clues about human infant abuse (Rock, 1978). "When they are caged alone with their babies, abuse by gorilla mothers seems to be the norm [Nadler, 1978, p. 58]." However, when gorilla mothers had the opportunity to share a compound and interact with other mothers, they raised their young with confidence and caring. The loneliness of the isolated gorilla mother appeared to be the key factor in the abusive families.

According to Kern (1978):

> A lot of things contribute to human child abuse, but I'm also inclined to think that the abuse we've been hearing so much about recently is indeed related to the loneliness experienced by today's young mothers. In years past, a human's family situation was like that of wild gorillas. Folks stuck together and there was always a grandma or an older sister to help when things got rough. Now the trend is to go it alone, out in the suburbs maybe, where the young mother is stranded all day with no company except that of her wailing child. No wonder she gets confused and depressed. She's like a captive gorilla in an isolation cage [p. 62].

Support groups for mothers such as Drop-In Centers, which are being organized in Michigan, and Parents Anonymous (P.A.), which is a national program, are responses to the isolated parent.

The Michigan Drop-In Center service began 9 years ago as a primary intervention program for those families who need temporary supportive help, who have few financial resources, or who might allow problems to magnify before they seek help. The service offers a combination of early childhood and parental education and parental respite (Raney, 1976). Because volunteers operate the centers, the program has a neighborhood self-help, mutual support theme. The centers are open for 3 hours, two or three times a week and welcome children from infancy through kindergarten. The older children experience typical nursery school activities that include free play, art projects, music, stories, snacks, etc. The infants receive almost individual care with lots of cuddling and rocking.

A special feature is the last hour of each Drop-In Session when parents are invited to participate in a sharing period. In addition to social visiting and recipe exchanges, parents are encouraged to discuss their anxieties and concerns about toilet training, aggression, sibling rivalry, etc., in a comfortable, nonthreatening situation. The trained volunteers model healthy parenting styles as another facet of the parent education component.

Because of the success of the first center in Ann Arbor, other centers in Michigan have developed—all steeped in the same theory of an informal, neighborhood helping system. At least two centers now have

Parents Anonymous groups meeting in conjunction with their other family-centered programs.

Parents Anonymous (P.A.) is a voluntary, self-help support group that meets weekly. There are no fees involved, it is not an extension of any agency, and confidentiality and anonymity of the members are protected. Parents can be referred to the program by a social service worker, but most parents come on their own and stay with the program because it meets their needs.

Parents Anonymous did not begin as a primary prevention concept and for most parents involved it is a secondary prevention resource. It is being included in this chapter for several reasons:

1. It is a unique and successful parent education process.
2. In its retraining techniques, often geared to the abuse of one child, it serves as a primary prevention force for other and future children.
3. Its equal emphasis on verbal abuse frequently prevents physical and emotional abuse and neglect before it ever occurs.
4. As its reputation spreads, many parents who recognize their potential to abuse become involved before a serious problem emerges.
5. It meets the special needs of the isolated, mistrusting parent.
6. Through its various publicity formats, it is helping to dissolve the stigma against child abusers, thus enabling more people to identify their own rageful and negative attitudes toward children in their care.

Parents Anonymous recognizes six forms of abuse and believes that each of the forms is equally destructive. They are (*a*) physical abuse; (*b*) physical neglect; (*c*) sexual abuse; (*d*) verbal abuse; (*e*) emotional abuse; and (*f*) emotional neglect. A parent who permits the other parent to engage in abuse and takes no action to deter such behavior is equally responsible in the P.A. view (*I Am a Parents Anonymous Parent*, 1974). The Parents Anonymous philosophy is two-fold: (*a*) to provide an accepting, caring atmosphere; and (*b*) to offer immediate do-it-now techniques to change parent behavior patterns. The goal of P.A. is to reduce abuse as quickly as possible, and their method has proven to be effective. Table 11.1 shows the results of a survey conducted in May 1975, for the National Center on Child Abuse and Neglect (Lieber & Baker, 1976).

Overall, after 2 months in Parents Anonymous, most daily physical abuse is reduced to zero. Of 15 demonstration grants evaluated by the National Center for Child Abuse and Neglect in 1976, Parents Anony-

TABLE 11.1
Frequency of Verbal and Physical Abuse as Reported by Parents

Frequency	Before P.A. (%)	After P.A. (%)
Verbal abuse		
Almost daily	48	12 of sample
Several times weekly	22	24[a]
Several times monthly	12	27[a]
Once a month	12	27[a]
Physical abuse		
Almost daily	19	1 of sample
Several times weekly	16	7[b]
Several times monthly	20	13[b]
Once a month	13	18[b]
Almost never	32	61[b]

[a]These are improvements from the "Daily" category of verbal abuse.
[b]These are improvements from the "Daily" category of physical abuse.

mous was determined to be the most cost-effective program. For some parents, however, private therapy is necessary in addition to the P.A. process, and P.A. staunchly supports those who decide to go into therapy.

The structure of P.A. is not complicated. Each group selects a chairperson from the group members. The sponsor's role is to help the chairperson be a strong and effective leader. Sponsors are frequently professionals and paraprofessionals who volunteer their skills and time to the P.A. chapter. There are 10 Guidelines for Achievement and 10 Guidelines for Allegiance that each member must agree to uphold to receive the privileges of anonymity.

A P.A. session is not a gripe session or a "show and tell" affair, nor is it a probing of private secrets. It is an opportunity to be completely honest, to accept advice from others who have been working on behavior alternatives, and to achieve self-confidence, self-esteem, respectability, and love. Specific advice might range from, "If you can't get control of your rage, lock yourself in the bathroom until you cool off," to "Toothpaste will take crayola marks off of painted walls" (Anonymous parent, personal communication, 1978).

Since its inception in 1970, when an abusive mother and a psychiatric social worker founded the first Mothers Anonymous meeting, the organization has grown to 800 chapters in 50 states. It was conceived as a place "where members who shared similar problems could meet together to obtain help from one another without moralizing, without stigma, without being judged [*I Am a Parents Anonymous Parent*, 1974, p. 7]." Meetings are held early in the evening and baby-sitting services are provided to make participation as easy as possible. Volunteer sitters do their part to keep the children eager to attend as the child will often urge the parent to go to P.A. For those who find a face-to-face meeting, anonymous as it is, still too threatening, telephone crisis lines manned by volunteers offer a practical alternative. In addition, part of the P.A. support system is exchange of phone numbers so that members can reach out to one another between meetings.

People Are Not for Hitting: Antiviolence Efforts

At the same time that many people promote bonding, spread information about children's needs, and support new families, some word must be mentioned about violence by parents against their children. Many people have difficulty believing that parents could inflict physical pain upon their own flesh and blood. Dr. John Caffey, a radiologist, tried to raise our consciousness about physical child abuse in the mid-1940s, but his professional peers discounted his evidence (Caffey, 1946). There were other physicians who suspected that the bruises, welts, burns, scars, lacerations, scaldings, punctures, fractures, and broken bones they were seeing in children couldn't have been accidents, but they also couldn't bring themselves to believe that parents were capable of such cruel behavior (Brodeur, 1976).

John Valusek, a crusading psychologist from Wichita, Kansas, has authored a book entitled *People Are Not for Hitting* (1974). He introduces his premise with a quote from Anthony Storrs' book, *Human Aggression* (1968), which states:

> That man is an aggressive creature will hardly be disputed. With the exception of certain rodents, no other vertebrate habitually destroys members of his own species. No other animal takes positive pleasure in the exercise of cruelty upon another of his own kind . . . in truth, the extremes of brutal behavior are confined to man; and there is no parallel in nature to our savage treatment of each other. The sombre fact is that we are the cruellest and most ruthless species that has ever walked the earth . . . [p. 9].

Why do parents use pain as a method of childrearing? How can the cycle be broken? Valusek points out that parents have been slapping and spanking their children for so long, that they never question the practice, even though the possible values are far outweighed by the potential harm. While adults are not allowed to use intentional physical pain as a means of resolving interpersonal problems with other people, lest they be subject to the laws of assault and battery, children are somehow not considered people.

Valusek believes that discipline without violence is a new idea and new ideas meet tough resistance. He finds that audiences frequently become defensive and disapproving when he attempts to include children in the view that people are not for hitting. Perhaps if Valusek took the position that spanking in moderation is acceptable, he would have more supporters, but he advocates abandonment of the practice of corporal punishment in the schools and homes as well. He maintains that "spankings firmly establish a non-helpful, blame-oriented, fault-finding, pain-provoking punishment principle which becomes an integral though usually undetected part of the child's being [Valusek, 1974, p. 22]." He further states that the punishment principle leads to approved forms of violence directed against others. A child who is hit will in all probability become a hitting adult.

Valusek wants to address a root cause of violence in our society and is devoting his considerable energies to convince some national organizations to adopt resolutions calling for the elimination or corporal punishment. To increase response to his idea, he uses humor, logic, anecdotes, and bumper stickers. He uses his educational and psychological background to persuade parents that discipline is important, but there are many ways to accomplish it without resorting to physical means. The essence of his message is summed up by a reviewer, Donald E. P. Smith (1974), who says: "Valusek's thesis is simple—and profound. Parent violence toward children is the well-spring of violence in the world [p. 34]."

As an example of the consequences of severe abuse and neglect, Valusek participated in making a film entitled *Some Wounds Never Heal* (Kansas Committee for Prevention of Child Abuse, 1978). Three prisoners at the Kansas State Penitentiary (KSP) at Lansing, Kansas, are interviewed by Valusek and discuss their personal histories of deprivation and brutalization. One of the men has conducted a survey of his cell block to discover the connection, if any, between prisoner status and childhood abuse. Terry McClain (1978), president of the Lifer's Club at KSP and author of the survey, published his findings in a prison newsletter and concluded his article with these words: "If you brutalize your children, don't be surprised if they grow up to become killers. If you allow your neighbor to brutalize his children, don't wail and gnash your teeth when those children grow up—and kill yours [p. 14]."

Education for Parenthood Curriculum

Of all the primary prevention strategies, the one that has gathered the most widespread support is education for parenthood. Several prominent groups have called for parent education as a national priority. The following "Resolution Relating to Parenting" was adopted at the 1975 National PTA Convention (National PTA, 1978):

> WHEREAS, the National PTA has designated Parenting as a PTA priority; and
> WHEREAS, the National PTA in cooperation with the National Foundation March of Dimes has drawn much attention to the critical need of prenatal and postnatal care of babies; and
> WHEREAS, one-third of the infants are born to teenage parents and of those babies born to teenage mothers the number who die in the first year of life is almost twice the national average; therefore be it
> RESOLVED, that the National PTA encourage its state congresses to urge local school districts to provide for strengthening family life by upgrading pre-parent education in elementary and secondary schools; be it further
> RESOLVED, that the National PTA encourage its state congresses to emphasize the need to enhance the quality of life through programming and parent education classes [p. 1].

The National Advisory Committee on Child Abuse and Neglect, formed by the Education Commission of the States (ECS), and chaired by former Governor Robert F. Bennett of Kansas, offered a number of recommendations to the federal government, state government, and education governing agencies (Education Commission of the States, 1978). Among the 16 recommendations are:

> To the federal government—
> In future legislation, allocate additional resources for prevention programs, particularly for parenting education. Encourage the states to include parenting education in their plans for career education.
>
> To state governments—
> Identify a resource center to provide technical assistance for developing and implementing parenting education programs.
>
> To education governing agencies—
> Include information on responsible parenting and appropriate parenting behavior in curricula from elementary through continuing education programs [p. 8].

In line with the ECS report, the Governor's Commission on Education for Parenthood in Kansas determined that an essential key to the widespread implementation of parenting education programs in schools and communities is the establishment of a centralized Parent Education Resource Center within the State Department of Education. A full-time education specialist/coordinator serves as a reference source for all films, curricula, texts, materials, etc., that promote parent education. This unique, statewide program was implemented during the latter part of 1979.

National PTA, in a resource kit for parents and community leaders (National PTA, 1978), spotlights programs in Utah, Texas, and Missouri and offers examples of existing programs that seem to be working well in Larkspur, California; Owensboro, Kentucky; Ferguson, Missouri; Lewisburg, Pennsylvania; McMinnville, Tennessee; and Slayton, Minnesota. In Slayton, Minnesota, for instance, "Parent Readiness" is a required course for graduation from high school. Each graduating senior must enroll in a trimester program that includes consumer management skills, interpersonal communication, and a section on parent readiness that includes engagement, marriage, divorce, separation, death, births, adoption, and child abuse (National PTA, 1978).

One popular program in the Midwest is the "raw egg" project. In classrooms where this activity is used, each student is charged with maintaining a raw egg for one week. Each egg is given a sexual identity, named, decorated, and entrusted to the care of its "parent." The egg has to be supervised at all times and the responsibilities are meant to be akin to those of a real parent. For instance, if a student attends a basketball game, a sitter must be engaged for the egg. If the egg should break, the issues of guilt, loss, and separation are dealt with. A typical response to the unusual assignment is reportedly a greater awareness of the sacrifices involved in parenting and a stated inclination to postpone parenthood for several years. This program has been passed around by word of mouth and the originator's identity is unknown.

Although a multitude of such activities and courses are springing up in school systems all across the country, they are for the most part being offered in home economics classes, which usually have very few boys enrolled. Little is being done to evaluate the effectiveness of these efforts, and it will probably be years before we have some definitive information about the effect on the prevention of child abuse and neglect (Tramontana, Sherrets, & Authier, 1979). There are many administrators who will prefer to wait for the research results before they adopt parenting curricula. It is to the credit of those who are willing to innovate parenting education at this time because they believe in the basic premise that parenting education, as with driver's education, will better equip students for the responsibilities involved.

Conclusion

If we are unable to design parent education programs that succeed, the alternatives are less than ideal. Severance of parents' rights, which allows for adoption, accounts for a small proportion of the resolution of child abuse cases. Foster care, which is employed with much greater frequency, is often a temporary solution but can present additional problems. Dr. Karl Menninger, founder of The Villages, a model juvenile group-care facility, stated that the average young person arriving at their group homes in Topeka, Kansas has already experienced six foster home settings (Menninger, 1979). It is obvious that even if the quality of care in each of these settings was excellent, the trauma of being uprooted so many times plays havoc with a youngster's emotional stability.

Therefore, it is extremely important to reiterate a premise that permeates all of the child abuse literature. Whenever possible, the family unit should be maintained. Because the overwhelming number of families that are investigated prove to be nonmalicious and nonpsychotic, it is crucial that those families be encouraged to stay together and that all community resources be brought to bear to strengthen those family ties.

All of the programs mentioned in this chapter are intended to strengthen family living. Clearly, it must be stated that these programs are not direct antidotes to the causes. No one program will inoculate the next generation against the pervasiveness of child abuse and neglect. Not even all the programs in combination would be the equivalent of a vaccine. But we can at least begin to understand the genesis of this problem and to explore the responses that are emerging to deal with it.

There are several other influences that deserve mention. Mental health centers are spearheading an important role in the wave of parent education information. There are excellent syndicated newspaper and magazine columns written by such notables as Dr. Lee Salk, Dr. Walter Menninger, and Joan Beck. A plethora of books, magazines, articles, and filmstrips dealing with child abuse have been produced for public consumption. The National Advertising Council, in cooperation with the National Committee for Prevention of Child Abuse has been conducting a 3-year public awareness campaign with the themes of "Child Abuse Hurts Everybody," "It Shouldn't Hurt to Be a Child," and "Help Destroy a Family Tradition—Prevent Child Abuse" (National Committee for Prevention of Child Abuse, 1978). Family and parent resource centers are operating in Illinois and Florida and new ideas and programs are blossoming every day. The whole field is in its infancy and can hardly be expected to have produced the hard data that would validate various interventions. But this should not be the only criterion in judging the value of parent education as a primary prevention strategy to ameliorate child abuse and neglect. The severity and pervasiveness of the problem and its devastation of human resources, argues for immediate and sustained intervention at all levels and continued accumulation of confirming data.

References

Albee, G. *The problems of primary prevention.* Speech presented at the Annenburg School of Communications Conference on "Child abuse: Cultural roots and policy options." Philadelphia, November 1978.

American Humane Association. *Annual statistical analysis of child neglect and abuse reporting: 1977.* Denver: American Humane Association, 1979.

American Medical Association. *Parent and newborn interaction.* Press release distributed December 21, 1978.

Anonymous parent. Personal communication, 1978.

Brodeur, A. Radiologic identification of abuse. *Proceedings of the Conference on Identification of Child Abuse and Neglect,* Jefferson City, Mo., June 1976.

Brown, L. Personal communication, March 19, 1979.

Caffey, J. Multiple fractures in the long bones of children suffering from chronic subdural hematoma. *American Journal of Roentology, Radiologic Therapy and Nuclear Medicine,* 1946, *56,* 163–173.

Dinkmeyer, D., & McCay, J. *Systematic training for effective parenting.* Circle Pines, Minn.: American Guidance Services, 1976.

Dugan, C. Personal communication, March 1979.

Education Commission of the States. *Report and recommendations of the National Advisory Committee on Child Abuse and Neglect,* Denver, April 1978.

Fontana, V. J., & Besharov, D. *The maltreated child.* Springfield, Ill.: Charles C. Thomas, 1977.

Footsteps: A discussion guide. Baltimore: University Park Press, 1979.

Footsteps: A publicity resource kit. Lexington, Ky.: Kentucky Educational Television, 1979.

Fraser, B. G. The child and his parents: A delicate balance of rights. In R. E. Helfer & C. H. Kempe (Eds.), *Child abuse and neglect: The family and the community.* Cambridge, Mass.: Ballinger Publishing, 1976.

Gelles, R. J. *A profile of violence towards children in the United States.* Paper presented at the Annenburg School of Communications Conference on "Child abuse: Cultural roots and policy options." Philadelphia, November 20, 1978.

Gordon, T. *Parent effectiveness training.* New York: Peter Wyden, 1970.

Helfer, R. E. Unpublished speech at Kansas Governor's Conference for the Prevention of Child Abuse, Wichita, Kans., October 1977.

Helfer, R. E. *Child abuse: A plan for prevention.* Chicago: National Committee for the Prevention of Child Abuse, 1978. (a)

Helfer, R. E. *Childhood comes first: A crash course in childhood for adults.* Lansing, Mich.: Ray E. Helfer, 1978. (b)

Helfer, R. E., & Kempe, C. H. *The battered child.* Chicago: University of Chicago Press, 1968.

Helfer, R. E., & Kempe, C. H. (Eds.). *Child abuse and neglect: The family and the community.* Cambridge, Mass.: Ballinger Publishing, 1976.

I Am a Parents Anonymous Parent. Torrance, Calif.: Parents Anonymous, 1974.

Kansas Committee for the Prevention of Child Abuse. *Some wounds never heal.* Wichita, Kans.: Harvest Communications, 1978.

Kempe, C. H. Preface. In R. E. Helfer, *Childhood comes first: A crash course in childhood for adults.* Lansing, Mich.: Ray E. Helfer, 1978.

Kempe, C. H., Silverman, F. N., Steele, B. F., Droegemeuller, W., & Silver, H. K. The battered child syndrome. *Journal of the American Medical Association,* 1962, *181,* 17.

Kempe, C. H., & Helfer, R. E. (Eds.). *Helping the battered child and his family.* Philadelphia: J. B. Lippincott, 1972.

Kennell, J., Voos, D., & Klaus, M. Parent–infant bonding. In R. E. Helfer & C. H. Kempe (Eds.), *Child abuse and neglect: The family and the community.* Cambridge, Mass.: Ballinger Publishing, 1976.

Kerne, R. Quoted in M. A. Rock, Gorilla mothers need some help from their friends. *Smithsonian,* July 1978, 58–62.

Klaus, M. *Parent–infant bonding.* Speech presented at a conference on "Child abuse and neglect: The role of physicians, nurses, and allied health personnel in its prevention." Wichita, Kans., June 1978.

Klaus, M. H., & Kennell, J. H. *Maternal–infant bonding.* St. Louis: C. V. Mosby, 1976.

Land, H. Commentary. In *Footsteps: A discussion guide.* Baltimore: University Park Press, 1979.

Lieber, L., & Baker, J. *P.A.—Self-help treatment for child abusing parents: A review and evaluation.* Paper presented at the International Congress on Child Abuse and Neglect, Geneva, September 22, 1976.

Martin, H. P. (Ed.). *The abused child: A multidisciplinary approach to developmental issues and treatment.* Cambridge, Mass.: Ballinger Publishing, 1976.

McClain, T. Editorial. *Concept,* Spring 1978, 14.

Menninger, K. Personal communication, April 1979.

Michigan Department of Mental Health. *A report of some aspects of the effectiveness of the "Pierre the Pelican" mental health pamphlets.* Lansing, Mich.: State Department of Mental Health, 1952. (Records of the Michigan Department of Mental Health, R. G. 62-41, records relating to research projects)

Nadler, R. Quoted in M. A. Rock, Gorilla mothers need some help from their friends. *Smithsonian,* July 1978, 58–62.

Nagi, S. Z. *Child maltreatment in the United States.* New York: Columbia University Press, 1977.

National Center on Child Abuse and Neglect. *Interdisciplinary glossary on child abuse and neglect: Legal, medical and social work terms.* Washington, D. C.: U. S. Department of Health, Education and Welfare [DHEW Publication No. (OHDS) 78-30137], 1978.

National Committee for Prevention of Child Abuse. *Prevent child abuse.* Chicago: NCPCA, 1978.

National PTA. *How to help children become better parents: A resource kit.* Chicago: National Congress of Parents and Teachers, 1978.

Raney, A. *A response to a request.* Ann Arbor, Mich., 1976.

Rock, M. A. Gorilla mothers need some help from their friends. *Smithsonian.* July 1978, 58–62.

Rowland, L. *Pierre the Pelican: Postnatal series.* New Orleans: Louisiana Association for Mental Health, 1947. (Revised 1957, 1967.)

Rowland, L. *Pierre the Pelican: Prenatal series.* New Orleans: Louisiana Association for Mental Health, 1950. (Revised 1969, 1978.)

Rowland, L. *Pierre the Pelican, Revised.* New Orleans: Family Publications Center, 1977.

Rowland, L. Personal communication, March 19, 1979.

Sandler, J. Commentary. In *Footsteps: A discussion guide.* Baltimore: University Park Press, 1979.

Smith, D. E. P. A review. In J. Valusek, *People are not for hitting.* Wichita, Kans.: John E. Valusek, 1974.

Storrs, A. *Human aggression.* New York: Atheneum, 1968.

Tramontana, M. G., Sherrets, S. D., & Authier, K. J. *Evaluation of parent education programs.* Lincoln, Neb.: University of Nebraska College of Medicine, 1979.

Uviller, R. *Save them from their saviors: Constitutional rights of the family.* Speech presented at the Annenburg School of Communications Conference on "Child abuse: Cultural roots and policy options." Philadelphia, November 20, 1978.

Valusek, J. *People are not for hitting.* Wichita, Kans.: John E. Valusek, 1974.

Young, L. *Wednesday's children.* New York: McGraw-Hill, 1964.

Zigler, E. *Controlling child abuse in America: An effort doomed to failure?* Speech presented at the Annenburg School of Communications Conference on "Child abuse: Cultural roots and policy options." Philadelphia, November 20, 1978.

Chapter 12

Parenting Education for Youth

KAREN W. BARTZ

Programs for youth who are not yet parents are the best examples of the preventive potential of effective parent education. What better time to instill the attitudes and skills that make for good parenting than before having children? Educational programs for youth can help prepare future parents rather than attempt to repair what has already gone wrong, as so many adult programs must do.

Many people have proposed some type of mandatory parenting education program for young people. Usually such plans revolve around a required course for every boy and girl in junior high or high school. Some have proposed that elementary school children should also experience a required course in parenting.

However, the concept of preparing youth for parenthood is deceptively simple. Several pragmatic and philosophical issues complicate the ultimate goal of preventing future problems. These include the fact that 1 out of every 10 17-year-old girls in the United States is already a mother. In 1974, 247,000 adolescent girls 17 years of age and under gave birth. About 13,000 births occurred among girls younger than 15 (Guttmacher Institute, 1976). How early must education for parenthood begin? Another issue revolves around motivation to learn about parenthood. Are adolescents motivated to prepare for a future life role or do their more immediate developmental tasks take priority?

Finally, there are the most basic questions of all. What are the at-

HANDBOOK ON
PARENT EDUCATION

titudes and skills that make for effective parenting? And is it feasible to think that these can be packaged into an effective educational program for youth?

All of these issues are interrelated and will be explored in more detail throughout this chapter. First, however, it is important to present the current "state of the art" in educating youth for parenthood.

The 1970s—Youth Needs Become Obvious

Youth have less opportunity for preparent education in the homes of today as compared with the past when families were larger and older children were expected to help with the younger members. The school and social world of today's youth involves them more often in activities with their peers than in cross-age relationships. And the nature of parenthood has changed so much in recent generations that what youth learn at home may be inadequate or, in some cases, detrimental to being good parents themselves. Thus, as with preparation for so many other roles in life, schools have been expected to take on more responsibility in this area also.

Educating for parenthood has been an implicit goal of home economics classes in child development and family relationships for many years. But not many students take these classes. Around 1970 less than one-ninth of all secondary school students were enrolled in vocational home economics classes, and many of these classes do not deal directly with child development or family relations. About 95% of the students in courses related to parenthood were young women (Kruger, 1973a).

In the late 1960s and early 1970s, several studies and reports drew public attention to an abysmal state of knowledge among our nation's youth about children and parenting. Facts on adolescent pregnancy, child abuse, and child health were disturbing. One of the most frequently mentioned studies was one by Vladimir de Lissovoy (1973). He interviewed several adolescent parents and reported that few had any realistic expectations of what their children were capable of doing and understanding. It is clear that frustration, anger, and perhaps abuse can easily develop when parents, for example, believe that an infant can understand the difference between right and wrong.

Around 1970, many professionals also became more aware of the problems of adolescent pregnancy. Out-of-wedlock births to girls 17 years of age and younger increased 75% between 1961 and 1974. Nine out of 10 teenage mothers decide to keep their babies rather than give them up for adoption. And failure to complete high school, an increasingly important indicator of future life-style, is very common among teenage mothers (Guttmacher, 1976).

All of these developments brought about a painful awareness of the need for preparent and adolescent parent education. For both groups of youth, many significant developments have occurred over the past 5 years.

Meeting the Needs of School-Age Parents

Since the 1960s there has been a dramatic change in attitudes and policies concerning the pregnant junior high or high school student. In the not-too-distant past, such students were automatically expelled from school. Then schools started to develop separate programs to provide these students with a means of at least completing their education. Now some schools are encouraging pregnant students to remain in regular classes as long as possible. In addition, some pregnant adolescent girls, their boyfriends or husbands, and their families have access to comprehensive education, health, and social service systems.

Two groups have been instrumental in bringing about these changes. They are the Consortium on Early Childbearing and Childrearing and the National Alliance Concerned with School-Age Parents. Both have sponsored conferences and workshops to make schools and communities aware of the needs of pregnant students.

Additional impetus to address the problems of school-age parents came in 1977 when the Department of Health, Education and Welfare appointed an Adolescent Pregnancy Task Force. Important new federal legislation to expand preventive and aftercare services and to encourage linkages between community service providers is now being implemented. It is too early to determine the direction that such services will take as a result of this current initiative.

A Place for Parenting Education

Dealing with the many needs of the pregnant school-age girl or school-age parent of either sex is a challenging proposition. Completing their formal education is only one concern. These students also need special vocational or career education to help in assuming the financial responsibilities of parenthood. A third need is for health care and social services for the girl while pregnant and for both mother and child after delivery. And finally they need education for parenthood, either as a single- or two-parent family.

Only comprehensive care programs for school-age pregnant girls and school-age parents, both girls and boys, can adequately address these many needs. In 1968, there were about 35 such programs in existence in our nations' schools. In 1976, there were approximately 350 comprehensive programs, most of them in alternative schools (U.S. Office of Education, 1978). This reflects significant, but certainly not sufficient, progress to meet the needs of all pregnant school-age girls.

At this time there is little statistical evidence that one method of programming for school-age parents is any more effective than another (Honig, 1978). But certainly some parenting education is essential for most of these youth. However, it is likely that in the press to meet the many needs of these youth, the parenting education offered has had little depth. An absolute minimum level of learning would include the physiological and psychological aspects of pregnancy and childbirth plus early infant care. Such knowledge and skills are often taught through classroom experiences or contact with community social and health services. A few exceptional programs offer supervised infant day care to give the young mother role models for effective parenting while also freeing the mother to continue her schooling. In infant care centers, much learning occurs by "osmosis." Young mothers can see new techniques of feeding, discipline, and stimulating infant development. They can practice these techniques themselves under the watchful eye of the center caregivers and at home after school.

Almost inevitably, however, a basic conflict is confronted. What happens when the technique a young mother prefers is not the same as that used by the center caregivers? The same principle must be dealt with by any parent educator who attempts to modify ethnic, racial, socioeconomic, or simply family idiosyncracies in parenting. Professional consensus appears to be that if a method is not blatantly harmful, center caregivers should try to adopt the mother's practices (Ogg, 1975; Weigle, 1974). The basic needs of children for a balanced diet, body care, physical loving, and stimulation of the senses must not be compromised, but parents can meet these needs in a variety of ways. The success of any program attempting to change child-care practices no doubt lies in how new ideas are presented. Respect for the values and past experiences of the young mother, and working gently within these parameters, will be infinitely more effective than pronouncing edicts or demanding that they follow certain rules.

Public school programs for school-age parents have been the primary focus of this discussion. It should not be assumed that schools are or should be the only agency providing services to the school-age parent. Hospitals, special homes for youth, private volunteer groups, such as the YWCA, and public social service agencies also provide individual or collaborative programs in many communities. At this time it is not possible to conclude that the programs under the auspices of any one institution are most effective in meeting the needs of school-age parents (Honig, 1978). The most effective model probably involves the cooperation of many such groups.

Programs for youth who are already parents are only part of the picture of parenting education for youth. As Ogg (1975) has stated, "For educators to concern themselves with an adolescent girl's parenting skills only after she has become pregnant, however, and to ignore those of the adolescent boy altogether, is now seen as 'too little, too late' [p. 9]." Consequently, the past 5 years have brought about significant developments in preparent education.

The "Education for Parenthood" Initiative

Credit for the current status of preparent education in our country must be given largely to the federal government. In 1972, the U.S. Office of Education, the Office of Child Development, and the National Institute of Mental Health cooperatively launched a major national initiative called "Education for Parenthood." The thrust of this initiative was toward the development of curriculum models for youth parenting education in both school and nonschool settings. The initiative not only stimulated public awareness of the need for parent education, but also provided the seed money to start many new programs.[1]

"Education for Parenthood" had two major components. One was the development of a classroom curriculum to provide adolescents with information about child development and to involve adolescents in regular personal contact with young children. The second component involved seven national voluntary youth-serving organizations in the development of nonschool curriculum models.

The first component of the project received the greatest commitment of resources and sustained follow-up from the federal government. Secondary schools were seen as the last opportunity to provide universal parenthood education. Further support for a secondary school emphasis was based upon Kruger's (1973b) observation that,

---

[1] Although the major thrust of the project is now completed, the U.S. Office of Education still serves as a clearing house for program materials and a source of technical assistance to schools and agencies.

When it comes to learning what it takes to be a good parent, the home is a decreasingly active, albeit still primary, source of instruction. Nor has the church or any other private organization been able to take up the slack. More and more, the job of reinforcing the home in this sensitive area is becoming the responsibility of the schools [p. 1].

However, both the school and nonschool components of the "Education for Parenthood" project were directed at achieving the same basic objectives. Although different programs developed in this project varied in their emphases, many, if not all, of the following objectives were apparent in each:

1. To help adolescents learn more about themselves—attitudes, values, future goals.
2. To promote understanding of others, especially younger children.
3. To impart knowledge of the developmental process—physical, social, emotional, and cognitive.
4. To teach specific skills of caring for and interacting with children.
5. To develop awareness of the impact of a family on a child and vice versa.
6. To help adolescents to appreciate the responsibilities involved in being a parent.
7. To create knowledge of and interest in careers involving children.

Since the "Education for Parenthood" initiative has been the major influence upon preparent education in recent years, some details of the goals, assumptions, teaching techniques, and results of typical programs will serve to illustrate the nature of much of today's preparenting education for youth.

A School Curriculum—"Exploring Childhood"

The school curriculum model developed under the auspices of "Education for Parenthood" is entitled "Exploring Childhood." It was designed by the Education Development Center (1978) in Cambridge, Massachusetts, for boys and girls in grades 7 through 12.

The basic curriculum model is designed to be used as a 1-year course with three major modules. One module focuses upon working with children and sets the stage for the students to have "hands-on" experience with youngsters. Students may work with children in such settings as Head Start programs, day-care centers, nursery schools, or parent cooperatives. The second module presupposes that when students actually start interacting with young children, they will be motivated to learn about child development. This module synthesizes general data about child growth and development with some major theories of development and perspectives on child care in other societies. The third module moves the students from perceiving the child as an individual to the child as a social member. It emphasizes the interaction of child with family, community, environment, and social values. An attempt is made to create some feeling for the systemic nature of the family.

COURSE FORMAT

The combination of classroom learning and practical experience with children, which is basic to the "Exploring Childhood" curriculum, deserves emphasis. Conceptually, it appears that this approach to parenting education for youth is the most valid. It addresses itself to the typical criticisms one hears of many high school courses, that is, they are too abstract, not relevant, and involve passive learning. In combination with the fact that the classroom materials include many audiovisual aids and workbooks, "Exploring Childhood" has great potential for capturing and keeping the interest of youth. However, it must be noted that the idea of field work with children originated many years before this particular curriculum. In the 1960s many schools introduced a laboratory approach to child development that combined classroom activities with time in a preschool or day-care setting.

In addition to making the course interesting and fun, practical experience with children carries with it other important benefits. It helps adolescents in their continuing struggle to establish a sense of identity. A young child's response of pure pleasure to an adolescent boosts the youth's self-confidence. A child's very candid reactions to an adolescent's appearance, language, or mannerisms can also be enlightening. Youth constantly test their perceptions of themselves against the feedback they get from others. Young children give back to the adolescent a relatively undistorted image.

Certainly direct experience with children is the most practical form of education for a career in child care. The curriculum materials emphasize the basic skills needed by a child-care worker. The emphasis given to the worker's influence upon children hopefully displaces the traditional view that such work is "not very important." The importance of the parental role is also given a boost in the process. Finally, practical experience in the school setting makes up, in part, for the lack of contact with young children at home or in their neighborhood. It assists in the translation of factual knowledge into usable skills and functional values.

COURSE EFFECTIVENESS

After 2 years of implementation, an evaluation of the "Exploring Childhood" curriculum was conducted by the Education Development Center (1976). This evaluation included attempts to determine changes in student knowledge, attitudes, and practical skills as a result of completing the course curriculum. Although "Exploring Childhood" is only one particular approach to parenting education for youth, the results of the evaluation can provide some insight into the effectiveness of any similar preparent education.

"Exploring Childhood," as with most parent education programs for adults or youth, reaches females primarily. Over 90% of the students in 1975 were females. This is despite concerted efforts to recruit boys into the classes. However, the curriculum has been relatively successful in attracting students of low socioeconomic status. Over half of the students gave self-reports that placed them in this group.

Compared with a control group, students who completed "Exploring Childhood" attained scores indicating greater knowledge of working with children and of ways to learn about children. Specific knowledge about child development concepts and issues seemed less influenced by the "Exploring Childhood" curriculum.

Attitudinal changes among course participants were found in the areas of expressing more tenderness and affection to children, allowing the expression of aggression, using mild rather than harsh punishment, and encouraging autonomy. The changes were small and not especially dramatic. They were often related to having taken a previous child development course, student age, sex, educational expectations, and ethnicity.

The sex-related differences illustrate some important cultural qualities that must be dealt with in any parent education program. Females favor expressing feelings and showing tenderness to children more than males, even before taking the "Exploring Childhood" course. Females also tend to be more tolerant of aggression. Males type themselves as more serious and severe with children and favor harsh punishment and strict rules more than females. "Exploring Childhood" may influence these attitudes a little, but it does not bring male and female participants into congruence on any of these issues. It appears that cultural conditioning of the sexes is difficult to impact.

Although it is possible to relate many highly impressive expressions by students about their learning and gaining insights from a parent education course, the factual analysis of "Exploring Childhood" is not overwhelmingly impressive. One of the major reasons for this may be the self-selective nature of the course. In most cases, any kind of parenting education course in the school is an elective. It generally attracts female students and students who already hold values consistent with the goals of the course. These students are already motivated to learn about children and to apply their learning to a future career or parent role. This is not to imply that the students are failing to learn valuable skills, knowledge, and attitudes as potential parents, but that the course experience may be only reinforcing that which is already a part of the student's repertoire in a vast majority of cases (Behavior Associates, 1977).

COURSE THEORY

Many of the models of parent education programs and their theoretical foundations previously presented in this book are reflected in the "Exploring Childhood" curriculum. However, no one model prevails in the curriculum, and the primary emphasis is not upon communication, as in many parent education models for adults, but upon development. The developmental perspective in the curriculum is described as:

> Human development is a process of continual growth and potential. From the moment of birth, the individual influences the people and the world around him or her, and is shaped by those people and that world. This view might be defined as "mutuality," "reciprocity," or "interaction"; its message is that one is influenced—but not bound by—one's past, one's peers and elders, and one's culture. Rather than promote any specific body or information or any particular skill, *Exploring Childhood* suggests an *attitude* toward development that stresses the capacity of the person—whether child, adolescent, or adult—to synthesize past experience and to continue to grow in relationship with others. We view the young child as an active being endowed from the start with resources for coping, for growth, and for human interaction [Education Development Center, 1978, p 6].

Thus, an emphasis upon developmental concepts and the total system within which the parent–child relationship exists are important differences between this approach to parent education and the models previously described. One might even question whether it is too ambitious as a conceptual framework. In some ways it is more difficult to teach this approach to parenting than it is to teach some relatively concrete techniques for communicating between parent and child. The fact that the concepts are subsequently translated and applied in practical field work is essential to the learning process.

Close inspection of the "Exploring Childhood" materials suggests, at least to this author, that many parent education programs for adults are philosophically and conceptually shallow. How many adult programs ask participants to compare their own values to that of other cultures?

How many use the field of art to show how children change physically and cognitively? How many help parents to experience the egocentricism of a child's world? How many involve parents interacting with children under the watchful eye of a trained observer? This is not to suggest that this particular curriculum, or other similar ones, is the most effective way of teaching youth about parenting, as will be discussed later. However, many of the concepts and activities can be appropriately and effectively used in adult programs. In actuality, the curriculum is now being used in over 300 colleges and universities and about 400 community agencies around the country (Behavior Associates, 1977). The curriculum has also been revised for use with parents involved in Head Start programs.

CURRENT STATUS OF PARENT EDUCATION IN SCHOOLS

In 1977, "Exploring Childhood" was being used in over 2300 schools around the country (Behavior Associates, 1977). In addition, no one knows for sure how many schools have been influenced to adapt or create classroom offerings in parenting education as a result of the "Education for Parenthood" initiative. Certainly there are more youth receiving some type of parenting education now through the public and private schools than before this government program, but it is also reasonable to predict that many, many more youth do not receive such an educational experience. In only six states and the District of Columbia are the public schools required to provide education about sexuality, parenting, and family life (Institute of Medicine, 1978, p. 16).

In 1976, family life professionals in 40 states were surveyed for their assessment of the amount of parent education offered in local secondary schools (Kerckhoff & Habig, 1976). One out of 10 could find no parent education in their local schools, and about 3 out of 10 could find courses in only a few schools. The remaining professionals said that parent education was a part of the curriculum in most or all secondary schools in their area, usually as a part of another course rather than as a separate offering. Many of these parent education courses primarily focused upon normal child growth and development or they were simply an extension of traditional family life education. The importance of this distinction is further discussed in the next section of this chapter entitled "What Do Youth Need to Know?"

A formal parenthood preparation experience for all youth attending public schools is certainly not a reality. Several factors are inhibiting the development of such programs for youth. One is a lack of good teaching materials. Aside from the "Exploring Childhood" curriculum, there are few textbooks, films or other materials appropriate for youth (Kerckhoff & Habig, 1976).

A second factor is a shortage of trained teachers. In most cases the responsibility for teaching family life education in the public schools belongs to the home economics teacher. In fewer cases a health educator, social science teacher, or counselor assumes the responsibility (Kerckhoff & O'Connor, 1978). The same pattern is probably true of parenting education. Even many home economists need further specialized training in parent education, as contrasted to traditional child development and family relations (Coward & Kerckhoff, 1978). Teachers using the "Exploring Childhood" curriculum do have access to special teacher workshops and opportunities for field site visits. The curriculum also has extensive support materials for teachers. Often such training and acquisition of resource material is financed through federal projects. At this time there appears to be little support among professionals or state education departments for specific certification of parent education teachers (Kerckhoff & O'Connor, 1978).

Some commonly held public attitudes are also preventing the teaching of parent education in some schools. The "back to basics" movement has shifted attention away from responding to social issues. For some people, parent education in the schools detracts from the family's responsibilities. They believe that such courses will reduce parental impact and influence upon children. To this argument, it can be stated that:

> Parent education has the opposite goal: it tries to increase parental influence on their children's behavior by making the parents more effective. The ultimate aim of parent education is to develop in parents the skills that will guide their children's behavior more effectively [Coward & Kerchkoff, 1978, p. 26].

Another fear is that large-scale parent education programs will produce homogeneity among parents and children. It is believed that parent education espouses only one way of rearing children. Thus all parents and ultimately all children will be the same. A review of the many models in this book alone should convince the skeptic that there is a little unanimity among parent educators!

Coward and Kerckhoff (1978) have stated that any attempt to increase the amount of parent education in the schools will fail unless attention is paid to both the lack of instructors and instructional materials and the existence of negative public attitudes. Progress on either issue alone will be negated by the other.

A further consideration in determining the future of school-based parent education for youth is that of making it a required or elective course. An elective course will probably not achieve the goal of reaching all youth. But required courses are often resented by students. It is often difficult to motivate students in required courses. In addition, a required course in parenting may imply that all students are going to be parents. Parenting education must prepare youth for many future alternatives, including singlehood, marriage without children, and even children without marriage (Kerckhoff & Habig, 1976). Parenting education for youth in any setting must give attention to the decision to be a parent or not.

Voluntary Youth-Serving Organizations Tackle the Problem

The second component of the "Education for Parenthood" project was the involvement of seven national voluntary youth-serving organizations in developing pilot programs for adolescents in nonschool settings. The organizations involved were Boy Scouts, Boys' Clubs, 4-H, Girl Scouts, National Federation of Settlements and Neighborhood Centers, Salvation Army, and Save the Children Federation. Each received 3-year grants. These are certainly not the only informal education groups teaching parent education to youth. Churches, social service agencies, and other youth groups have similar goals. However, the programs of these seven agencies are the most extensively developed and evaluated. Data from these programs provide the most reliable assessment of parenting education for youth outside the formal school system.

Although each organization created a slightly different approach to the challenge of preparing youth for parenthood, some commonalities in content are apparent. One-quarter of all training sessions across all of these programs were devoted to child development information. The next most commonly mentioned purposes of the training sessions were to assist in self-understanding and to impart sex education. Exploring child-care jobs or careers was the purpose of less than 5% of all sessions (Behavior Associates, 1977).

Thus, as a whole, the approach of the national voluntary youth organizations to parenting education appears to differ somewhat from that of the school-based curriculum, especially with the inclusion of sex education and de-emphasis upon career exploration. However, the programs of the youth organizations differed a great deal from one another. A brief description of some of them gives an idea of the diversity of approach to the basic goal of education for parenthood.

PROGRAM FORMATS

The Boy Scouts developed a career education program around the Explorer Post concept, a basic program model for older youth. To explore careers in child care, posts were created in schools, day-care nurseries, centers for the handicapped, and other locations. This aspect of the program was supplemented by a seminar on children and family dynamics and publications to spread parent education concepts throughout the organization's programs.

The 4-H programs varied greatly in content and technique. In one program young mothers were paired with pregnant teenagers to serve as friend and confidante. Another used a peer-leader model to train adolescents to teach other adolescents about human development, child care, and interpersonal skills. These two youth organizations, along with the Girl Scouts, primarily reached girls with their parenting programs. Even in the Boy Scouts, less than 5% of the participants in this program have been boys (Behavior Associates, 1977).

However, the Boys' Clubs and the National Federation of Settlements and Neighborhood Centers were successful in attracting about equal numbers of girls and boys to their parenting classes. The Boys' Clubs' program trained older youth members to help work with younger children in clubs and their communities. Developing such leadership skills involved communication techniques from Gordon's Parent Effectiveness Training (1970) and practical skills for childrearing and homemaking. Youth were involved in the actual planning and coordinating of activities and training. The National Federation program aimed at youth from low-income families and emphasized self-development rather than specific parenting skills. The medical and emotional aspects of pregnancy, prenatal development, and childbirth were important aspects of this program.

The Save the Children Federation trained youth in parenting skills and then deployed them in the community to contact and teach parents of infants and toddlers. During regular visits to the homes of young children, the youth left information, toys, and play ideas with the parents. The youth were paid a small amount for their work in this project. Thus, in addition to learning personal parenting skills, the youth were also performing a community service in rural areas that had few social services. Actual observation and care of children appear to have played a less significant role in the programs of the youth agencies than in the classroom curriculum, except for the program of the Save the Children Federation.

The voluntary agencies used a variety of techniques to obtain the trainers needed for their programs. Some used existing staff, whereas others hired special staff for this project alone. However, all relied to some extent upon community resource people who volunteered to teach the programs. The Boy Scout and Girl Scout programs relied heavily upon this source of trainers.

PROGRAM EFFECTIVENESS

An independent evaluation of all the youth agency programs was completed during each of the 3 years the agencies were involved in the "Education for Parenthood" initiative (Behavior Associates, 1977). A long-term effect study is also underway at this time to assess the impact up to 4 years after the program.

The evaluation included comparison groups at each site that were given pretests and posttests, as were groups of youth involved in the educational programs. Both opinion and knowledge change were assessed. Although there were some differences among the youth group programs in their effect upon opinions and/or knowledge, the youth group programs as a whole had only a slight effect upon participants' opinions about children, parenthood, themselves, and careers in child care. The participants' opinions of their own child-care skills changed the most as a result of the programs. Self-ratings of child-care skills by participants in the parenthood programs increased from pretest to posttest, whereas those in the comparison groups did not change over time. Although questions about child-care skills were phrased as opinions about one's self, they indirectly reflect behavioral change, rather than attitudinal change. This indicates that the educational programs, as a whole, may have more impact on behavior than on attitudes.

In knowledge about prenatal development, infant behavior, children's needs, and family life, there were very small but significant changes among those participants in the parenthood programs. In general, the parenthood programs were most effective in bringing about increased knowledge of prenatal development and understanding children's needs, including the general nature of children, effect of environmental stimuli, and health needs.

Females in these programs of the national youth organizations started and ended their educational experience with more knowledge about children than did males. In fact, after the programs, the males involved still did not exhibit a level of knowledge about children as great as that of females before starting the program.

The evaluation attempted to determine which program format of the national voluntary youth agencies was the most effective. After controlling for all the differences in age, sex, race, and family composition, no program stood out as significantly more effective than others. Within all programs, however, it appears that the use of rap sessions and role playing were characteristic of the more effective sessions.

CURRENT STATUS OF PARENTHOOD EDUCATION IN YOUTH ORGANIZATIONS

No recent assessment has been made of the parenthood programs offered by the national youth groups participating in the "Education for Parenthood" initiative. With loss of funding for staff and new material development, it can be predicted that the programs have either leveled off or declined in impact. Those youth groups that attempted to integrate parenting education into their ongoing program efforts have probably been most effective beyond the 3 years of the grant.

However, in the final analysis, the parenthood programs of the national voluntary youth organizations and the public schools with the "Exploring Childhood" and other development courses can claim to have had only a small impact upon the attitudes and skills of the future parents they attempted to train. Education *for* parenthood is obviously not an easy undertaking.

What Do Youth Need to Know?

The most logical question to ask at this time seems to be, "What do youth need to know to become effective parents?" A wide variety of topic areas has already been mentioned in describing the programs of schools and youth agencies. The "Exploring Childhood" program is, as the title implies, largely slanted toward child development and child care. In fact, in many programs it seems as though parent education is synonymous with child development. An understanding of child development is an essential part of parenting education for youth. Then from this foundation must be built other understanding related to self-development, personal values, interpersonal responsibility, and love. One of the most difficult concepts to teach is that of the lifelong commitment involved in being a parent.

In their published evaluation of the youth agency programs described earlier, Behavior Associates (1977) created a materials matrix combining major topics related to parenting with three nonhierarchical levels of learning—feelings, facts, and skills. The following list of topics is a summary and synthesis of that matrix.[2] Only a few specifics are listed

---

[2] Some topics have been expanded to reflect needs that the author feels should be addressed in preparent education.

after each topic. In almost every case, each topic area is adequately taught only through all three levels of learning—feelings, facts, and skills. Altogether, the list gives a picture of the many facets of a comprehensive parenthood education program.

1. Topics related to self-understanding and interpersonal relationships:
   a. *Self-awareness.* Self-confidence, recognition of values, understanding own capabilities, appreciation of individuality, ability to make decisions.
   b. *Relating to others.* Knowing the value of spending time with children, how to show love and affection, the systemic nature of family living.
   c. *Attitudes and approaches to life.* Willingness to seek help, positive attitudes toward parenting, approaching problems with humor, realistic expectations.
   d. *Human sexuality.* Sex roles, human reproduction, family planning, parental sexuality.
2. Topics related to children:
   a. *Prenatal development.* Heredity, genetic abnormalities, nutrition, drugs, pregnancy, childbirth.
   b. *Physical, intellectual, social development.* Building self-esteem, differences between children and adults, a child's view of things, expected behaviors of different ages, theories of development, positive motivation, individuality, early childhood stimulation, toys, play.
   c. *Behavior and discipline.* Accepting a child's problems, discipline versus punishment, parents as models, consistency, encouraging self-reliance.
   d. *Children with special needs.* Learning disabilities, physical handicaps, mental retardation.
   e. *Child health and safety.* Nutrition, health care, legal requirements.
3. Topics related to family and environment:
   a. *Parent needs and styles.* Value of time with children and away from children, styles of relating to children, parental expectations, handling stress.
   b. *Family life-styles.* Choosing to be a parent or nonparent, importance of the parent–child relationship, the joys of parenting, selecting child care, role of TV.
   c. *Community resources.* Where and how to seek assistance.
   d. *Children's and parent's rights.* Balancing the legal and ethical rights of parents and children.

    e. *Family management.* Decision making, economics of raising a
      child, time management, homemaking, purchasing services
      and goods related to children.
    f. *Family communication.* Communicating love, general communi-
      cation skills with children of all ages and adults.
    g. *Children's needs.* Value of play, exposing the child to a variety of
      learning opportunities, helping children to make decisions.

This list is a composite. No one program in existence now adequately
addresses all the topics in the list. It is probably unrealistic to think that
any such program could be developed.

Basically what this illustrates is the fallacy of conceptualizing parenting education for youth as a self-contained school course or youth
agency program. Effective education for parenthood must be comprehensive, interdisciplinary, experience-based, long-range, multigoal,
competency-based and equally appropriate for both young men and
women (Kruger, 1975). There will be no easy, short-term, media-
packaged program to solve the problems presented by youth in-
adequately prepared for parenthood.

What Do Youth Want to Learn?

Before proceeding to suggest how we may more effectively approach
the delivery of parenting education to our youth, a final issue remains
unresolved. Are youth who are not yet parents developmentally ready
to learn about children and parenthood? If the interests and needs of
youth are not taken into account, parenthood education becomes just
another "required course" that must be endured before youth can
escape the formal education system. At least in the national youth
organizations, an adolescent can generally choose what he or she wants
to learn. But even the best parenting program, by professional standards, will be avoided if it is not designed around the primary needs
of youth.

There are some critics of the current direction that parenting education for youth is taking in our country. De Lissovoy (1978), who ironically instigated much of the furor with his studies of adolescent parents,
has recently published a critical commentary on the "Exploring Childhood" curriculum. He admits that the curriculum itself is the best
available but claims that it is being used with the wrong audience.
De Lissovoy suggests that most adolescents are not maturationally ready
to understand what it means to be a parent. He cites polls of youth
interests and the theoretical concepts of adolescent egocentrism and ego

identity to show that youth are really not interested in parent education. Youth are eager to learn about children only when they are prospective parents-to-be.

De Lissovoy suggests that an experience such as the "Exploring Childhood" course should be saved for young parents and parents-to-be. This approach would capitalize on maximum motivation to learn and would facilitate the involvement of both parents in an experience that would build family ties. So what is needed for all the other high school students?

A pre-parent education program to facilitate the adolescents' resolution of the identity crisis; the need is to assist the adolescent to move towards the identification of occupational choices and an ideological commitment, both of which are the precursors in the epigenesis to generativity and parental sense. . . . The goals of a program oriented to adolescent development should center around the issues of self, interpersonal relationships and skills, and values within a democratic milieu [de Lissovoy, 1978, p. 331].

Cohen (1973) has also cautioned educators about assuming that youth will respond to what adults think they should be thinking and planning. Cohen agrees with de Lissovoy that the parental role is not developmentally suitable to adolescents and that few place priority on learning about the role. Some adolescents may even become quite disturbed by close involvement with young children and discussions of family relationships. However, Cohen still sees the value of a parenting education experience for most youth, even those who have no immediate future prospect of becoming parents. He believes that such an educational experience can meet some of an adolescent's current developmental needs. Emphasis must be upon the present as an adolescent rather than upon some nebulous future as a parent.

For example, a basic developmental task of adolescence is to begin to understand the feelings and behaviors of themselves and others. Exposure to young children through a parent education program in school or some other setting can facilitate learning that is deeply relevant to this task.

They will learn that the existence of pain and confusion during certain developmental phases is natural, that behavior can be understood, that it is not easy to be a parent, that the child is not entirely the product of what his parents do with or for him, and that there are caring people who have professional competence in understanding people's lives [Cohen, 1973, p. 29].

Adolescents also need to feel helpful and useful. The opportunity to work with young children uses their energy and idealism toward a rewarding goal for both the adolescents and youngsters involved.

A Focus for the Future

All of this suggests two closely interrelated recommendations for the future direction of parenting education for youth. First, the appropriate developmental needs of youth must be considered before youth will enter a parenting education program with enthusiasm, interest, and motivation to learn. The emphasis must be upon helping youth with today's problems. A skillfully designed program will, in the process of addressing today's problems, also help youth to gain basic skills of decision making, communication, and empathy, all of which are valuable attributes for youth who choose to become parents in the future.

Second, the development of the skills, attitudes, and knowledge for effective parenting must be "decentralized." Just the term "parent education" may turn off the interest of youth. In many cases there should be no need for a separate entity called "parent education." Almost everything in an effective parenting education program can be integrated into other aspects of the school curriculum, youth agency program, or other educational experience. And this integration should start at an early age. When 7-year-olds learn about family roles and responsibilities in their own and their friends' families, they are learning about parenting. A 10-year-old helping a 6-year-old with mathematics is learning about parenting. The older child learns how to motivate, how to reinforce behaviors, and how to communicate in simple language. The older child also learns about cognitive development processes. When high school students study literature, they can study children's literature. They can learn about a child's imagination, how children interpret words and pictures, how books can be used to stimulate language development, and how to read a story to children. A social studies class or club of adolescents can discuss the issues of childrens' and parents' rights and what would constitute a federal family policy.

The opportunities are endless. The potential impact upon future parents is exhilarating. By providing youth an opportunity for personal growth, social involvement, and commitment, a strong foundation will be laid upon which the very specific skills of being a parent can be more easily built when the need is felt.

References

Behavior Associates. *Education for parenthood: A program, curriculum and evaluation guide.* DHEW Publication No. [OHDS] 77-30125). Washington, D.C.: U.S. Government Printing Office, 1977.

Cohen, D. J. Meeting adolescents' needs. *Children Today*, 1973, 2(2), 28–29.

Coward, R. C., & Kerckhoff, F. G. Parent education in the public schools. *Journal of Home Economics*, 1978, *72*, 24–27.

de Lissovoy, V. Child care by adolescent parents. *Children Today*, 1973, 2(4), 22–25.

de Lissovoy, V. Parent education: White elephant in the classroom? *Youth & Society*, 1978, *9*, 315–338.

Education Development Center. *Summary of evaluation findings, year two*. Newton, Mass.: Education Development Center, 1976.

Education Development Center. *Exploring childhood: Program overview and catalog of materials*. Newton, Mass.: Education Development Center, 1978.

Gordon, T. *Parent effectiveness training*. New York: Peter H. Wyden, 1970.

Guttmacher Institute. *11 million teenagers: What can be done about the epidemic of adolescent pregnancies in the United States.?* New York: Planned Parenthood Federation of America, 1976.

Honig, A. S. What we need to know to help the teenage parent. *The Family Coordinator*, 1978, *27*, 113–119.

Institute of Medicine. *Adolescent behavior and health: A conference summary*. Washington, D.C.: National Academy of Sciences, 1978.

Kerckhoff, R. K., & Habig, M. Parent education as provided by secondary schools. *The Family Coordinator*, 1976, *25*, 127–130.

Kerckhoff, R. K., & O'Connor, T. Certification of high school family life teachers. *The Family Coordinator*, 1978, *27*, 59–61.

Kruger, W. S. Education for parenthood and the schools. *Children Today*, 1973, *2*(2), 4–7. (a)

Kruger, W. S. Teaching parenthood (DHEW Publication No. [DE] 74-01005). Washington, D.C.: U.S. Government Printing Office, 1973. (b)

Kruger, W. S. Education for parenthood and school-age parents. *Journal of School Health*, 1975, *45*, 292–295.

Ogg, E. *Preparing tomorrow's parents*. New York: Public Affairs Committee, 1975.

U.S. Office of Education. Survey of programs for school-age parents. Draft paper. June 1978.

Weigle, J. W. Teaching child development to teenage mothers. *Children Today*, 1974, *3*(5), 23–25.

PART IV

IMPLEMENTATION AND EVALUATION

Chapter 13

Parent Education Programs: Ready, Set, Go!

JERRY L. WYCKOFF

This chapter deals with the issues of how to organize and teach parenting skills to groups of parents. The ideas presented herein are a distillation of how-to's found in successful parent training programs. Of major concern in working with parents is the question of groups versus individual consultation and which format is more efficient in the end. Furthermore, the question of the characteristics of parents to select for the sort of parenting program you may wish to conduct is of importance. Such issues as location of a meeting place, whether or not to have a sponsor, or the kind of sponsor to select are of concern when conducting parent education groups. Advertising a group's existence and deciding on the cost per family or per participant is also of importance in parenting education, as is the selection of the program format and the issue of generalization at the conclusion of the training sequence. All these areas of concern are considered in this chapter.

In reviewing the parent training literature, it must be noted that there is a general lack of detailed "how-to" information for setting up and carrying out parent training groups. One of the most detailed of the parent training programs reported in the early literature was that of Walder and his associates (Hirsch & Walder, 1969; Walder, Breiter, Cohen, Daston, Forbes, & McIntire, 1966; Walder, Cohen, Breiter, Daston, Hirsch, & Leibowitz, 1967a; Walder, Cohen, & Datson, 1967b; Walder, Cohen, Daston, Breiter, & Hirsch, 1967c). The Walder *et al.*

293

HANDBOOK ON
PARENT EDUCATION

parent training program was described as a 15-week program aimed at building operant-oriented family therapy that focused on the complex interactions among family members. The researchers developed a program to teach parents skills in the analysis of behavior and the application of operant principles to parent–child relationship problems. They stressed the generalized value of such skills for parents of "normal" as well as "deviant" children and discussed the potential preventive value of training couples before they become parents. Problems cited by the researchers ranged from school conduct problems to those of children labeled "autistic" or "psychotic."

The Walder parent training program is important because it is one of the few programs cited in the literature that has experimentally tested the various components of a training program, and also because it outlined the various steps taken to ensure success in training parents. The Walder parent training program included: (a) a "contract" with each family, specifying details of their participation; (b) weekly group meetings of several families aimed at teaching basic general behavior theory and technology through the use of reading assignments, written homework, films, lectures, group discussions, modeling, and role playing; (c) weekly individual family sessions (with the therapist-consultant) held for specific application to their own children; and (d) before and after testing of parents using videotapes, standard personality tests, and parental reports of behavior observations.

The parents had the major responsibility for applying home programs and identifying, observing, and recording problem behaviors. They were also taught to continue the application of principles to new behavior problems as they arose. Contingencies aimed at maintaining parental involvement were systematically applied, which included a system of "debits" for incomplete work resulting in a loss of previously written checks; weekly home visits by the therapist-consultant; weekly group meetings with two other families; and weekly coffee socials with all other families and staff. Walder's major importance in family training lies not only in his development and illustration of an approach to family therapy and parenting education, but also, unlike nearly all others in family training, he set up a coordinated, clearly sequenced teaching process for working with large numbers of families.

Group versus Individual Instruction

Although parent training may take many forms, ranging from clinical intervention on an individual basis to large parent training groups, the more popular mode of delivery has been the group approach (O'Dell, 1974). Group parent training appears to offer a more efficient delivery system than does the individual training session. It has been found that individually trained parents required an average of 24 hours per parent to demonstrate competence on the pre- and post-measures used, whereas group-trained parents reached competence with only an average of 8 hours per parent (Behrens, 1970). The time saving noted with the group delivery over the individual delivery has been attributed to the opportunity the grouped parents had to exchange ideas and learn how others solved problems with their own children.

Thus it would appear that the group interaction is of prime importance for parents. This opportunity to exchange ideas helps parents appreciate that they are not alone in having problems in the area of childrearing. In addition, parents discussing various methods of problem solving may feel more confident to try new things when they hear of the successful application by other parents. A major problem can develop, however, that does not occur in individual sessions when a group leader is faced with a parent who is either challenging the group leader's knowledge and ability or is espousing childrearing practices that are totally inappropriate. Such confrontations may serve to damage the group process if not curtailed. In such cases, a technique taught by behaviorists called "shaping" is quite useful.

Shaping can be defined as the reinforcing of approximations to the desired behavior in such a way as to lead the person step by step to the goal. A group leader under these circumstances may simply say, "That's an interesting idea and the most relevant points you seem to be making are . . ." At this point, the group leader can delineate the right way to approach the issue without putting down the problem parent. If a parent in a group continues to challenge and in that way erode the effectiveness of the group instruction, it may be necessary to isolate that parent and deal with him or her on an individual basis. During individual conferences, many parents drop the challenging approach to the professional staff member and respond to a logical presentation of factual information.

Another factor favoring the group approach to parent training is, of course, the cost factor with parent training groups providing a realistic low-cost means of producing therapeutic change (Clark, 1975; Galloway & Galloway, 1970; Howard, 1970; Peine, 1972; Rose, 1969). Parent education groups also provide an efficient, low-cost way to provide information about basic parenting skills to parents seeking to improve the way they relate to their children.

Setting Up a Parent Education Program

In the Beginning

The first step to be taken in setting up a parent education program is to decide upon the particular group of parents to which the parent training program is to be directed. There are many possible types of parent groups to which a parent training program might be oriented: single parents, couples, parents with preschool children, parents with school-age children, parents with adolescents, parents-to-be, parents of exceptional children, parents who are interested in improving their parenting skills, parents of deviant children, and all possible combinations.

Each group of parents with whom you may choose to work has a set of special problems with which the parent group staff must cope. Parents with preschool children are often most concerned with developmental issues such as feeding, sleeping, toileting, and basic independence/dependence conflicts. Parents of preschool children are often caught up in the trap of making excessive demands on their children when the problems cited are often of a developmental nature and will be solved naturally as a result of maturation. In order to adequately deal with the problems presented by parents of preschoolers, basic information about child development is of prime necessity.

Parents of adolescents may present some problems similar to those found in preschoolers; that is, issues of independence/dependence and of a basic struggle for power. Very often parents of adolescents have become highly critical of their children and as a result have compounded the problems presented by the adolescents. Recently, a father of a 16-year-old boy who had a reputation as a troublesome child presented a situation that serves to exemplify the very critical nature of the interaction that may develop between an adolescent and his or her parents.

The boy called his father to ask for permission to ride two family motorcycles with a friend for about an hour or so. The father granted permission without further clarifying the time limit that had only been loosely established. Upon arriving home, the father discovered the boys had been gone over an hour and had left a note stating a later return time. While the father was complaining to the mother about the boy violating his trust by not returning at the originally established time, the boy called home with the information that one of the bikes was not running and asked the father to come to help fix it so they could return home. The father agreed to help, but when he arrived at the appointed place, he found the bikes but not the boys, who had wandered off. When they finally returned, the father discovered the friend was wearing the father's boots and helmet. The father then exploded and levied punishment for all the infractions.

In analyzing this highly critical father's interaction with his son, it is obvious that the appropriate components of the interaction, that is, the asking of permission, the leaving of a note, the use of safety gear, and the calling for help were not seen because of the father's focus on the elements of time, not being at the bikes when the father arrived, and the unauthorized use of the father's equipment. Over 50% of the elements of the situation were appropriate, but the father didn't pay any attention to these. This kind of highly critical interaction between parents and their adolescent children constitutes a major problem that leaders in parenting programs in which parents of adolescents participate must learn to manage.

Each of the other parent categories have their own special problems. Parents in single-parent families often feel overwhelmed by their responsibility and often spend a great deal of time bemoaning their marital status rather than focusing on improving their parenting skills. Mothers in families in which the father works long hours or is absent from the home for extended periods of time present the same kinds of problems generally found in single-parent families, with the exception that instead of blaming the single status for their problems, they often blame the absent father. Parents of exceptional children are also very often overwhelmed by their child's exceptionality and tend very often to overcompensate in some way for the handicapping condition. Parents of a blind 9-year old were so convinced that blindness was such an overwhelming handicap that they did not expect any form of compliance from the child in the home, although school staff managed to achieve good compliance at school. Even after it was demonstrated that the child could do what was expected of him at home, the parents had difficulty generalizing and consistently expecting their child to function at a level he was able to achieve. All problems encountered were blamed on the boy's blindness rather than on the parent's skills in parenting.

Keeping parent groups fairly homogeneous tends to result in higher levels of success. When variables such as intelligence, reading level, and educational level have been kept fairly constant within a group, the success of the group has been found to be higher (Salzinger, Feldman, & Portnoy, 1970). Training some uneducated parents from the lower socioeconomic levels has proven to be difficult perhaps because of their lack of even the most rudimentary child management skills and the limited availability of reinforcers (Patterson, Cobb, & Ray, 1972). Or-

ganizing and maintaining groups among lower socioeconomic populations is very difficult because of what appears to be a general lack of
interest in parenting education by this population. Often massive recruitment campaigns among lower socioeconomic groups of parents
have resulted in a very low attendance rate regardless of the incentives
offered by the program. If lower socioeconomic groups are selected for
parent training, the parent education staff must be prepared for problems such as understanding concepts, attendance, and completion of
any projects that may be assigned.

Working with parents without spouses or working in homes with
parental conflicts requires considerably more time and effort to achieve
success than working with couples in nonconflict homes. Parents in
these categories obviously need parenting education, so it would be an
inequity to screen them out of a parenting program. It must be recognized, however, that these parents will present special problems and
will require what seems at times to be an excessive amount of individual attention. On the other hand, parents showing obvious signs of
personality disorder or psychopathology should generally be screened
out of parent groups because of the extremely limited success traditionally found with this population (Bernal, Williams, Miller, &
Reagor, 1972; Patterson, 1965).

The problem with screening parents with personality disorders or
psychopathology out of parenting programs is that these problems
often become apparent only after several group sessions. By that time, it
becomes a problem of coping with the pathology while trying to convince the parent that he or she would be better off not attending any
more group sessions or could best be served on a one-to-one basis.
Sometimes ignoring the inappropriateness of the responses of a disturbed parent and using that moment as an opportunity to pursue a
related issue is a useful technique that allows the group leader to retain
control of the group without getting involved with the obvious pathology. In a parent training group recently, a mother began asking questions and challenging the group leader each time a statement was made
that did not fit her scheme of things. The group leader acknowledged
the questions and met the challenges for a few moments until it became
obvious that the person's problem was not related to the discussion but
to her own mental state. At that point, the group leader acknowledged
that her questions were far beyond the scope of his expertise and
invited the person to pursue the question with an assistant in private.
This effectively eliminated the problem from the group and allowed the
group leader to move on with the discussion.

Screening interviews prior to enrollment of a parent in a group can be the best and least aversive way of eliminating those parents who show obvious signs of personality disorder. Some parent trainers advocate the use of tests that would assess personality, marital adjustment, and child behavior as well as interviews and in-home observations prior to accepting parents for family training (Miller, 1975). These procedures are, of course, quite laborious and may need to be restricted to use with those families who are seeking help for a highly deviant child. Much milder screening procedures would probably suffice for entry into those parenting programs designed to be informative and geared to improving parenting skills rather than those designed for correcting obvious deviant family interactions.

Another individual parent characteristic that may need to be considered when establishing the criteria for parent group selection is that of locus of control (Rotter, 1972), a concept having emerged from social learning theory that refers to the extent to which an individual feels that he or she has control over his or her own behavior and its consequences. Individuals who believe that outcomes are controlled by chance, fate, or powerful others are said to have an external locus of control, whereas those who believe events are contingent on their own behavior have an internal locus of control. Abramowitz, Abramowitz, Roback, and Jackson (1974) found that the overall therapeutic outcome of a treatment program was more favorable for those with an external locus who were presented with a directive mode of presentation than with a nondirective mode. Conversely, those with an internal locus evidenced greater gains when assigned to a nondirective group. Parents matched on the basis of locus of control to parental training in behavior management can be expected to make greater gains than those randomly assigned to parent groups regardless of the type of presentation made (Brewer, 1977).

The only reliable method to screen for locus of control is to use one of the several tests available. The real question is, however, how functional such screening may be for your individual needs. If you must revise your total program in order to take into account those who operate from a locus of control opposite to that of the majority, it may be more trouble than the results may warrant to make such a revision. An alternate strategy to massive screening and grouping is an individualization of approach that can be utilized based on the degree to which each participant exhibits problems in the area of locus of control. Group leaders can become more or less directive in their approach to individuals within the program rather than to revise an entire program in order to provide a separate track for directive and nondirective teaching approaches.

As can be seen from this discussion, basic desirable family character- istics are a responsiveness to training in at least one of the parents that results in a strong motivation to improve the family interaction, a capability to function in a predictable manner, and a sensitivity about other family member's needs. A desirable family characteristic would also include the absence of excessive rigidity about avoiding new methods of childrearing or maintaining negative pessimistic attitudes about their children (Miller, 1975).

Now That We Know Who We Want to Teach, Where Do We Meet?

Once the type of group desired has been established and the format has been selected, the next step should be to approach likely organiza- tions that may act as a sponsor to your group. Because of the vested interest in children, all schools, whether preschool, public, or private, appear to lend themselves to the establishment of parent education programs. Some parent education programs rely almost exclusively on the public schools for their financial support as well as for the parent population and the meeting places (Clark-Hall, Blattenberg, Collier, Leiker, Grinstead, Kerns, Rotton, & Wyckoff, 1976). Other social in- stitutions that may sponsor parenting education and may be able to provide the necessary space in which to meet are churches and other religious organizations, YMCA or YWCA organizations, local junior colleges, mental health associations, and community centers. It must be noted, however, that selecting a sponsor and a meeting site may mean that you have also selected a built-in population that may not be the population of your choice.

If you choose to approach a school, it is often better to work through an individual principal or PTA and to sell them on the idea of a parenting education program rather than to approach the school board or superintendant directly. Once the local school patrons and adminis- tration have decided to use your program, they will often be able to convince the central office administration to allow them to implement the program within their school. Gaining financial support from schools is, a different matter, however, and requires approval by the school board. Approval for major budgetary expenditures must be obtained at least a year prior to the actual time the program is to start because of the advance budget planning necessary in school districts and other public agencies.

How Much Does It Cost?

One of the more important issues in parenting education is the establishing and maintaining of a program budget. Parent training programs can derive all or only a part of the program budget from tuition fees charged the participating parents. Establishing the tuition fee charged, then, must be based on the total program budget. Parent education programs are currently available that range from costing nothing to costing several hundred dollars for a 10-week course. Fees must be based on the needs and policies of the sponsoring agency or group and must fit the group's budgetary requirements. Most sponsoring agencies are of a nonprofit nature and as a result, discourage "for profit" parent training groups within their organization. Fees based on the cost of the program materials, rental of the meeting space, child care, refreshments, and staff time may total more than a given population feels ready to spend on parent education. Interestingly enough, free parent group offerings appear to be no more well attended than do groups that cost an average of $2 or more per session, even when nursery facilities are available at only $1 per family.

Obtaining funds from sources other than tuition or the sponsoring group requires an ability to review available grant sources from federal as well as private agencies. Also needed are the time and skills necessary to submit a grant application, and the time and skills to conduct the needed lobbying efforts required to be funded adequately. Often detailed research data derived from the parenting program is required by the granting agency that would support the particular program you advocate. Even with successful research citations, sometimes purely political considerations prevent the funding of even the most worthwhile programs. Research is often included as one of the demands made of the programs that have obtained grant funding, so a parent training organization must be prepared to continue collecting satisfactory data in order to continue obtaining funds.

Noting the problems of obtaining funds from school districts, other governmental agencies, or from granting institutions, it would appear that most parenting education programs must ultimately become totally self-sufficient and operate only on the tuition collected from the participants. Because many parents may not feel they can afford to spend much on acquiring new or improved parenting skills, the program costs must be kept at a minimum in order to keep parent enrollment as high as possible. One of the most obvious areas in which costs can be reduced is in staff time, because over 85% of most educational budgets is in staff salaries. The use of volunteer staff is perhaps the best way to reduce staff cost, but volunteers can create difficulty in the area of quality control. Getting and keeping good volunteer help is very difficult, and a decision must be made in order to determine if the time and effort taken for recruitment and training justifies the use of volunteer help. The training of volunteer staff will be discussed in a later section.

Getting the Word Out

Once the site and population have been selected and a sponsor lined up, the next step is to arrange for the necessary publicity. Promotion may often be arranged within the sponsoring organization and is often carried out through the organization's newsletter, by posted announcements, or by direct invitation to members. When establishing a parent education group independently, it is often necessary to promote it through the use of radio and TV spot announcements, mental health bulletins, PTA newsletters, direct mailings, press interviews, and speaking engagements. An interesting concept used by the Responsive Parenting Program as a promotion tool is the "teaser" show, which is given before groups of parents and demonstrates the content and goals of the parent training program (Clark-Hall et al., 1976). Another promotion technique utilized by the Responsive Parenting Program is the showing of a film that depicts the training program in action. In this way prospective parents may see how the group is conducted, the concepts taught, and the wide range of behavior problems solved by the parents who have taken the course in the past.

Direct mail has been a popular way of disseminating information and of promotion, but because of increased postage rates, it can be a very expensive method of advertising a parenting group. This is particularly relevant in view of the fact that only about 1% of the mailing on a single mailing basis results in a sale. Based on current postal rates, one might expect one response out of every 100 letters, which means in postage alone each person eventually signing up for a parenting program would cost about $15 in solicitation fees.

Newspaper coverage is apparently an effective promotion too, but it also results in a fairly low rate of return for the number of available subscribers. Recently a parent education program was described in glowing terms in an article published in a Sunday news magazine in a major metropolitan newspaper covering an area with a population of over 1 million. As a result of the article and the accompanying invitation for any and all to join the parent education group, which was totally free of charge, only 75 new members joined the group, and of the 75 new members, 25 dropped out after the first session. Based on this kind of response to a news story, it is doubtful that newspaper advertising, which is quite expensive, would draw the kind of response desired for the expenditure necessary.

One of the least expensive means of dissemination is through the sponsoring agency. Often school districts will allow flyers to be given to students that advertise worthwhile, nonprofit programs such as parent education groups. Based on a cost of less than 1¢ per flyer, the cost of each respondent would be less than $1, a figure much easier to absorb in the limited budget most parenting education programs are forced to live with.

Publicity remains a major problem for parent training programs. Consumer satisfaction, which leads to word-of-mouth advertising, has perhaps been consistently the least expensive and the most effective recruitment tool yet. Once a program gains a reputation and receives referrals from teachers, physicians, satisfied parents, and other community agencies, a regular enrollment is almost assured with a slow but steady increase in population the general rule. Lean years are generally followed by ample numbers of parents seeking a program if the program meets the needs of those parents.

Those Little Details

Once the sponsor and meeting place have been selected and the finances arranged, the details of the program can be developed. Many who sponsor groups as well as many group leaders feel that it is important to provide refreshments (coffee and tea) during a meeting, although parents when polled did not feel that refreshments were important to the meeting (Wyckoff, 1975). If refreshments are desired, however, the meeting place must include a place to prepare the refreshments before the meeting and a place to clean up afterward. Special trips must be made to purchase necessary supplies (cups, coffee, tea, cream, sugar) and a budget must be established for such items. Assigning someone to prepare and to clean up further complicates the refreshment issue. Special permission must often be obtained from the sponsoring organization or the custodian in charge of the meeting site in order to take drinks into the meeting area. As a related issue, the question of allowing smoking during the meeting or in the meeting area must be considered and local ordinances must be consulted.

Selection of the time of day for the meeting is also of great importance, because the time of day the meeting is held will determine the make-up of the parent population. Day meetings will almost always be restricted to mothers, unless they are held on a weekend so fathers can attend. Evening meetings, on the other hand, will allow both parents or working parents to attend. Evening meetings, however, necessitate the consideration of child care, a major problem for some parents.

A good evening starting time is from 7:00 to 7:30 P.M. which usually allows most parents to eat dinner before coming to the meeting and to be home by a reasonable time. For daytime meetings, late morning, 9:30 to 11:30 A.M. or early afternoons, 1:00 to 3:00 P.M., are often preferred. Late morning times allow parents sufficient time to get children off to school before going to the meeting in the morning and to return home by noon. The early afternoon time allows the parent ample time to return home before school is out in order to avoid children being left unattended.

The day of the week selected should be determined by the various schedules of meetings held by religious groups, schools, and service organizations in order to avoid conflict. Recently a PTA group in a public school contracted for an early afternoon parent education group meeting. After the meetings were underway, the PTA sponsor was dismayed at the extremely poor turnout. It was only after someone reminded her of the PTA bowling league meeting time that she realized the conflict and rescheduled the parent group meeting time. Scheduling a course of study to begin just prior to a vacation period at school will disrupt the continuity of the program and cause valuable time to be devoted to review of the previously covered material. Scheduling a course of study during the summer months often results in lowered attendance because of conflicting vacation schedules.

Offering child care during the meetings can have advantages and disadvantages. More couples may be able to attend together when one member is not forced to stay home with the children. On the other hand, time must be spent recruiting skilled child-care staff, local ordinances and insurance must be considered, budget must be established, and fee schedules determined. Child care provided on a "reservation only" basis takes more staff time than simply hiring a number of child-care workers to be subsidized by the program budget, regardless of the number of children served. The latter tends to be more expensive, however, and often forces a single child-care worker to be in charge of excessive numbers of children. A further disadvantage to providing child care is that it may narrow considerably the range of possible meeting sites because of the lack of adequate child-care facilities located at the meeting site.

The Content of a
Parent Education Program

Now That I Have Them, What Do I Teach Them?

As demonstrated in the earlier chapters of this book, program content can be widely varied. Selection of program content can be based on the target population and on the goals of the program staff. Many excellent program materials are on the market today, all of which lend themselves to parent education groups. It should be noted, however, that whatever the materials selected, they should be considered as supplemental to and not the total program. Program format and sequence may be provided by the materials selected, but the content should be greatly elaborated by the program staff. A frequent complaint heard from parents attending parent education programs is the redundancy encountered when the program staff only reiterates what was written in the manual or text used. Program staff members who "ad lib" parenting examples and who seek active discussion of problem areas are often favored in "consumer satisfaction" surveys.

Some parenting programs have determined that giving parents a complete program at the beginning of the series tends to encourage dropouts who no longer feel the need to attend weekly when they have the complete program in hand, whereas giving the parents the written material a chapter at a time keeps attendance up (Clark, 1975). Having parents drop out of group participation does not allow for support by the group staff when questions or problems arise, and it renders impossible any individualization that may be necessary to help the parents learn the necessary parenting skills.

Other methods of discouraging parent dropouts is through the use of reinforcement or paying parents to attend the class meetings. Although there is little agreement as to the effectiveness of this method of encouraging parent participation in a parent education program, the use of contingency contracting within a parent education program is certainly worth exploring. A contingency contract should contain the elements of *who* is to carry out the behavior, *what* the behavior is, *when* the behavior is to be emitted, and *what* reinforcement will be given. The most obvious reinforcers available to parents in a parent education program are staff time and fee reimbursement. If a contract were established for specific homework assignments to be completed before the next meeting, with group leader time and a percentage of the workshop fee contingent upon completion of the homework, an increase in homework completion might be expected. The contracts must be stated clearly and explicitly prior to invoking them, however, and contracts should be in writing in order to obtain compliance and to reduce questions about contract content.

Once the program content is selected, the program staff must spend ample time becoming thoroughly familiar with the materials and the sequence to be followed in presenting the material to the parents. Staff training may take several sessions or several months, depending on the level of familiarity the staff has with the selected program. Simply having a background in the content area, however, cannot be considered enough training for staff members. A knowledge of the use of behavioral principles in the classroom or laboratory does not ensure being able to teach those concepts to parents in such a way that they can use them effectively in the home.

Knowledge in child development is a necessary part of the training the staff of a parenting education group should have. Parent training staff is constantly required to make decisions about what behavior can be reasonably expected of variously aged children. Experience and training in the accepted social, emotional, and behavioral milestones of normal child development can greatly facilitate the application of parent training procedures. Other characteristics desired in staff members, in addition to training background, would be empathy, a genuine desire to help others, and an openness to constructive retraining.

A method of staff training that has been demonstrated to be successful is that of "on-the-job" training or apprenticeship. In this method of training, staff members may begin as program participants, become apprentice group leaders, group leaders, apprentice program directors, and finally, program directors. The entire program is taught and supervised by a core of professional staff acting as field coordinators (Clark-Hall *et al.*, 1976). This training sequence ensures that the staff will be familiar with all aspects of the program before being placed in a position of leadership. Furthermore, an apprenticeship program can greatly increase the number of parents who can benefit from the training of the professional supervisory staff. If, for example, one professional staff member monitored one meeting weekly, answered group leader questions, and offered direction to the program directors, that professional staff member's time could be effectively multiplied by the number of group leaders at the program site. Each professional staff member, then, could work with a group of paraprofessional staff members who in turn would work with groups of parents. Finally, the most convincing reason for having volunteer paraprofessional staff is the simple fact that there are not enough trained professionals to do the job required. Being a volunteer paraprofessional does, however, require considerable dedication on the part of the trainee, for the whole process from apprentice group leader to program director can take as long as 2 years of concentrated effort and training. Maintaining adequately trained staff becomes for most programs a major problem area.

In order to provide supplemental training to staff members, training workshops may be utilized. These workshops are generally held at regular intervals and can be used to solve problems and to expand staff knowledge. Because we learn and can function at two levels, cognitive or verbal and performance or behavioral, training must take place at both levels. It is not enough to train through discussion and to stop training when staff members can parrot the discussion. All staff members must also be able to assume and to carry out the role of program director or group leader when working with parents. Role modeling by professional staff and active role playing of problem situations by paraprofessional staff are techniques that can bring staff members functionally closer to the skills needed to carry out the program goals. Because parent training involves "performance" skills rather than verbal skills, the use of the "performance" approach to staff training should help staff members utilize the same approach in parent training.

Now That I Know What to Teach . . .

Perhaps the most frequently used parent training techniques have been the various forms of didactic instruction. Some trainers utilize simple advice and verbal directions (Allen & Harris, 1971; Patterson, 1965; Wahler, 1969), whereas others utilize lectures and movies (Hall, Cristler, Cranston, & Tucker, 1970; Walder et al., 1967a, b, c). Written material in the form of programmed texts that present the basic principles employed in the training program have been utilized in many of the parent training programs (Cohen, 1970; Lindsley, 1966; Mathis, 1971; Patterson et al., 1972, Rose, 1969).

One of the most successful techniques used in parent training programs has been "modeling," a visual or verbal demonstration of the techniques to be used (Johnson & Brown, 1969; Patterson & Brodsky, 1966; Rose, 1969; Sherman & Baer, 1969; Straughn, 1964). Some experimenters use combinations of the most widely employed techniques including interviews, lectures, individual instruction, discussion, home assignments, modeling, behavioral rehearsal, and contracts with the parents (Rose, 1969). Lindsley (1970) discussed the use of humor and speed of presentation of information as important to holding the interest of groups. Patterson et al. (1972) emphasized the importance of positive reinforcement feedback to parents as they develop their skills.

Reinforcement feedback to parents is considered very important because although improved behavior on the part of the child should be an
inherent reinforcer for parents, it may not be sufficient. Obtaining full
cooperation of parents to collect data, do the assigned homework,
attend the meetings, and fulfill all the requirements of the parent training program may require the use of reinforcement on a programmed
basis. Parent trainers have made fulfilling course requirements as the
ticket to see the behavior therapist (Mira, 1970) and have allowed
parents to earn back a part of their workshop fee as a reward for having
collected the required data and fulfilled the course requirements (Clark,
1975; Wyckoff, 1975). Although research suggests better attendance
when parents are reimbursed for attendance (Hirsch & Walder, 1969),
no definitive studies have been done to demonstrate the necessity of
providing reinforcement for parent cooperation. Although it has been
demonstrated that parent behavior can be shaped using contingencies,
the literature in parent education is generally lacking in research that
suggests ways to deal with reluctant or oppositional parents who say
they want to change but who consistently oppose stated requirements
and/or sabotage the therapist. Again virtually every successful study in
the literature attests to the importance of having highly cooperative
parents (Johnson, 1972).

A suggested course format, then, would include the use of short
lectures about course content, a written text that is disseminated chapter by chapter to prevent parents from reading ahead, quizzes over the
course content, home-behavior-change projects, small-group discussion, and reinforcement by group leaders of each small step taken by the
parents (Clark-Hall *et al.*, 1976). Programs that contain the widest array
of presentation forms as well as those that allow parents to actively
participate in the learning process should experience the highest rate of
success. Keeping in mind such issues as the socioeconomic levels of the
participants and the research cited earlier regarding locus of control, a
parent training program can be made to be optimally successful.

How to Keep Them Doing What I Taught Them

A major problem noted in reviewing parent training literature is the
failure of the researchers to cite follow-up data indicating maintenance
of induced change. Success usually has been measured by improvements found only at the termination of the treatment or the parent
training program (Miller, 1975). We all recognize the need for generalization to occur over time and we hope that learning is maintained by
parents who undergo parent training, however, generalization does not

always occur naturally (Budd, Green, & Baer, 1976; Miller & Sloane, 1976; Wahler, 1969; Walker & Buckley, 1972).

As a possible solution to the dilemma of ensuring generalization and maintenance, it has been suggested that training be conducted in a setting similar to that in which the behaviors are expected to be produced, that careful fading of the instructions be carried out within that setting, and that intensive reprogramming of the environment in which the behaviors are to occur be included in the training package (Walker & Buckley, 1972). Although some attention has been given to similarity of stimulus conditions as a means of producing generalization of training, Miller and Sloane (1976) contend that in order to ensure generalization across settings, training must be programmed across settings. Because the ability of the parent to generalize to other behaviors in other settings has not been demonstrated, parent training must include training in the setting in which parents function and must teach the management of a variety of behaviors. It is essential, therefore, to include the systematic use of homework to be carried out in the home setting as well as the demonstrated application of the basic behavioral principles across as many behaviors as possible in order to ensure some degree of generalization.

Stokes and Baer (1977), in their monumental review of the effects of generalization found in the literature, cited the most frequent method of examining generalization as the "train and hope" method, which was defined as the documenting but not actively pursuing of generalization after behavior change was effected. This method, although sadly lacking in its ability to deal with the need for behavioral generalization in parenting programs, constituted almost half the generalization noted in the literature. A more effective method of dealing with the generalization issue was found to be the "sequential modification" approach, which was seen by Stokes and Baer as an approach through which behavior change is effected, generalization is assessed, and if generalization is absent, procedures are initiated to accomplish the desired generalization.

Stokes and Baer (1977) suggested we assume that generalization does not occur naturally without some sort of programming. Therefore, in . teaching behavioral skills, Stokes and Baer described a set of tactics that may be useful in bringing about generalization and that has been expanded upon here:

1. Teach parents to supply their own cues in their natural setting, which will stimulate and reinforce their own desirable behavior. Methods used to help parents supply cues for themselves in the variety of settings in which they find themselves with their children are the use

of signs and posters to be used at home, data sheets and recorders that fit in pocket or purse, and stimulus words or phrases that have been carefully practiced in vivo by the parents.

2. Train for a diverse set of exemplars that may occur in the natural setting. This would involve the discussion of as many different examples of behavior as can be thought of that may occur wherever the parents and child find themselves and a discussion of ways of dealing with those problems. An example that may be used is that of the occurrence of attention-getting behaviors, the most frequent times and places in which that behavior may occur, and the best ways of dealing with that particular behavior in each of the diverse settings.

3. Train for different examples concurrently as well as vary instruction, stimuli, social reinforcers, and back-up reinforcers. As the program staff cites examples of various techniques used, it is often easy to demonstrate, through a series of examples, how those techniques may be used. The use of a single-ring kitchen timer may serve as our example here. When suggesting the use of a single-ring timer as the behavior change agent, different examples may be used that explain the use of the kitchen timer during time-out, during dinner to decrease dawdling and leaving the table early, to help children get ready for bed, to help them get dressed in the morning, and to help teach children independent play skills. Citing as many possible examples of the uses of a kitchen timer to parents should help those parents generalize the uses of that technique more easily. In addition, it is useful to discuss the variety of stimuli, for example, getting out the timer, which can be used to manage the array of behaviors dealt with in all settings. It is also important to discuss the range of reinforcers available and all possible back-up reinforcers that could be utilized to teach specific behaviors.

4. Use stimuli in the training settings that are likely to be found in the generalization settings. Also, use peer tutors who understand the setting most. In teaching home-based management systems, it is advisable to use people who are familiar with the home setting and who understand the array of stimuli available there to use in management systems. Furthermore, as management systems are taught, vary the instructional cues the parents are taught to use with their children in order for then to have a wider range of stimuli for the specific behaviors they are seeking.

5. Encourage through reinforcement accurate self-reports of desirable behavior and apply self-recording and self-reinforcement techniques whenever possible. One way to increase the frequency and accuracy of self-reports is to request self-reports weekly during the training period and to encourage through shaping, accuracy of reports. In addition, the

recording of self-behavior can be encouraged by requiring the completion of data sheets that are turned in weekly. Another device used to encourage self-monitoring is the use of daily recording of positive feedback statements made to each child and the requirement that the number be increased daily. Daily progress in behavioral areas can be assumed to be self-reinforcing if the data indicate an increase in the desired behaviors.

6. When generalizations do occur, reinforce at least some of them as if "to generalize" were an operant response class. In addition to reinforcing generalizations as they appear in parent reports, it is also useful to program generalization as an exercise. One possible exercise is the naming of as many possible stimuli, reinforcers, and basic techniques that can be used in the home setting. Asking how to bring about generalization across settings and as a continuance across time is also a useful exercise as specific management systems are taught or hone management systems are designed and carried out.

In order to ensure adequate generalizations across settings, across behavior managers, and across time when working with parents, it would appear that some of the training should be conducted in the settings in which the problems most frequently occur (O'Leary, Becker, Evans, & Saudargas, 1969; Patterson, 1965). Because it is not feasible to carry out training in the setting in which the behavior generally occurs, teaching basic concepts and helping parents design a system that is then carried out in the setting in which the behavior occurs is the next most useful way of helping generalization to occur. As parents conduct behavior change projects and report back to the program staff, alterations can be made and generalization of the behavior can be designed into the behavior change procedure.

The parents and other potential behavior managers should be actively involved in the application of behavioral change procedures (Christophersen, Bernard, Ford, & Wolf, 1976) and careful fading procedures should be utilized to allow the parents to become more and more independent of the behavior therapist (Walker & Buckley, 1972). Although Christophersen *et al.* (1976) demonstrated a method of training parents in vivo and fading the training in a systematic way, the in-home training of parents is not economically feasible. Again, the use of home-management projects with data collection and weekly monitoring by program staff can substitute for in-home training and still meet the criteria for generalization of training. The use of "sequential modification" in which behavior change is effected, generalization is assessed and, if absent, procedures initiated to accomplish the desired generalization, would appear to be practical in most parent training programs. Sequential modification would allow whatever generalizatiom is inherent in the procedure to occur naturally and would offer sufficient monitoring to help in the programming of any generalization that did not occur as a natural result of the modification procedure used.

A major problem with generalization in dealing with parent groups is that of measurement of the generalization over time. Usually after the group has terminated, a small percentage of the parents who attended will return for a "maintenance meeting" (Clark-Hall et al., 1976). Follow-up by mail has also been utilized, but getting an adequate number of responses from the parents is difficult (Sirridge, 1975). Telephone follow-up is a laborious procedure that has been used to assess maintenance, but telephone reports are often sketchy and difficult to evaluate (Christophersen et al., 1976; Wyckoff, 1978). Unless program staff is willing and able to conduct extensive follow-up that may need to be conducted in the home, follow-up measures of maintenance may not be available. Under such conditions, the trainers are forced to rely on the "train and hope" method of generalization in which all possible training measures are utilized, and it is hoped that they are sufficient to bring about adequate generalization.

A method that has been utilized to provide a setting in which generalization can be aided as well as monitored is that of the maintenance group, a continuous, ongoing resource group to which parents who have completed the parent training course can go to get further suggestions about new child management problems. This kind of group fulfills the suggestions by Stokes and Baer (1977) for training different examples concurrently, reinforcing generalizations, use of peers as trainers, and the use of diverse exemplars. In that respect, as parents attend the group, they are able to see principles being applied to a diverse and varied population concurrently. For example, if a discussion involves toilet training problems and the positive practice techniques of Azrin and Foxx (1974) are discussed, the same positive practice may be generalized to a school-aged child for hanging up a jacket or to an adolescent who is having difficulty with peer interactions. Furthermore, open discussion in such groups offers peer instruction that is elaborated on by the group leader, and it allows for the group reinforcement of appropriate parent behavior as well as appropriate reports of generalization. The preparation and cost of such a maintenance group is relatively low, and such groups tend to be popular community programs.

The establishment of ongoing maintenance or resource groups can be made a natural extension of the parent training program and can be held in the same setting in which the parent training program was held. The maintenance group requires only a meeting room, an established weekly time, and a professional group leader who can field questions and deal with the stated problems in an effective, coherent way. In order to stimulate discussion in the ongoing resource group, the group leader can ask for successful experiences by parents attending the group, which can then serve as examples of effective procedures that can be generalized into other settings. Furthermore, the group leader can state problem solutions in such a way as to exemplify their use in a variety of settings and with a diverse population.

Unfortunately missing in the maintenance group is the data monitoring that is often available in the original training group. Because a maintenance group is ongoing, with no definite beginning or end, parents with a wide range of experience may attend. Those parents with adequate data collection skills may be able to continue their data collection when they feel it necessary and may report their accomplishments to the group with supportive data. However, those parents who do not fully understand or who are not always able to carry out data collection would not be able to collect or present meaningful data to the group. The lack of an established training sequence may be a detriment, but the overall maintenance group format is quite functional and does provide a place for parents to go to get needed assistance and to fade out as their needs are met.

Conclusion

A successful parent eduction group can be organized and conducted if such variables as who to teach, what to teach, and how to teach are taken into consideration in the planning stages. Other important issues are the obtaining of a sponsor, a site, and the recruitment of a parent population. Such details as the time and day, child care, and refreshments must also be considered in order to minimize problems and to make the group experience as enjoyable as possible for the participants. Finally, the question of ensuring maintenance of the training is of great importance. Successful parent training is not a simple matter, but it can be carried out successfully with sufficient attention given to the major issues. Because parenting is such a dynamic, ongoing concern, it is important to constantly reevaluate, modify, and continually upgrade a parent training program. In this way a parent training program may continue to be able to help parents deal in more effective ways with the constantly changing problems of childrearing.

References

Abramowitz, C. V., Abramowitz, S. I., Roback, H. B., & Jackson, C. Differential effectiveness of directive and nondirective group therapies as a function of client internal–external control. *Journal of Consulting and Clinical Psychology*, 1974, *42*, 849–853.

Allen, K. E., & Harris, F. R. Eliminating a child's excessive scratching by training the mother in reinforcement procedures. In A. M. Graziano (Ed.), *Behavior therapy with children*. Chicago: Aldine, 1971.

Azrin, N. R., & Foxx, R. M. *Toilet training in less than a day*. New York: Simon and Schuster, 1974.

Behrens, E. M. *Individual vs. group training of parents in behavior modification techniques*. Unpublished master's thesis, University of Utah, 1970.

Bernal, M. E., Williams, D. E., Miller, W. H., & Reagor, P. A. The use of videotape feedback and operant learning principles in training parents in management of deviant children. In R. D. Rubin, H. Festerheim, J. D. Henderson, & L. P. Ullman (Eds.), *Advances in behavior therapy*. New York: Academic Press, 1972.

Brewer, S. *The effects of locus of control and presentation mode congruence and incongruence upon parent training effectiveness*. Unpublished doctoral dissertation, University of Kansas, 1977.

Budd, K. S., Green, D. R., & Baer, D. M. An analysis of multiple misplaced parental social contingencies. *Journal of Applied Behavior Analysis*, 1976, *9*, 459.

Christophersen, E. R., Bernard, J. D., Ford, D., & Wolf, M. M. The family training program: Improving parent–child interaction patterns. In E. J. Mash, L. A. Hamerlynck, & L. C. Handy (Eds.), *Behavior modification approaches to parenting*. New York: Brunner/Mazel, 1976.

Clark, M. L. *Teaching parents applied behavior analysis: A training program for the prevention and remediation of problem behaviors*. Unpublished doctoral dissertation, University of Kansas, 1975.

Clark-Hall, M., Blattenberg, E., Collier, H., Leiker, K. F., Grinstead, J., Kerns, L., Rotton, M. J., & Wyckoff, J. *Program director manual for the responsive parenting program, group leader manual for the responsive parenting program and parent manual for the responsive parenting program*. Lawrence, Kans.: H and H Enterprises (P.O. Box 3342), 1976.

Cohen, H. C. *The P.I.C.A. Project. Year 2. Project interim report. Programming interpersonal curricula for adolescents*. Silver Springs, Md.: Institute for Behavioral Research, 1970. (ERIC Document Reproduction Service, No. ED 044 717)

Galloway, C., & Galloway, K. Parent groups with a focus on precise behavior management. *IMRID Paper and Reports* (Vol. 2). Nashville: George Peabody College, John F. Kennedy Center, 1970.

Hall, R. V., Cristler, C., Cranston, S. S., & Tucker, B. Teachers and parents as researchers using multiple baseline designs. *Journal of Applied Behavior Analysis*, 1970, *3*, 247–255.

Hirsch, I., & Walder, L. O. *Training mothers in groups as reinforcement therapists for their own children*. Proceedings of the 77th Annual Convention of the American Psychological Association, 1969.

Howard, O. F. *Teaching a class of parents as reinforcement therapists to treat their own children*. Paper presented at the Annual Meeting of the Southeastern Psychological Association, Louisville, Ky., 1970.

Johnson, M. R. *Operant techniques in parent training: A critical review.* Unpublished review paper for the Department of Human Development, University of Kansas, 1972.

Johnson, S. A., & Brown, R. A. Producing behavior change in parents of disturbed children. *Journal of Child Psychology and Psychiatry*, 1969, 10, 107–121.

Lindsley, O. R. An experiment with parents handling behavior at home. *Johnstone Bulletin*, 1966, 9, 27–36.

Lindsley, O. R. Procedures in common described by a common language. In C. Neuringer & J. L. Michael (Eds.), *Behavior modification in clinical psychology.* New York: Appleton-Century-Crofts, 1970.

Mathis, H. I. Training a disturbed boy using the mother as therapist: A case study. *Behavior Therapy*, 1971, 2, 233–239.

Miller, W. H. *Systematic parent training.* Champaign, Ill.: Research Press, 1975.

Miller, S. J., & Sloane, H. N., Jr. The generalization effects of parent training across stimulus settings. *Journal of Applied Behavior Analysis*, 1976, 9, 355–370.

Mira, M. Results of a behavior modification training program for parents and teachers. *Behavior Research and Therapy*, 1970, 8, 309–311.

O'Dell, S. Training parents in behavior modification. *Psychological Bulletin*, 1974, 81, 408–433.

O'Leary, K. D., Becker, W. C., Evans, M. B., & Saudargas, R. A. A token reinforcement program in a public school: A replication and systematic analysis. *Journal of Applied Behavior Analysis*, 1969, 2, 3–13.

Patterson, G. R. A learning theory approach to the treatment of the school phobic child. In L. P. Ullman & L. Krasner (Eds.), *Case studies in behavior modification.* New York: Holt, Rinehart and Winston, 1965.

Patterson, G. R., & Brodsky, M. Behavior modification for a child with multiple problem behaviors. *Journal of Child Psychology and Psychiatry*, 1966, 7, 277–295.

Patterson, G. R., Cobb, J. A., & Ray, R. S. A social engineering technology for retraining the families of aggressive boys. In H. E. Adam & I. P. Unikel (Eds.), *Issues and trends in behavior therapy.* Springfield, Ill.: Charles C Thomas, 1972.

Peine, H. A. Effects of training models on the modification of parent behavior. *Dissertation Abstracts*, 1972, 32, 1341.

Rose, S. D. A behavioral approach to group treatment of parents. *Social Work*, 1969, 14, 21–29.

Rotter, J. B. Generalized expectancies for internal versus external control of reinforcement. In J. Rotter, J. Chance, & J. Phares (Eds.), *Application of a social learning theory of personality.* New York: Holt, Rinehart and Winston, 1972.

Salzinger, K., Feldman, R. S., & Portnoy, S. Training parents of brain-injured children in the use of operant conditioning procedures. *Behavior Therapy*, 1970, 1, 4–32.

Sherman, M., & Baer, D. M. Appraisal of operant therapy techniques with children and adults. In C. M. Franks (Ed.), *Behavior therapy: Appraisal and status.* New York: McGraw-Hill, 1969.

Sirridge, S. T. *Parent training: Assessment of parent attitudes, parent management skills, and child target behavior.* Unpublished doctoral dissertation, University of Kansas, 1975.

Stokes, T. F., & Baer, D. M. An implicit technology of generalization. *Journal of Applied Behavior Analysis*, 1977, 10, 349–367.

Straughn, J. H. Treatment with mother and child in the playroom. *Behavior Research and Therapy*, 1964, 2, 37–41.

Wahler, R. G. Setting generality: Some specific and general effects of child behavior therapy. *Journal of Applied Behavior Analysis*, 1969, 2, 239–246.

Walder, L. O., Breiter, D. E., Cohen, S. I., Daston, P. G., Forbes, J. A., & McIntyre, R. W.

Teaching parents to modify the behaviors of their autistic children. Paper presented at the 74th Annual Convention of the American Psychological Association, New York, 1966.

Walder, L. O., Cohen, S. I., Breiter, D. E., Daston, P. G., Hirsch, I. S., & Leibowitz, J. M. *Teaching behavioral principles to parents of disturbed children.* Paper presented at the meeting of the Eastern Psychological Association, Boston, 1967.(a)

Walder, L. O., Cohen, S. I., & Daston, P. G. *Teaching parents and others principles of behavior control for modifying the behavior of children.* Progress Report, U.S. Office of Education, 32-31-7515-5024, 1967.(b) (Available from the U.S. Office of Education)

Walder, L. O., Cohen, S. I., Daston, P. G., Breiter, D. E., & Hirsch, J. S. *Behavior therapy of children through their parents.* Revision of a paper presented at the meeting of the American Psychological Association, Washington, D.C., 1967.(c)

Walker, H. M., & Buckley, N. K. Programming generalization and maintenance of treatment effects across time and across settings. *Journal of Applied Behavior Analysis,* 1972, *2,* 209–224.

Wyckoff, J. L. *An assessment of the results of behavior modification workshops for parents through the analysis of behavior records and self-reporting.* Unpublished master's thesis, University of Kansas, 1975.

Wyckoff, J. L. *A clinical replication of the dry-bed enuresis procedure with parents as the trainers.* Unpublished doctoral dissertation, University of Kansas, 1978.

Chapter 14

Evaluating Parent
Education Programs

MARVIN S. KAPLAN

Several years ago a professional colleague lamented that he was again being evaluated. "Does this process of evaluation never cease?" he complained. Fortunately or unfortunately, depending on your perspective, the answer is that evaluation—of individuals and programs—is an ever-present fact of life. (Reportedly the first evaluation, "It was good," was associated with the creation of the heavens and the earth.) Furthermore, evaluation often comes from more than one source (e.g., parent education programs are "graded" by participants, professional peers, superiors, and sometimes by the larger community) and occurs without systematic planning or data.

For example, the writer once proposed comprehensive evaluation of a program for gifted children. The superintendent of the school system responded, "The parents like it, the kids like it, the teachers like it—why should we evaluate it?" In fact, the evaluation of this program had already taken place: The criteria of evaluation was the superintendent's subjective impression that there was a consensus of "liking it." The issue of evaluation, then, is not *whether* a program should be evaluated but rather *how* it will be evaluated.

Although the major focus of this chapter is on the various stages of a systematic evaluation, it should be noted that the intended uses of such an evaluation will inevitably influence its content and methods. For example, the specific strategies involved, including data selection and

317

HANDBOOK ON
PARENT EDUCATION

analysis, will vary, depending on whether the projected use of the data is to decide (*a*) to improve internal program practices and procedures; (*b*) to continue or discontinue the program; or (*c*) to allocate resources among competing programs. Others factors influencing the evaluation process are the availability of technical, financial, and human resources as well as the time interval available before the information is needed.

Evaluation—What Is It?

Program evaluation is a relatively new concept that provides a model for the study of program effectiveness in complicated real-life settings. This model emerged because the logic of the existing research-experiment system was often neither relevant nor readily applicable to the assessment of educational programs.

Perhaps the evaluation viewpoint is best expressed by Guba and Stufflebeam (1970):

> It is not just being unable to control all variables posed by experimental design; it is a matter of being unwilling to do so. The need is to know what is happening in the real world where there are many influences. . . . Thus far from wishing to screen out possible sources of interference, evaluation is actually concerned with inviting interference, so that results under the worst possible circumstances can also be assessed [p. 12].

The experimental model seeks to add to the general store of knowledge and to assess the relationships among variables, whereas program evaluation attempts to determine whether an intervention has helped participants achieve previously selected program goals. Evaluation seeks information for immediate application, whereas experimental research generally is unconcerned with the immediate use of the information derived from the data (Bloom, Hastings, & Madaus, 1971; Burck, 1978; Nuttall & Ivey, 1978).

These differences in purpose dictate different design strategies. Contributing to knowledge regarding the relationships among variables requires assurance that unknown influences are not at work (whereas the evaluation of goal attainment is far less concerned with the impact of unknown influences). The necessary strategies for eliminating such influences in experimental research require the use of random assignment of participants to treatment and control conditions as well as the assurance of the representativeness of the participant sample vis-à-vis the population to which generalization is intended (Campbell & Stanley, 1963). These experimental design requirements are frequently unfulfilled in evaluation studies. This is so partly because program planners often want to provide help to those most in need and are therefore reluctant to delay help by making assignments based on the demands of experimental research methodology. There is an ethical tension between the demands of the research experiment and the perceived needs of potential participants (Gilbert, Light, & Mosteller, 1975).

These considerations have led Apple (1974) to describe program evaluation as a process for systematically obtaining data in order to permit a social judgment regarding the worth of a particular set of actions or objectives. In other words, that which is worth attaining as well as the level of attainment are value judgments made prior to the collection of data. This is especially significant because it implies that evaluation is not neutral.

As contrasted with the experimental model, program evaluation yields some gains and some losses. The gains include assessing more aspects of the program, the ability to provide immediate feedback to increase program effectiveness, greater latitude in participant selection, and greater certainty that participants have or have not achieved criterion goals. The potential losses include decreased certainty that the participants achieved the goals *because of the program intervention itself* and decreased ability to generalize the program's effects to other people and settings.

Once this major distinction between the research and program evaluation models is understood, the evaluation model can be further analyzed in its component parts. The following sections of this chapter discuss the types and stages of evaluation (need, input, process, and outcome evaluation) and critique some of the tools of evaluation.

Need Evaluation

Let us assume that based on discussion with others or as the result of his or her own individual perceptions, the program planner concludes that a certain group of parents in the community needs information, skills, altered attitudes, and/or altered behaviors. Typically in such cases an implicit rather than explicit presumption exists, namely that if one or more such needs are supplied to the parents, life will somehow be better for the children. The program planner is operating from the theoretical position that if X is provided to parents, children will gain Y. The planner is also assuming a value stance, that is, that the children in question will be better off if they gain Y, even though many Y's may be controversial in a specific community given our pluralistic society. For example, Gordon's Parent Effectiveness Training (1970) and Dreikurs and Stoltz's proposals (1964) that children be treated as equals (Y) may be more acceptable to the planners of parent education programs than to the parents participating in such programs.

Other goals that may seem to be self-evidently desirable contain procedural assumptions, which in turn may prove controversial. Undoubtedly many parent educators were surprised by the negative response to initial federal government proposals for the establishment of day-care centers for children. (Some citizens apparently viewed government-supported day-care centers as interference in family life.)

If the preceding analysis is correct, it is evident that program planners must first determine whether parents *want* to achieve the same goals as the planner and whether the means chosen for implementing these goals (and more indirectly the theories involved) are fundamentally acceptable. The importance of this question of means was underscored by Anchor and Thomason's (1977) account of parent resistance to the concepts and technology of a behavior modification program (expressed by comments that the program was not meeting individual participants' needs and by a high dropout rate). Given the potentially negative consequences of mismatched planner-participant values, it seems prudent for the program planner to test his or her plans by interviewing or surveying a sample of potential participants.

A different but equally significant value issue arises from the fact that educational as well as treatment programs produce a variety of unintended consequences (Anchor & Thomason, 1977). For example, few will any longer dispute that in addition to positive results, psychotherapy can also have negative and unanticipated outcomes (Bergin & Lambert, 1978). Accordingly, the program planner must attempt to predict possible negative consequences, make plans for detecting their appearance, and provide necessary services if undesirable results occur.

Even if such precautions are taken, a fundamental value question remains: If programs can lead to negative or unintended consequences, to what extent should potential participants be informed? Legally, in the area of "treatment" the principle involved is referred to as "informed consent" (Waltz & Scheunerman, 1969). Consent is only possible given the absence of duress (e.g., no institutional pressure to participate) and the provision of adequate knowledge regarding the goals, procedures, and potential side effects or negative consequences of the particular treatment regimen.

Thus, participants have a legal "right to know" before they commit themselves to any program defined as "treatment." In the area of educational programs, however, such a right—for now at least—remains in the realm of ethical requirement rather than legal mandate. This hardly makes the critical issues at stake any simpler. For example, consider the question of institutional encouragement (pressure) for parental partici- pation (either attend or your child will be placed—or not placed—in a special class). What kind of community sanction—legal, moral, or social—does the institution have to create such pressure? Some of the worst abuses of individual rights have historically been justified on the grounds, "It's for your own good." Justice Brandeis once noted

> Experience should teach us to be most on our guard to protect liberty when the governnent's purposes are beneficent. . . . The greatest dangers to liberty lurk in insidious encroachment of men of zeal, well meaning but without understanding [*Olmstead* v. *United States* 1928].

In addition, the evaluation must consider a variety of legal and ethical issues related to the process of intervention (If the participant may be harmed, is the program justifiable?), the collection of information (May the evaluator invade the privacy of the participant?), and the protection of the data acquired (Who may obtain access to the information?). An interesting review of these issues is provided by Bersoff (1978). In summary, program evaluators and planners must carefully consider the values, beliefs, and rights of their prospective clients and such consid- eration must begin at the earliest stages of program planning and development.

The value questions raised earlier are not the only problems relating to program goals that require a great deal of attention yet often do not get it. The very process of defining formal objectives often meets with great resistance. As Dressel (1976) comments, "The difficulties include confused terminology, basic philosophical differences regarding the nature of learning, difficulties in translating global concerns into realis- tic objectives, and skepticism over the usefulness of stating objectives [pp. 27–28]." Dressel also observes that some educators oppose state- ments of objectives because they are convinced that individuals pursue many differing objectives simultaneously and worthwhile outcomes invariably exceed those consciously perceived. Indeed, they believe that learning may actually be restricted by the awareness of limited objectives.

Opponents of more general statements of program goals sometimes make just the opposite charge: Objectives are not specific enough. The precise specification of goals—in a form that is measurable—is a difficult task and one often poorly achieved. How difficult it apparently is becomes clear in the following list of outcome goals proposed by such a widely used parent program as that prepared by Gordon (1970).

1. Parents will avoid being fired by their children.
2. Parents and children will develop a warm, intimate relationship of mutual love and respect.
3. Avoid war in the home.
4. Bring parents and children closer together rather than grouped against each other.
5. Maintain effective relationships with the children in any and all circumstances.

Note that the goals are vague and their achievement may not be measurable. That more specificity is possible, however, was shown by Gordon on another occasion when he focused on parent component objectives as contrasted to parent–child relationship outcomes (e.g., see discussion of input evaluation in the next section).

Some assistance is available with the problem of defining measurable goals in behavioral terms. Mager (1962, p. 53) provides a framework for conceptualizing and formulating instructional goals in behavioral terms.

"1. A statement of instructional objectives is a collection of words or symbols describing one of your educational intents.
"2. An objective will communicate your intent to the degree you have described what the learner will be DOING when demonstrating his achievement and how you will know when he is doing it.
"3. To describe terminal behavior (what the learner will be DOING):
   a. Identify and name the overall behavior act.
   b. Define the important conditions under which the behavior is to occur (givens or restrictions, or both).
   c. Define the criterion of acceptable performance.
"4. Write a separate statement for each objective: The more statements you have, the better chance you have of making clear your intent [p. 53]."

Thus, there are three steps in selecting behavioral goals, namely description of the specific behavior to be demonstrated by the learner, the conditions in which the behavior should occur, and the level of acceptable performance.

Measurement, however, need not be limited to goals expressed in terms of behavior change. Bloom (1956) in his taxonomy of objectives includes an analysis of the hierarchy of acquisition including knowledge, comprehension, and skill attainment. This taxonomy may be useful in separating objectives into their component parts and levels of complexity and as an aid to the clear formulation of sub-objectives. Further discussion of the use of the taxonomy in curriculum building is provided by Krathwohl (1978).

Input Evaluation

The assessment of the specific plan of intervention has been called input evaluation. At this stage the evaluator seeks to determine whether the projected program strategies are likely to achieve the outcome goals desired. The evaluator also seeks to select or design measures of the achievement of component objectives.

The achievement of outcome goals, according to Bloom (1956), requires "the analysis of a complex final product into components which must be attained separately and in some sequence. To teach anything is to have in view the final model to be attained while concentrating on one step at a time in movement toward the goal [p. 13]." Essentially agreeing with this analysis, Weiss (1972) recommends the construction of a model of the intended processes of the program to identify the steps and means by which the program is intended to work. Such a model will indicate the kinds of effects that should be investigated. As soon as ways are established to measure each identified set of events and the appropriate measurements are made, it becomes possible to "see what happens, what works and what doesn't, for whom it works, and for whom it doesn't" (Weiss, 1972, pp. 50–51).

The specification of a particular group of component objectives is described by Gordon (1970) for his program. He identifies a number of essentially hierarchical objectives to achieve the outcome goals of improved family relationships.

1. Understanding the effects of unaccepting language.
2. Recognizing the language of acceptance and unacceptance.
3. Distinguishing between parent needs and child needs.
4. Use of passive and active listening as the language of acceptance.
5. Exploring alternative solutions when there is conflict with the child.

These steps are consistent with the concepts of Carl Rogers and the theory and empirical data supporting client-centered counseling (Rogers & Dymond, 1954) including the belief in the individual's (in this case the child's) potential for growth and adaptation when provided with conditions of acceptance. The program planner in developing his or her evaluation procedures must decide how the steps of the planned intervention process are related to one another (in theory and logic) and ultimately to the desired outcome goals. He or she should review the specific activities, lectures, and material planned for each component objective to determine whether they facilitate movement toward the desired ends. These assumptions of cause and effect relationships may be tested against the evidence of the empirical and theoretical literature regarding the known connection between skills and knowledge and interpersonal relationships (assuming the program goals are seeking to attain an improvement in parent–child interactions).

The measurement of the achievement of *component objectives* should be more closely related to the specifics of the curriculum content than to generalized extrapolations manifest in the natural or home environment. Devices for measurement at this level should be closely tied to the curriculum and generally are assessed in the program environment (e.g., acquisition of knowledge, ability to achieve discriminations, etc.). Returning to the *Parent Effectiveness Training* program model (Gordon, 1970) as an example, the following questions may be evaluated:

1. Can the parent distinguish unaccepting and accepting language?
2. Has the parent learned the skills of passive and active listening?
3. Can the parent distinguish between his or her needs and those of the child?
4. Can the parents use the learning to create alternative solutions to disagreements with the child?

Data from this analysis can be immediately fed back to the instructional process to increase its effectiveness. Step by step assessment permits the change of any process that is not achieving its prescribed goal. "Evaluation is a part of the intervention program development, not a process applied after its development [Burck, 1978, p. 345]."

Process Evaluation

Process evaluation involves the monitoring of program strategies and activities that can have an effect on the adequacy of participant learning. Such continuous monitoring has two purposes: (*a*) to periodically feed back information for immediate refinement of plans and procedures; and (*b*) to provide information for subsequent understanding of the final outcome data. Some of the questions to be considered at this stage of process evaluation are:

1. Did the participants arrive as scheduled? (Brewer, 1978, reported that less than 50% of those parents who agreed to participate actually arrived.)
2. Did the participants accept the goals and methods of the program? (Anchor & Thomason, 1977, reported that parents resisted behavior modification classes, said the program was not fulfilling their needs, and several dropped out.)
3. Did the leader carry out the implementation as planned or were there alterations?
4. Were there problems in interpersonal relationships among the participants?
5. Were there unique and intense experiences within the group (e.g., a child's death shared with the group; a divorce shared with the group)?
6. Were there unique events occurring in the society or community during the program implementation (e.g., a television special on child management or abuse or a unique tragedy in the community affecting the participants)?

Sources of information might include:

1. Participant-written statements regarding what was learned, which are completed after each session.
2. Participant diary data regarding interactions with children.
3. Nonparticipant descriptive data regarding child–parent interactions in the home.
4. Nonparticipant observer data regarding program process and implementation.
5. Participant achievements assessed at the end of each session or component unit.
6. Measures of skills attained during each session.
7. Measures of attitude toward the process and content.

It should be noted that in addition to anticipated effects of the program, there will be many unanticipated effects. Knight (1975) reported that Gordon's Parent Effectiveness Training (1970) actually resulted in deterioration (beyond that of the control group) of parent–child relationships. As noted earlier, similar unintended negative effects have been reported as outcomes of various psychotherapies (Bergin & Lambert, 1978; Strupp, 1978). Thus, some of the measures utilized should be relatively open ended (allowing participants the opportunity to indicate unintended consequences) rather than being limited to the measurement of predetermined objectives of knowledge or skill acquisition.

Outcome Evaluation

Outcome evaluation assesses whether the larger and more generalized goals of the program have been achieved. While the data obtained at earlier stages may well be applicable at this point, the inquiry made for outcome evaluation is distinctive in the proportion of the program material evaluated (total overview), the expected uses of the data (including external decision making), and the site of data collection (natural environments, such as the home, are often preferable to the earlier program-based setting).

A major decision facing the program planner at the outcome evaluation stage is whether to measure the program's effects on the parent-participants and/or on their children. Whether the planners' theoretical stance is behavioral or what Tavormina (1974) calls "reflective" (feeling emphasis) will affect whose behavior is measured and how it is measured. O'Dell (1974) reports that most of the behaviorally oriented programs he reviewed carefully defined and measured child behavior but seldom defined or measured the parent behaviors producing the change. Reflective approaches are more concerned with cognitively mediated variables such as warmth and understanding and are therefore more likely to measure cognitive and attitudinal changes in the parent-participant (Tavormina, 1974).

The theoretical framework of the program may also influence the choice of "objective" measures (e.g., observation) or subjective measures (e.g., self-rating or self-appraisal), although both kinds of data are usually necessary to fully understand program effects (Burck, Cottingham, & Reardon, 1972). If behavior change is viewed as unitary, then, as has been proposed by some behaviorists, single criterion measures are all that are necessary. However, most evaluators believe that program impact is better understood through the use of multiple measurements of different types (Weiss, 1972). It may also be useful to measure along the chain of expected impact such as the following (adapted from Bloom, 1956, in the handbook entitled *Cognitive Domain*, and Krathwohl, Bloom, & Masia, 1964, in *Affective Domain*):

Parental knowledge obtained—leading to understanding the implications of the knowledge—leading to valuing the new understanding—leading to learning the new skills—leading to valuing the new skills—leading to preferring the new skills—leading to commitment to the use of the new skills and understanding—leading to change in parental behavior—leading to child perception of altered parental behavior—leading to child change in behavior.

If measurement takes place along such a chain of expected effects, the evaluator will better understand how the program achieves (or why it does not achieve) its goals and where to make program changes. (Some of the data along the chain of expected effect will have been collected at prior stages of the evaluation.)

A number of other decisions must be made:

1. Is it expected that the program will have the same effect on everyone? Oetting and Hawkes (1974) suggest that "it should be assumed that a particular intervention will not have the same effect on everyone [p. 37]." If the evaluator is concerned with differential effects he or she may desire to analyze results in terms of common demographic variables: sex, intact marriages, number of children, and parent and child educational levels. Such data may help in the decision as to whether the program is likely to be effective with other groups (Croake & Glover, 1977; O'Dell, 1974; Tavormina, 1974). Burck et al. (1972) also suggest that the individual participant as well as the general outcome goals should be measured. They recommend that participants be encouraged to specify their own goals and that such goal achievement become part of the program outcome data.

2. Is it expected that the program will have long-term consequences? Evaluators generally study short-term outcomes because of the time and expense of follow-up studies. However, it is possible that program effects may increase or decrease over time and such information, especially when compared with alternate program models, may be very helpful in decision making.

Finally, it should be noted that interpreting the meaning of outcome data requires at least one comparison (Campbell & Stanley, 1963); in program evaluation this is often accomplished by pretest and posttest assessment. Such a procedure unfortunately has a number of deficiencies including pretest effects on posttest data and the unreliability of difference scores. Scriven (1974) suggests that a more meaningful approach, which also overcomes the deficiencies of the pretest and posttest strategy, is the comparison of program outcomes with those of other promising programs covering roughly the same territory.

Devices and Sources for Data Acquisition

Frequent reference has been made in the preceding sections to the critical data associated with the various stages of evaluating parent education programs. Such data can be obtained by using a wide array of sources and devices. Weiss (1972) identified some of the possible sources, but she also commented that such a list is only limited by the ingenuity and imagination of the planner and evaluator. Following are just some of the sources Weiss identified:

1. Interviews
2. Questionnaires
3. Observations
4. Ratings (by peers, staff; experts)
5. Psychometric tests of attitudes, values, personality, preferences, norms, beliefs
6. Institutional records
7. Government statistics
8. Tests of information, interpretation, skills, application of knowledge
9. Projective tests
10. Situation tests presenting the respondent with simulated life situations
11. Diary records
12. Physical evidence
13. Clinical examination
14. Financial records
15. Documents (minutes of board meetings, newspaper accounts of policy actions, transcripts of trials)

While the evaluator may be tempted to construct a new evaluation device specifically tailored to the program objectives, this is often a difficult and time-consuming task requiring considerable technical skill. Instead, consideration might be given to evaluation devices reported in published studies or those described in standard references such as the *Eighth Mental Measurements Yearbook* (Buros, 1978). In addition, a number of books provide basic information about unpublished devices used by other evaluators. *Tests and Measurements in Child Development: A Handbook,* edited by Johnson and Bommarito (1971), and *Handbook II,* edited by Johnson (1976), provide detailed information about a wide array of useful instruments focusing on the parent, the child, and the environment. Observation and interview guides, rating scales, and questionnaires are also described. Some examples include: a variety of parent attitude scales; the Parental Dissatisfaction with Instrumental Behavior Scale; the Index of Parental Dissatisfaction with Social-Emotional Behavior; the Child Responsibility Inventory; Self-

Concept Report Scale; Children's Perceptions of Their Classmates Scale; Observation Record of Discipline Scale, etc.

The works cited earlier (Buros, 1978; Johnson, 1976; Johnson & Bommarito, 1971) also provide references and descriptions of the content of other source books on measuring devices. In addition, evaluators may request computer searches of recent studies such as those provided by *Resources in Education*, Journal Supplement Abstract Service, or The Information Clearing House of HEW, each of which provides information about types of instruments (as well as evaluation designs and study outcomes) evaluators have used.

Perhaps the chief danger in this review of existing instruments is that there is so much literature and so many sources that the reviewer may become bogged down in descriptions of measurement tools and studies. Nevertheless, this activity should prove worthwhile. It is very likely that somebody has already constructed the instrument the program evaluator needs. Indeed, three or four such devices are probably available. Nuttall and Ivey (1978) suggest the following guidelines for instrument selection: (*a*) measures what you are interested in; (*b*) has reasonable reliability; (*c*) has been used in a program similar to your own; (*d*) seems to have some relation to a larger body of theory; and (*e*) is not offensive to the general public (pp. 99–100). They also note that an instrument with a history of use provides the program evaluator with a comparative data base sample.

Some Problems of Questionnaire, Interview, and Observational Data

Inevitably, each type of measuring instrument has its advantages and disadvantages, and these have been documented in the research literature (Cox, 1975). O'Dell (1974) reports that paper and pencil tests are frequently major sources of data used to measure parent education program effectiveness, "despite evidence that they have been shown to relate little to actual behavior changes [p. 428]." Similarly, research—for example, using the carefully developed Parent Attitude Research Instrument (Schaefer & Bell, 1958)—has not supported the usefulness of expressed parental attitudes and values for making predictions about parental behavior (Becker & Krug, 1965; Hess, 1970). Ratings based on notes made during home observations also introduce unknown degrees of distortion into the data (Martin, 1975). Interviews, too, have been subject to considerable criticism because they depend upon parent memory, capacity for verbal articulation, interviewer skill, and judgments by ego-involved parental reporters (Martin, 1975).

In addition to supporting these conclusions, Yarrow (1963) found that agreement—parent–parent and child–parent—regarding items on authority relations ranged from 26 to 72%, making evident the need for multiple sources of information. Hetherington and Martin (1972) found that mothers who knew the father was also going to be interviewed gave more favorable reports concerning the father's behavior than did mothers who believed that they alone would be interviewed. Hetherington and Martin (1972) suggest that in addition to interviewing more than one member of the family, focusing on contemporary practices rather than on retrospective attitudes will improve the validity of the self-report.

Regarding the currently favored observation method, Yarrow (1963) comments

> Observations do not necessarily yield valid data. They do so only to the extent that the phenomena to be observed have not been destroyed, missed or misinterpreted by the observer. The avoidance of such calamities requires awareness by the investigator of new kinds of data sampling problems, judicious selection of categories and framework for observation, and the working out of a relationship with the observed that is neither destructive nor unduly confining for the research [p. 219].

Zegiob and Forehand (1975) similarly report that observed (as contrasted with seemingly unobserved) mothers played more with their children and were more informal and positive in their verbal behavior. Hetherington and Martin (1972) report that in general the more unknown and structured the situation, the more socially desirable are the parental behaviors. The reactive effects of observation are so consistent (increase of appropriate behaviors) that they have been called the "girdle on/girdle off" phenomena (Evans & Nelson, 1977). These effects can be minimized if observations occur in the home and the observers are similar to those observed in sex, age, and race. It is also helpful if the observers are inconspicuous and friendly, and visit regularly (Clarke-Stewart, 1977).

Although the structuring of observed parent and child behaviors may make behavior less than typical, providing structure assures that the interactions of interest occur during the observational interval. Bell (1964) proposed that structuring can be designed to give either the parent or the child behavioral latitude (e.g., the child given a block-building task with the parents instructed that they may only respond verbally). The interaction can thus be designed to elicit the behaviors the evaluator desires to measure. Further suggestions for structuring are offered by Evans and Nelson (1977); Lytton (1971); Mash, Terdal, and Anderson (1973); and Yarrow (1963).

In summary, the validity of questionnaire and interview data can be improved if questions focus on the present and take into account the tendency of parents to respond in socially approved ways. It is helpful to obtain at least part of the data in the home in a conversational (seemingly unstructured) format, with each member of the family being informed that the others will be interviewed or will complete similar questionnaires.

Observational data can be improved if the data are obtained in the home, if behaviors are not apparently structured, if observers are friendly and familiar to the family as the result of frequent visits, and if observers are similar in demographic characteristics. However, the failure to structure may prevent the appearance of the specific behavior the evaluator wishes to measure.

This brief review indicates some of the weaknesses and possible means for improving questionnaires, interviews, and observational measurement. Research data supports the argument for careful consideration of the methodology chosen and for utilizing multiple sources of information.

Summary and Conclusions

The evaluation model has been proposed for use in nonlaboratory field settings. It seeks primarily to measure the attainment of previously selected goals and objectives. On the one hand, this model provides a means for determining total program effectiveness; on the other hand, it serves as a management tool to audit ongoing program operations (Riecken, 1977). Thus, a major task of program planners and evaluators is to obtain general consensus among responsible institutional leaders regarding desired program outcomes.

Since the term "evaluation" as used in this chapter refers to systematic data collection for a specific use, another task of the program evaluator involves the careful determination during the early planning stages of the intended uses of the evaluation data. It will be recalled that such data—as contrasted to research data—are not value neutral, and consequently part of the evaluation process involves the assignment of value to activities, procedures, and goals.

Any assessment process requires the consideration of participant rights. Before committing themselves to a program, participants have the right to know the program's goals and the methods planned for achieving them. Participants also have the right to protect their privacy. They may choose to do so by refusing to complete evaluation materials that they consider an infringement on this right, either as it applies to them individually or as it applies to the family unit. Furthermore, participants have the right to know who will have access to the data collected as well as how that data will be used. Finally, they have the right to information about potential undesirable consequences of the program and existing policy regarding assistance should such negative results occur.

As late as 1977 Croake and Glover (1977) were discouraged about the available data on parent education program effectiveness. They found that the literature in this area has "historically been very inadequate both in terms of amount and quality [p. 151]." The clear charge to those currently engaged in program planning is to provide continuing and careful reporting of the characteristics of participants, description of program assessment devices and program operation, as well as successes and failures of goal attainment.

References

Anchor, K. N., & Thomason, T. C. A comparison of two parent training models with educated parents. *Journal of Community Psychology*, 1977, *5*, 134–141.

Apple, M. W. The process and ideology of valuing in educational settings. In M. W. Apple, J. J. Subkoviak, H. S. Lufler, Jr. (Eds.), *Educational evaluation: Analysis and responsibility*. Berkeley: McCutchan Publishing, 1974.

Becker, W. C., & Krug, R. S. The parent attitude research instrument. A review of research. *Child Development*, 1965, *36*, 329–365.

Bell, R. D. Structuring parent–child interaction situations for direct observation. *Child Development*, 1964, *35*, 1009–1020.

Bergin, A. E., & Lambert, M. The evaluation of therapeutic outcomes. In S. L. Garfied & A. E. Bergin (Eds.), *Handbook of psychotherapy & behavior change: An empirical analysis* (2nd ed.). New York: Wiley, 1978.

Bersoff, D. N. Ethical concerns in research. In L. Goldman (Ed.), *Research methods for counselors: A practical approach for field settings*. New York: Wiley, 1978.

Bloom, B. S. (Ed.). *Taxonomy of educational objectives: The classification of educational goals. Handbook 1. Cognitive domain*. New York: McKay, 1956.

Bloom, B. S., Hastings, J. T., & Madaus, G. F. *Handbook on formative and summative evaluation of student learning*. New York: McGraw-Hill, 1971.

Brewer, S. *The effects of locus of control and presentation mode upon parent training effectiveness*. Unpublished doctoral dissertation, University of Kansas, 1978.

Burck, H. D. Evaluation programs, models and strategies. In L. Goldman (Ed.), *Research methods for counselors, a practical approach for field settings*. New York: Wiley, 1978.

Burck, H. D., Cottingham, H. F., & Reardon, R. C. *Counseling and accountability: Methods & critique*. New York: Pergamon Press, 1972.

Buros, O. K. (Ed.). *The eighth mental measurements yearbook.* Edison, N. J.: Gryphon Press, 1978.

Campbell, D. T., & Stanley, J. C. Experimental and quasi-experimental designs for research on teaching. In N. L. Gage (Ed.), *Handbook of research on teaching.* Chicago: Rand McNally, 1963.

Clarke-Stewart, K. A. *Child care in the family.* New York: Academic Press, 1977.

Cox, A. The assessment of parental behavior. *Journal of Child Psychology and Psychiatry,* 1975, *16,* 255–259.

Croake, J. W., & Glover, K. E. A history and evaluation of parent education. *The Family Coordinator,* 1977, *26,* 151–158.

Dreikurs, R., & Stolz, V. *Children the challenge.* New York: Hawthorne Books, 1964.

Dressel, P. *Handbook of academic evaluation.* San Francisco: Jossey-Bass, 1976.

Evans, I. M., & Nelson, R. O. Assessment of child behavior problems. In A. R. Ciminero, K. Calhoun, & H. Adams (Eds.), *Handbook of behavioral assessment.* New York: Wiley-Interscience, 1977.

Gilbert, J. P., Light, R. J., & Mosteller, F. Assessing social innovations: An empirical base for policy. In C. A. Bennett & A. A. Lumsdaine (Eds.), *Evaluation and experiment. Some critical issues in assessing social programs.* New York: Academic Press, 1975.

Gordon, T. *Parent effectiveness training.* New York: Peter Wyden, 1970.

Guba, E. G., & Stufflebeam, D. L. Evaluation: The process of stimulating, aiding and abetting insightful action. *Monograph Series in Readings in Education.* Indiana University, Bloomington, Indiana, 1970.

Hess, R. D. Social class and ethnic influences on socialization. In P. H. Mussen (Ed.), *Carmichael's handbook of child psychology.* New York: Wiley, 1970.

Hetherington, E. M., & Martin, B. Family interaction and psychopathology in children. In H. C. Quay & J. S. Werry (Eds.), *Psychopathological disorders of childhood.* New York: Wiley, 1972.

Information Clearing House. U.S. Department of Health, Education and Welfare, Rockville, Maryland.

Johnson, O. G. *Tests and measurements in child development: Handbook II.* San Francisco: Jossey-Bass, 1976.

Johnson, O. G., & Bommarito, J. W. *Tests and measurements in child development.* San Francisco: Jossey-Bass, 1971.

Journal Supplement Abstract Service. American Psychological Association, Washington, D.C.

Knight, N. A. The effects of changes in family interpersonal relationships on the behavior of enuretic children and their parents. (Doctoral Dissertation, University of Hawaii, 1975). *Dissertation Abstracts International,* 1974, *36,* 383a.

Krathwohl, D. R. The taxonomy of educational objectives—Its uses in curriculum building. In J. R. Gress & D. E. Purpel (Eds.), *Curriculum: An introduction to the field.* Berkeley: McCutchan Publishing, 1978.

Krathwohl, D. R., Bloom, B. S., & Masia, B. B. *Taxonomy of educational objectives: The classification of educational goals. Handbook 2. Affective domain.* New York: McKay, 1964.

Lytton, H. Observational studies of parent–child interaction: A methodological review. *Child Development,* 1971, *42,* 651–682.

Mager, R. F. *Preparing instructional objectives,* Palo Alto: Fearon Publishers, 1962.

Martin, B. Parent–child relations. In F. D. Horowitz & E. M. Hetherington (Eds.), *Review of child development research* (Vol. 4). Chicago: University of Chicago Press, 1975.

Mash, E. J., Terdal, L., & Anderson, K. The response class matrix: A procedure for recording parent–child interaction. *Journal of Consulting and Clinical Psychology*, 1973, *40*, 163–164.

Nuttall, E. V., & Ivey, A. E. Research for action: The tradition and its implementation. In L. Goldman (Ed.), *Research methods for counselors: Practical approaches in field settings*. New York: Wiley, 1978.

O'Dell, S. Training parents in behavior modification. A review. *Psychological Bulletin*, 1974, *81*, 418–433.

Oetting, E. R., & Hawkes, F. J. Training professionals for evaluation. *Personnel and Guidance Journal*, 1974, *52*, 435–438.

Olmstead v. *United States*, 277 U.S. 438 (1928).

Reardon, D. F. A model for communicating about program evaluation. *Journal of Community Psychology*, 1977, *5*, 350–358.

Resources in Education. National Institute of Education, U.S. Department of Health, Education and Welfare, Washington, D.C.

Riecken, H. W. Principal components of the evaluation process. *Professional Psychology*, 1977, *8*, 392–410.

Rogers, C. L., & Dymond, R. *Psychotherapy and behavior change*. Chicago: University of Chicago Press, 1954.

Schaefer, E. S., & Bell, R. Q. The development of a parental attitude research instrument. *Child Development*, 1958, *29*, 339–361.

Scriven, M. The concept of evaluation. In M. W. Apple, M. J. Subkoviak, H. S. Lufler, Jr. (Eds.), *Educational evaluation: Analysis and responsibility*. Berkeley: McCutchan Publishing, 1974.

Strupp, H. H. Psychotherapy research and practice: An overview. In S. L. Garfield & A. E. Bergin (Eds.), *Handbook of psychotherapy and behavior change: An empirical analysis* (2nd ed.). New York: Wiley, 1978.

Tavormina, J. B. Basic models of parent counseling: A critical review. *Psychological Bulletin*, 1974, *81*, 827–835.

Waltz, J. R., & Scheunerman, T. W. Informed consent in therapy. *Northwest Law Review*, 1969, *64*, 628–650.

Weiss, C. *Evaluation research. A method of assessing program effectiveness*. Englewood Cliffs, N.J.: Prentice-Hall, 1972.

Yarrow, M. R. Problems of nethods in parent–child research. *Child Development*, 1963, *34*, 215–226.

Zegiob, L. E., & Forehand, R. An examination of observer effects on parent–child relationships. *Child Development*, 1975, *46*, 509–512.

Index

EDUCATIONAL PSYCHOLOGY

continued from page ii

Donald J. Treffinger, J. Kent Davis, and Richard E. Ripple (eds.). Handbook on Teaching Educational Psychology

Harry L. Hom, Jr. and Paul A. Robinson (eds.). Psychological Processes in Early Education

J. Nina Lieberman. Playfulness: Its Relationship to Imagination and Creativity

Samuel Ball (ed.). Motivation in Education

Erness Bright Brody and Nathan Brody. Intelligence: Nature, Determinants, and Consequences

António Simões (ed.). The Bilingual Child: Research and Analysis of Existing Educational Themes

Gilbert R. Austin. Early Childhood Education: An International Perspective

Vernon L. Allen (ed.). Children as Teachers: Theory and Research on Tutoring

Joel R. Levin and Vernon L. Allen (eds.). Cognitive Learning in Children: Theories and Strategies

Donald E. P. Smith and others. A Technology of Reading and Writing (in four volumes).
> *Vol. 1. Learning to Read and Write: A Task Analysis (by Donald E. P. Smith)*
> *Vol. 2. Criterion-Referenced Tests for Reading and Writing (by Judith M. Smith, Donald E. P. Smith, and James R. Brink)*
> *Vol. 3. The Adaptive Classroom (by Donald E. P. Smith)*
> *Vol. 4. Designing Instructional Tasks (by Judith M. Smith)*

Phillip S. Strain, Thomas P. Cooke, and Tony Apolloni. Teaching Exceptional Children: Assessing and Modifying Social Behavior